D0088000

Study Guide and Student's Solutions Manual

Pin Ng, *Northern Arizona University*

Business Statistics: A First Course

Sixth Edition

David M. Levine
Timothy C. Krehbiel
Mark L. Berenson

PEARSON

Boston   Columbus   Indianapolis   New York   San Francisco   Upper Saddle River

Amsterdam   Cape Town   Dubai   London   Madrid   Milan   Munich   Paris   Montreal   Toronto

Delhi   Mexico City   Sao Paulo   Sydney   Hong Kong   Seoul   Singapore   Taipei   Tokyo

Editor in Chief: Donna Battista
Senior Executive Editor: Chuck Synovec
Editorial Project Manager: Mary Kate Murray
Production Project Manager: Jane Bonnell
Operations Specialist: Cathleen Petersen

Copyright © 2013 Pearson Education, Inc., publishing as Prentice Hall, One Lake Street, Upper Saddle River, New Jersey 07458. All rights reserved. Manufactured in the United States of America. This publication is protected by Copyright, and permission should be obtained from the publisher prior to any prohibited reproduction, storage in a retrieval system, or transmission in any form or by any means, electronic, mechanical, photocopying, recording, or likewise. To obtain permission(s) to use material from this work, please submit a written request to Pearson Education, Inc., Permissions Department, One Lake Street, Upper Saddle River, New Jersey 07458, or you may fax your request to 201-236-3290.

Many of the designations by manufacturers and sellers to distinguish their products are claimed as trademarks. Where those designations appear in this book, and the publisher was aware of a trademark claim, the designations have been printed in initial caps or all caps.

10 9 8 7 6 5 4 3 2 1

PEARSON

ISBN-13: 978-0-13-280732-6
ISBN-10: 0-13-280732-7

Table of Contents

Preface

The ***Study Guide and Student's Solutions Manual*** consists of three major sections. The ***Objective*** section summarizes what is expected of a student after reading a chapter. The ***Overview and Key Concepts*** section provides an overview of the major topics covered in a chapter and lists the important key concepts. The overview and listing of the key concepts are meant not to replace but to supplement the textbook and to reinforce understanding. The ***Solutions to End of Section and Chapter Review Even Problems*** section provides extra detail in the problem solutions.

CHAPTER 1

OBJECTIVES

In this chapter, you learn:

- What statistics is
- How statistics is fundamental to business
- The basic concepts and vocabulary of statistics
- How to use Microsoft Excel and/or Minitab with this book

OVERVIEW AND KEY CONCEPTS

The Growth and Development of Modern Statistics

Needs of government to collect data on its citizens

The development of the mathematics of probability theory

The advent of the computer

Key Definitions

- **Population (universe):** The whole collection of things under consideration, e.g., all the students enrolled at a university.
- **Sample:** A portion of the population selected for analysis, e.g., all the freshmen at a university.
- **Parameter:** A summary measure computed to describe a characteristic of the population, e.g., the population average weight of all the students enrolled at a university.
- **Statistic:** A summary measure computed to describe a characteristic of the sample, e.g., the average weight of a sample of freshmen at a university.
- **Variable:** A characteristic of an item or individual.
- **Data:** The set of individual values associated with a variable.

Relationship between Population and Sample

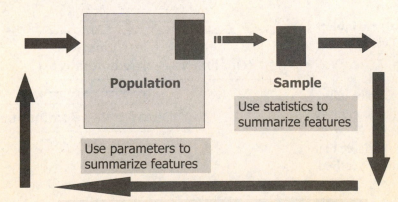

The Difference between Descriptive Statistics and Inferential Statistics
- **Descriptive statistics:** Deal with collecting, presenting, summarizing, and analyzing data.
- **Inferential statistics:** Deal with drawing conclusions and/or making decisions concerning a population based only on sample data.

The Primary Goal of the Text

To understand how the methods of statistics can be used in the decision-making process. This understanding includes the following objectives:
- Visualize and summarize data (a use of descriptive methods)
- Reach conclusions about a large group based on data collected from a small group (a use of inferential methods)
- Make reliable forecasts from statistical models that infer information (another use of inferential methods)
- Improve business processes using managerial approaches such as Six Sigma that focus on quality improvement (a use of both descriptive and inferential methods)

The Different Types of Data Sources

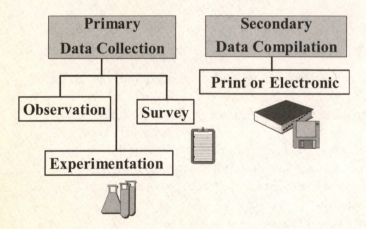

The Different Types of Data
- **Qualitative (categorical) variable**: A nonnumeric variable, e.g., male or female.
- **Quantitative (numerical) variable:** A numeric variable, e.g., weight, exam score.
- **Discrete variable:** A variable with only certain values, there are usually gaps between values, e.g., the number of cars a company owns.
- **Continuous variable:** A variable that can have any value within a specified range, e.g., atmospheric temperature.

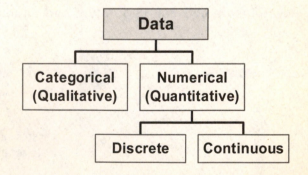

SOLUTIONS TO END OF SECTION
AND CHAPTER REVIEW EVEN PROBLEMS

1.2   Three sizes of soft drink are classified into distinct categories—small, medium, and large—and, hence, is an example of categorical variable.

1.4   (a)   The number of landline telephones is a numerical variable that is discrete because the outcome is a count.
        (b)   The length of the longest telephone call is a numerical variable that is continuous because any value within a range of values can occur.
        (c)   Whether someone in the household owns a Wi-Fi–capable cell phone is a categorical variable because the answer can be only yes or no.
        (d)   Same answer as in (c).
        (e)   Same answer as (c).
        (f)   Same answer as (a).

1.6   (a)   categorical
        (b)   numerical, continuous
        (c)   numerical, discrete
        (d)   numerical, discrete
        (e)   categorical

1.8   (a)   numerical, continuous *
        (b)   numerical, discrete
        (c)   numerical, continuous *
        (d)   categorical
        *Some researchers consider money as a discrete numerical variable because it can be "counted."

1.10   The underlying variable, ability of the students, may be continuous, but the measuring device, the test, does not have enough precision to distinguish between the two students.

1.12   A population contains all the items of interest whereas a sample contains only a portion of the items in the population.

1.14   Descriptive statistical methods deal with the collection, presentation, summarization, and analysis of data whereas inferential statistical methods deal with decisions arising from the projection of sample information to the characteristics of a population.

1.16   Discrete variables produce numerical responses that arise from a counting process. Continuous variables produce numerical responses that arise from a measuring process.

1.18   Data are the values associated with a trait or property that help distinguish the occurrences of something while a variable is one of those traits or properties that helps distinguish the occurrence of something. A variable describes a characteristic of an item or individual while data are the set of individual values associated with a variable.

Answers for 1.20 through 1.24 provided below are just some of the many different possible answers.

1.20   (a)   The population of interest was all the fulltime first-year students at the Midwestern
               United States university when the survey was conducted.
       (b)   The sample that was collected consisted of those 2821 students who responded to the
               survey.
       (c)   An example of a parameter of interest could be the proportion in the population of all
               the fulltime first-year students at this Midwestern United States university who had
               studied with other students.
       (d)   The statistic that could be used to estimate the parameter in (c) was the 90.1% of
               students in the sample who indicated that they had studied with other students.

1.22   (a)   The population of interest was all adults living in the United States, aged 18 and
               older.
       (b)   The sample was the 1,000 or more adults living in the United States, aged 18
               and older that responded to the telephone interviews.
       (c)   The 74% is a statistic.
       (d)   The 40% is a statistic.

1.24   (a)   The answer to "In 2007, did another company or organization own more than 50% of
               this business?" is an example of a categorical variable.
       (b)   The "percentage owned" is an example of numerical variable.

1.26   (a)   (i)   categorical   (iii) numerical, discrete
               (ii)   categorical   (iv) categorical
       (b)   The answers will vary.
       (c)   The answers will vary.

1.28   (a)   Categorical variables: gender, graduate major, undergrad major, and employment
               status.
       (b)   Numerical variables: age, graduate GPA, undergrad GPA, number of full-time jobs,
               expected salary, spending, advisory rating, the number of text messages sent and
               wealth.
       (c)   Discrete numerical variables: age (in years), number of jobs, expected salary (in
               thousands of dollars), spending (in dollars), advisory rating (from 1 to 7), the number
               of text messages sent and wealth.

CHAPTER 2

OBJECTIVES

In this chapter, you learn:
- The sources of data used in business
- To construct tables and charts for categorical data
- To construct tables and charts for numerical data
- The principles of properly presenting graphs

OVERVIEW AND KEY CONCEPTS

Organizing Numerical Data

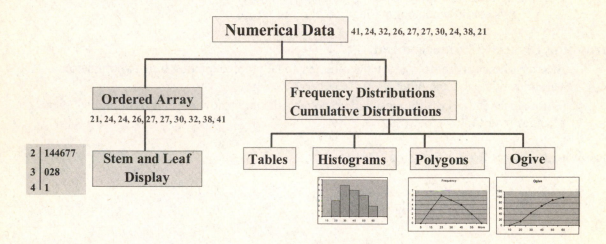

- **Ordered array:** Ordered sequence of raw data.
  - Ordered array makes it easier to pick out extremes, typical values, and concentrations of values.
- **Stem-and-leaf display:** Data are separated into leading digits (stems) and trailing digits (leaves).
  - Allows easy understanding of how the values distribute and cluster over the range of the observations in the data set.
- **Frequency distribution:** A summary table in which the data are arranged into numerically ordered class groupings or categories.
  - Makes the process of data analysis and interpretation much more manageable and meaningful
  - **Selecting the number of classes**: At least 5 but no more than 15 groupings
  - **Obtaining the class intervals:** $\text{width of interval} = \dfrac{\text{range}}{\text{number of desired class groupings}}$.
  - **Establishing the boundaries of the classes**: Non-overlapping classes must include the entire range of observations
  - **Class midpoint:** The point halfway between the boundaries of each class and is representative of the data within that class

- **Relative frequency distribution**: Formed by dividing the frequencies in each class of the frequency distribution by the total number of observations
  - Essential whenever one set of data is being compared with other sets of data if the number of observations in each set differs
- **Percentage distribution:** Formed by multiplying the relative frequencies by 100%
- **Cumulative distribution:** Formed from the frequency distribution, relative frequency distribution or percentage distribution by accumulating the frequencies, relative frequencies or percentages
  - It shows the number of observations below given values (lower boundaries)
- **Histogram:** Vertical bar chart in which the rectangular bars are constructed at the boundaries of each class
- **Percentage polygon:** Formed by having the midpoint of each class represent the data in that class and then connecting the sequence of midpoints at their respective class percentages
  - Useful when comparing two or more sets of data
- **Cumulative polygon (Ogive):** Formed by plotting cumulative percentages against the lower boundaries of the classes and connecting the cumulative percentages
  - It is useful when comparing two or more sets of data

Graphing Bivariate Numerical Data

- **Scatter diagram (scatter plot):** Two-dimensional graph depicting how two numerical variables relate to each other
- **Time-series plot:** Two-dimensional graph that illustrates how a series of numerical data changes over time

Table and Charts for Categorical Data

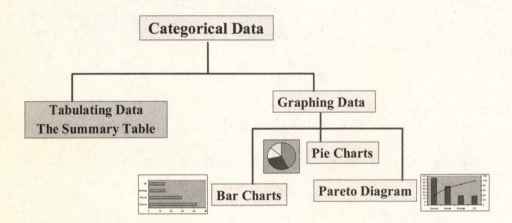

- **Summary table:** Similar to frequency distribution table for numerical data except there is no natural order of the classes
- **Bar chart:** Each category is depicted by a bar, the length of which represents the frequency or percentage of observations falling into a category
- **Pie chart:** The circle of 360^0 is divided into slices according to the percentage in each category
- **Pareto diagram**: A special type of vertical bar chart in which the categorized responses are plotted in the descending rank order of their frequencies and combined with a cumulative polygon on the same scale
  - Useful when the number of classification increases. Enables the separation of the "vital few" from the "trivial many"

Tabulating Bivariate Categorical Data
- Contingency table (cross-classification table): Two-way table of cross-classification

Principles of Graphical Excellence
- Well-designed presentation of data that provides substance, statistics and design
- Communicates complex ideas with clarity, precision and efficiency
- Gives the viewer the largest number of ideas in the shortest time with the least ink
- Almost always involves several dimensions
- Requires telling the truth about the data

Common Errors in Presenting Data
- Using "chart junk"
- No relative basis in comparing data between groups
- Compressing the vertical axis
- No zero point on the vertical axis

SOLUTIONS TO END OF SECTION
AND CHAPTER REVIEW EVEN PROBLEMS

2.2   The answer depends on the specific story.

2.4   The information presented there is based on surveys.

2.6   (a)   Table frequencies for all student responses

Student Major Categories

Gender	A	C	M	Totals
Male	14	9	2	25
Female	6	6	3	15
Totals	20	15	5	40

(b)   Table percentages based on overall student responses

Student Major Categories

Gender	A	C	M	Totals
Male	35.0%	22.5%	5.0%	62.5%
Female	15.0%	15.0%	7.5%	37.5%
Totals	50.0%	37.5%	12.5%	100.0%

Table based on row percentages

Student Major Categories

Gender	A	C	M	Totals
Male	56.0%	36.0%	8.0%	100.0%
Female	40.0%	40.0%	20.0%	100.0%
Totals	50.0%	37.5%	12.5%	100.0%

Table based on column percentages

Student Major Categories

Gender	A	C	M	Totals
Male	70.0%	60.0%	40.0%	62.5%
Female	30.0%	40.0%	60.0%	37.5%
Totals	100.0%	100.0%	100.0%	100.0%

2.8   (a)

Region	Oil Consumption (millions of barrels a day)	Percentage
Developed Europe	14.5	17.18%
Japan	4.4	5.21%
United States	18.8	22.27%
Rest of the world	46.7	55.33%
Total	84.4	100.00%

(b)   More than half the oil consumed is from countries other than the U.S., Japan, and developed Europe. More than 20% is consumed by the U.S. and slightly less than 20% is consumed by developed Europe.

2.10   (a)   Table of total percentages

ENJOY SHOPPING FOR CLOTHING FOR YOURSELF	GENDER		
	Male	Female	Total
Yes	22%	25%	47%
No	28%	25%	53%
Total	50%	50%	100%

Table of row percentages

ENJOY SHOPPING FOR CLOTHING FOR YOURSELF	GENDER		
	Male	Female	Total
Yes	46%	54%	100%
No	53%	47%	100%
Total	50%	50%	100%

Table of column percentages

ENJOY SHOPPING FOR CLOTHING FOR YOURSELF	GENDER		
	Male	Female	Total
Yes	44%	51%	47%
No	56%	49%	53%
Total	100%	100%	100%

(b)   A higher percentage of females enjoy shopping for clothing for themselves.

2.12   Table of row percentages

	Need => 3 Clicks		
Year	Yes	No	
2009	39%	61%	100%
2008	7%	93%	100%

According to the row percentages table, 32% more online retailers were requiring three or more clicks in 2009 than in 2008.

2.14   Ordered array: 73 78 78 78 85 88 91

2.16   (a)   The class boundaries of the 9 classes can be "10 to less than 20", "20 to less than 30", "30 to less than 40", "40 to less than 50", "50 to less than 60", "60 to less than 70", "70 to less than 80", "80 to less than 90", and "90 to less than 100".

(b)   The class-interval width is $= \dfrac{97.8 - 11.6}{9} = 9.58 \cong 10$.

(c)   The nine class midpoints are: 15, 25, 35, 45, 55, 65, 75, 85, and 95.

2.18   (a)

Electricity Costs	Frequency	Percentage
$80 to $99	4	8%
$100 to $119	7	14
$120 to $139	9	18
$140 to $159	13	26
$160 to $179	9	18
$180 to $199	5	10
$200 to $219	3	6

(b)

Electricity Costs	Frequency	Percentage	Cumulative %
$99	4	8%	8%
$119	7	14%	22%
$139	9	18%	40%
$159	13	26%	66%
$179	9	18%	84%
$199	5	10%	94%
$219	3	6%	100%

(c)   The majority of utility charges are clustered between $120 and $180.

2.20   (a), (b)

Bin	Frequency	Percentage	Cumulative %
8.310 -- 8.329	3	6.12%	6.12%
8.330 -- 8.349	2	4.08%	10.20%
8.350 -- 8.369	1	2.04%	12.24%
8.370 -- 8.389	4	8.16%	20.41%
8.390 -- 8.409	5	10.20%	30.61%
8.410 -- 8.429	16	32.65%	63.26%
8.430 -- 8.449	5	10.20%	73.46%
8.450 -- 8.469	5	10.20%	83.66%
8.470 -- 8.489	6	12.24%	95.90%
8.490 -- 8.509	2	4.08%	100.00%

(c)   All the troughs will meet the company's requirements of between 8.31 and 8.61 inches wide.

2.22   (a)

Bulb Life (hrs)	Frequency Manufacturer A		Bulb Life (hrs)	Frequency Manufacturer B
650 -- 749	3		750 -- 849	2
750 -- 849	5		850 -- 949	8
850 -- 949	20		950 -- 1049	16
950 -- 1049	9		1050 -- 1149	9
1050 -- 1149	3		1150 -- 1249	5

2.22 (a), (b)
cont.

Bulb Life (hrs)	A		B	
	Percentage	Cumulative %	Percentage	Cumulative %
650 – 749	7.50%	7.50%	.00%	0.00%
750 – 849	12.50%	20.00%	5.00%	5.00%
850 – 949	50.00%	70.00%	20.00%	25.00%
950 – 1049	22.50%	92.50%	40.00%	65.00%
1050 – 1149	7.50%	100.00%	22.50%	87.50%
1150 – 1249	0.00%	100.00%	12.50%	100.00%

(c) Manufacturer B produces bulbs with longer lives than Manufacturer A. The cumulative percentage for Manufacturer B shows 65% of its bulbs lasted less than 1,050 hours, contrasted with 70% of Manufacturer A's bulbs, which lasted less than 950 hours. None of Manufacturer A's bulbs lasted more than 1,149 hours, but 12.5% of Manufacturer B's bulbs lasted between 1,150 and 1,249 hours. At the same time, 7.5% of Manufacturer A's bulbs lasted less than 750 hours, whereas all of Manufacturer B's bulbs lasted at least 750 hours

2.24 (a) Note: %s converted to counts. $n = 1264$

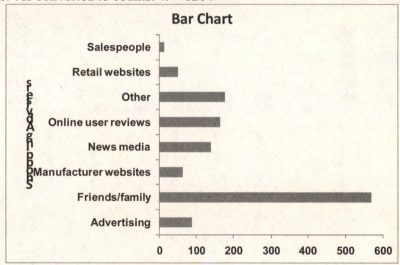

2.24   (a)
cont.

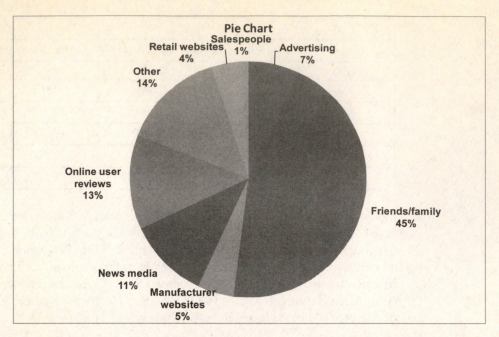

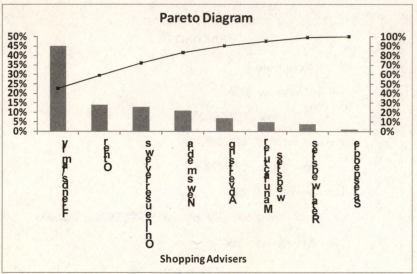

(b)   The Pareto diagram is better than the pie chart to portray these data because it not
only sorts the frequencies in descending order, it also provides the cumulative
polygon on the same scale.

(c)   You can conclude that friends/family account for the largest percentage of 45%.
When other, news media, and online user reviews are added to friends/family, this
accounts for 83%.

2.26   (a)

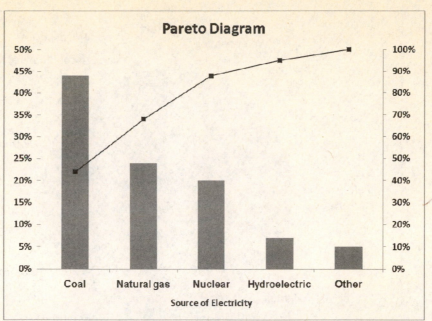

(b)   According to the Pareto chart, slightly less than 90% of the power is derived from coal, nuclear, or natural gas.

(c)

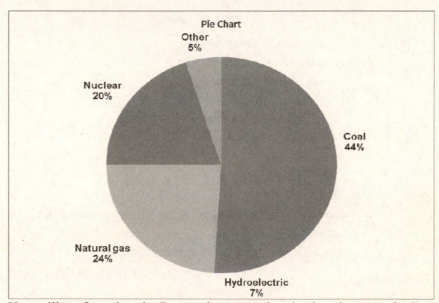

(d)   You will prefer using the Pareto chart over the pie chart because the Pareto chart not only sorts the frequencies in descending order, it also provides the cumulative polygon on the same scale.

2.28   (a)

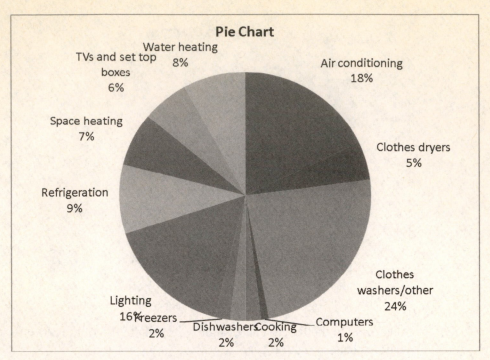

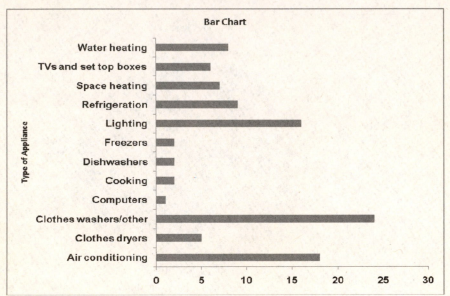

2.28   (a)
cont.

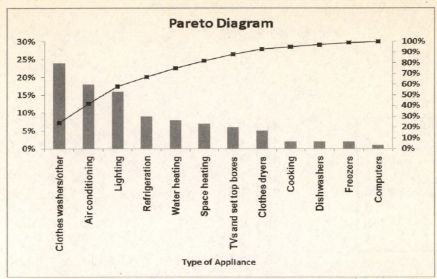

(b)   The Pareto diagram is better than the pie chart and bar chart because it not only sorts the frequencies in descending order, it also provides the cumulative polygon on the same scale.

(c)   Almost 60% of the residential electricity consumption in the United States is on "Clothes washers/other", "Air conditioning", and "Lighting".

2.30   (a)

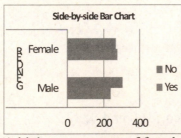

(b)   A higher percentage of females enjoy shopping for clothing.

2.32   (a)

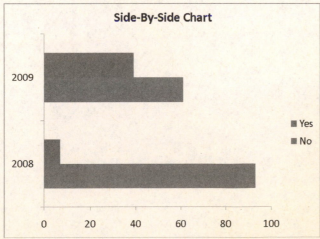

(b)   32% more online retailers were requiring three or more clicks in 2009 than in 2008.

2.34   Ordered array: 50 74 74 76 81 89 92

2.36   (a)

Stem-and-Leaf Display

Stem unit: 10

Statistics	
Sample Size	30
Mean	194.7
Median	179
Std.	56.8210
Deviation	4
Minimum	115
Maximum	335

```
11 | 5
12 | 1 7
13 | 2
14 | 1
15 | 1 8

16 | 0 1 2 8
17 | 0 2 3 8
18 | 0 4
19 |
20 | 7 8
21 | 2 6 7
22 | 1 2 7 7
23 |
24 |
25 | 0
26 |
27 |
28 |
29 |
30 |
31 | 6
32 |
33 | 0 5
```

(b)   The results are concentrated between $160 and $227.

2.38   (a)

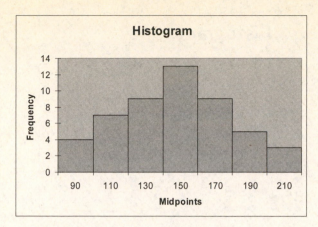

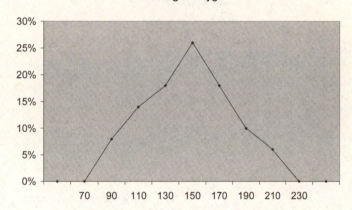

(b)

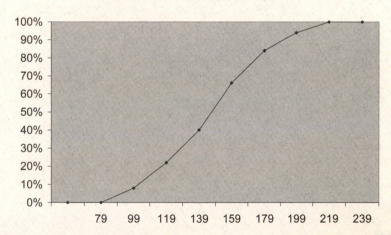

(c)   The majority of utility charges are clustered between $120 and $180.

2.40   The property taxes per capita appear to be right-skewed with approximately 90% falling between $399 and $1,700, and the remaining 10% fall between $1,700 and $2,100. The center is at about $1,000.

2.42   (a)

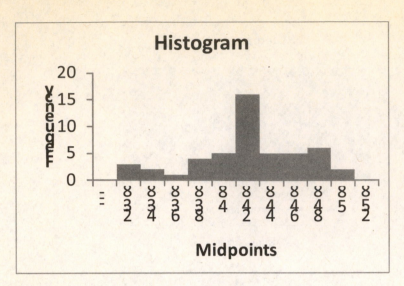

(b)

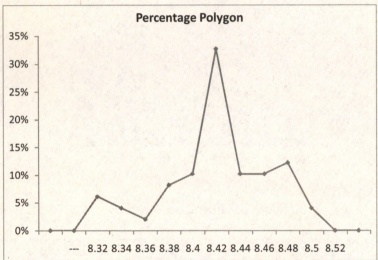

(c)   All the troughs will meet the company's requirements of between 8.31 and 8.61 inches wide.

2.44   (a)

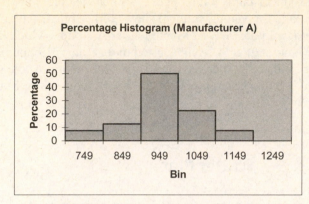

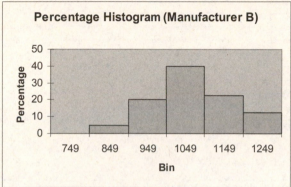

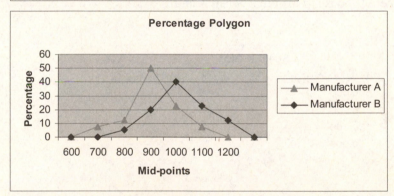

(b)

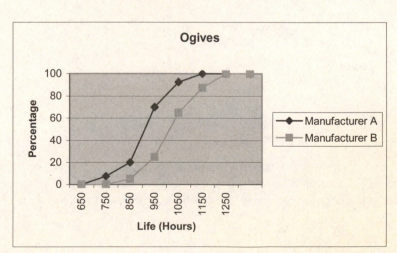

2.44   (c)   Manufacturer B produces bulbs with longer lives than Manufacturer A. The
cont.   cumulative percentage for Manufacturer B shows 65% of their bulbs lasted 1049
                 hours or less contrasted with 70% of Manufacturer A's bulbs which lasted 949 hours
                 or less. None of Manufacturer A's bulbs lasted more than 1149 hours, but 12.5% of
                 Manufacturer B's bulbs lasted between 1150 and 1249 hours. At the same time, 7.5%
                 of Manufacturer A's bulbs lasted less than 750 hours, while all of Manufacturer B's
                 bulbs lasted at least 750 hours.

2.46   (a)

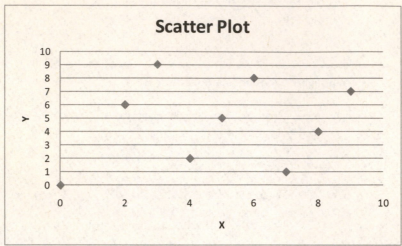

        (b)   There is no relationship between *X* and *Y*.

2.48   (a)

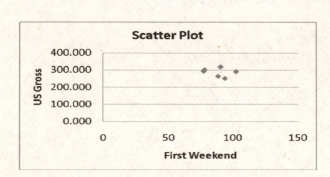

        (b)

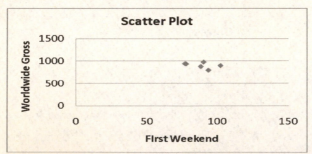

        (c)   There appears to be a rather weak negative relationship between first weekend gross
               and U. S. gross and between first weekend gross and worldwide gross. However,
               due to the small sample size, the relationships should not be taken as conclusive.

2.50   (a)   Yes, schools with higher revenues will also have higher coaches' salaries.
        (b)

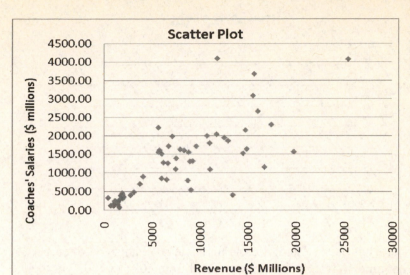

        (c)   There appears to be a positive relationship between coaches' salary and revenue.
               Yes, this is borne out by the data.

2.52   (a)   Excel output:

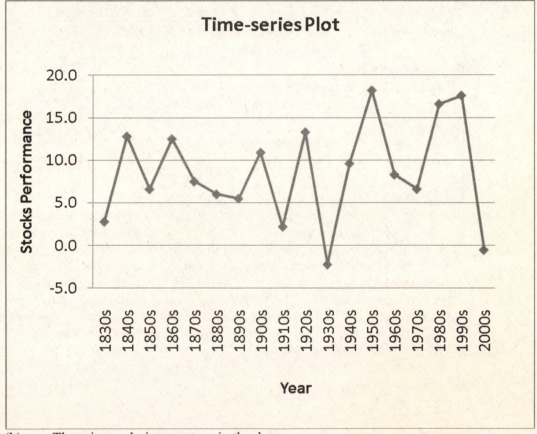

        (b)   There is no obvious pattern in the data.

2.54   (a)

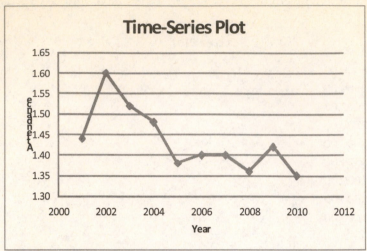

(b)   There has been a slight decline in movie attendance between 2001and 2010. During that time, movie attendance increased from 2001 to 2002 but then decreased to a level below that in 2001.

2.56   (a)

Count of Risk		Fees		
Risk	Type	No	Yes	Grand Total
Above Average	Intermediate Government	9.44%	8.89%	18.33%
	Short Term Corporate	11.11%	2.78%	13.89%
Above Average Total		20.56%	11.67%	32.22%
Average	Intermediate Government	10.56%	5.56%	16.11%
	Short Term Corporate	12.78%	4.44%	17.22%
Average Total		23.33%	10.00%	33.33%
Below Average	Intermediate Government	10.56%	5.00%	15.56%
	Short Term Corporate	16.67%	2.22%	18.89%
Below Average Total		27.22%	7.22%	34.44%
Grand Total		71.11%	28.89%	100.00%

(b)   Although the ratio of fee-yes to fee-no bond funds for intermediate government category seems to be about 2-to-3 (19% to 31%), the ratio for above average risk intermediate government bond funds is closer to 1-to-1 (8.9% to 9.4%). While the group "intermediate government funds that do not charge a fee" has nearly equal numbers of above average risk, average risk, and below risk funds, the group "short term corporate bond funds that do not charge a fee" contains about fifty percent more below average risk funds than above average ones. The pattern of risk percentages differs between the fee-yes and fee-no funds in each bond fund category.

(c)   The results for type, fee, and risk, in the two years are similar.

2.58   (a)

Count of Risk		Fees		
Category	Risk	No	Yes	Grand Total
⊟ Large Cap Average	Average	95	79	174
	High	76	51	127
	Low	80	69	149
Large Cap Total		251	199	450
⊟ Mid Cap	Average	33	22	55
	High	41	45	86
	Low	23	10	33
Mid Cap Total		97	77	174
⊟ Small Cap	Average	52	30	82
	High	84	58	142
	Low	16	4	20
Small Cap Total		152	92	244
Grand Total		500	368	868

Count of Risk		Fees		
Category	Risk	No	Yes	Grand Total
⊟ Large Cap	Average	10.94%	9.10%	20.05%
	High	8.76%	5.88%	14.63%
	Low	9.22%	7.95%	17.17%
Large Cap Total		28.92%	22.93%	51.84%
⊟ Mid Cap	Average	3.80%	2.53%	6.34%
	High	4.72%	5.18%	9.91%
	Low	2.65%	1.15%	3.80%
Mid Cap Total		11.18%	8.87%	20.05%
⊟ Small Cap	Average	5.99%	3.46%	9.45%
	High	9.68%	6.68%	16.36%
	Low	1.84%	0.46%	2.30%
Small Cap Total		17.51%	10.60%	28.11%
Grand Total		57.60%	42.40%	100.00%

(b)   Large cap funds without fees are fairly evenly spread in risk while large cap funds with fees are more likely to have average or low risk. Mid cap and small cap funds regardless of fees are more likely to have average or high risk.

2.68   (a)

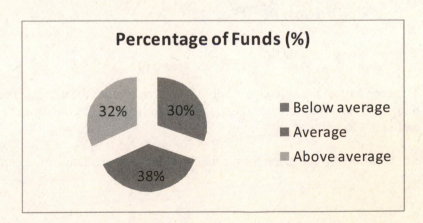

2.68   (a)
cont.

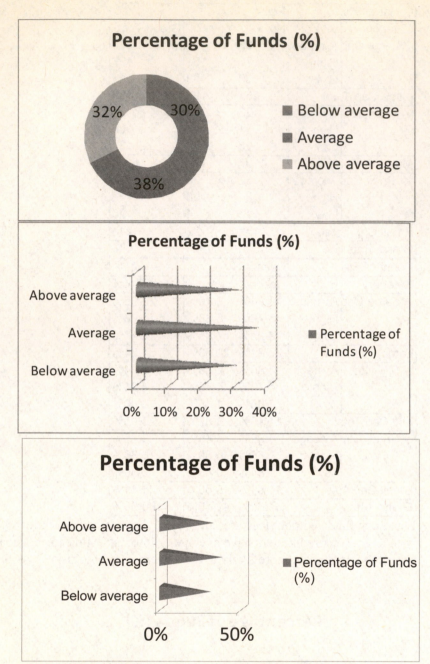

(b)   The bar chart and the pie chart should be preferred over the exploded pie chart, doughnut chart, the cone chart and the pyramid chart since the former set is simpler and easier to interpret.

2.70   A summary table allows one to determine the frequency or percentage of occurrences in each category.

2.72   The bar chart for categorical data is plotted with the categories on the vertical axis and the frequencies or percentages on the horizontal axis. In addition, there is a separation between categories. The histogram is plotted with the class grouping on the horizontal axis and the frequencies or percentages on the vertical axis. This allows one to more easily determine the distribution of the data. In addition, there are no gaps between classes in the histogram.

2.74   Because the categories are arranged according to frequency or importance, it allows the user to focus attention on the categories that have the greatest frequency or importance.

2.76   A contingency table contains information on two categorical variables whereas a multidimensional table can display information on more than two categorical variables.

2.78   (a)

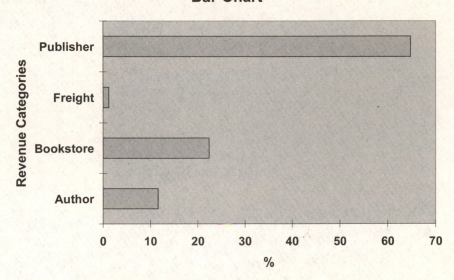

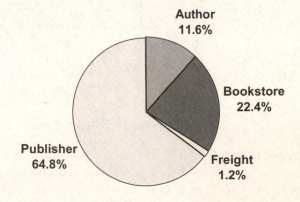

2.78   (a)
cont.

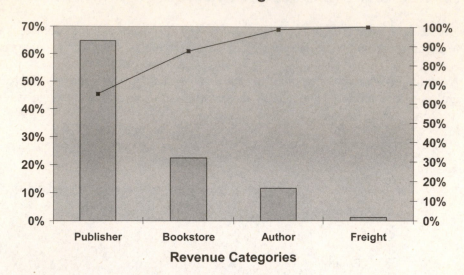

(b)

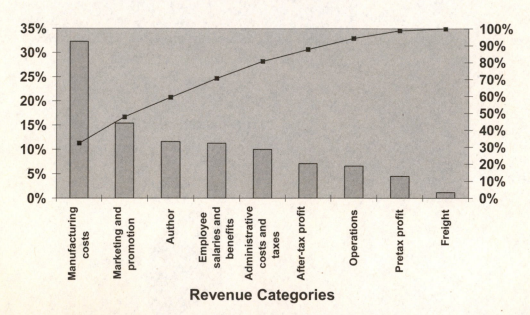

(c)   The publisher gets the largest portion (64.8%) of the revenue. About half (32.3%) of
        the revenue received by the publisher covers manufacturing costs. The publisher's
        marketing and promotion account for the next largest share of the revenue, at 15.4%.
        Author, bookstore employee salaries and benefits, and publisher administrative costs
        and taxes each account for around 10% of the revenue, whereas the publisher after-
        tax profit, bookstore operations, bookstore pretax profit, and freight constitute the
        "trivial few" allocations of the revenue. Yes, the bookstore gets twice the revenue of
        the authors.

2.80   (a)

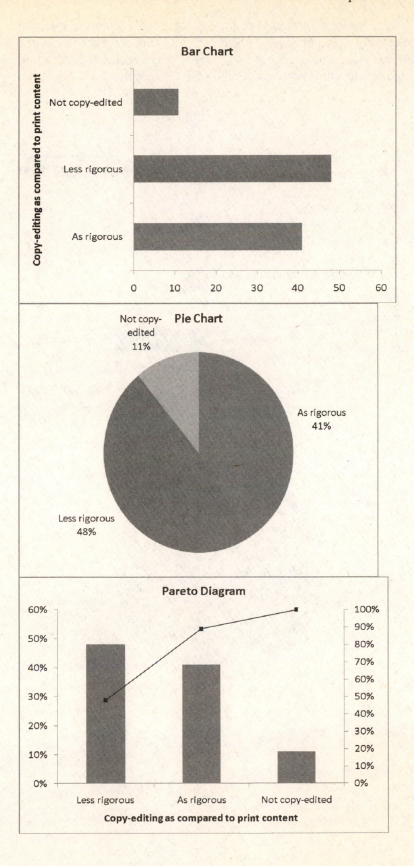

2.80   (b)   Since there are only three categories, all the three graphical methods are capable of
cont.   portraying these data well. The Pareto diagram, however, is better than the pie chart
                    and bar chart because it not only sorts the frequencies in descending order, it also
                    provides the cumulative polygon on the same scale.

        (c)

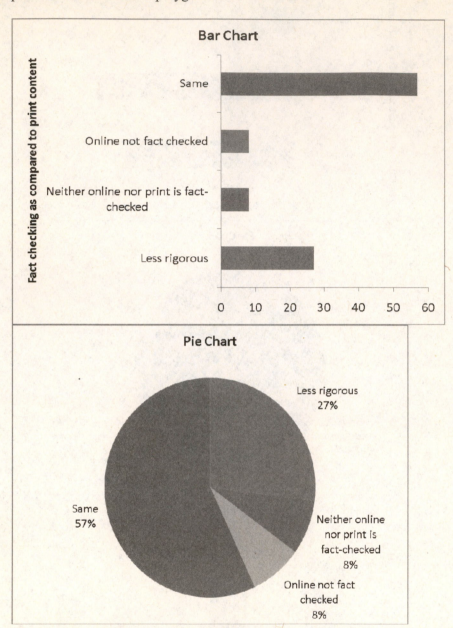

2.80   (c)
cont.

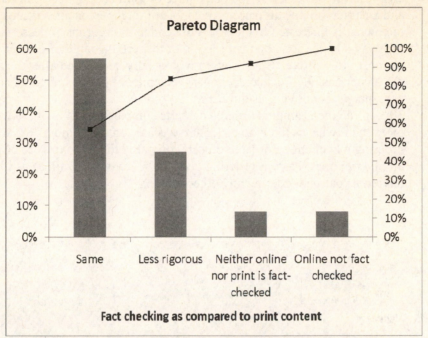

(d)   Since there are only four categories, all the three graphical methods are capable of portraying these data well. The Pareto diagram, however, is better than the pie chart and bar chart because it not only sorts the frequencies in descending order, it also provides the cumulative polygon on the same scale.

(e)   Based on the Pareto chart for copy-editing, about 50% of the contents in online consumer magazines receive less rigorous copy-editing. Based on the Pareto chart for fact-checking, more than 50% of the contents in online consumer magazines receive the same amount of fact-checking.

2.82   (a)

Dessert Ordered	Gender			Dessert Ordered	Beef Entrée		
	Male	Female	Total		Yes	No	Total
Yes	71%	29%	100%	Yes	52%	48%	100%
No	48%	52%	100%	No	25%	75%	100%
Total	53%	47%	100%	Total	31%	69%	100%

Dessert Ordered	Gender			Dessert Ordered	Beef Entrée		
	Male	Female	Total		Yes	No	Total
Yes	30%	14%	23%	Yes	38%	16%	23%
No	70%	86%	77%	No	62%	84%	77%
Total	100%	100%	100%	Total	100%	100%	100%

Dessert Ordered	Gender			Dessert Ordered	Beef Entrée		
	Male	Female	Total		Yes	No	Total
Yes	16%	7%	23%	Yes	12%	11%	23%
No	37%	40%	77%	No	19%	58%	77%
Total	53%	47%	100%	Total	31%	69%	100%

2.82   (b)   If the owner is interested in finding out the percentage of joint occurrence of gender
cont.   and ordering of dessert or the percentage of joint occurrence of ordering a beef entrée
               and a dessert among all patrons, the table of total percentages is most informative. If
               the owner is interested in the effect of gender on ordering of dessert or the effect of
               ordering a beef entrée on the ordering of dessert, the table of column percentages will
               be most informative. Since dessert will usually be ordered after the main entree and
               the owner has no direct control over the gender of patrons, the table of row
               percentages is not very useful here.

        (c)   30% of the men sampled ordered desserts compared to 14% of the women. Men are
               more than twice as likely to order desserts as women. Almost 38% of the patrons
               ordering a beef entree ordered dessert compared to less than 16% of patrons ordering
               all other entrees. Patrons ordering beef are better than 2.3 times as likely to order
               dessert as patrons ordering any other entree.

2.84   (a)

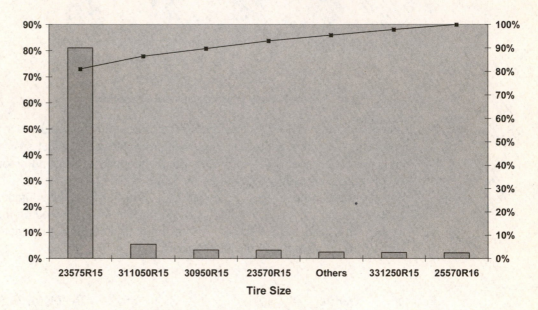

23575R15 accounts for over 80% of the warranty claims.

2.84   (b)
cont.

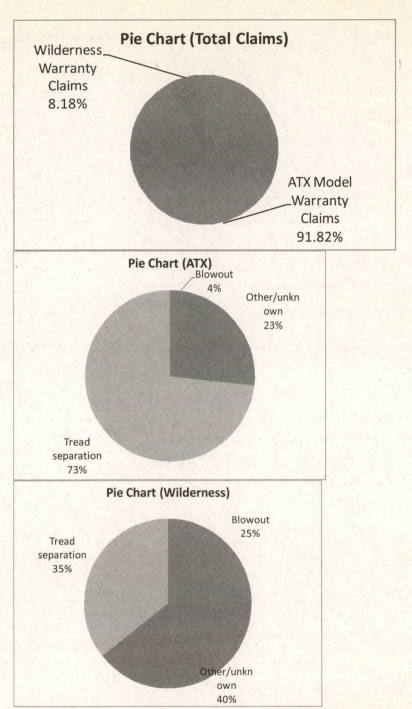

91.82% of the warranty claims are from the ATX model.

2.84   (c)
cont.

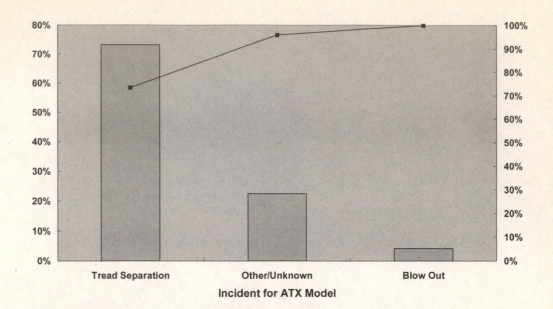

Tread separation accounts for 73.23% of the warranty claims among the ATX model..

(d)

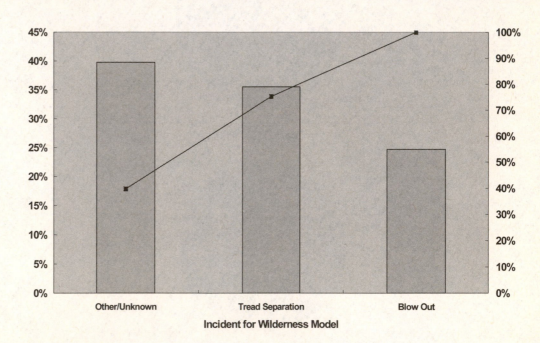

The number of claims is fairly evenly distributed among the three incidents; other/unknown incidents account for almost 40% of the claims, tread separation accounts for about 35% of the claims, and blowout accounts for about 25% of the claims.

2.86   (a)

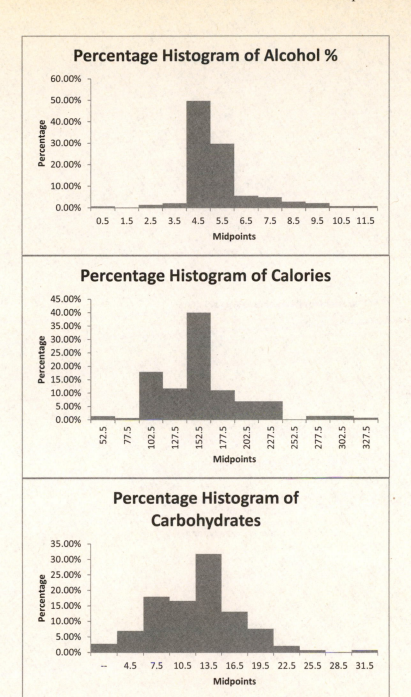

2.86   (b)
cont.

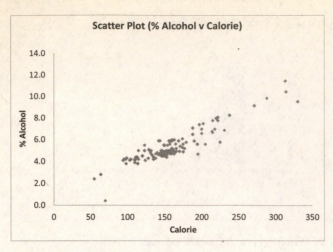

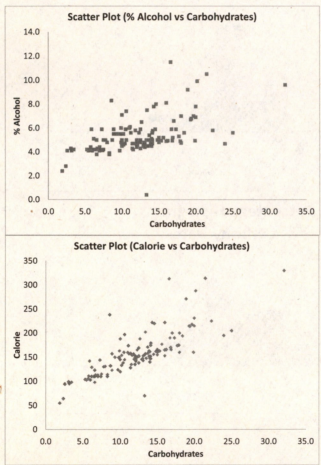

2.86 (c) cont.   The alcohol percentage is concentrated between 4% and 6%, with the largest concentration between 4% and 5%. The calories are concentrated between 140 and 160. The carbohydrates are concentrated between 12 and 15. There are outliers in the percentage of alcohol in both tails. The outlier in the lower tail is due to the non-alcoholic beer O'Doul's with only a 0.4% alcohol content. There are a few beers with alcohol content as high as around 11.5%. There are a few beers with calorie content as high as 330 and carbohydrates as high as 32.1. There is a strong positive relationship between percentage alcohol and calories, and calories and carbohydrates and a moderately positive relationship between percentage alcohol and carbohydrates.

There is a strong positive relationship between percentage alcohol and calories, and calories and carbohydrates and a moderately positive relationship between percentage alcohol and carbohydrates.

2.88 (a)   1-year CD

Stem-and-Leaf Display

Stem unit: 0.1

Statistics	
Sample Size	23
Mean	1.046957
Median	1.16
Std. Deviation	0.219968
Minimum	0.6
Maximum	1.26

```
 6 | 0 0
 7 | 5
 8 | 0 0 5
 9 | 0 1
10 | 0
11 | 1 5 6
12 | 0 0 0 0 0 1 4 4 5 5
   | 6
```

5-year CD

Stem-and-Leaf Display

Stem unit: 0.1

Statistics	
Sample Size	23
Mean	2.307391
Median	2.3
Std. Deviation	0.183333
Minimum	1.9
Maximum	2.65

```
19 | 0
20 | 0 0
21 | 2
22 | 0 2 5 5 7 8
23 | 0 0 5 8 9 9
24 | 0 0 3 9
25 | 5 5
26 | 5
```

2.88   (b)
cont.

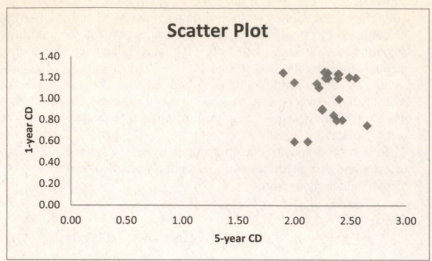

(c)   The one-year CD return is concentrated between 1.2%. The five-year CD return is concentrated between 2.2% and 2.5%. In general, the five-year CD has the higher yield.

There does not appear to be a positive relationship between the yield of the money market and the five-year CD.

2.90   (a)

Frequencies (Boston)

Weight (Boston)	Frequency	Percentage
3015 but less than 3050	2	0.54%
3050 but less than 3085	44	11.96%
3085 but less than 3120	122	33.15%
3120 but less than 3155	131	35.60%
3155 but less than 3190	58	15.76%
3190 but less than 3225	7	1.90%
3225 but less than 3260	3	0.82%
3260 but less than 3295	1	0.27%

(b)

Frequencies (Vermont)

Weight (Vermont)	Frequency	Percentage
3550 but less than 3600	4	1.21%
3600 but less than 3650	31	9.39%
3650 but less than 3700	115	34.85%
3700 but less than 3750	131	39.70%
3750 but less than 3800	36	10.91%
3800 but less than 3850	12	3.64%
3850 but less than 3900	1	0.30%

2.90   (c)
cont.

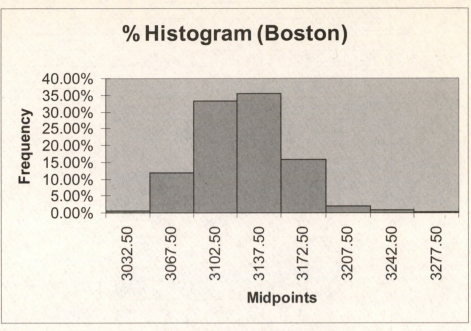

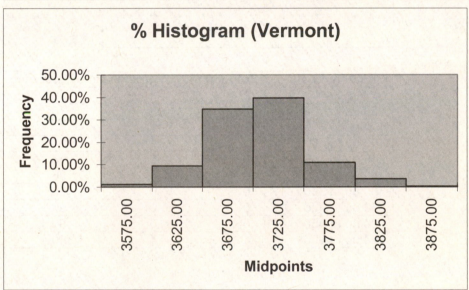

(d)   0.54% of the "Boston" shingles pallets are underweight while 0.27% are overweight. 1.21% of the "Vermont" shingles pallets are underweight while 3.94% are overweight.

2.92   (a)

Calories	Frequency	Percentage	Percentage Less Than
50 up to 100	3	12%	12%
100 up to 150	3	12	24
150 up to 200	9	36	60
200 up to 250	6	24	84
250 up to 300	3	12	96
300 up to 350	0	0	96
350 up to 400	1	4	100

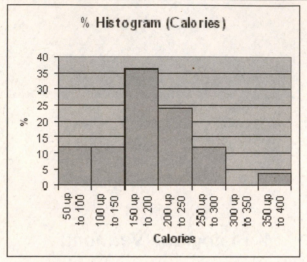

(b)

Cholesterol	Frequency	Percentage	Percentage Less Than
0 up to 50	2	8	8%
50 up to 100	17	68	76
100 up to 150	4	16	92
150 up to 200	1	4	96
200 up to 250	0	0	96
250 up to 300	0	0	96
300 up to 350	0	0	96
350 up to 400	0	0	96
400 up to 450	0	0	96
450 up to 500	1	4	100

2.92   (b)
cont.

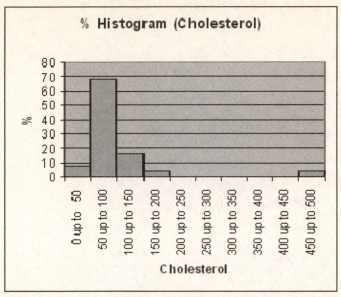

(c)   The sampled fresh red meats, poultry, and fish vary from 98 to 397 calories per serving, with the highest concentration between 150 to 200 calories. One protein source, spareribs, with 397 calories, is more than 100 calories above the next highest caloric food. The protein content of the sampled foods varies from 16 to 33 grams, with 68% of the data values falling between 24 and 32 grams. Spareribs and fried liver are both very different from other foods sampled—the former on calories and the latter on cholesterol content.

2.94   (a)

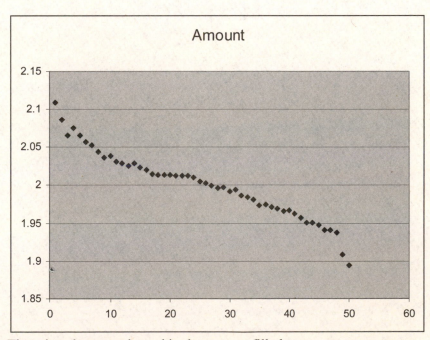

(b)   There is a downward trend in the amount filled.
(c)   The amount filled in the next bottle will most likely be below 1.894 liter.
(d)   The scatter plot of the amount of soft drink filled against time reveals the trend of the data, whereas a histogram only provides information on the distribution of the data.

2.100   (a) **Expense Ratio**

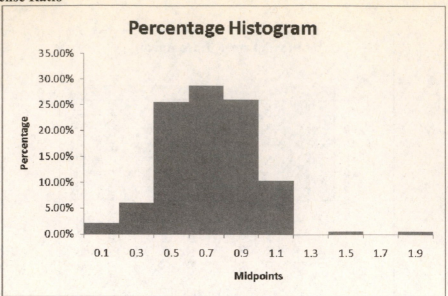

(b)

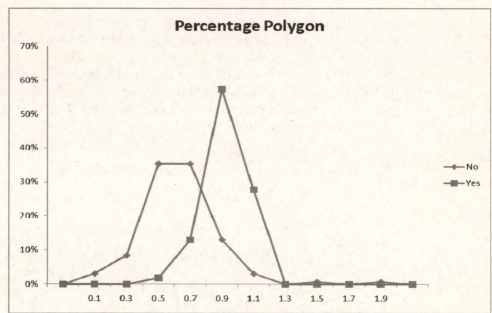

(c)   The expense ratio of all bond funds is scattered around 0.75. Bond funds with fees have expense ratios scattered around 0.9 while bond funds without fees have expense ratios scattered around 0.6.

2.102   (a) **Five-year Annualized Return**

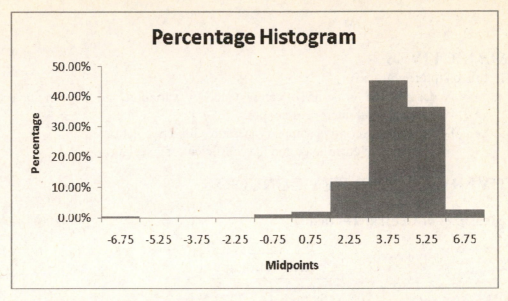

(b)

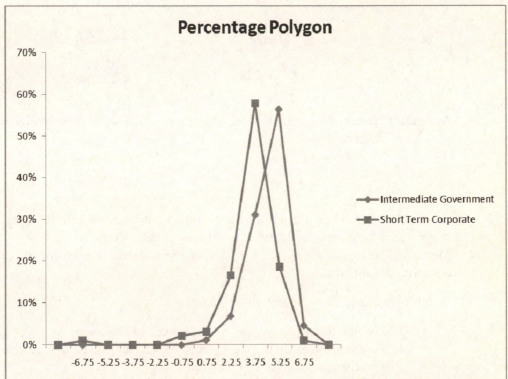

(c)   The five-year annualized return of all the bond funds is left-skewed with majority of them (about 93%) scattered between 1.5% and 6%. About 1.6% of the bond funds have a negative five-year annualized return while about 2.7% of them have a return higher than 6%. In general, the intermediate government funds have higher five-year annualized returns than short term corporate funds. Both types of mutual funds have five-year annualized returns skewed to the left.

CHAPTER 3

OBJECTIVES

In this chapter, you learn:

- To describe the properties of central tendency, variation, and shape in numerical data
- To construct and interpret a boxplot
- To compute descriptive summary measures for a population
- To compute the covariance and the coefficient of correlation

OVERVIEW AND KEY CONCEPTS

Measures of Central Tendency

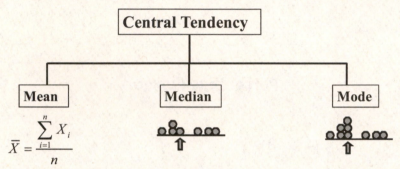

- **Arithmetic mean:** The sum of all the observations in a set of data divided by the total number of observations.

  - $$\bar{X} = \frac{\sum_{i=1}^{n} X_i}{n}$$

  - The arithmetic mean is the most common measure of central tendency.
  - It is very sensitive to extreme values, called outliers.
- **Median:** The value such that 50% of the observations are smaller and 50% of the observations are larger.

  - Median $= \dfrac{n+1}{2}$ ranked observation.

  - If n is odd, the median is the middle ranked observation.
  - If n is even, the median is the average of the two middle ranked observations.
  - The median is not affected by extreme values.
- **Mode:** The value that occurs most often in a set of data.
  - It is not affected by extreme values.
  - There may be several modes or there may be no mode in a set of data.
  - It can be used for either numerical or categorical data.
- **Quartiles:** The most widely used measures of noncentral location.
  - The ordered data is split into four equal portions.
  - The first quartile (Q_1) is the value for which 25% of the observations are smaller and 75% are larger.

  - $Q_1 = \dfrac{n+1}{4}$ ordered observation.

- The third quartile (Q_3) is the value for which 75% of the observations are smaller and 25% are larger.

  $Q_3 = \dfrac{3(n+1)}{4}$ ordered observation.

- The median is the second quartile.

  $Q_2 = \dfrac{(n+1)}{2}$ ordered observation.

Measures of Variation

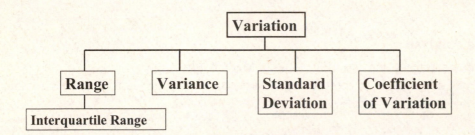

- **Range:** The largest value minus the smallest value.
  - The range ignores how the data are distributed.
  - It is very sensitive to extreme values.
- **Interquartile range (mid-spread):** The 3rd quartile minus the 1st quartile.
  - It is not affected by extreme values.
  - It measures the spread of the middle 50% of the observations.
- **Sample variance:** The sum of the squared differences around the arithmetic mean divided by the sample size minus 1.

  - $S^2 = \dfrac{\sum\limits_{i=1}^{n}\left(X_i - \bar{X}\right)^2}{n-1}$

  - Sample variance measures the average scatter around the mean.
- **Sample standard deviation:** The square root of the sample variance.

  - $S = \sqrt{\dfrac{\sum\limits_{i=1}^{n}\left(X_i - \bar{X}\right)^2}{n-1}}$

  - Sample standard deviation has the same units of measurement as the original data.
- **Coefficient of Variation:** The standard deviation divided by the arithmetic mean, multiplied by 100%.

  - $CV = \left(\dfrac{S}{\bar{X}}\right)100\%$

  - It is a relative measure of variation.
  - It is used in comparing two or more sets of data measured in different units.

Shape of a Distribution

- The shape describes how data is distributed.
- Measures of shapes can be symmetric or skewed.

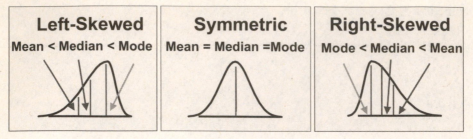

Exploratory Data Analysis

- A five-number summary consists of $X_{smallest}$, Q_1, Median, Q_3, $X_{largest}$.
- **Box plot:** Provides a graphical representation of the data based on the five-number summary.

Distribution Shape and Box Plot

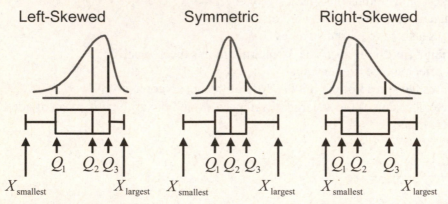

- In right-skewed distributions, the distance from the median to $X_{largest}$ is greater than the distance from $X_{smallest}$ to the median.
- In right-skewed distribution, the distance from Q_3 to $X_{largest}$ is greater than the distance from $X_{smallest}$ to Q_1.
- In left-skewed distributions, the distance from the median to $X_{largest}$ is smaller than the distance from $X_{smallest}$ to the median.
- In left-skewed distribution, the distance from Q_3 to $X_{largest}$ is smaller than the distance from $X_{smallest}$ to Q_1.

Obtaining Descriptive Summary Measures from a Population

- **Population mean:** $\mu = \dfrac{\sum_{i=1}^{N} X_i}{N}$

- **Population variance:** $\sigma^2 = \dfrac{\sum_{i=1}^{N}(X_i - \mu)^2}{N}$

- **Population standard deviation:** $\sigma = \sqrt{\dfrac{\sum_{i=1}^{N}(X_i - \mu)^2}{N}}$

- **The empirical rule:** In bell-shaped distributions, roughly 68% of the observations are contained within a distance of ± 1 standard deviation around the mean, approximately 95% of the observations are contained within a distance of ± 2 standard deviation around the mean and approximately 99.7% are contained within a distance of ± 3 standard deviation around the mean.

- **The Chebyshev rule:** Regardless of how skewed a set of data is distributed, the percentage of observations that are contained within distances of k standard deviations around the mean must be at least $\left(1 - \dfrac{1}{k^2}\right)100\%$

  - At least 75% of the observations must be contained within distances of ± 2 standard deviation around the mean.
  - At least 88.89% of the observations must be contained within distances of ± 3 standard deviation around the mean.
  - At least 93.75% of the observations must be contained within distances of ± 4 standard deviation around the mean.

Covariance and Correlation Coefficient as a Measure of Strength between Two Numerical Variables

- **The sample covariance:** $\mathrm{cov}(X, Y) = \dfrac{\sum_{i=1}^{n}(X_i - \bar{X})(Y_i - \bar{Y})}{n-1}$

  - Measures the strength of a linear relationship between 2 numerical variables X and Y.
  - Can have any value.
  - Unsuitable for determining the relative strength of the relationship.

- **The sample coefficient of correlation:** $r = \dfrac{\sum_{i=1}^{n}(X_i - \bar{X})(Y_i - \bar{Y})}{\sqrt{\sum_{i=1}^{n}(X_i - \bar{X})^2 \sum_{i=1}^{n}(Y_i - \bar{Y})^2}}$

  - Measures the strength of a linear relationship between 2 numerical variables X and Y.
  - Is unit free.
  - Suitable for determining the relative strength of the relationship.

- The values are between −1 and +1.
- The closer r is to −1, the stronger the negative linear relationship.
- The closer r is to +1, the stronger the positive linear relationship.
- If r is close to 0, little or no linear relationship exists.

SOLUTIONS TO END OF SECTION
AND CHAPTER REVIEW EVEN PROBLEMS

3.2   (a)   Excel output:

X	
Mean	7
Median	7
Mode	7
Standard Deviation	3.286335
Sample Variance	10.8
Range	9
Minimum	3
Maximum	12
Sum	42
Count	6
First Quartile	4
Third Quartile	9
Interquartile Range	5
Coefficient of Variation	46.9476%

Mean = 7   Median = 7   Mode = 7

(b)   Range = 9   Variance = 10.8
        Standard deviation = 3.286
        Coefficient of variation = (3.286/7)•100% = 46.948%

(c)   Z scores: 0, -0.913, 0.609, 0, -1.217, 1.522
        None of the Z scores is larger than 3.0 or smaller than -3.0. There is no outlier.

(d)   Since the mean equals the median, the distribution is symmetrical.

3.4   Excel output:

X	
Mean	2
Median	7
Mode	7
Standard Deviation	7.874007874
Sample Variance	62
Range	17
Minimum	-8
Maximum	9
Sum	10
Count	5
First Quartile	-6.5
Third Quartile	8
Interquartile Range	14.5
Coefficient of Variation	393.7004%

(a)   Mean = 2   Median = 7   Mode = 7

3.4   (b)   Range = 17   Variance = 62
cont.   Standard deviation = 7.874   Coefficient of variation = $(7.874/2) \cdot 100\% = 393.7\%$
       (c)   Z scores: 0.635, -0.889, -1.270, 0.635, 0.889. No outliers.
       (d)   Since the mean is less than the median, the distribution is left-skewed.

3.6   (a)

	Grade X	Grade Y
Mean	575	575.4
Median	575	575
Standard deviation	6.4	2.1

(b) If quality is measured by central tendency, Grade X tires provide slightly better quality
because X's mean and median are both equal to the expected value, 575 mm. If, however,
quality is measured by consistency, Grade Y provides better quality because, even though
Y's mean is only slightly larger than the mean for Grade X, Y's standard deviation is
much smaller. The range in values for Grade Y is 5 mm compared to the range in values
for Grade X, which is 16 mm.

(c) Excel output:

Grade X		Grade Y	
Mean	575	Mean	577.4
Median	575	Median	575
Mode	#N/A	Mode	#N/A
Standard Deviation	6.403124	Standard Deviation	6.107373
Sample Variance	41	Sample Variance	37.3
Range	16	Range	15
Minimum	568	Minimum	573
Maximum	584	Maximum	588
Sum	2875	Sum	2887
Count	5	Count	5

	Grade X	Grade Y, Altered
Mean	575	577.4
Median	575	575
Standard deviation	6.4	6.1

When the fifth Y tire measures 588 mm rather than 578 mm, Y's mean inner diameter
becomes 577.4 mm, which is larger than X's mean inner diameter, and Y's standard
deviation increases from 2.07 mm to 6.11 mm. In this case, X's tires are providing better
quality in terms of the mean inner diameter, with only slightly more variation among the
tires than Y's.

3.8   (a), (b)

Amount	
Mean	7.028888889
Median	7.38
Mode	#N/A
Standard Deviation	1.812487548
Sample Variance	3.285111111
Range	5.67
Minimum	4.2
Maximum	9.87
Sum	63.26
Count	9
First Quartile	5.445
Third Quartile	8.465
CV	25.79%

(c)   The mean is only slightly smaller than the median, so the data are only slightly left-skewed.

(d)   The mean amount spent is $7.03 and the median is $7.38. The average scatter of the amount spent around the mean is $1.81. The difference between the highest and the lowest amount spent is $5.67.

3.10   (a), (b)

MPG	
Mean	21.12
Median	22
Mode	22
Standard Deviation	2.2971
Sample Variance	5.276667
Range	10
Minimum	16
Maximum	26
Sum	528
Count	25
First Quartile	19.5
Third Quartile	22
CV	10.88%

3.10   (a),(b)
cont.

MPG	Z Score	MPG	Z Score
20	-0.48757	19	-0.9229
24	1.253755	19	-0.9229
22	0.383092	23	0.818423
23	0.818423	24	1.253755
20	-0.48757	21	-0.05224
22	0.383092	21	-0.05224
21	-0.05224	19	-0.9229
22	0.383092	21	-0.05224
22	0.383092	22	0.383092
19	-0.9229	22	0.383092
22	0.383092	16	-2.2289
22	0.383092	16	-2.2289
26	2.124418		

(c)   The data appears to be symmetrical since the median is about the same as the mean.

(d)   The distributions of MPG of the sedans is slightly right-skewed while the SUVs are symmetrical. The mean MPG of sedans is 4.67 higher than that of SUVs. The average scatter of the MPG of sedans is more than three times higher than that for SUVs. The range of sedans is more than 2 times higher than that for SUVs.

3.12   Excel output:

Cost($)	
Mean	0.925714
Standard Error	0.087472
Median	0.88
Mode	0.57
Standard Deviation	0.32729
Sample Variance	0.107119
Kurtosis	-0.73366
Skewness	0.698782
Range	0.96
Minimum	0.55
Maximum	1.51
Sum	12.96
Count	14
Minimum	0.55
First Quartile	0.68
Median	0.88
Third Quartile	1.14
Maximum	1.51
CV	35.36%

3.12   Excel output:
cont.

Cost($)	Z Score
0.68	-0.75075
0.72	-0.62854
0.92	-0.01746
1.14	0.654728
1.42	1.510238
0.94	0.043649
0.77	-0.47577
0.57	-1.08685
1.51	1.785224
0.57	-1.08685
0.55	-1.14796
0.86	-0.20078
1.41	1.479684
0.90	-0.07857

(a)   mean = 0.9257, median = 0.88, mode = 0.57

(b)   variance = 0.1071, standard deviation = 0.3273, range = 0.96,
        coefficient of variation = 35.36%.
        There is no outlier since none of the Z-scores has an absolute value that is greater
        than 3.0.

(c)   The data appear to be skewed to the right because the mean is greater than the
        median.

3.14   (a), (b)

Cost(English Pounds)	
Mean	82.33333
Median	77
Mode	#N/A
Standard Deviation	18.08498
Sample Variance	327.0667
Range	48
Minimum	62
Maximum	110
Sum	494
Count	6

(c)   Since the average room price is slightly higher than the median price, the room price
        is slightly right-skewed.

3.14   (d)   (a), (b)
cont.

Cost(English Pounds)	
Mean	90.66666667
Median	77
Mode	#N/A
Standard Deviation	36.01481177
Sample Variance	1297.066667
Range	98
Minimum	62
Maximum	160
Sum	544
Count	6

(c)   Since the average room price is greater than the median price, the room price is right-skewed.

3.16   Excel output:

Waiting Time	
Mean	7.114667
Standard Error	0.537619
Median	6.68
Mode	#N/A
Standard Deviation	2.082189
Sample Variance	4.335512
Kurtosis	-1.05627
Skewness	0.072493
Range	6.67
Minimum	3.82
Maximum	10.49
Sum	106.72
Count	15
First Quartile	5.64
Third Quartile	8.73
Interquartile Range	3.09
Coefficient of Variation	29.2662%

(a)   Mean = 7.114   Median = 6.68

3.16   (b)   Variance = 4.336   Standard deviation = 2.082   Range = 6.67
cont.   Coefficient of variation = 29.27%

Waiting Time	Z Score
9.66	1.222431
5.90	-0.58336
8.02	0.434799
5.79	-0.63619
8.73	0.775786
3.82	-1.58231
8.01	0.429996
8.35	0.593286
10.49	1.62105
6.68	-0.20875
5.64	-0.70823
4.08	-1.45744
6.17	-0.45369
9.91	1.342497
5.47	-0.78987

There is no outlier since none of the observations are greater than 3 standard deviations away from the mean.

(c)   Because the mean is greater than the median, the distribution is right-skewed.

(d)   The mean and median are both greater than 5 minutes. The distribution is right-skewed, meaning that there are some unusually high values. Further, 13 of the 15 bank customers sampled (or 86.7%) had waiting times greater than 5 minutes. So the customer is likely to experience a waiting time in excess of 5 minutes. The manager overstated the bank's service record in responding that the customer would "almost certainly" not wait longer than 5 minutes for service.

3.18   (a) $Q_1 = 4$, $Q_3 = 9$, interquartile range = 5
       (b)   Five-number summary: 3 4 7 9 12
       (c)

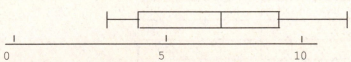

The distances between the median and the extremes are close, 4 and 5, but the differences in the tails are different (1 on the left and 3 on the right), so this distribution is slightly right-skewed.

(d)   In 3.2 (d), because the mean and median are equal , the distribution is symmetric. The box part of the graph is symmetric, but the tails show right-skewness.

3.20   (a) $Q_1 = -6.5$, $Q_3 = 8$, interquartile range = 14.5
        (b)   Five-number summary: -8 -6.5 7 8 9
        (c)

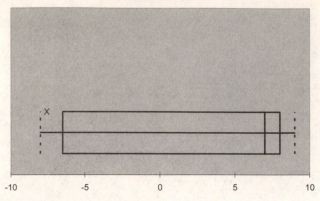

Box-and-whisker Plot

The distribution is left-skewed.
        (d)   This is consistent with the answer in 3.4 (d).

3.22   (a)   Excel output:

Cost($)	
Mean	0.925714286
Mode	0.57
Standard Deviation	0.327289904
Sample Variance	0.107118681
Range	0.96
Minimum	0.55
First Quartile	0.68
Median	0.88
Third Quartile	1.14
Maximum	1.51
CV	35.36%
Interquartile Range	0.46

$Q_1 = 0.68$, $Q_3 = 1.14$
Interquartile range = 0.46

        (b)

Minimum	0.55
First Quartile	0.68
Median	0.88
Third Quartile	1.14
Maximum	1.51

3.22   (c)
cont.

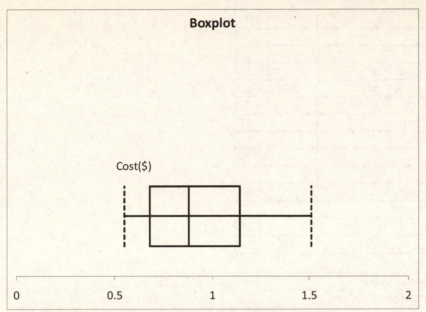

The distribution is slightly skewed to the right.

3.24   (a), (b)

Five-Number Summary	
Minimum	16
First Quartile	19.5
Median	22
Third Quartile	22
Maximum	26
Interquartile Range	2.5

(c)

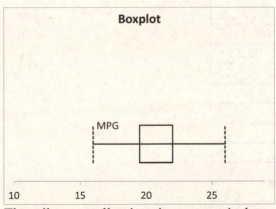

The miles per gallon is quite symmetrical.

3.26   Excel output for Residential Area:

Waiting Time	
Mean	7.114667
Median	6.68
Mode	#N/A
Standard Deviation	2.082189
Sample Variance	4.335512
Range	6.67
Minimum	3.82
Maximum	10.49
Sum	106.72
Count	15
First Quartile	5.64
Third Quartile	8.73
Interquartile Range	3.09
Coefficient of Variation	29.2662%

Box-and-whisker Plot	
Five-number Summary	
Minimum	3.82
First Quartile	5.64
Median	6.68
Third Quartile	8.73
Maximum	10.49

Excel output for Commercial District:

Waiting Time	
Mean	4.286667
Standard Error	0.422926
Median	4.5
Mode	#N/A
Standard Deviation	1.637985
Sample Variance	2.682995
Kurtosis	0.832925
Skewness	-0.83295
Range	6.08
Minimum	0.38
Maximum	6.46
Sum	64.3
Count	15
First Quartile	3.2
Third Quartile	5.55
Interquartile Range	2.35
Coefficient of Variation	38.2112%

3.26
cont.

Box-and-whisker Plot	
Five-number Summary	
Minimum	0.38
First Quartile	3.2
Median	4.5
Third Quartile	5.55
Maximum	6.46

(a)   **Commercial district**: Five-number summary: 0.38 3.2 4.5 5.55 6.46

       Residential area: Five-number summary: 3.82 5.64 6.68 8.73 10.49

(b)   **Commercial district:**

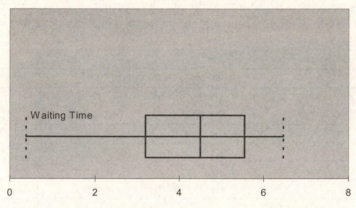

The distribution is skewed to the left.

Residential area:

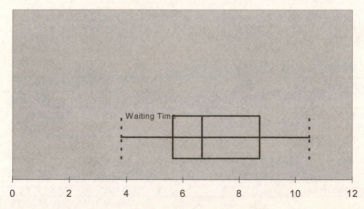

The distribution is skewed slightly to the right.

(c)   The central tendency of the waiting times for the bank branch located in the commercial district of a city is lower than that of the branch located in the residential area. There are a few longer than normal waiting times for the branch located in the residential area whereas there are a few exceptionally short waiting times for the branch located in the commercial area.

3.28   (a)

Average of 3-Year Return	Risk			
Type	Above Average	Average	Below Average	Grand Total
Intermediate Government	5.651515152	5.786206897	4.821428571	5.43666666
Short Term Corporate	-0.044	2.635483871	3.229411765	2.11555555
Grand Total	3.196551724	4.158333333	3.948387097	3.77611111

(b)

StdDev of 3-Year Return	Risk			
Type	Above Average	Average	Below Average	Grand Total
Intermediate Government	2.461722112	1.145713794	1.278412541	1.80657040
Short Term Corporate	3.605791638	1.703437385	1.488649869	2.68030314
Grand Total	4.119656157	2.149283812	1.600076016	2.82268076

(c)   Across the 3 different risk levels, intermediate government funds have the highest average 3-year returns but the lowest standard deviation.

(d)   **2007-2009 3-year Returns**

Average of 3-Year Return	Risk			
Type	Above average	Average	Below average	Grand Total
Intermediate Government	5.544827586	5.565625	5.711538462	5.6022988
Short Term Corporate	2.833333333	4.535135135	3.923333333	3.8195876
Grand Total	4.166101695	5.013043478	4.753571429	4.66

StdDev of 3-Year Return	Risk			
Type	Above average	Average	Below average	Grand Total
Intermediate Government	2.097717502	1.370097565	1.099209506	1.5702893
Short Term Corporate	4.579288706	1.527928194	1.442861939	2.888541
Grand Total	3.805060613	1.536125095	1.567390917	2.5164065

Similar to the 2006-2008 3-year returns, intermediate government funds have the highest average 3-year returns but the lowest standard deviation across the 3 different risk levels.

3.30   (a)

Average of Return 2008		Risk			
Type	Fees	Above Average	Average	Below Average	Grand
Intermediate Government	No	9.029411765	6.905263158	4.036842105	6.570
	Yes	3.88625	7.17	4.544444444	4.993
Intermediate Government Total		6.535757576	6.996551724	4.2	5.957
Short Term Corporate	No	-10.7315	-1.617391304	0.46	-3.260
	Yes	-10.2	-1.625	0.725	-3.594
Short Term Corporate Total		-10.6252	-1.619354839	0.491176471	-3.323
Grand Total		-0.861206897	2.545	2.166129032	1.316

3.30
cont.

(b)

StdDev of Return 2008		Risk			
Type	Fees	Above Average	Average	Below Average	Grand T
Intermediate Government	No	5.66345353	3.699770816	3.517766104	4.7321
	Yes	6.577828289	2.874427479	3.205507413	5.0712
Intermediate Government Total		6.567539032	3.387000649	3.369360858	4.8998
Short Term Corporate	No	8.607600849	4.06130881	3.350306213	7.1587
	Yes	7.292804673	5.401256468	3.578989615	6.9785
Short Term Corporate Total		8.219881954	4.34775186	3.32204461	7.0873
Grand Total		11.23186571	5.823052522	3.802326447	7.6529

(c)   The intermediate government funds have the highest average 2008 returns but the lowest standard deviation among all different combinations of risk level and whether there is a fee charged with the exception that they have the highest average 2008 returns and the highest standard deviation among the below average risk funds that do not charge a fee.

(d)   **2009 Returns**

Average of Return 2009		Risk			
Type	Fees	Above average	Average	Below average	Grand
Intermediate Government	No	1.407142857	3.736842105	7.17	4.416
	Yes	4.886666667	3.392307692	5.983333333	4.508
Intermediate Government Total		3.206896552	3.596875	6.896153846	4.452
Short Term Corporate	No	12.4173913	9.663333333	5.629166667	9.228
	Yes	15.98571429	9.871428571	6.533333333	
Short Term Corporate Total		13.25	9.702702703	5.81	9.595
Grand Total		8.313559322	6.871014493	6.314285714	7.164

StdDev of Return 2009		Risk			
Type	Fees	Above average	Average	Below average	Grand
Intermediate Government	No	6.160102932	3.311631106	3.097894021	4.723
	Yes	9.267444298	2.189543917	1.979309644	6.302
Intermediate Government Total		7.980732648	2.872841055	2.887418331	5.360
Short Term Corporate	No	7.737726479	3.567814296	2.361370119	5.578
	Yes	7.009857006	2.753612346	3.037542867	6.022
Short Term Corporate Total		7.612048073	3.394807022	2.479620383	5.686
Grand Total		9.2392054	4.389931711	2.707459633	6.090

In contrast to the 2008 returns, the intermediate government funds have the lowest average 2008 returns for all combinations of risk level and whether the funds charged a fee with the except of the below average risk funds that do not charge a fee where the intermediate government funds have the highest average 2008 returns. Unlike the 2008 returns, the intermediate government funds have the lowest standard deviations only among the above average risk funds that do not charge a fee, the average risk funds that either charge a fee or do not charge a fee, and the below average risk funds that charge a fee.

3.32   (a)   Population Mean $= 6$

      (b) $\sigma^2 = 2.8$ $\sigma = 1.67$

3.34   (a)   68%   (b)   95%   (c)   not calculable   75%   88.89%

      (d) $\mu - 4\sigma$ to $\mu + 4\sigma$ or -2.8 to 19.2

3.36   Excel output:

Kilowatt Hours	
Mean	12999.22
Standard Error	546.9863
Median	13255
Mode	#N/A
Standard Deviation	3906.264
Sample Variance	15258895
Kurtosis	0.232784
Skewness	0.468115
Range	18171
Minimum	6396
Maximum	24567
Sum	662960
Count	51

(a)   mean = 12999.2158,   variance = 14959700.52,   std. dev. = 3867.7772

(b)   64.71%, 98.04% and 100% of these states have average per capita energy consumption within 1, 2 and 3 standard deviations of the mean, respectively.

(c)   This is consistent with the 68%, 95% and 99.7% according to the empirical rule.

(d)   Excel output:

Kilowatt Hours	
Mean	12857.74
Standard Error	539.0489
Median	12999
Mode	#N/A
Standard Deviation	3811.651
Sample Variance	14528684
Kurtosis	0.464522
Skewness	0.494714
Range	18171
Minimum	6396
Maximum	24567
Sum	642887
Count	50

(d)   (a)   mean = 12857.7402, variance = 14238110.67, std. dev. = 3773.3421

        (b)   66%, 98% and 100% of these states have average per capita energy consumption within 1, 2 and 3 standard deviation of the mean, respectively.

(c)   This is consistent with the 68%, 95% and 99.7% according to the empirical rule.

3.38   (a) $cov(X, Y) = 65.2909$

(b) $S_X^2 = 21.7636$, $S_Y^2 = 195.8727$

$$r = \frac{\text{cov}(X,Y)}{\sqrt{S_X^2}\sqrt{S_Y^2}} = \frac{65.2909}{\sqrt{21.7636}\sqrt{195.8727}} = +1.0$$

(c)   There is a perfect positive linear relationship between X and Y; all the points lie exactly on a straight line with a positive slope.

3.40   (a) $cov(X, Y) = 133.3333$

(b) $S_X^2 = 2200$, $S_Y^2 = 11.4762$

$$r = \frac{\text{cov}(X,Y)}{S_X S_Y} = 0.8391$$

(c)   The correlation coefficient is more valuable for expressing the relationship between calories and sugar because it does not depend on the units used to measure calories and sugar.

(d)   There is a strong positive linear relationship between calories and sugar.

3.42   (a) $cov(X, Y) = 4473270.3$

(b) $S_X^2 = 956812.1336$, $S_Y^2 = 33480836.07$

$$r = \frac{\text{cov}(X,Y)}{S_X S_Y} = 0.7903$$

(c)   There is a positive linear relationship between the coaches' salary and revenue.

3.44   We should look for ways to describe the typical value, the variation, and the distribution of the data within a range.

3.46   The arithmetic mean is a simple average of all the values, but is subject to the effect of extreme values. The median is the middle ranked value, but varies more from sample to sample than the arithmetic mean, although it is less susceptible to extreme values. The mode is the most common value, but is extremely variable from sample to sample.

3.48   Variation is the amount of dispersion, or "spread," in the data.

3.50   The range is a simple measure, but only measures the difference between the extremes. The interquartile range measures the range of the center fifty percent of the data. The standard deviation measures variation around the mean while the variance measures the squared variation around the mean, and these are the only measures that take into account each observation. The coefficient of variation measures the variation around the mean relative to the mean. The range, standard deviation, variance and coefficient of variation are all sensitive to outliers while the interquartile range is not.

3.52   The Chebyshev rule applies to any type of distribution while the empirical rule applies only to data sets that are approximately bell-shaped. The empirical rule is more accurate than the Chebyshev rule in approximating the concentration of data around the mean.

3.54   The covariance measures the strength of the linear relationship between two numerical variables while the coefficient of correlation measures the relative strength of the linear relationship. The value of the covariance depends very much on the units used to measure the two numerical variables while the value of the coefficient of correlation is totally free from the units used.

3.56   Excel output:

Time	
Mean	43.88889
Standard Error	4.865816
Median	45
Mode	17
Standard Deviation	25.28352
Sample Variance	639.2564
Range	76
Minimum	16
Maximum	92
First Quartile	18
Third Quartile	63
interquartile range	45
c.v	57.61%

(a)   mean = 43.89   median = 45   1st quartile = 18 3rd quartile = 63

(b)   range = 76   interquartile range = 45   variance = 639.2564
       standard deviation = 25.28   coefficient of variation = 57.61%

(c)

Box-and-whisker Plot

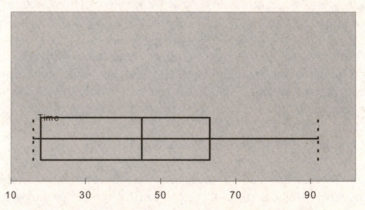

The distribution is skewed to the right because there are a few policies that require an exceptionally long period to be approved even though the mean is smaller than the median.

(d)   The mean approval process takes 43.89 days with 50% of the policies being approved in less than 45 days. 50% of the applications are approved between 18 and 63 days. About 67% of the applications are approved between 18.6 to 69.2 days.

3.58   Excel output:

Width	
Mean	8.420898
Standard Error	0.006588
Median	8.42
Mode	8.42
Standard Deviation	0.046115
Sample Variance	0.002127
Kurtosis	0.035814
Skewness	-0.48568
Range	0.186
Minimum	8.312
Maximum	8.498
Sum	412.624
Count	49
First Quartile	8.404
Third Quartile	8.459
Interquartile Range	0.055
CV	0.55%

(a)   mean = 8.421, median = 8.42, range = 0.186 and standard deviation = 0.0461. On average, the width is 8.421 inches. The width of the middle ranked observation is 8.42. The difference between the largest and smallest width is 0.186 and majority of the widths fall between 0.0461 inches around the mean of 8.421 inches.

(b)   Minimum = 8.312, 1st quartile = 8.404, median = 8.42, 3rd quartile = 8.459 and maximum = 8.498

Box-and-whisker Plot

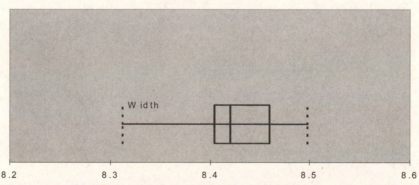

(c)   Even though the median is equal to the mean, the distribution is not symmetrical but skewed to the left.

(d)   All the troughs fall within the limit of 8.31 and 8.61 inches.

3.60   (a), (b)

	Calories	Fat
Mean	108.3333	3.375
Median	110	3.25
Mode	120	3.5
Standard Deviation	19.46247	1.759713
Sample Variance	378.7879	3.096591
Kurtosis	0.004224	-0.79267
Skewness	-0.34199	0.083521
Range	70	5.5
Minimum	70	0.5
Maximum	140	6
Count	12	12
First Quartile	90	1.5
Third Quartile	120	5
Interquartile Range	30	3.5
Coefficient of Variation	17.97%	52.14%

(c)

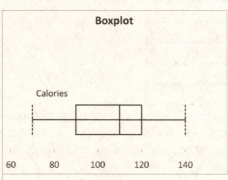

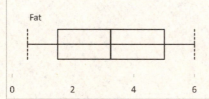

The distribution of calories and total fat are quite symmetrical.

(d) $$r = \frac{\text{cov}(X, Y)}{S_X S_Y} = 0.6969$$

(e)   The amount of calories of the veggie burgers centers around 110 and its distribution is quite symmetrical. The amount of fat centers around 3.3 grams per serving and its distribution is very symmetrical. There is a positive linear relationship between calories and fat.

3.62   (a)   Excel output:
                   Five-number Summary

	Boston	Vermont
Minimum	0.04	0.02
First Quartile	0.17	0.13
Median	0.23	0.2
Third Quartile	0.32	0.28
Maximum	0.98	0.83

(b)

Box-and-whisker Plot

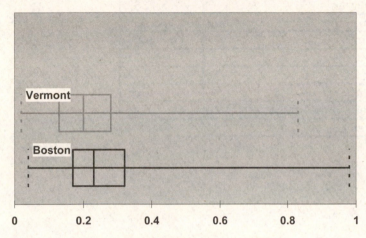

Both distributions are right skewed.

(c)   Both sets of shingles did quite well in achieving a granule loss of 0.8 gram or less.
The Boston shingles had only two data points greater than 0.8 gram. The next
highest to these was 0.6 gram. These two data points can be considered outliers.
Only 1.176% of the shingles failed the specification. In the Vermont shingles, only
one data point was greater than 0.8 gram. The next highest was 0.58 gram. Thus,
only 0.714% of the shingles failed to meet the specification.

3.64   (a), (b), (c)

	Calories	Protein	Cholesterol
Calories	1		
Protein	0.464411	1	
Cholesterol	0.177665	0.141673	1

(d)   There is a rather weak positive linear relationship between calories and protein with
a correlation coefficient of 0.46. The positive linear relationship between calories
and cholesterol is quite weak at .178.

3.66   (a), (b)

Property Taxes Per Capita ($)	
Mean	1040.863
Median	981
Mode	963
Standard Deviation	428.5385
Sample Variance	183645.2
Kurtosis	-0.11136
Skewness	0.604297
Range	1732
Minimum	367
Maximum	2099
Sum	53084
Count	51
First Quartile	713
Third Quartile	1306
Interquartile Range	593
Coefficient of Variation	41.17%

(c)

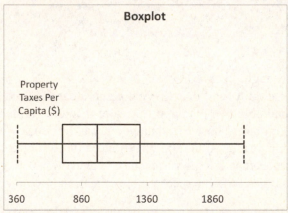

(d)   The distribution of the property taxes per capita is right-skewed with an average value of $1,040.83 thousands, a median of $981 thousands and an average spread around the mean of $428.54 thousands. There is an outlier in the right tail at $2,099 thousands while the standard deviation is about 41.17% of the average. Twenty-five percent of the states have property taxes that fall below $713 thousands while twenty-five percent have property taxes higher than $1,306 thousands.

3.70   (a), (b)

	Expense Ratio	3-Year Return	5-Year Return
Mean	0.711793478	4.6625	3.985869565
Standard Error	0.018897433	0.185511952	0.109492889
Median	0.7	5.1	4.3
Mode	0.6	5.5	4.4
Standard Deviation	0.256337254	2.516406548	1.485233806
Sample Variance	0.065708788	6.332301913	2.205919458
Kurtosis	2.406321172	16.19316748	18.48495505
Skewness	0.596580991	-2.902127021	-3.058311976
Range	1.82	23.2	14.1
Minimum	0.12	-13.8	-7.3
Maximum	1.94	9.4	6.8
Sum	130.97	857.9	733.4
Count	184	184	184
First Quartile	0.52	3.9	3.6
Third Quartile	0.91	6.1	4.9
Interquartile Range	0.39	2.2	1.3
CV	36.01%	53.97%	37.26%

(c)

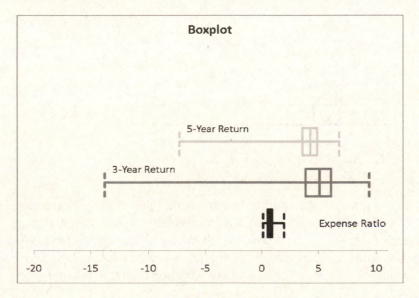

The 3-year return and 5-year return are left-skewed while the expense ratio is right-skewed.

(d)   In general, the 3-year return is higher than the 5-year return. Half of the 3-year returns are higher than 5.1; half of the 5-year returns are higher than 4.3 and half of the expense ratios are higher than 0.7. The 3-year return has the highest variation, followed by the 5-year return and, finally, the expense ratio. Expense ratio is right-skewed and has the smallest variation. Relative to the mean, the 3-year return has the largest average spread at 53.97%, followed by the 5-year at 37.26% and, finally, the expense ratio at 36.01%.

3.72   **Expense Ratio:**
(a), (b)

	Intermediate Government	*Short Term Corporate*
Mean	0.757816092	0.670515464
Median	0.75	0.66
Mode	1	0.7
Standard Deviation	0.300741043	0.201475656
Sample Variance	0.090445175	0.04059244
Range	1.82	0.96
Minimum	0.12	0.14
Maximum	1.94	1.1
First Quartile	0.55	0.52
Third Quartile	0.96	0.815
Interquartile Range	0.41	0.295
CV	39.69%	30.05%

(c)

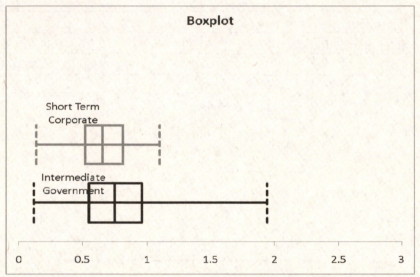

Expense ratio for short-term corporate bond funds is quite symmetrical while the expense ratio for intermediate government bond funds is right-skewed.

(d)   Intermediate government bonds funds have a higher central tendency based on the median and mean, and a higher variation based on the standard deviation, range, interquartile range and coefficient of variation than the short-term corporate bond funds.

3.72   **3-year Return:**
cont.   (a),(b)

	Intermediate Government	Short Term Corporate
Mean	5.602298851	3.819587629
Median	6	4.6
Mode	6	5.5
Standard Deviation	1.570289339	2.88854199
Sample Variance	2.465808607	8.343674828
Range	9.5	22.7
Minimum	-0.1	-13.8
Maximum	9.4	8.9
First Quartile	5.1	3.2
Third Quartile	6.4	5.45
Interquartile Range	1.3	2.25
CV	28.03%	75.62%

(c)

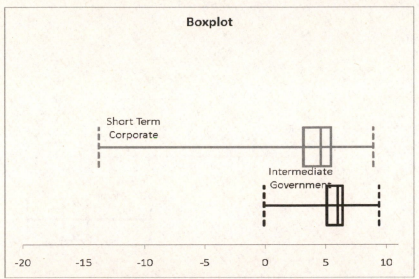

The 3-year return of both intermediate government bond funds and short term corporate bond funds is left-skewed.

(d)   The 3-year return of intermediate government bonds funds has a higher central tendency based on the median and mean, but a lower variation based on the standard deviation, range, interquartile range and coefficient of variation when compared to the short term corporate bond funds.

3.72   **5-year Return:**
cont.   (a),(b)

	Intermediate Government	Short Term Corporate
Mean	4.557471264	3.473195876
Median	4.7	3.9
Mode	5.1	4
Standard Deviation	0.979633556	1.66842712
Sample Variance	0.959681903	2.783649055
Range	5.6	13.7
Minimum	1.2	-7.3
Maximum	6.8	6.4
First Quartile	4.1	3.05
Third Quartile	5.2	4.4
Interquartile Range	1.1	1.35
CV	21.50%	48.04%

(c)

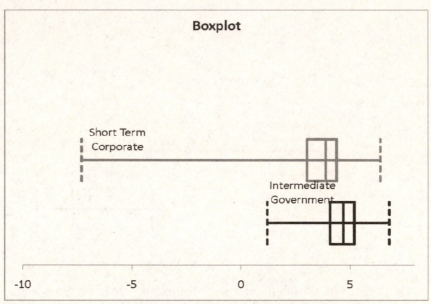

The 5-year return of both types of bond funds is left-skewed.

(d)   The 5-year return of intermediate government bonds funds has a higher central tendency based on the median and mean, but a lower variation based on the standard deviation, range, interquartile range and coefficient of variation when compared to the short term corporate bond funds.

3.74   (a),(b)

	Age	GPA	Salary	Social Networking
Mean	21.12903226	3.126290323	48.5483871	1.516129032
Standard Error	0.181776693	0.048050979	1.534277386	0.107226798
Median	21	3.135	50	1
Mode	21	3.4	40	1
Standard Deviation	1.431311115	0.378353785	12.08091222	0.844304651
Sample Variance	2.048651507	0.143151586	145.94844	0.712850344
Kurtosis	1.396512749	-0.577675236	0.424263618	1.104052341
Skewness	0.736532768	-0.278085839	0.534700844	0.961056334
Range	8	1.56	55	4
Minimum	18	2.34	25	0
Maximum	26	3.9	80	4
Sum	1310	193.83	3010	94
Count	62	62	62	62
First Quartile	20	2.9	40	1
Third Quartile	22	3.4	55	2
Interquartile Range	2	0.5	15	1
CV	6.77%	12.10%	24.88%	55.69%

	Satisfaction	Spending	Text Messages	Wealth
Mean	3.741935484	482.016129	246.2096774	7.151209677
Standard Error	0.154151923	28.18816142	27.23720293	2.490282305
Median	4	500	200	1
Mode	4	500	300	1
Standard Deviation	1.213793456	221.953805	214.4659503	19.60850248
Sample Variance	1.473294553	49263.49154	45995.64384	384.4933694
Kurtosis	0.46941975	4.559914424	1.135685207	16.98386711
Skewness	-0.50543694	1.585914741	1.295807973	4.15826833
Range	5	1300	900	99.9
Minimum	1	100	0	0.1
Maximum	6	1400	900	100
Sum	232	29885	15265	443.375
Count	62	62	62	62
First Quartile	3	300	100	0.75
Third Quartile	4	600	300	5
Interquartile Range	1	300	200	4.25
CV	32.44%	46.05%	87.11%	274.20%

3.74   (c)
cont.

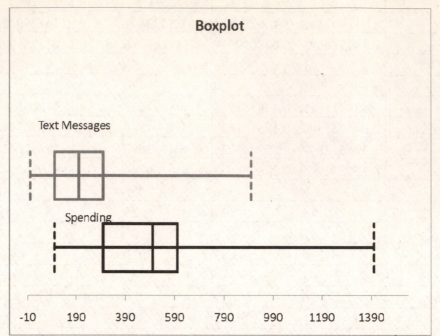

Both the number of text messages sent and spending for textbooks and supplies are right skewed.

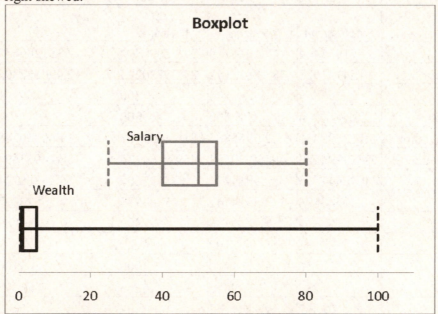

Both wealth and expected starting annual salary are right skewed.

3.74   (c)
cont.

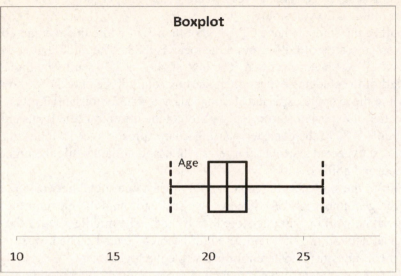

Age is right-skewed.

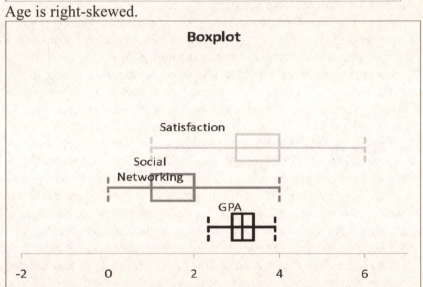

Social networking is right-skewed while satisfaction and GPA are quite
symmetical.

3.74   (d)   The middle ranked age of the students is 21 while the average age is 21.13. The
cont.   average scatter of the age around the mean is 1.43 years. The middle 50% of the
                students have age spread over 2 years. The youngest student is 18 years old while
                the oldest is 26 years old.

                Half of the students have GPA higher than 3.14 while the average GPA is 3.13. The
                average scatter of GPA around the mean is 0.38. The middle 50% of the students
                have GPAs spread over 0.5. The lowest GPA is 2.34 while the highest is 3.9.

                Half of the students expect their starting salary to be at least 50 thousand dollars
                while the average expected starting salary is 48.55 thousand dollars. The average
                scatter of expected starting salary around the mean is 12.08 thousand dollars. The
                middle 50% of the expected starting salary spreads over 15 thousand dollars. The
                lowest expected starting salary is 25 thousand dollars while the highest is 80
                thousand dollars.

                Half of the students are registered for at least one social networking site while the
                average number is 1.52. The average scatter around the mean of the number of
                social networking site registered for is 0.84. The middle 50% of the number of
                social networking sites registered for is spread over 1. The lowest number of social
                networking sites registered for is 0 while the highest is 4.

                Half of the students have satisfaction rating on the food and dining services on
                campus of at least 4 while the average rating is 3.74. The average scatter of the
                rating around the mean is 1.21. Ratings of the middle 50% of the students spread
                over 1. The lowest rating is 1 while the highest is 6.

                Half of the students spend at least $ 500 on textbooks and supplies, while the
                average spending is $482.01. The average scatter of spending around the mean is
                221.95. Spending by the middle 50% of the students spreads over $300. The lowest
                amount of spending is $100 while the highest is $1400.

                The middle ranked number of text messages sent in a typical week is 200 while the
                average is 246.21. The average scatter of the number of text messages sent in a
                typical week around the mean is 214.47. The number of text messages sent in a
                typical week by the middle 50% of the students spreads over 200. The lowest
                number of text messages sent in a typical week is 0 while the highest is 900.

                Half of the students say they have to accumulate at least one million dollars before
                they would say they are rich while the average amount of wealth needed to
                accumulate before they would say they are rich is 7.1512 million dollars. The
                average scatter around the mean of the amount of wealth needed to accumulate
                before they would say they are rich is 19.6085 million dollars. The middle 50% of
                the students say that the amount of wealth needed to accumulate before they would
                say they are rich spreads over 4.25 million dollars. The lowest amount of wealth
                needed to accumulate before they would say they are rich is 0.1 million dollars while
                the highest is 100.

3.76   (a), (b)

	Age	G- GPA	U-GPA	FT Jobs
Mean	26.45454545	3.329545455	3.368181818	1.727272727
Standard Error	0.805277614	0.060962986	0.048199367	0.153753724
Median	25.5	3	3.4	2
Mode	26	3	3.6	2
Standard Deviation	5.341607394	0.404382702	0.319718428	1.019886824
Sample Variance	28.53276956	0.16352537	0.102219873	1.040169133
Kurtosis	6.232765898	-1.343008579	-1.279108415	0.067158672
Skewness	2.361148742	0.654559987	-0.170725641	0.44754573
Range	26	1	1.1	4
Minimum	21	3	2.8	0
Maximum	47	4	3.9	4
Sum	1164	146.5	148.2	76
Count	44	44	44	44
First Quartile	23	3	3	1
Third Quartile	27	3.7	3.7	2
Interquartile Range	4	0.7	0.7	1
CV	20.19%	12.15%	9.49%	59.05%
	Expected Salary	Spending	Advisory Rating	Text Messages
Mean	82.97727273	363.8636364	4.590909091	232.4545455
Standard Error	6.701127878	54.20988878	0.146553722	44.75936902
Median	70	300	5	100
Mode	70	300	4	100
Standard Deviation	44.45025369	359.587722	0.972127416	296.9000658
Sample Variance	1975.825053	129303.3298	0.945031712	88149.64905
Kurtosis	12.9346988	17.69405816	0.495590571	3.230509207
Skewness	3.131929021	3.968429285	-0.029587874	1.833591049
Range	260	2130	5	1250
Minimum	40	70	2	0
Maximum	300	2200	7	1250
Sum	3651	16010	202	10228
Count	44	44	44	44
First Quartile	60	200	4	20
Third Quartile	100	400	5	400
Interquartile Range	40	200	1	380
CV	53.57%	98.82%	21.18%	127.72%

3.76   (c)
cont.

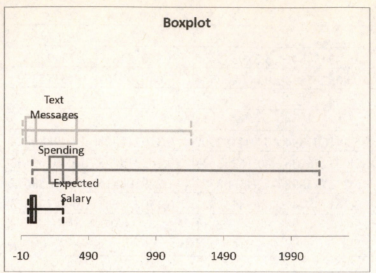

The number of text messages sent in a typical week, spending and expected salary
are all right-skewed.

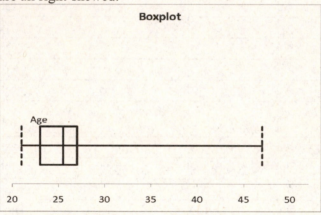

Age is right skewed.

The number of different full-time jobs held in the past 10 years is right-skewed. The
advisory rating and undergraduate GPA are quite symmetrical. The graduate GPA is
right-skewed.

3.76   (d)   The middle ranked age of the students is 25.5 while the average age is 26.45. The
cont.   average scatter of the age around the mean is 5.34 years. The middle 50% of the
               students have age spread over 4 years. The youngest student is 21 years old while
               the oldest is 47 years old.
               Half of the students have graduate GPA higher than 3.0 while the average graduate
               GPA is 3.33. The average scatter of graduate GPA around the mean is 0.40. The
               middle 50% of the students have graduate GPA spread over 0.7. The lowest
               graduate GPA is 3.0 while the highest is 4.0.
               Half of the students have undergraduate GPA higher than 3.4 while the average
               undergraduate GPA is 3.37. The average scatter of undergraduate GPA around the
               mean is 0.32. The middle 50% of the students have undergraduate GPA spread over
               0.7. The lowest undergraduate GPA is 2.8 while the highest is 3.9.
               Half of the students have held more than 2 full-time jobs in the past 10 years while
               the average is 1.73. The average scatter of the number of full-time jobs held in the
               past 10 years around the mean is 1.02. The number of full-time jobs held in the past
               10 years by the middle 50% of the students spread over 1. The lowest number of
               full-time jobs held in the past 10 years is 0 while the highest is 4.
               Half of the students expected their starting salary to be 70 thousand dollars while the
               average expected starting salary is 82.98 thousand dollars. The average scatter of
               expected starting salary around the mean is 44.45 thousand dollars. The middle 50%
               of the expected starting salary spreads over 40 thousand dollars. The lowest
               expected starting salary is 40 thousand dollars while the highest is 300 thousand
               dollars.
               Half of the students spend $300 on textbooks and supplies while the average
               spending is $ 363.86. The average scatter of spending around the mean is $359.59.
               Spending by the middle 50% of the students spreads over $200. The lowest amount
               of spending is $70 while the highest is $2200.
               The middle ranked advisory rating is 5 while the average is 4.59. The average
               scatter of advisory rating around the mean is 0.97. Rating by the middle 50% of the
               students spreads over 1. The lowest rating is 2 while the highest is 7.
               The middle ranked number of text messages sent in a typical week is 100 while the
               average is 232.45. The average scatter of the number of text messages sent in a
               typical week around the mean is 296.90. The number of text messages sent in a
               typical week by the middle 50% of the students spreads over 380. The lowest
               number of text messages sent in a typical week is 0 while the highest is 1250.
               Half of the students say they have to accumulate at least 2.75 million dollars before
               they would say they are rich while the average amount of wealth needed to
               accumulate before they would say they are rich is 10.6409 million dollars. The
               average scatter around the mean of the amount of wealth needed to accumulate
               before they would say they are rich is 22.3537 million dollars. The middle 50% of
               the students say that the amount of wealth needed to accumulate before they would
               say they are rich spreads over 9 million dollars. The lowest amount of wealth
               needed to accumulate before they would say they are rich is 0.1 million dollars while
               the highest is 100.

CHAPTER 4

OBJECTIVES

In this chapter, you learn:
- Basic probability concepts
- Conditional probability
- Bayes' theorem to revise probabilities
- Various counting rules

OVERVIEW AND KEY CONCEPTS

Some Basic Probability Concepts

- **A priori probability:** The probability is based on prior knowledge of the process involved.
- **Empirical probability:** The probability is based on observed data.
- **Subjective probability:** Chance of occurrence assigned to an event by particular individual.
- **Sample space:** Collection of all possible outcomes, e.g., the set of all six faces of a die.
- **Simple event:** Outcome from a sample space with one characteristic, e.g., a red card from a deck of cards.
- **Joint event:** Involves two or more characteristics simultaneously, e.g., an Ace that is also a Red Card from a deck of cards.
- **Impossible event:** Event that will never happen, e.g., a club and diamond on a single card.
- **Complement event:** The complement of event A, denoted as A', includes all events that are not part of event A, e.g., If event A is the queen of diamonds, then the complement of event A is all the cards in a deck that are not the queen of diamonds.
- **Mutually exclusive events:** Two events are mutually exclusive if they cannot occur together. E.g., If event A is the queen of diamonds and event B is the queen of clubs, then both event A and event B cannot occur together on one card. An event and its complement are always mutually exclusive.
- **Collectively exhaustive events:** A set of events is collectively exhaustive if one of the events must occur. The set of collectively exhaustive events covers the whole sample space. E.g., Event A: all the aces, event B: all the black cards, event C: all the diamonds, event D: all the hearts. Then events A, B, C, and D are collectively exhaustive and so are events B, C, and D. An event and its complement are always collectively exhaustive.
- **Rules of probability:** (1) Its value is between 0 and 1; (2) the sum of probabilities of all collectively exhaustive and mutually exclusive events is 1.
- **The addition rule:** $P(A \text{ or } B) = P(A) + P(B) - P(A \text{ and } B)$
    - For two mutually exclusive events: $P(A \text{ and } B) = 0$
- **The multiplication rule:** $P(A \text{ and } B) = P(A|B)P(B) = P(B|A)P(A)$
- **Conditional probability:** $P(A|B) = \dfrac{P(A \text{ and } B)}{P(B)}$; $P(B|A) = \dfrac{P(A \text{ and } B)}{P(A)}$
- **Statistically independent events:** Two events are statistically independent if $P(A|B) = P(A)$, $P(B|A) = P(B)$ or $P(A \text{ and } B) = P(A)P(B)$. That is, any information about a given event does not affect the probability of the other event.

- **Bayes' theorem:** $P(B_i \mid A) = \dfrac{P(A \mid B_i) P(B_i)}{P(A \mid B_1) P(B_1) + \cdots + P(A \mid B_k) P(B_k)} = \dfrac{P(B_i \text{ and } A)}{P(A)}$

  - **E.g.** We know that 50% of borrowers repaid their loans. Out of those who repaid, 40% had a college degree. Ten percent of those who defaulted had a college degree. What is the probability that a randomly selected borrower who has a college degree will repay the loan?

    Solution: Let R represent those who repaid and C represent those who have a college degree. $P(R) = 0.50$, $P(C \mid R) = 0.4$, $P(C \mid R') = 0.10$.

    $$P(R \mid C) = \frac{P(C \mid R) P(R)}{P(C \mid R) P(R) + P(C \mid R') P(R')} = \frac{(.4)(.5)}{(.4)(.5) + (.1)(.5)} = \frac{.2}{.25} = .8$$

  - Bayes' theorem is used if $P(A \mid B)$ is needed when $P(B \mid A)$ is given or vice-versa.

Viewing and Computing Marginal (Simple) Probability and Joint Probability Using a Contingency Table

Event	Event B₁	B₂	Total
A₁	P(A₁ and B₁)	P(A₁ and B₂)	P(A₁)
A₂	P(A₂ and B₁)	P(A₂ and B₂)	P(A₂)
Total	P(B₁)	P(B₂)	1

Joint Probability

Marginal (Simple) Probability

Viewing and Computing Compound Probability Using a Contingency Table

$$P(A_1 \text{ or } B_1) = P(A_1) + P(B_1) - P(A_1 \text{ and } B_1)$$

Event	Event B₁	B₂	Total
A₁	P(A₁ and B₁)	P(A₁ and B₂)	P(A₁)
A₂	P(A₂ and B₁)	P(A₂ and B₂)	P(A₂)
Total	P(B₁)	P(B₂)	1

For Mutually Exclusive Events: P(A or B) = P(A) + P(B)

Viewing and Computing Conditional Probability Using a Contingency Table

First setup the contingency table.

Type	Color Red	Color Black	Total
Ace	2	2	4
Non-Ace	24	24	48
Total	26	26	52

Revised Sample Space

To find $P(\text{Ace|Red})$, we only need to focus on the revised sample space of $P(\text{Red}) = 26/52$. Out of this, 2/52 belongs to Ace and Red.

Hence, $P(\text{Ace|Red})$ is the ratio of 2/52 to 26/52 or 2/26.

Likewise, $P(\text{Red | Ace}) = \dfrac{P(\text{Ace and Red})}{P(\text{Ace})} = \dfrac{2/52}{4/52} = \dfrac{2}{4}$

Applying Bayes' Theorem Using a Contingency Table

- **E.g.** We know that 50% of borrowers repaid their loans. Out of those who repaid, 40% had a college degree. Ten percent of those who defaulted had a college degree. What is the probability that a randomly selected borrower who has a college degree will repay the loan? **Solution:** Let R represents those who repaid and C represents those who have a college degree. We know that $P(R) = 0.50$, $P(C \mid R) = 0.4$, $P(C \mid R') = 0.10$.

	Repay	Repay'	Total
College	0.2	0.05	0.25
College'	0.3	0.45	0.75
Total	0.5	0.5	1

First we fill in the marginal probabilities of $P(R) = 0.5$ and $P(R') = 0.5$ in the contingency table. Then we make use of the conditional probability $P(C \mid R) = 0.4$. It says that if R has already occurred, the probability of C is 0.4. Since R has already occurred, we are restricted to the revised sample space of $P(R) = 0.5$. Forty percent or 0.4 of this $P(R) = 0.5$ belongs to $P(C \text{ and } R)$. Hence, the $0.4(0.5) = 0.2$ for $P(C \text{ and } R)$ in the contingency table. Likewise, given that R' has already occurred, the probability of C is 0.10. Hence, $P(C \text{ and } R')$ is 10% of $P(R') = 0.5$, which is 0.05. Utilizing the fact that the joint probabilities add up vertically and horizontally to their respective marginal probabilities, the contingency table is completed.

We want the probability of R given C. Now we are restricted to the revised sample space of $P(C) = 0.25$ since we know that C has already occurred. Out of this 0.25, 0.2 belongs to $P(C \text{ and } R)$. Hence, $P(R \mid C) = \dfrac{0.2}{0.25} = 0.8$

SOLUTIONS TO END OF SECTION
AND CHAPTER REVIEW EVEN PROBLEMS

4.2 (a) Simple events include selecting a red ball.
   (b) Selecting a white ball
   (c) The sample space is the collection of "a red ball being selected" and "a white ball being selected".

4.4 (a) $60/100 = 3/5 = 0.6$ (b) $10/100 = 1/10 = 0.1$
   (c) $35/100 = 7/20 = 0.35$ (d) $\dfrac{60}{100} + \dfrac{65}{100} - \dfrac{35}{100} = \dfrac{90}{100} = \dfrac{9}{10} = 0.9$

4.6 (a) Mutually exclusive, not collectively exhaustive. "Registered voters in the United States were asked whether they registered as Republicans, Democrats, or none of the above." will be mutually exclusive and collectively exhaustive.
   (b) Not mutually exclusive, not collectively exhaustive. "Respondents were classified by country of manufacture of car owned and used for majority of their driving into the categories American, European, Japanese, or none of the above." will be mutually exclusive and collectively exhaustive. People can own more than one car but only one car can be used for majority of their driving.
   (c) Mutually exclusive, not collectively exhaustive. "People were asked, "Do you currently live in (i) an apartment, (ii) a house or (iii) none of the above?" will be mutually exclusive and collectively exhaustive.
   (d) Mutually exclusive, collectively exhaustive

4.8 (a) "Need three or more clicks to be removed from an email list".
   (b) "Need three or more clicks to be removed from an email list in 2008".
   (c) "Need less than three clicks to be removed from an email list".
   (d) "Needs three or more clicks to be removed from an email list in 2009" is a joint event because it consists of two characteristics or attributes.

4.10 (a) "Users over 70 years of age"
   (b) "Users over 70 years of age who believe that e-mail message should be answered quickly."
   (c) "A respondent who does not answer quickly."
   (d) A respondent who answers quickly and is over 70 years old is a joint event because the respondent is over 70 years old and also answers quickly.

4.12 (a) P(is engaged with his or her workplace) = (550+246)/3790 = 0.2100
   (b) P(is a U.S. worker) = (550+1345)/3790 = 0.5
   (c) P(is engaged with his or her workplace or is a U.S. worker) = (796+1895-550)/3790 = 0.5649
   (d) The probability of "is engaged with his or her workplace or is a U.S. worker" includes the probability of "is engaged with his or her workplace", the probability of "is a U.S. worker", minus the joint probability of "is engaged with his or her workplace" and "is a U.S. worker".

4.14

Enjoy Shopping	Male	Female	Total
Yes	238	276	514
No	304	267	571
Total	542	543	1085

(a) P(enjoys clothes shopping) = 514/1085 = 0.4737
(b) P(female *and* enjoys clothes shopping) = 276/1085 = 0.2544
(c) P(female *or* enjoys clothes shopping) = (238+276+267)/1085= 0.7198
(d) P(male *or* female) = 1085/1085 = 1.00

4.16   (a) $P(A \mid B) = 10/30 = 1/3 = 0.33$
(b) $P(A \mid B') = 20/60 = 1/3 = 0.33$
(c) $P(A' \mid B') = 40/60 = 2/3 = 0.67$
(d)   Since $P(A \mid B) = P(A) = 1/3$, events A and B are statistically independent.

4.18 $P(A \mid B) = \dfrac{P(A \text{ and } B)}{P(B)} = \dfrac{0.4}{0.8} = \dfrac{1}{2} = 0.5$

4.20   Since $P(A \text{ and } B) = .20$ and $P(A)\, P(B) = 0.12$, events A and B are not statistically independent.

4.22   (a) P(answers quicklly | 12-50) = 536/1000 = 0.5360
(b) P(answers quickly | over 70) = 707/1000 = 0.707
(c)   Since P(answers quickly) = 1243/2000 = 0..6215 is not equal to P(answers quicklly | 12-50) = 0.5360, answering quickly is not statistically independent of age category.

4.24   (a) P(is engaged | is from U.S.) = 550/1895 = 0.2902
(b) P(is not engaged | is from U.S.) = 1345/1895 = 0.7098
(c) P(is engaged | is from Germany) = 246/1895 = 0.1298
(d) P(is not engaged | is from Germany) = 1649/1895 = 0.8702

4.26   (a) P(needs warranty repair | manufacturer based in U.S.) = 0.025/0.6 = 0.0417
(b) P(needs warranty repair | manufacturer not based in U.S.) = 0.015/0.4
       = 0.0375
(c)   Since P(needs warranty repair | manufacturer based in U.S.) = 0.0417 and P(needs warranty repair) = 0.04, the two events are not statistically independent.

4.28   (a) P(both queens) = $\dfrac{4}{52} \cdot \dfrac{3}{51} = \dfrac{12}{2,652} = \dfrac{1}{221} = 0.0045$

(b) P(10 followed by 5 or 6) = $\dfrac{4}{52} \cdot \dfrac{8}{51} = \dfrac{32}{2,652} = \dfrac{8}{663} = 0.012$

(c) P(both queens) = $\dfrac{4}{52} \cdot \dfrac{4}{52} = \dfrac{16}{2,704} = \dfrac{1}{169} = 0.0059$

(d) P(blackjack) = $\dfrac{16}{52} \cdot \dfrac{4}{51} + \dfrac{4}{52} \cdot \dfrac{16}{51} = \dfrac{128}{2,652} = \dfrac{32}{663} = 0.0483$

4.30

$$P(B \mid A) = \frac{P(A \mid B) \cdot P(B)}{P(A \mid B) \cdot P(B) + P(A \mid B') \cdot P(B')}$$

$$= \frac{0.8 \cdot 0.05}{0.8 \cdot 0.05 + 0.4 \cdot 0.95} = \frac{0.04}{0.42} = 0.095$$

4.32   (a) D = has disease T = tests positive

$$P(D \mid T) = \frac{P(T \mid D) \cdot P(D)}{P(T \mid D) \cdot P(D) + P(T \mid D') \cdot P(D')}$$

$$= \frac{0.9 \cdot 0.03}{0.9 \cdot 0.03 + 0.01 \cdot 0.97} = \frac{0.027}{0.0367} = 0.736$$

(b)

$$P(D' \mid T') = \frac{P(T' \mid D') \cdot P(D')}{P(T' \mid D') \cdot P(D') + P(T' \mid D) \cdot P(D)}$$

$$= \frac{0.99 \cdot 0.97}{0.99 \cdot 0.97 + 0.10 \cdot 0.03} = \frac{0.9603}{0.9633} = 0.997$$

4.34   (a) B = Base Construction Co. enters a bid
        O = Olive Construction Co. wins the contract

$$P(B' \mid O) = \frac{P(O \mid B') \cdot P(B')}{P(O \mid B') \cdot P(B') + P(O \mid B) \cdot P(B)}$$

$$= \frac{0.5 \cdot 0.3}{0.5 \cdot 0.3 + 0.25 \cdot 0.7} = \frac{0.15}{0.325} = 0.4615$$

(b) $P(O) = 0.175 + 0.15 = 0.325$

4.36   (a) P(huge success | favorable review) = 0.099/0.459 = 0.2157
        P(moderate success | favorable review) = 0.14/0.459 = 0.3050
        P(break even | favorable review) = 0.16/0.459 = 0.3486
        P(loser | favorable review) = 0.06/0.459 = 0.1307
(b) P(favorable review) = 0.99(0.1) + 0.7(0.2) + 0.4(0.4) + 0.2(0.3) = 0.459

4.38 $3^{10} = 59049$

4.40   (a) $2^7 = 128$ (b) $6^7 = 279936$
(c)   There are two mutually exclusive and collectively exhaustive outcomes in (a) and six
        in (b).

4.42 $(8)(4)(3)(3) = 288$

4.44 $5! = (5)(4)(3)(2)(1) = 120$. Not all these orders are equally likely because the players are
different in each team.

4.46 $n! = 6! = 720$

4.48 $_{10}C_4 = \dfrac{10!}{4!(6!)} = 210$

4.50 $\dfrac{n!}{X!(n-X)!} = \dfrac{100!}{2!(98!)} = \dfrac{(100)(99)}{2} = 4950$

4.52   With a priori probability, the probability of success is based on prior knowledge of the process involved. With empirical probability, outcomes are based on observed data. Subjective probability refers to the chance of occurrence assigned to an event by a particular individual.

4.54   The general addition rule is used by adding the probability of A and the probability of B and then subtracting the joint probability of A and B.

4.56   If events A and B are statistically independent, the conditional probability of event A given B is equal to the probability of A.

4.58   Bayes' theorem uses conditional probabilities to revise the probability of an event in the light of new information.

4.60   (a)

		Age		
		18-25	26-40	Total
Goals	Getting Rich	405	310	715
	Other	95	190	285
	Total	500	500	1000

(b)   Simple event: "Has a goal of getting rich".
       Joint event: "Has a goal of getting rich and is between 18-25 years old.
(c) P(Has a goal of getting rich) = 715/1000 = 0.715
(d) P(Has a goal of getting rich and is in the 26-40 year old group) = 310/1000 = 0.31
(e) P(Has a goal of getting rich | in the 26-40 year old group) = 310/500 = 0.62
       Since P(Has a goal of getting rich | in the 26-40 year old group) $\neq$ P(Has a goal of getting rich), the events "age group" and "has getting rich as a goal" are not statistically independent.

4.62   (a) P(prefers ordering lunch at the drive-thru) = 99/200 = 0.495
        (b) P(prefers ordering breakfast or lunch at the drive-thru) = (28+99)/200 = 0.635
        (c) P(is a male or prefers ordering dinner at the drive-thru) = (100+58-29)/200 = 0.645
        (d) P(is a male and prefers ordering dinner at the drive-thru) = 29/200 = 0.145
        (e) P(prefers ordering breakfast at the drive-through | female) = 10/100 = 0.10

4.64 A = fatality involved an SUV, van or pickup
B = fatality involved a rollover
(a) $P(B \mid A) = (0.158)(0.24)/((0.158)(0.24)+(0.056)(0.76)) = 0.4712$
(b)   Since the probability that a fatality involved a rollover given that the fatality
involved an SUV, van or pickup is 0.4712, which is almost twice the probability that
a fatality involved a rollover with any vehicle type at 0.24, SUVs, vans or pickups
are generally more prone to rollover accidents.

4.66 **Type and Fees:**

Count of Type	Type		
Fees	Intermediate Government	Short Term Corporate	Grand Total
No	53	77	130
Yes	34	20	54
Grand Total	87	97	184

(a) P(No Fees) = 0.7065, P(Fees) = 0.2935
P(Intermediate Government) = 0.4728, P(Short Term Corporate) = 0.5272
P(No Fees | Intermediate Government) = 0.6092
P(Fees | Intermediate Government) = 0.3908
P(No Fees | Short Term Corporate) = 0.7938
P(Fees | Short Term Corporate) = 0.2062
P(Intermediate Government | No Fees) = 0.4077
P(Short Term Corporate | No Fees) = 0.5923
P(Intermediate Government | Fees) = 0.6296
P(Short Term Corporate | Fees) = 0.3704
(b)   Type and fees are not statistically independent.

Type and Risk:

Count of Risk	Type		
Risk	Intermediate Government	Short Term Corporate	Grand Total
Above average	29	30	59
Average	32	37	69
Below average	26	30	56
Grand Total	87	97	184

(a) P(Above Average) = 0.3207, P(Average) = 0.375, P(Below Average) = 0.3043
P(Intermediate Government) = 0.4728, P(Short Term Corporate) = 0.5272
P(Above Average | Intermediate Government) = 0.3333
P(Average | Intermediate Government) = 0.3678
P(Below Average | Intermediate Government) = 0.2989
P(Above Average | Short Term Corporate) = 0.3093
P(Average | Short Term Corporate) = 0.3814
P(Below Average | Short Term Corporate) = 0.3093
P(Intermediate Government |Above Average) = 0.4915
P(Short Term Corporate | Above Average) = 0.5085
P(Intermediate Government | Average) = 0.4638
P(Short Term Corporate | Average) = 0.5362
P(Intermediate Government | Below Average) = 0.4643
P(Short Term Corporate | Below Average) = 0.5357
(b)   Type and risk are not statistically independent.

4.66   **Risk and Fees:**
cont.

Count of Risk	Fees		
Risk	No	Yes	Grand Total
Above average	37	22	59
Average	49	20	69
Below average	44	12	56
Grand Total	130	54	184

(a) $P(\text{No Fees}) = 0.7065$, $P(\text{Fees}) = 0.2935$
$P(\text{Above Average}) = 0.3207$, $P(\text{Average}) = 0.375$, $P(\text{Below Average}) = 0.3043$
$P(\text{No Fees} \mid \text{Above Average}) = 0.6271$
$P(\text{Fees} \mid \text{Above Average}) = 0.3729$
$P(\text{No Fees} \mid \text{Average}) = 0.7101$
$P(\text{Fees} \mid \text{Average}) = 0.2899$
$P(\text{No Fees} \mid \text{Below Average}) = 0.7857$
$P(\text{Fees} \mid \text{Below Average}) = 0.2143$
$P(\text{Above Average} \mid \text{No Fees}) = 0.2846$
$P(\text{Average} \mid \text{No Fees}) = 0.3769$
$P(\text{Below Average} \mid \text{No Fees}) = 0.3385$
$P(\text{Above Average} \mid \text{Fees}) = 0.4074$
$P(\text{Average} \mid \text{Fees}) = 0.3704$
$P(\text{Below Average} \mid \text{Fees}) = 0.2222$

(b)   Risk and fees are not statistically independent.

CHAPTER 5

OBJECTIVES

In this chapter, you learn:
- The properties of a probability distribution
- To compute the expected value and variance of a probability distribution
- To compute probabilities from the binomial and Poisson distributions
- How to use the binomial and Poisson distributions to solve business problems

OVERVIEW AND KEY CONCEPTS

Some Basic Concepts of Discrete Probability Distribution
- **Random variable:** Outcomes of an experiment expressed numerically, e.g., Toss a die twice and count the number of times the number four appears (0, 1 or 2 times).
- **Discrete random variable:** A random variable that can have only certain distinct values. It is usually obtained by counting. E.g., Toss a coin five times and count the number of tails (0, 1, 2, 3, 4 or 5 tails).
- **Discrete probability distribution:** A mutually exclusive listing of all possible numerical outcomes for a discrete random variable such that a particular probability of occurrence is associated with each outcome.

Concepts of Expectation for a Discrete Random Variable
- **Expected value of a discrete random variable:** A weighted average over all possible outcomes.
  - The weights being the probabilities associated with each of the outcomes.
  - $$\mu = E(X) = \sum_{i=1}^{N} X_i P(X_i)$$
- **Variance of a discrete random variable:** The weighted average of the squared differences between each possible outcome and its mean
  - The weights being the probabilities of each of the respective outcomes.
  - $$\sigma^2 = \sum_{i=1}^{N} \left[X_i - E(X) \right]^2 P(X_i)$$
- **Standard deviation of a discrete random variable:** The square root of the variance.
  - $$\sigma = \sqrt{\sum_{i=1}^{N} \left[X_i - E(X) \right]^2 P(X_i)}$$

The Binomial Distribution

- **Properties of the binomial distribution:**
  - The sample has n observations.
  - Each observation is classified into one of the two mutually exclusive and collectively exhaustive categories, usually called *items of interest and items not of interest.*
  - The probability of getting an *item of interest* is p while the probability of an *item not of interest* is (1-p).
  - The outcome (i.e., *interest* or *not of interest*) of any observation is independent of the outcome of any other observation. This can be achieved by selecting each observation randomly either from an *infinite population without replacement* or from a *finite population with replacement*.
- **The binomial probability distribution function:**

  - $$P(X) = \frac{n!}{X!(n-X)!} p^X (1-p)^{n-X}$$

    where

    $P(X=x)$: probability that $X = x$ events of interest, given n and π

    x : number of events of interest in the sample $(x = 0,1,\cdots,n)$

    π : the probability of an event of interest

    $(1-\pi)$: the probability of not having an event of interest

    n : sample size

- **The mean and variance of a binomial distribution:**
  - $\mu = E(X) = np$
  - $\sigma^2 = np(1-p)$
  - $\sigma = \sqrt{np(1-p)}$
- **Applications:** Useful in evaluating the probability of X items of interest in a sample of size n drawn with replacement from a finite population or without replacement from an infinite population.

The Poisson Distribution

- **Properties of the Poisson distribution:**
  1. The area of opportunity, in which the number of times a particular event of interest occurs is defined by time, length, surface area, etc.
  2. The probability that an event occurs in a given area of opportunity is the same for all of the areas of opportunity.
  3. The number of events that occur in one area of opportunity is independent of the number of events that occur in other areas of opportunity.
  4. The probability that two or more events will occur in an area of opportunity approaches zero as the area of opportunity becomes smaller.

- **The Poisson probability distribution function:**

  - $$P(X) = \frac{e^{-\lambda}\lambda^{X}}{X!}$$

    where

    $P(X = x)$: probability that $X = x$ events in an area of opportunity given λ

    X: number of events $(x == 0, 1, 2, \cdots, \infty)$

    λ: expected (average) number of events

    e: 2.71828 (base of natural logs)

- **The mean and variance of a Poisson Distribution**

  - $\mu = E(X) = \lambda$

  - $\sigma^2 = \lambda$

  - $\sigma = \sqrt{\lambda}$

- **Applications:** Useful in modeling the number of items of interest in a given continuous interval of time, length, surface area, etc.

SOLUTIONS TO END OF SECTION
AND CHAPTER REVIEW EVEN PROBLEMS

5.2   PHStat output:

Probabilities & Outcomes:	P	X
	0.1	0
	0.2	1
	0.45	2
	0.15	3
	0.05	4
	0.05	5
Statistics		
E(X)	2	
E(Y)	0	
Variance(X)	1.4	
Standard Deviation(X)	1.183216	
Variance(Y)	0	
Standard Deviation(Y)	0	
Covariance(XY)	0	
Variance(X+Y)	1.4	
Standard Deviation(X+Y)	1.183216	

(a)-(b)

X	P(x)	X*P(X)	$(X-\mu)^2$	$(X-\mu)^2*P(X)$
0	0.10	0.00	4	0.40
1	0.20	0.20	1	0.20
2	0.45	0.90	0	0.00
3	0.15	0.45	1	0.15
4	0.05	0.20	4	0.20
5	0.05	0.25	9	0.45
	(a) Mean =	2.00	Variance =	1.40
			(b) Stdev =	1.18321596

5.4   (a)

X	P(X)
$-1	21/36
$+1	15/36

(b)

X	P(X)
$-1	21/36
$+1	15/36

(c)

X	P(X)
$-1	30/36
$+4	6/36

(d) $ – 0.167 for each method of play

5.6   PHStat output:

Probabilities & Outcomes:	P	X
	0.125	0
	0.240385	1
	0.307692	2
	0.163462	3
	0.086538	4
	0.057692	5
	0.009615	6
	0.009615	7
Statistics		
E(X)	2.105769	
Variance(X)	2.152274	
Standard Deviation(X)	1.467063	

(a) $\mu = E(X) = 2.1058$

(b) $\sigma = 1.4671$

5.8   (a)   PHStat output:

Covariance Analysis			
Probabilities & Outcomes:	P	X	Y
	0.01	-200	-999
	0.09	-70	-300
	0.15	30	-100
	0.35	80	100
	0.3	100	150
	0.1	120	350
Weight Assigned to X	0.5		
Statistics			
E(X)	66.2		
E(Y)	63.01		
Variance(X)	3273.56		
Standard Deviation(X)	57.21503		
Variance(Y)	38109.75		
Standard Deviation(Y)	195.2172		
Covariance(XY)	10766.74		
Variance(X+Y)	62916.79		
Standard Deviation(X+Y)	250.8322		
Portfolio Management			
Weight Assigned to X	0.5		
Weight Assigned to Y	0.5		
Portfolio Expected Return	64.605		
Portfolio Risk	125.4161		

Let X = corporate bond fund, Y = common stock fund.

(a) $E(X) = \$66.2$ $E(Y) = \$63.01$.

(b) $\sigma_X = \$57.2150$ $\sigma_Y = \$195.2172$

5.8   (c) $CV(X) = 86.43\%$ $CV(Y) = 309.82\%$

cont.   The corporate bond fund gives the investor a slightly higher expected return than the common stock fund, and has a standard deviation about 1/3 of that of the common stock fund. An investor who does not like risk but desires a high expected return should invest in the corporate bond fund.

(d)   According to the probability of 0.01, it is highly unlikely that you will lose $999 of every $1,000 invested.

5.10   PHstat output:

Binomial Probabilities						
Data						
Sample size	5					
Probability of an event of interest	0.4					
Statistics						
Mean	2					
Variance	1.2					
Standard deviation	1.095445					
Binomial Probabilities Table						
	X	P(X)	P(<=X)	P(<X)	P(>X)	P(>=X)
	0	0.07776	0.07776	0	0.92224	1
	1	0.2592	0.33696	0.07776	0.66304	0.92224
	2	0.3456	0.68256	0.33696	0.31744	0.66304
	3	0.2304	0.91296	0.68256	0.08704	0.31744
	4	0.0768	0.98976	0.91296	0.01024	0.08704
	5	0.01024	1	0.98976	0	0.01024

(a) $P(X = 4) = 0.0768$
(b) $P(X \leq 3) = 0.9130$
(c) $P(X < 2) = 0.3370$
(d) $P(X > 1) = 0.6630$

5.12   Partial PHStat output:

Binomial Probabilities						
Data						
Sample size	6					
Probability of an event of interest	0.825					
Statistics						
Mean	4.95					
Variance	0.86625					
Standard deviation	0.930726					
Binomial Probabilities Table						
	X	P(X)	P(<=X)	P(<X)	P(>X)	P(>=X)
	0	2.87E-05	2.87E-05	0	0.999971	1
	1	0.000812	0.000841	2.87E-05	0.999159	0.999971
	2	0.009575	0.010416	0.000841	0.989584	0.999159
	3	0.060187	0.070604	0.010416	0.929396	0.989584
	4	0.212806	0.28341	0.070604	0.71659	0.929396
	5	0.401291	0.6847	0.28341	0.3153	0.71659
	6	0.3153	1	0.6847	0	0.3153

Let X = number of on-time flights.

(a) $P(X = 4) = 0.2128$.

(b) $P(X = 6) = 0.3153$

(c) $P(X > 5) = 0.9294$

(d) $E(X) = 4.95$ $\sigma_X = 0.9307$

(e)   The four assumptions are (i) the sample consists of a fixed number of observations, n, (ii) each observation can be classified into one of two mutually exclusive and collectively exhaustive categories, usually called "an event of interest" and "not an event of interest", (iii) the probability of an observation being classified as "an event of interest", π, is constant from observation to observation and (iv) the outcome (i.e., "an event of interest" or "not an event of interest") of any observation is independent of the outcome of any other observation.

5.14   Partial PHStat output:

Data						
Sample size	10					
Probability of an event of interest	0.22					
Statistics						
Mean	2.2					
Variance	1.716					
Standard deviation	1.309962					
Binomial Probabilities Table						
	X	P(X)	P(<=X)	P(<X)	P(>X)	P(>=X)
	0	0.083358	0.083358	0	0.916642	1
	1	0.235112	0.318469	0.083358	0.681531	0.916642
	2	0.298411	0.61688	0.318469	0.38312	0.681531
	3	0.224446	0.841326	0.61688	0.158674	0.38312

(a) $P(X = 0) = 0.0834$
(b) $P(X = 1) = 0.2351$
(c) $P(X \leq 2) = 0.6169$
(d) $P(X \geq 3) = 0.3831$

5.16   PHStat output:

Binomial Probabilities						
Data						
Sample size	3					
Probability of an event of interest	0.848					
Statistics						
Mean	2.544					
Variance	0.386688					
Standard deviation	0.621842					
Binomial Probabilities Table						
	X	P(X)	P(<=X)	P(<X)	P(>X)	P(>=X)
	0	0.003512	0.003512	0	0.996488	1
	1	0.058777	0.062288	0.003512	0.937712	0.996488
	2	0.327911	0.3902	0.062288	0.6098	0.937712
	3	0.6098	1	0.3902	0	0.6098

Given $\pi = 0.848$ and $n = 3$,
(a) $P(X = 3) = 0.6098$
(b) $P(X = 0) = 0.0035$
(c) $P(X \geq 2) = 0.9377$
(d) $E(X) = n\pi = 2.544$

$$\sigma_X = \sqrt{n\pi(1-\pi)} = 0.6218$$

You can expect 2.544 orders to be filled with an average spread around the mean of 0.6218 orders.

5.18   (a)   Partial PHStat output:

Poisson Probabilities					
Data					
Average/Expected number of successes:			2.5		
Poisson Probabilities Table					
	X	P(X)	P(<=X)	P(<X)	P(>X)	P(>=X)
	2	0.256516	0.543813	0.287297	0.456187	0.712703

Using the equation, if $\lambda = 2.5$, $P(X = 2) = \dfrac{e^{-2.5} \cdot (2.5)^2}{2!} = 0.2565$

(b)   Partial PHStat output:

Poisson Probabilities					
Data					
Average/Expected number of successes:			8		
Poisson Probabilities Table					
	X	P(X)	P(<=X)	P(<X)	P(>X)	P(>=X)
	8	0.139587	0.592547	0.452961	0.407453	0.547039

If $\lambda = 8.0$, $P(X = 8) = 0.1396$

(c)   Partial PHStat output:

Poisson Probabilities					
Data					
Average/Expected number of successes:			0.5		
Poisson Probabilities Table					
	X	P(X)	P(<=X)	P(<X)	P(>X)	P(>=X)
	0	0.606531	0.606531	0.000000	0.393469	1.000000
	1	0.303265	0.909796	0.606531	0.090204	0.393469

If $\lambda = 0.5$, $P(X = 1) = 0.3033$

(d)   Partial PHStat output:

Poisson Probabilities					
Data					
Average/Expected number of successes:			3.7		
Poisson Probabilities Table					
	X	P(X)	P(<=X)	P(<X)	P(>X)	P(>=X)
	0	0.024724	0.024724	0.000000	0.975276	1.000000

If $\lambda = 3.7$, $P(X = 0) = 0.0247$

5.20   PHStat output for (a) – (d)

Poisson Probabilities Table						
	X	P(X)	P(<=X)	P(<X)	P(>X)	P(>=X)
	0	0.006738	0.006738	0.000000	0.993262	1.000000
	1	0.033690	0.040428	0.006738	0.959572	0.993262
	2	0.084224	0.124652	0.040428	0.875348	0.959572
	3	0.140374	0.265026	0.124652	0.734974	0.875348
	4	0.175467	0.440493	0.265026	0.559507	0.734974
	5	0.175467	0.615961	0.440493	0.384039	0.559507
	6	0.146223	0.762183	0.615961	0.237817	0.384039
	7	0.104445	0.866628	0.762183	0.133372	0.237817
	8	0.065278	0.931906	0.866628	0.068094	0.133372
	9	0.036266	0.968172	0.931906	0.031828	0.068094
	10	0.018133	0.986305	0.968172	0.013695	0.031828
	11	0.008242	0.994547	0.986305	0.005453	0.013695
	12	0.003434	0.997981	0.994547	0.002019	0.005453
	13	0.001321	0.999302	0.997981	0.000698	0.002019
	14	0.000472	0.999774	0.999302	0.000226	0.000698
	15	0.000157	0.999931	0.999774	0.000069	0.000226
	16	0.000049	0.999980	0.999931	0.000020	0.000069
	17	0.000014	0.999995	0.999980	0.000005	0.000020
	18	0.000004	0.999999	0.999995	0.000001	0.000005
	19	0.000001	1.000000	0.999999	0.000000	0.000001
	20	0.000000	1.000000	1.000000	0.000000	0.000000

Given $\lambda = 5.0$,

(a) $P(X = 1) = 0.0337$
(b) $P(X < 1) = 0.0067$
(c) $P(X > 1) = 0.9596$
(d) $P(X \leq 1) = 0.0404$

5.22   (a) – (c) Portion of PHStat output

Data					
Average/Expected number of successes:			6		
Poisson Probabilities Table					
X	P(X)	P(<=X)	P(<X)	P(>X)	P(>=X)
0	0.002479	0.002479	0.000000	0.997521	1.000000
1	0.014873	0.017351	0.002479	0.982649	0.997521
2	0.044618	0.061969	0.017351	0.938031	0.982649
3	0.089235	0.151204	0.061969	0.848796	0.938031
4	0.133853	0.285057	0.151204	0.714943	0.848796
5	(b) 0.160623	0.445680	(a) 0.285057	0.554320	(c) 0.714943
6	0.160623	0.606303	0.445680	0.393697	0.554320
7	0.137677	0.743980	0.606303	0.256020	0.393697
8	0.103258	0.847237	0.743980	0.152763	0.256020
9	0.068838	0.916076	0.847237	0.083924	0.152763
10	0.041303	0.957379	0.916076	0.042621	0.083924
11	0.022529	0.979908	0.957379	0.020092	0.042621
12	0.011264	0.991173	0.979908	0.008827	0.020092
13	0.005199	0.996372	0.991173	0.003628	0.008827
14	0.002228	0.998600	0.996372	0.001400	0.003628
15	0.000891	0.999491	0.998600	0.000509	0.001400
16	0.000334	0.999825	0.999491	0.000175	0.000509
17	0.000118	0.999943	0.999825	0.000057	0.000175

(a) $P(X < 5) = P(X = 0) + P(X = 1) + P(X = 2) + P(X = 3) + P(X = 4)$

$$= \frac{e^{-6}(6)^0}{0!} + \frac{e^{-6}(6)^1}{1!} + \frac{e^{-6}(6)^2}{2!} + \frac{e^{-6}(6)^3}{3!} + \frac{e^{-6}(6)^4}{4!}$$

$$= 0.002479 + 0.014873 + 0.044618 + 0.089235 + 0.133853 = 0.2851$$

(b) $P(X = 5) = \dfrac{e^{-6}(6)^5}{5!} = 0.1606$

(c) $P(X \geq 5) = 1 - P(X < 5) = 1 - 0.2851 = 0.7149$

(d) $P(X = 4 \text{ or } X = 5) = P(X = 4) + P(X = 5) = \dfrac{e^{-6}(6)^4}{4!} + \dfrac{e^{-6}(6)^5}{5!} = 0.2945$

5.24   Partial PHStat outputu:

Poisson Probabilities					
Data					
Mean/Expected number of events of interest:			3.52		
Poisson Probabilities Table					
X	P(X)	P(<=X)	P(<X)	P(>X)	P(>=X)
0	0.029599	0.029599	0.000000	0.970401	1.000000
1	0.104190	0.133789	0.029599	0.866211	0.970401
2	0.183374	0.317164	0.133789	0.682836	0.866211

$\lambda = 3.52$

(a) $P(X = 0) = 0.0296$ (b) $P(X \geq 1) = 0.9704$

(c) $P(X \geq 2) = 0.8662$

5.26   (a)   Partial PHStat output:

Poisson Probabilities					
Data					
Average/Expected number of successes:			0.2		
Poisson Probabilities Table					
	X	P(X)	P(<=X)	P(<X)	P(>X)	P(>=X)
	2	0.016375	0.998852	0.982477	0.001148	0.017523

If $\lambda = 0.2$, $P(X \geq 2) = 1 - [P(X = 0) + P(X = 1)] = 1 - [0.8187 + 0.1637]$
$= 0.0176$

(b)   Partial PHStat output:

Poisson Probabilities					
Data					
Average/Expected number of successes:			2.4		
Poisson Probabilities Table					
	X	P(X)	P(<=X)	P(<X)	P(>X)	P(>=X)
	0	0.090718	0.090718	0.000000	0.909282	1.000000
	1	0.217723	0.308441	0.090718	0.691559	0.909282

If there are 0.2 flaws per foot on the average, then there are 0.2•(12) or 2.4 flaws on the average in a 12-foot roll.
If $\lambda = 2.4$, $P(X \geq 1) = 1 - P(X = 0) = 1 - 0.0907 = 0.9093$

(c)   Partial PHStat output:

Poisson Probabilities					
Data					
Average/Expected number of successes:			10		
Poisson Probabilities Table					
	X	P(X)	P(<=X)	P(<X)	P(>X)	P(>=X)
	5	0.037833	0.067086	0.029253	0.932914	0.970747
	6	0.063055	0.130141	0.067086	0.869859	0.932914
	7	0.090079	0.220221	0.130141	0.779779	0.869859
	8	0.112599	0.332820	0.220221	0.667180	0.779779
	9	0.125110	0.457930	0.332820	0.542070	0.667180
	10	0.125110	0.583040	0.457930	0.416960	0.542070
	11	0.113736	0.696776	0.583040	0.303224	0.416960
	12	0.094780	0.791556	0.696776	0.208444	0.303224
	13	0.072908	0.864464	0.791556	0.135536	0.208444
	14	0.052077	0.916542	0.864464	0.083458	0.135536
	15	0.034718	0.951260	0.916542	0.048740	0.083458

If there are 0.2 flaws per foot on the average, then there are 0.2•(50) or 10 flaws on the average in a 50-foot roll.
If $\lambda = 10$, $P(5 \leq X \leq 15) = 0.9220$

5.28   Partial PHStat output:

Poisson Probabilities Table

X	P(X)	P(<=X)	P(<X)	P(>X)	P(>=X)
0	0.261846	0.261846	0.000000	0.738154	1.000000
1	0.350873	0.612719	0.261846	0.387281	0.738154
2	0.235085	0.847804	0.612719	0.152196	0.387281

(a) $\lambda = 1.34$, $P(X = 0) = 0.2618$

(b) $\lambda = 1.34$, $P(X \leq 2) = 0.8478$

(c)   Because Ford had a lower mean rate of problems per car in 2009 compared to Dodge, the probability of a randomly selected Ford having zero problems and the probability of no more than 2 problems are both higher than their values for Dodge.

5.30   PHStat output:

Poisson Probabilities Table

X	P(X)	P(<=X)	P(<X)	P(>X)	P(>=X)
0	0.244143	0.244143	0.000000	0.755857	1.000000
1	0.344242	0.588385	0.244143	0.411615	0.755857
2	0.242691	0.831076	0.588385	0.168924	0.411615

(a) $\lambda = 1.41$, $P(X = 0) = 0.2441$

(b) $P(X \leq 2) = 0.8311$

(c)   Because Dodge had a lower mean rate of problems per car in 2009 compared to 2008, the probability of a randomly selected Dodge having zero problems and the probability of no more than 2 problems are both higher in 2009 than their values in 2008.

5.32   The expected value is the average of a probability distribution. It is the value that can be expected to occur on the average, in the long run.

5.34   The four properties of a situation that must be present in order to use the Poisson distribution are (i) you are interested in counting the number of times a particular event occurs in a given area of opportunity (defined by time, length, surface area, and so forth), (ii) the probability that an event occurs in a given area of opportunity is the same for all of the areas of opportunity, (iii) the number of events that occur in one area of opportunity is independent of the number of events that occur in other areas of opportunity and (iv) the probability that two or more events will occur in an area of opportunity approaches zero as the area of opportunity becomes smaller.

5.36   Partial PHstat output:

Binomial Probabilities						
Data						
Sample size	5					
Probability of an event of interest	0.64					
Statistics						
Mean	3.2					
Variance	1.152					
Standard deviation	1.073313					
Binomial Probabilities Table						
	X	P(X)	P(<=X)	P(<X)	P(>X)	P(>=X)
	0	(d) 0.006047	0.006047	0	0.993953	1
	4	(c) 0.30199	0.892626	0.590636	0.107374	0.409364

(a)   0.64
(b)   0.64
$\pi = 0.64, \ n = 5$
(c) $P(X = 4) = 0.3020$ (d) $P(X = 0) = 0.0060$
(e)   Stock prices tend to rise in the years when the economy is expanding and fall in the years of recession or contraction. Hence, the probability that the price will rise in one year is not independent from year to year.

5.38   (a)   Partial PHStat output:

Data						
Sample size	12					
Probability of an event of interest	0.5					
Statistics						
Mean	6					
Variance	3					
Standard deviation	1.732051					
Binomial Probabilities Table						
	X	P(X)	P(<=X)	P(<X)	P(>X)	P(>=X)
	9	0.053711	0.980713	0.927002	0.019287	0.072998

If $\pi = 0.50$ and $n = 12$, $P(X \geq 9) = 0.0730$

5.38   (b)   Partial PHStat output:
cont.

Data						
Sample size	12					
Probability of an event of interest	0.75					
Statistics						
Mean	9					
Variance	2.25					
Standard deviation	1.5					
Binomial Probabilities Table						
	X	P(X)	P(<=X)	P(<X)	P(>X)	P(>=X)
	9	0.258104	0.609325	0.351221	0.390675	0.648779

If $\pi = 0.75$ and $n = 12$, $P(X \geq 9) = 0.64878$

5.40   (a)-(d) Portion of the PHStat output:

Binomial Probabilities						
Data						
Sample size	10					
Probability of success	0.2					
Statistics						
Mean	(d) 2					
Variance	1.6					
Standard deviation	(d) 1.2649					
Binomial Probabilities Table						
	X	P(X)	P(<=X)	P(<X)	P(>X)	P(>=X)
	0	(a) 0.107374	0.107374	0	0.892626	1
	1	(b) 0.268435	0.37581	0.107374	0.62419	0.892626
	2	0.30199	0.6778	0.37581	0.3222	(c) 0.62419

(d)   Because the percentage of bills containing an error is lower in this problem than that in Problem 5.57, the probability of containing a smaller number of errors as in (a) and (b) if 10 bills are processed is higher than that in Problem 5.57 (a) and (b). Likewise, the probability of containing a larger number of errors as in (c) if 10 bills are processed is lower than that in Problem 5.57 (c).

5.42   Partial PHStat output:

Data						
Sample size	20					
Probability of an event of interest	0.68					
Statistics						
Mean	13.6					
Variance	4.352					
Standard deviation	2.086145					
Binomial Probabilities Table						
	X	P(X)	P(<=X)	P(<X)	P(>X)	P(>=X)
	10	0.043973	0.071899	0.027926	0.928101	0.972074
	15	0.159892	0.817277	0.657385	0.182723	0.342615

(a) $\mu = n\pi = 13.6$ (b) $\sigma = \sqrt{n\pi(1-\pi)} = 2.0861$

(c) $P(X = 15) = 0.1599$ (d) $P(X \le 10) = 0.0719$

(e) $P(X \ge 10) = 0.9721$

5.44   (a) $\pi = 0.5, P(X \ge 34) = 1.21 \times 10^{-6}$

Partial PHStat output:

Binomial Probabilities						
Data						
Sample size	39					
Probability of an event of interest	0.5					
Statistics						
Mean	19.5					
Variance	9.75					
Standard deviation	3.122499					
Binomial Probabilities Table						
	X	P(X)	P(<=X)	P(<X)	P(>X)	P(>=X)
	34	1.05E-06		1	0.999999	1.68E-07	1.21E-06

5.44   (b) $\pi = 0.7, P(X \geq 34) = 0.0109$
cont.   Partial PHStat output:

Binomial Probabilities						
Data						
Sample size	39					
Probability of an event of interest	0.7					
Statistics						
Mean	27.3					
Variance	8.19					
Standard deviation	2.861818					
Binomial Probabilities Table						
	X	P(X)	P(<=X)	P(<X)	P(>X)	P(>=X)
	34	0.007571	0.996682	0.989111	0.003318	0.010889

(c) $\pi = 0.9, P(X \geq 34) = 0.8097$
Partial PHStat output:

Binomial Probabilities						
Data						
Sample size	39					
Probability of an event of interest	0.9					
Statistics						
Mean	35.1					
Variance	3.51					
Standard deviation	1.873499					
Binomial Probabilities Table						
	X	P(X)	P(<=X)	P(<X)	P(>X)	P(>=X)
	34	0.160134	0.350394	0.190259	0.649606	0.809741

(d)   Based on the results in (a)-(c), the probability that the Standard & Poor's 500 index
will increase if there is an early gain in the first five trading days of the year is very
likely to be close to 0.90 because that yields a probability of 80.97% that at least 34
of the 39 years the Standard & Poor's 500 index will increase the entire year.

5.46   (a)   The assumptions needed are (i) the probability that a golfer loses a golf ball in a given interval in a game is constant, (ii) the probability that a golfer loses more than one golf ball in this interval approaches zero as the interval gets smaller, (iii) the probability that a golfer loses a golf ball is independent from interval to interval.

Partial PHStat output:

Poisson Probabilities					
Data					
Mean/Expected number of events of interest:			5		
Poisson Probabilities Table					
	X	P(X)	P(<=X)	P(<X)	P(>X)	P(>=X)
	0	0.006738	0.006738	0.000000	0.993262	1.000000
	5	0.175467	0.615961	0.440493	0.384039	0.559507
	6	0.146223	0.762183	0.615961	0.237817	0.384039

$\lambda = 5.0$

(b) $P(X = 0) = 0.0067$

(c) $P(X \leq 5) = 0.6160$

(d) $P(X \geq 6) = 0.3840$

CHAPTER 6

OBJECTIVES
In this chapter, you learn:
- To compute probabilities from the normal distribution
- How to use the normal distribution to solve business problems
- To use the normal probability plot to determine whether a set of data is approximately normally distributed

OVERVIEW AND KEY CONCEPTS

Some Basic Concepts of Continuous Probability Density Function
- **Continuous random variable:** A variable that can take an infinite number of values within a specific range, e.g. Weight, height, daily changes in closing prices of stocks, and time between arrivals of planes landing on a runway.
- **Continuous probability density function:** A mathematical expression that represents the continuous phenomenon of a continuous random variable, and can be used to calculate the probability that the random variable occurs within certain ranges or intervals.
- The probability that a continuous random variable is equal to a *particular value* is 0. This distinguishes continuous phenomena, which are measured, from discrete phenomena, which are counted. For example, the probability that a task can be completed in between 20 and 30 seconds can be measured. With a more precise measuring instrument, we can compute the probability that the task can be completed between a very small interval such as 19.99 to 20.01. However, the probability that the task can be completed in *exactly* 20 seconds is 0.
- Obtaining probabilities or computing expected values and standard deviations for continuous random variables involves mathematical expressions that require knowledge of integral calculus. In this book, these are achieved with special probability tables or computer statistical software like Minitab or PHStat2.

The Normal Distribution
- **Properties of the normal distribution:**
  - Bell-shaped (and thus symmetrical) in its appearance.
  - Its measures of central tendency (mean, median, and mode) are all identical.
  - Its "middle spread" (interquartile range) is equal to 1.33 standard deviations.
  - Its associated random variable has an infinite range $\left(-\infty < X < +\infty\right)$.

- **The normal probability density function:**

    - $f(X) = \dfrac{1}{\sqrt{2\pi\sigma^2}} e^{-\frac{1}{2\sigma^2}(X-\mu)^2}$ where

        $f(X)$: density of random variable X

        $\pi = 3.14159;\quad e = 2.71828$

        μ: population mean

        σ: population standard deviation

        X: value of random variable $(-\infty < X < \infty)$

    - A particular combination of μ and σ will yield a particular normal probability distribution.

- **Standardization or normalization of a normal continuous random variable:** By standardizing (normalizing) a normal random variable, we need only one table to tabulate the probabilities of the whole family of normal distributions.

- **The transformation (standardization) formula:** $Z = \dfrac{X - \mu}{\sigma}$

    - The standardized normal distribution is one whose random variable Z always has a mean 0 and a standard deviation 1.

- **Finding range probability of a normal random variable:**
    1.   Standardize the value of X into Z.
    2.   Look up the cumulative probabilities from the cumulative standardized normal distribution table.

    E.g., For $\mu = 5$ and $\sigma = 10$, $P(2.9 < X < 7.1) = ?$

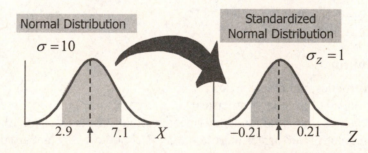

$$Z = \frac{X-\mu}{\sigma} = \frac{2.9-5}{10} = -.21 \qquad Z = \frac{X-\mu}{\sigma} = \frac{7.1-5}{10} = .21$$

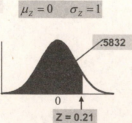
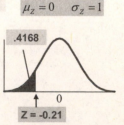

$$P(2.9 < X < 7.1) = P(-0.21 < Z < 0.21) = 0.5832 - 0.4168 = 0.1664$$

E.g., For $\mu = 5$ and $\sigma = 10$, $P(X \geq 8) = ?$

$$Z = \frac{X - \mu}{\sigma} = \frac{8-5}{10} = .30$$

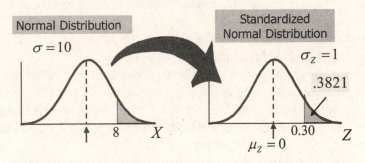

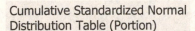

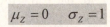

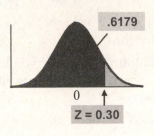

Z	.00	.01	.02
0.0	.5000	.5040	.5080
0.1	.5398	.5438	.5478
0.2	.5793	.5832	.5871
0.3	**.6179**	.6217	.6255

$$P(X \geq 8) = P(Z \geq 0.30) = 1 - 0.6179 = 0.3821$$

- **Finding X values for known probabilities:**
    1. Look up the Z value from the cumulative standardized normal distribution table.
    2. Find the value of X using the formula $X = \mu + Z\sigma$

  E.g., For $\mu = 5$ and $\sigma = 10$, $P(X \leq A) = 0.6179$, what is the value of A?

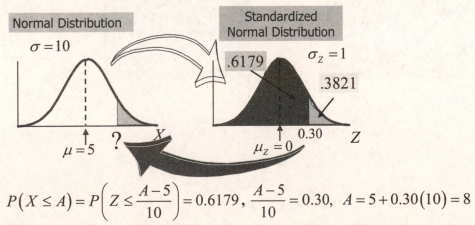

$$P(X \leq A) = P\left(Z \leq \frac{A-5}{10}\right) = 0.6179, \quad \frac{A-5}{10} = 0.30, \quad A = 5 + 0.30(10) = 8$$

- **Applications:** Many continuous random phenomena are either normally distributed or can be approximated by a normal distribution. Hence, it is important to know how to assess whether a distribution is normally distributed.

Evaluating the Normality Assumption

- For small and moderate-sized data sets, construct a stem-and-leaf display and box plot. For large data sets, construct the frequency distribution and plot the histogram or polygon.
- Obtain the mean, median, and mode, and note the similarities or differences among these measures of central tendency.
- Obtain the interquartile range and standard deviation. Note how well the interquartile range can be approximated by 1.33 times the standard deviation.
- Obtain the range and note how well it can be approximated by 6 times the standard deviation.
- Determine whether approximately 2/3 of the observations lie between the mean ± 1 standard deviation. Determine whether approximately 4/5 of the observations lie between the mean ± 1.28 standard deviations. Determine whether approximately 19/20 of the observations lie between the mean ± 2 standard deviations.
- Construct a normal probability plot and evaluate the likelihood that the variable of interest is at least approximately normally distributed by inspecting the plot for evidence of linearity (i.e., a straight line).

The Normal Probability Plot

- **The normal probability plot:** A two-dimensional plot of the observed data values on the vertical axis with their corresponding quantile values from a standardized normal distribution on the horizontal axis.

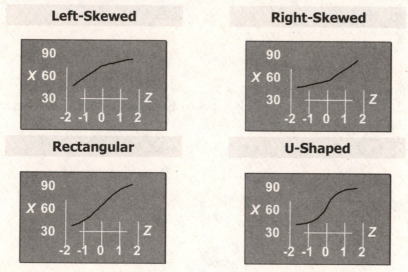

SOLUTIONS TO END OF SECTION
AND CHAPTER REVIEW EVEN PROBLEMS

6.2   PHStat output:

Normal Probabilities					
Common Data					
Mean	0				
Standard Deviation	1				
			Probability for a Range		
Probability for X <=			From X Value		1.57
X Value	-1.57		To X Value		1.84
Z Value	-1.57		Z Value for 1.57		1.57
P(X<=-1.57)	0.0582076		Z Value for 1.84		1.84
			P(X<=1.57)		0.9418
Probability for X >			P(X<=1.84)		0.9671
X Value	1.84		P(1.57<=X<=1.84)		0.0253
Z Value	1.84				
P(X>1.84)	0.0329		**Find X and Z Given Cum. Pctage.**		
			Cumulative Percentage		84.13%
Probability for X<-1.57 or X >1.84			Z Value		0.999815
P(X<-1.57 or X >1.84)	0.0911		X Value		0.999815

(a) $P(-1.57 < Z < 1.84) = 0.9671 - 0.0582 = 0.9089$
(b) $P(Z < -1.57) + P(Z > 1.84) = 0.0582 + 0.0329 = 0.0911$
(c)   If $P(Z > A) = 0.025$, $P(Z < A) = 0.975$. $A = +1.96$.
(d)   If $P(-A < Z < A) = 0.6826$, $P(Z < A) = 0.8413$. So 68.26% of the area is captured between $-A = -1.00$ and $A = +1.00$.

6.4   PHStat output:

Normal Probabilities					
Common Data					
Mean	0				
Standard Deviation	1				
			Probability for a Range		
Probability for X <=			From X Value		-1.96
X Value	-0.21		To X Value		-0.21
Z Value	-0.21		Z Value for -1.96		-1.96
P(X<=-0.21)	0.4168338		Z Value for -0.21		-0.21
			P(X<=-1.96)		0.0250
Probability for X >			P(X<=-0.21)		0.4168
X Value	1.08		P(-1.96<=X<=-0.21)		0.3918
Z Value	1.08				
P(X>1.08)	0.1401		**Find X and Z Given Cum. Pctage.**		
			Cumulative Percentage		84.13%
Probability for X<-0.21 or X >1.08			Z Value		0.999815
P(X<-0.21 or X >1.08)	0.5569		X Value		0.999815

(a) $P(Z > 1.08) = 1 - 0.8599 = 0.1401$

6.4   (b) $P(Z < -0.21) = 0.4168$

cont.   (c) $P(-1.96 < Z < -0.21) = 0.4168 - 0.0250 = 0.3918$

       (d) $P(Z > A) = 0.1587, P(Z < A) = 0.8413.$ $A = +1.00.$

6.6   (a)   Partial PHStat output:

Common Data				
Mean	50			
Standard Deviation	4			
			Probability for a Range	
Probability for X <=			From X Value	42
X Value	42		To X Value	43
Z Value	-2		Z Value for 42	-2
P(X<=42)	0.0227501		Z Value for 43	-1.75
			P(X<=42)	0.0228
Probability for X >			P(X<=43)	0.0401
X Value	43		P(42<=X<=43)	0.0173
Z Value	-1.75			
P(X>43)	0.9599		Find X and Z Given Cum. Pctage.	
			Cumulative Percentage	5.00%
Probability for X<42 or X >43			Z Value	-1.644854
P(X<42 or X >43)	0.9827		X Value	43.42059

$P(X > 43) = P(Z > -1.75) = 1 - 0.0401 = 0.9599$

(b) $P(X < 42) = P(Z < -2.00) = 0.0228$

(c) $P(X < A) = 0.05,$

$$Z = -1.645 = \frac{A - 50}{4} \qquad A = 50 - 1.645(4) = 43.42$$

(d)   Partial PHStat output:

Find X and Z Given Cum. Pctage.	
Cumulative Percentage	80.00%
Z Value	0.841621
X Value	53.36648

$P(X_{lower} < X < X_{upper}) = 0.60$

$P(Z < -0.84) = 0.20$ and $P(Z < 0.84) = 0.80$

$$Z = -0.84 = \frac{X_{lower} - 50}{4} \qquad Z = +0.84 = \frac{X_{upper} - 50}{4}$$

$X_{lower} = 50 - 0.84(4) = 46.64$ and $X_{upper} = 50 + 0.84(4) = 53.36$

6.8   Partial PHStat output:

Common Data	
Mean	50
Standard Deviation	12

Probability for X <=	
X Value	30
Z Value	-1.666667
P(X<=30)	0.0477904

Probability for X >	
X Value	60
Z Value	0.8333333
P(X>60)	0.2023

Probability for X<30 or X >60	
P(X<30 or X >60)	0.2501

Probability for a Range	
From X Value	34
To X Value	50
Z Value for 34	-1.333333
Z Value for 50	0
P(X<=34)	0.0912
P(X<=50)	0.5000
P(34<=X<=50)	0.4088

Find X and Z Given Cum. Pctage.	
Cumulative Percentage	20.00%
Z Value	-0.841621
X Value	39.90055

(a) $P(34 < X < 50) = P(-1.33 < Z < 0) = 0.4082$

(b) $P(X < 30) + P(X > 60) = P(Z < -1.67) + P(Z > 0.83)$
       $= 0.0475 + (1.0 - 0.7967) = 0.2508$

(c) $P(X > A) = 0.80$ $P(Z < -0.84) \cong 0.20$ $Z = -0.84 = \dfrac{A - 50}{12}$

       $A = 50 - 0.84(12) = 39.92$ thousand miles or 39,920 miles

(d)   Partial PHStat output:

Common Data	
Mean	50
Standard Deviation	10

Probability for X <=	
X Value	30
Z Value	-2
P(X<=30)	0.0227501

Probability for X >	
X Value	60
Z Value	1
P(X>60)	0.1587

Probability for X<30 or X >60	
P(X<30 or X >60)	0.1814

Probability for a Range	
From X Value	34
To X Value	50
Z Value for 34	-1.6
Z Value for 50	0
P(X<=34)	0.0548
P(X<=50)	0.5000
P(34<=X<=50)	0.4452

Find X and Z Given Cum. Pctage.	
Cumulative Percentage	20.00%
Z Value	-0.841621
X Value	41.58379

The smaller standard deviation makes the Z-values larger.

(a) $P(34 < X < 50) = P(-1.60 < Z < 0) = 0.4452$

(b) $P(X < 30) + P(X > 60) = P(Z < -2.00) + P(Z > 1.00)$
       $= 0.0228 + (1.0 - 0.8413) = 0.1815$

(c) $A = 50 - 0.84(10) = 41.6$ thousand miles or 41,600 miles

6.10   PHStat output:

Common Data	
Mean	73
Standard Deviation	8

Probability for X <=	
X Value	91
Z Value	2.25
P(X<=91)	0.9877755

Probability for X >	
X Value	81
Z Value	1
P(X>81)	0.1587

Probability for X<91 or X >81	
P(X<91 or X >81)	1.1464

Probability for a Range	
From X Value	65
To X Value	89
Z Value for 65	-1
Z Value for 89	2
P(X<=65)	0.1587
P(X<=89)	0.9772
P(65<=X<=89)	0.8186

Find X and Z Given Cum. Pctage.	
Cumulative Percentage	95.00%
Z Value	1.644854
X Value	86.15883

(a) $P(X < 91) = P(Z < 2.25) = 0.9878$

(b) $P(65 < X < 89) = P(-1.00 < Z < 2.00) = 0.9772 - 0.1587 = 0.8185$

(c) $P(X > A) = 0.05$ $P(Z < 1.645) = 0.9500$

$$Z = 1.645 = \frac{A - 73}{8} \qquad A = 73 + 1.645(8) = 86.16\%$$

(d)   Option 1: $P(X > A) = 0.10$ $P(Z < 1.28) \cong 0.9000$

$$Z = \frac{81 - 73}{8} = 1.00$$

Since your score of 81% on this exam represents a Z-score of 1.00, which is below the minimum Z-score of 1.28, you will not earn an "A" grade on the exam under this grading option.

Option 2: $Z = \dfrac{68 - 62}{3} = 2.00$

Since your score of 68% on this exam represents a Z-score of 2.00, which is well above the minimum Z-score of 1.28, you will earn an "A" grade on the exam under this grading option. You should prefer Option 2.

6.12   (a)   Partial PHStat output:

Probability for X >	
X Value	10
Z Value	-1.608
P(X>10)	0.9461

$P(X > 10) = P(Z > -1.608) = 0.9461$

6.12   (b)   Partial PHStat output:
cont.

Probability for a Range	
From X Value	3
To X Value	5
Z Value for 3	-3.008
Z Value for 5	-2.608
P(X<=3)	0.0013
P(X<=5)	0.0046
P(3<=X<=5)	0.0032

$P(3 < X < 5) = P(-3.008 < Z < -2.608) = 0.0032$

(c)   Partial PHStat output:

Probability for X <=	
X Value	5
Z Value	-2.608
P(X<=5)	0.0045536

$P(X < 5) = P(Z < -2.608) = 0.0046$

(d)

Find X and Z Given Cum. Pctage.	
Cumulative Percentage	99.00%
Z Value	2.326348
X Value	29.67174

$P(X < A) = 0.99$ $Z = 2.3263$ $A = 29.6717$

6.14   With 39 values, the smallest of the standard normal quantile values covers an area under the normal curve of 0.025. The corresponding Z value is -1.96. The middle (20th) value has a cumulative area of 0.50 and a corresponding Z value of 0.0. The largest of the standard normal quantile values covers an area under the normal curve of 0.975, and its corresponding Z value is +1.96.

6.16   (a)   Excel output:

MPG	
Mean	21.12
Median	22
Mode	22
Standard Deviation	2.2971
Sample Variance	5.276667
Range	10
Minimum	16
Maximum	26
Sum	528
Count	25
First Quartile	19.5
Third Quartile	22
Interquartile Range	2.5
CV	10.88%
6*std dev	13.7826
1.33 * std dev	3.055142

mean = 21.12, median = 22, range = 10, standard deviation = 2.2971,
$(6\times \text{std dev}) = 13.7826$, interquartile range $= Q_3 - Q_1 = 2.5$,

$(1.33\times \text{std dev}) = 3.0551$. The mean is slightly less than the median. The range is
much less than 6S, and the interquartile range is less than 1.33S.

(b)

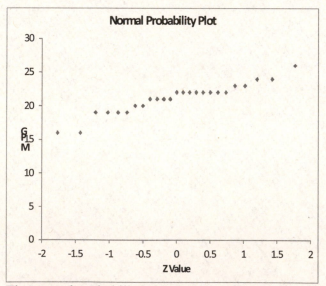

The normal probability plot does not appear to be skewed. The data may be
symmetrical but not normally distributed.

6.18   Excel output:

Property Taxes Per Capita ($)	
Mean	1040.863
Median	981
Mode	963
Standard Deviation	428.5385
Sample Variance	183645.2
Range	1732
Minimum	367
First Quartile	713
Median	981
Third Quartile	1306
Maximum	2099
Interquartile Range	593
6 * std. dev.	2571.231
1.33 std. dev.	569.9562

(a)   mean = 1040.863, median = 981, range = 1732,

$(6 \times$ std dev$) = 2571.2310$, interquartile range $= 593$, $(1.33 \times$ std dev$)$ 569.9562

There are 62.75% , 78.43% and 94.12% of the observations that fall within 1, 1.28 and 2 standard deviations of the mean, respectively, as compared to the approximate theoretical 66.67%, 80% and 95%.

Since the mean is slightly larger than the median, the interquartile range is slightly larger than 1.33 times the standard deviation, the range is much smaller than 6 times the standard deviation, the data appear to deviate slightly from the normal distribution.

(b)

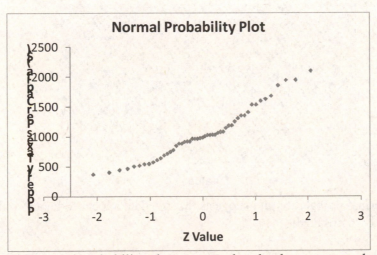

The normal probability plot suggests that the data appear to be slightly right-skewed.

6.20   Excel output:

Error	
Mean	-0.00023
Median	0
Mode	0
Standard Deviation	0.001696
Sample Variance	2.88E-06
Range	0.008
Minimum	-0.003
Maximum	0.005
First Quartile	-0.0015
Third Quartile	0.001
1.33 Std Dev	0.002255
Interquartile Range	0.0025
6 Std Dev	0.010175

(a) $\bar{X}$ = -0.00023   median = 0

Interquartile range = 0.0025 S = 0.0017   Range = 0.008

$(1.33 \times \text{ std dev}) = 0.0023$ $((6 \times \text{ std dev})) = 0.0102$

Between $\bar{X} \pm 1S_X = 61\%$ Between $\bar{X} \pm 1.28S_X = 72\%$

Between $\bar{X} \pm 2S_X = 98\%$

Since the interquartile range is quite close to $(1.33 \times \text{ std dev})$ and the range is also

quite close to $(6 \times \text{ std dev})$, the data appear to be approximately normally

distributed.

(b)

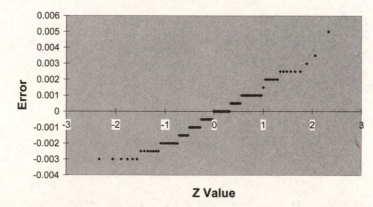

Normal Probability Plot

The normal probability plot suggests that the data appear to be approximately
normally distributed.

6.22   (a)   Five-number summary: 82   127   148.5   168   213   mean = 147.06
range = 131   interquartile range = 41   standard deviation = 31.69
The mean is very close to the median. The five-number summary suggests that the distribution is quite symmetrical around the median. The interquartile range is very close to 1.33 times the standard deviation. The range is about $50 below 6 times the standard deviation. In general, the distribution of the data appears to closely resemble a normal distribution.
Note: The quartiles are obtained using PHStat without any interpolation.

(b)

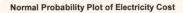

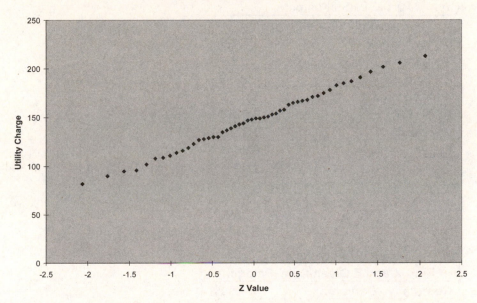

The normal probability plot confirms that the data appear to be approximately normally distributed.

6.24   Using Table E.2, first find the cumulative area up to the larger value, and then subtract the cumulative area up to the smaller value.

6.26   The normal distribution is bell-shaped; its measures of central tendency are all equal; its middle 50% is within 1.33 standard deviations of its mean; and 99.7% of its values are contained within three standard deviations of its mean.

6.28   If the distribution is normal, the plot of the Z values on the horizontal axis and the original values on the vertical axis will be a straight line.

6.30   (a)   Partial PHStat output:

Probability for a Range	
From X Value	1.9
To X Value	2
Z Value for 1.9	-2
Z Value for 2	0
P(X<=1.9)	0.0228
P(X<=2)	0.5000
P(1.9<=X<=2)	0.4772

$P(1.90 < X < 2.00) = P(-2.00 < Z < 0) = 0.4772$

(b)   Partial PHStat output:

Probability for a Range	
From X Value	1.9
To X Value	2.1
Z Value for 1.9	-2
Z Value for 2.1	2
P(X<=1.9)	0.0228
P(X<=2.1)	0.9772
P(1.9<=X<=2.1)	0.9545

$P(1.90 < X < 2.10) = P(-2.00 < Z < 2.00) = 0.9772 - 0.0228 = 0.9544$

(c)   Partial PHStat output:

Probability for X<1.9 or X >2.1	
P(X<1.9 or X >2.1)	0.0455

$P(X < 1.90) + P(X > 2.10) = 1 - P(1.90 < X < 2.10) = 0.0456$

(d)   Partial PHStat output:

Find X and Z Given Cum. Pctage.	
Cumulative Percentage	1.00%
Z Value	-2.326348
X Value	1.883683

$P(X > A) = P(Z > -2.33) = 0.99$ $A = 2.00 - 2.33(0.05) = 1.8835$

(e)   Partial PHStat output:

Find X and Z Given Cum. Pctage.	
Cumulative Percentage	99.50%
Z Value	2.575829
X Value	2.128791

$P(A < X < B) = P(-2.58 < Z < 2.58) = 0.99$

$A = 2.00 - 2.58(0.05) = 1.8710$ $B = 2.00 + 2.58(0.05) = 2.1290$

6.32   (a)   Partial PHStat output:

Probability for a Range	
From X Value	4.7
To X Value	5
Z Value for 4.7	0
Z Value for 5	0.75
P(X<=4.7)	0.5000
P(X<=5)	0.7734
P(4.7<=X<=5)	0.2734

$$P(4.70 < X < 5.00) = P(0 < Z < 0.75) = 0.2734$$

(b)

Probability for a Range	
From X Value	5
To X Value	5.5
Z Value for 5	0.75
Z Value for 5.5	2
P(X<=5)	0.7734
P(X<=5.5)	0.9772
P(5<=X<=5.5)	0.2039

$$P(5.00 < X < 5.50) = P(0.75 < Z < 2.00) = 0.9772 - 0.7734 = 0.2038$$

(c)

Find X and Z Given Cum. Pctage.	
Cumulative Percentage	23.00%
Z Value	-0.7388
X Value	4.40446

$$P(X > A) = P(Z > -0.74) = 0.77 \qquad A = 4.70 - 0.74(0.40) = 4.404 \text{ ounces}$$

(d)

Find X and Z Given Cum. Pctage.	
Cumulative Percentage	90.00%
Z Value	1.28155
X Value	5.21262

$$P(A < X < B) = P(-1.28 < Z < 1.28) = 0.80$$
$$A = 4.70 - 1.28(0.40) = 4.188 \text{ ounces}$$
$$B = 4.70 + 1.28(0.40) = 5.212 \text{ ounces}$$

6.34   (a)   Waiting time will more closely resemble an exponential distribution.
        (b)   Seating time will more closely resemble a normal distribution.
        (c)

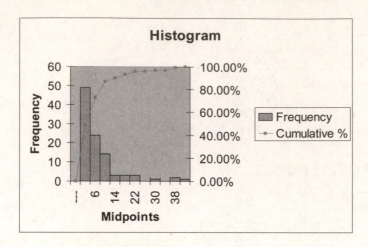

(c)

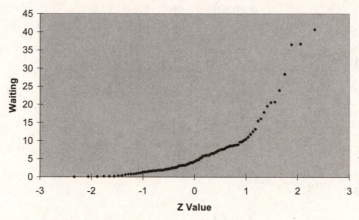

Both the histogram and normal probability plot suggest that waiting time more closely resembles an exponential distribution.

(d)

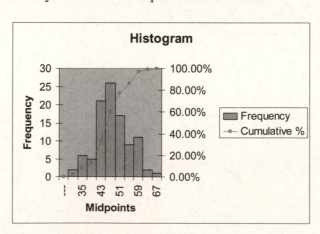

6.34
cont.

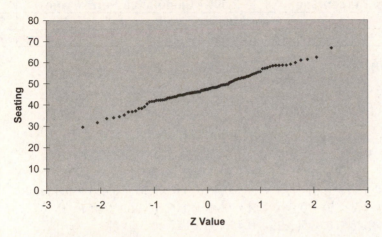

Normal Probability Plot

Both the histogram and normal probability plot suggest that seating time more closely resembles a normal distribution.

6.36   (a)   Partial PHStat output:

Probability for X <=	
X Value	2
Z Value	4
P(X<=2)	0.9999683

$P(X < 2) = P(Z < 4) = 0.99997$

(b)   Partial PHStat output:

Probability for a Range	
From X Value	1.5
To X Value	2.5
Z Value for 1.5	1.5
Z Value for 2.5	6.5
P(X<=1.5)	0.9332
P(X<=2.5)	1.0000
P(1.5<=X<=2.5)	0.0668

$P(1.5 < X < 2.5) = P(1.5 < Z < 6.5) = 0.0668$

(c)   Partial PHStat output:

Probability for X >	
X Value	1.8
Z Value	3
P(X>1.8)	0.0013

$P(X > 1.8) = P(Z > 3) = 0.0013$

(d)   Partial PHStat output:

Find X and Z Given Cum. Pctage.	
Cumulative Percentage	1.00%
Z Value	-2.326348
X Value	0.73473

$P(A < X) = 0.01$ $\dfrac{A - 1.2}{0.2} = -2.3263$ $A = 0.7347$

6.36   (e)   Partial PHStat output:
cont.

Find X and Z Given Cum. Pctage.		Find X and Z Given Cum. Pctage.	
Cumulative Percentage	2.50%	Cumulative Percentage	97.50%
Z Value	-1.959964	Z Value	1.959964
X Value	0.808007	X Value	1.591993

$P(A < X < B) = 0.95$ $\dfrac{A - 1.2}{0.2} = -1.960$ $A = 0.8080$

$\dfrac{B - 1.2}{0.2} = 1.96$ $B = 1.5920$

(f)   (a) $P(X < 2) = (1.95 - 0.45)/(1.95 - 0.45) = 1.0$

(b) $P(1.5 < X < 2.5) = (1.95 - 1.5)/(1.95 - 0.45) = 0.3020$

(c) $P(X > 1.8) = (1.95 - 1.8)/(1.95 - 0.45) = 0.1$

(d) $P(A < X) = 0.01$ $A = 0.45 + 0.01(1.95 - 0.45) = 0.465$

(e) $P(A < X < B) = 0.95$ $A = 0.45 + 0.025(1.95 - 0.45) = 0.4875$

$B = 0.45 + 0.975(1.95 - 0.45) = 1.9125$

6.40   Excel output:

	Age	GPA	Salary	Social Networking	Satisfaction	Spending	Text Messages	Wealth
Mean	21.12903226	3.126290323	48.5483871	1.516129032	3.741935484	482.016129	246.2096774	7.151209677
Median	21	3.135	50	1	4	500	200	1
Mode	21	3.4	40	1	4	500	300	1
Standard Deviation	1.431311115	0.378353785	12.08091222	0.844304651	1.213793456	221.953805	214.4659503	19.60850248
Sample Variance	2.048651507	0.143151586	145.94844	0.712850344	1.473294553	49263.49154	45995.64384	384.4933694
Range	8	1.56	55	4	5	1300	900	99.9
Minimum	18	2.34	25	0	1	100	0	0.1
Maximum	26	3.9	80	4	6	1400	900	100
First Quartile	20	2.9	40	1	3	300	100	0.75
Third Quartile	22	3.4	55	2	4	600	300	5
Interquartile Range	2	0.5	15	1	1	300	200	4.25
6 * std dev	8.587866688	2.270122709	72.4854733	5.065827906	7.282760734	1331.72283	1286.795702	117.6510149
1.33 * std dev	1.903643783	0.503210534	16.06761325	1.122925186	1.614345296	295.1985606	285.2397139	26.0793083

Age:

(a)   The mean is approximately equal to the median; the range is slightly smaller than 6 times the standard deviation and the interquartile range is approximately equal to 1.33 times the standard deviation.

(b)

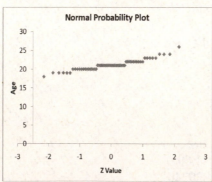

The normal probability plot suggests that the data appear to be normally distributed.

6.40   **GPA:**
cont.   (a)   The mean is approximately equal to the median; the range is smaller than 6 times the standard deviation and the interquartile range is approximately equal to 1.33 times the standard deviation.

(b)

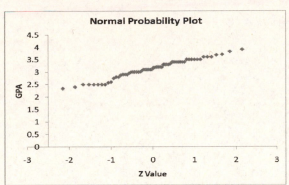

The normal probability plot suggests that the data are normally distributed.

Expected Salary:
(a)   The mean is slightly smaller than the median; the range is smaller than 6 times the standard deviation and the interquartile range is slightly smaller than 1.33 times the standard deviation.

(b)

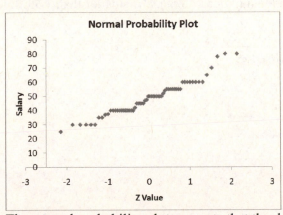

The normal probability plot suggests that the data appear to be normally distributed.

6.40   **Social Networking:**
cont.   (a)   The mean is larger than the median; the range is slightly smaller than 6 times the standard deviation and the interquartile range is approximately equal to 1.33 times the standard deviation.

(b)

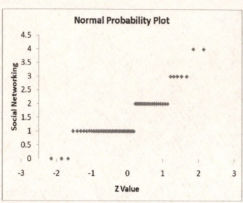

The normal probability plot suggests that the data do not appear to be normally distributed.

Satisfaction:

(a)   The mean is slightly smaller than the median; the range is smaller than 6 times the standard deviation and the interquartile range is smaller than 1.33 times the standard deviation.

(b)

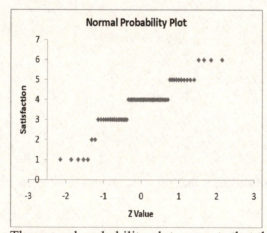

The normal probability plot suggests that the data do not appear to be normally distributed.

6.40   **Spending:**
cont.   (a)   The mean is slightly smaller than the median; the range is approximately equal to 6 times the standard deviation and the interquartile range is approximately equal 1.33 times the standard deviation.
         (b)

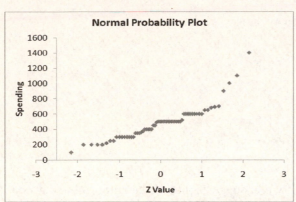

The normal probability plot suggests that the data do not appear to be normally distributed.

Text Messages:
(a)   The mean is larger than the median; the range is smaller than 6 times the standard deviation and the interquartile range is smaller than 1.33 times the standard deviation.
(b)

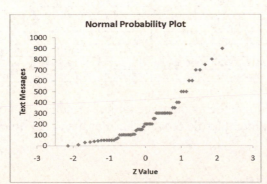

The normal probability plot suggests that the data appear to be right-skewed.

6.40   **Wealth:**
cont.   (a)   The mean is larger than the median; the range is smaller than 6 times the standard deviation and the interquartile range is smaller than 1.33 times the standard deviation.

(b)

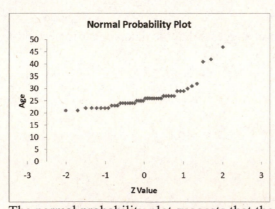

The normal probability plot suggests that the data are right-skewed.

6.42   Excel output:

	Age	G- GPA	U-GPA	FT Jobs	Expected Salary	Spending	Advisory Rating	Text Messages	Wealth
Mean	26.45454545	3.329545455	3.368181818	1.727272727	82.97727273	363.8636364	4.590909091	232.4545455	10.64090909
Median	25.5	3	3.4	2	70	300	5	100	2.75
Mode	26	3	3.6	2	70	300	4	100	1
Standard Deviation	5.341607394	0.404382702	0.319718428	1.019886824	44.45025369	359.587722	0.972127416	296.9000658	22.35365137
Sample Variance	28.53276956	0.16352537	0.102219873	1.040169133	1975.825053	129303.3298	0.945031712	88149.64905	499.6857294
Range	26	1	1.1	4	260	2130	5	1250	99.9
Minimum	21	3	2.8	0	40	70	2	0	0.1
Maximum	47	4	3.9	4	300	2200	7	1250	100
First Quartile	23	3	3	1	60	200	4	20	1
Third Quartile	27	3.7	3.7	2	100	400	5	400	10
Interquartile Range	4	0.7	0.7	1	40	200	1	380	9
6 * std dev	32.04964437	2.426296214	1.918310568	6.119320942	266.7015221	2157.526332	5.832764495	1781.400395	134.1219082
1.33 * std dev	7.104337835	0.537828994	0.425225509	1.356449476	59.1188374	478.2516703	1.292929463	394.8770875	29.73035632

Age:
(a)   The mean is slightly larger than the median; the range is smaller than 6 times the standard deviation and the interquartile range is smaller than 1.33 times the standard deviation.

(b)

The normal probability plot suggests that the data are right-skewed.

6.42   **Graduate-GPA:**
cont.   (a)   The mean is slightly larger than the median; the range is smaller than 6 times the standard deviation and the interquartile range is larger than 1.33 times the standard deviation.

(b)

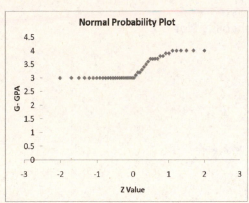

The normal probability plot suggests that the data do not appear to be normally distributed.

Undergrad GPA:

(a)   The mean is approximately equal to the median; the range is smaller than 6 times the standard deviation and the interquartile range is larger than 1.33 times the standard deviation.

(b)

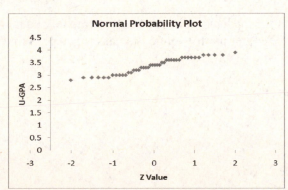

The normal probability plot suggests that the data are roughly normally distributed.

6.42   **Full-time Job:**
cont.   (a)   The mean is slightly smaller than the median; the range is smaller than 6 times the standard deviation and the interquartile range is smaller than 1.33 times the standard deviation.

(b)

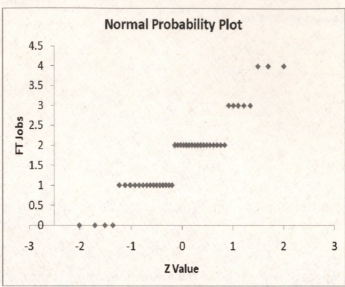

The normal probability plot suggests that the data are not normally distributed.

Expected Salary:

(a)   The mean is larger than the median; the range is approximately equal to 6 times the standard deviation and the interquartile range is smaller than 1.33 times the standard deviation.

(b)

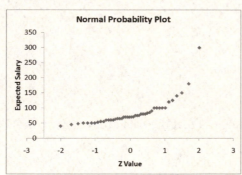

The normal probability plot suggests that the data are right-skewed.

6.42   **Spending:**
cont.   (a)   The mean is slightly larger than the median; the range is slightly smaller than 6 times the standard deviation and the interquartile range is much smaller than 1.33 times the standard deviation.

(b)

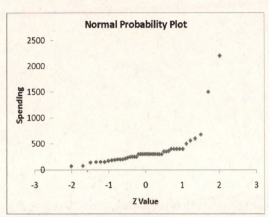

The normal probability plot suggests that the data are right-skewed.

Advisory Rating:

(a)   The mean is slightly smaller than the median; the range is slightly smaller than 6 times the standard deviation and the interquartile range is slightly smaller than 1.33 times the standard deviation.

(b)

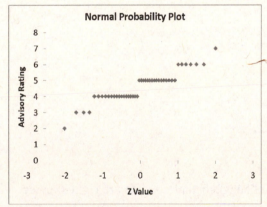

The normal probability plot suggests that the data do not deviate much from the normal distribution.

6.42   **Text Message:**

cont.   (a)   The mean is much larger than the median; the range is smaller than 6 times the standard deviation and the interquartile range is slightly smaller than 1.33 times the standard deviation.

(b)

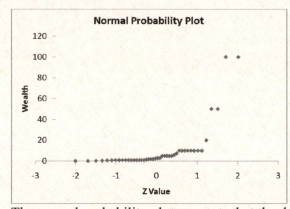

The normal probability plot suggests that the data are right-skewed.

Wealth:

(a)   The mean is much larger than the median; the range is smaller than 6 times the standard deviation and the interquartile range is much smaller than 1.33 times the standard deviation.

(b)

The normal probability plot suggests that the data are right-skewed.

CHAPTER 7

OBJECTIVES

In this chapter, you learn:
- About different sampling methods
- The concept of the sampling distribution
- To compute probabilities related to the sample mean and the sample proportion
- The importance of the Central Limit Theorem

OVERVIEW AND KEY CONCEPTS

Some Basic Concepts on Sampling Distribution
- **Why do we study sampling distribution?**
    - Sample statistics are used to estimate population parameters, but different samples yield different estimates. The solution is to develop a theoretical basis based on sampling distribution.
- **What is a sampling distribution?**
    - A sampling distribution is a theoretical probability distribution of a sample statistic. A sample statistic (e.g., sample mean, sample proportion) is a random variable because a different sample will yield a different value for the statistic, and, hence, a different estimate for the parameter of interest. The sampling distribution is the probability distribution of the sample statistic as a result of taking all possible samples of the same size from the population.

Sampling Distribution of the Sample Mean
- **Population mean of the sample mean**
    - $\mu_{\bar{X}} = \mu$
    - This is the unbiased property of the sample mean.
- **Standard error (population standard deviation) of the sample mean**
    - $\sigma_{\bar{X}} = \dfrac{\sigma}{\sqrt{n}}$
    - Standard error of the sample mean is smaller than the standard deviation of the population.
    - The larger the sample size, the smaller the standard error.
- **The central limit theorem:** As the sample size (i.e., the number of the observations in a sample) gets *large enough*, the sampling distribution of the mean can be approximated by the normal distribution regardless of the distribution of the individual values in the population.
- **The distribution of the sample mean**
    - If the population is normally distributed, the sampling distribution of the mean is normally distributed regardless of the sample size.
    - If the population distribution is fairly symmetrical, the sampling distribution of the mean is approximately normal if sample size is at least 15.
    - For most population distributions, regardless of the shape, the sampling distribution of the mean is approximately normally distributed if the sample size is at least 30.

Finding Range Probability of the Sample Mean

1. Standardize the value of the sample mean using $Z = \dfrac{\overline{X} - \mu_{\overline{X}}}{\sigma_{\overline{X}}} = \dfrac{\overline{X} - \mu}{\dfrac{\sigma}{\sqrt{n}}}$.

2. Look up the cumulative probabilities from the cumulative standardized normal distribution table.

E.g., for $\mu = 8$, $\sigma = 2$, $n = 25$ and X normally distributed. $P(7.8 < \overline{X} < 8.2) = ?$

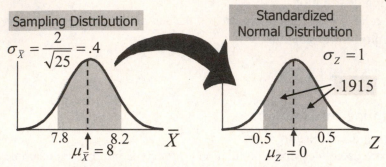

$$P(7.8 < \overline{X} < 8.2) = P\left(\frac{7.8 - 8}{2/\sqrt{25}} < \frac{\overline{X} - \mu_{\overline{X}}}{\sigma_{\overline{X}}} < \frac{8.2 - 8}{2/\sqrt{25}} \right) = P(-.5 < Z < .5) = .3830$$

Sampling Distribution of the Sample Proportion

- **Sample proportion:** $p = \dfrac{X}{n} = \dfrac{\text{number of items having the characteristic of interest}}{\text{sample size}}$

- **Population mean of the sample proportion**
    - $\mu_p = \pi$ where π is the population proportion.

- **Standard error of the sample proportion**
    - $\sigma_p = \sqrt{\dfrac{\pi(1-\pi)}{n}}$

- **The distribution of the sample proportion**
    - When $n\pi$ and $n(1-\pi)$ are each at least 5, the sampling distribution of the sample proportion can be approximated by the normal distribution with mean μ_p and standard deviation σ_p.

Finding Range Probability of the Sample Proportion

1. Standardize the value of the sample proportion using $Z = \dfrac{p - \mu_p}{\sigma_p} = \dfrac{p - \pi}{\sqrt{\dfrac{\pi(1-\pi)}{n}}}$.

2. Look up the cumulative probabilities from the cumulative standardized normal distribution table.

E.g., for $n = 200$, $\pi = 0.4$. $P(p < 0.43) = ?$

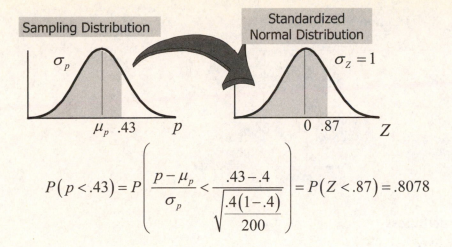

$$P(p<.43)=P\left(\frac{p-\mu_p}{\sigma_p}<\frac{.43-.4}{\sqrt{\frac{.4(1-.4)}{200}}}\right)=P(Z<.87)=.8078$$

Reasons for Drawing Sample
- Less time consuming than a census
- Less costly to administer than a census
- Less cumbersome and more practical to administer than a census of the targeted population

The Different Methods of Sample Selection
- **A nonprobability sample:** Items or individuals are chosen without regard to their probability of occurrence.
- **A probability sample:** The subjects of the sample are chosen on the basis of known probability.
- **A simple random sample:** Every individual or item from the frame has an equal chance of being selected. Selection may be with replacement or without replacement.
- **A systematic sample:** Decide on a sample size, n; divide frame of N individuals into groups of k individuals, $k = N/n$; randomly select one individual from the first group; select every k^{th} individual thereafter.
- **A stratified sample:** The population is divided into two or more groups according to some common characteristic, e.g., whether an employee is full-time or part-time; simple random sample is selected from each group; the two or more samples are combined into one.
- **A cluster sample:** The population is divided into several "clusters", e.g., counties or election districts, in which each is representative of the population; a simple random sample is selected from each cluster; the samples are combined into one.

Evaluating Survey Worthiness

- What is the purpose of the survey?
- Is the survey based on a probability sample?
- **Coverage error:** Certain groups of subjects are excluded from the frame and have no chance of being selected in the sample.
- **Nonresponse error:** Failure to collect data on all subjects in the sample.
- **Measurement error:** Inaccuracies in the recorded responses that occur because of a weakness in question wording, an interviewer's effect on the respondent, or the effort made by the respondent.
- **Sampling error:** The chance differences from sample to sample based on the probability of particular individuals or items being selected in the particular samples. Sampling error always exists in a survey.

SOLUTIONS TO END OF SECTION
AND CHAPTER REVIEW EVEN PROBLEMS

7.2   Sample without replacement: Read from left to right in 3-digit sequences and continue
       unfinished sequences from end of row to beginning of next row.
       Row 05: 338 505 855 551 438 855 077 186 579 488 767 833 170
       Rows 05-06: 897
       Row 06: 340 033 648 847 204 334 639 193 639 411 095 924
       Rows 06-07: 707
       Row 07: 054 329 776 100 871 007 255 980 646 886 823 920 461
       Row 08: 893 829 380 900 796 959 453 410 181 277 660 908 887
       Rows 08-09: 237
       Row 09: 818 721 426 714 050 785 223 801 670 353 362 449
       Rows 09-10: 406
       Note: All sequences above 902 and duplicates are discarded.

7.4   A simple random sample would be less practical for personal interviews because of travel
       costs (unless interviewees are paid to attend a central interviewing location).

7.6   Here all members of the population are equally likely to be selected and the sample selection
       mechanism is based on chance. But not every sample of size 2 has the same chance of being
       selected. For example the sample "B and C" is impossible.

7.8   (a)   Row 16: 2323 6737 5131 8888 1718 0654 6832 4647 6510 4877
              Row 17: 4579 4269 2615 1308 2455 7830 5550 5852 5514 7182
              Row 18: 0989 3205 0514 2256 8514 4642 7567 8896 2977 8822
              Row 19: 5438 2745 9891 4991 4523 6847 9276 8646 1628 3554
              Row 20: 9475 0899 2337 0892 0048 8033 6945 9826 9403 6858
              Row 21: 7029 7341 3553 1403 3340 4205 0823 4144 1048 2949
              Row 22: 8515 7479 5432 9792 6575 5760 0408 8112 2507 3742
              Row 23: 1110 0023 4012 8607 4697 9664 4894 3928 7072 5815
              Row 24: 3687 1507 7530 5925 7143 1738 1688 5625 8533 5041
              Row 25: 2391 3483 5763 3081 6090 5169 0546
              Note: All sequences above 5000 are discarded. There were no repeating sequences.

       (b)   089   189   289   389   489   589   689   789   889   989
              1089 1189 1289 1389 1489 1589 1689 1789 1889 1989
              2089 2189 2289 2389 2489 2589 2689 2789 2889 2989
              3089 3189 3289 3389 3489 3589 3689 3789 3889 3989
              4089 4189 4289 4389 4489 4589 4689 4789 4889 4989

       (c)   With the single exception of invoice #0989, the invoices selected in the simple
              random sample are not the same as those selected in the systematic sample. It would
              be highly unlikely that a random process would select the same units as a systematic
              process.

7.10   Before accepting the results of a survey of college students, you might want to know, for
        example:
        Who funded the survey? Why was it conducted?
        What was the population from which the sample was selected?
        What sampling design was used?
        What mode of response was used: a personal interview, a telephone interview, or a mail
            survey? Were interviewers trained? Were survey questions field-tested?
        What questions were asked? Were they clear, accurate, unbiased, valid?
        What operational definition of "vast majority" was used?
        What was the response rate?
        What was the sample size?

7.12   (a)   The four types of survey errors are: (a) coverage error, (b) nonresponse error, (c)
                sampling error and (d) measurement error.

        (b)   When people who answer the survey tell you what they think you want to hear,
                rather than what they really believe, it introduces the halo effect, which is a source of
                measurement error. Also, every survey will have sampling error which reflects the
                chance differences from sample to sample based on the probability of particular
                individuals being selected in the particular sample.

7.14   Before accepting the results of the survey, you might want to know, for example:
        Who funded the study? Why was it conducted?
        What was the population from which the sample was selected?
        What sampling design was used?
        What mode of response was used: a personal interview, a telephone interview, or a mail
            survey? Were interviewers trained? Were survey questions field-tested?
        What other questions were asked? Were they clear, accurate, unbiased, and valid?
        What was the response rate?
        What was the margin of error?
        What was the sample size?
        What was the frame being used?

7.16   PHStat output:

Common Data	
Mean	50
Standard Deviation	0.5

Probability for X <=	
X Value	47
Z Value	-6
P(X<=47)	9.866E-10

Probability for X >	
X Value	51.5
Z Value	3
P(X>51.5)	0.0013

Probability for X<47 or X >51.5	
P(X<47 or X >51.5)	0.0013

Probability for a Range	
From X Value	47
To X Value	49.5
Z Value for 47	-6
Z Value for 49.5	-1
P(X<=47)	0.0000
P(X<=49.5)	0.1587
P(47<=X<=49.5)	0.1587

Find X and Z Given Cum. Pctage.	
Cumulative Percentage	65.00%
Z Value	0.38532
X Value	50.19266

Probability for X >	
X Value	51.1
Z Value	2.2
P(X>51.1)	0.0139

(a) $P(\overline{X} < 47) = P(Z < -6.00) =$ virtually zero
(b) $P(47 < \overline{X} < 49.5) = P(-6.00 < Z < -1.00) = 0.1587 - 0.00 = 0.1587$
(c) $P(\overline{X} > 51.1) = P(Z > 2.20) = 1.0 - 0.9861 = 0.0139$
(d) $P(\overline{X} > A) = P(Z > 0.39) = 0.35$ $\overline{X} = 50 + 0.39(0.5) = 50.195$

7.18   (a)   Sampling Distribution of the Mean for $n = 2$ (without replacement)

Sample Number	Outcomes	Sample Means $\overline{X}_i$
1	1, 3	$\overline{X}_1 = 2$
2	1, 6	$\overline{X}_2 = 3.5$
3	1, 7	$\overline{X}_3 = 4$
4	1, 9	$\overline{X}_4 = 5$
5	1, 10	$\overline{X}_5 = 5.5$
6	3, 6	$\overline{X}_6 = 4.5$
7	3, 7	$\overline{X}_7 = 5$
8	3, 9	$\overline{X}_8 = 6$
9	3, 10	$\overline{X}_9 = 6.5$
10	6, 7	$\overline{X}_{10} = 6.5$
11	6, 9	$\overline{X}_{11} = 7.5$
12	6, 10	$\overline{X}_{12} = 8$
13	7, 9	$\overline{X}_{13} = 8$
14	7, 10	$\overline{X}_{14} = 8.5$
15	9, 10	$\overline{X}_{15} = 9.5$

7.18   (a)   Mean of All Possible Sample Means: Mean of All Population Elements:

cont.
$$\mu_{\bar{X}} = \frac{90}{15} = 6 \qquad\qquad \mu = \frac{1+3+6+7+9+10}{6} = 6$$

Both means are equal to 6. This property is called unbiasedness.

(b)   Sampling Distribution of the Mean for $n = 3$ (without replacement)

Sample Number	Outcomes	Sample Means $\bar{X}_i$
1	1, 3, 6	$\bar{X}_1 = 3\ 1/3$
2	1, 3, 7	$\bar{X}_2 = 3\ 2/3$
3	1, 3, 9	$\bar{X}_3 = 4\ 1/3$
4	1, 3, 10	$\bar{X}_4 = 4\ 2/3$
5	1, 6, 7	$\bar{X}_5 = 4\ 2/3$
6	1, 6, 9	$\bar{X}_6 = 5\ 1/3$
7	1, 6, 10	$\bar{X}_7 = 5\ 2/3$
8	3, 6, 7	$\bar{X}_8 = 5\ 1/3$
9	3, 6, 9	$\bar{X}_9 = 6$
10	3, 6, 10	$\bar{X}_{10} = 6\ 1/3$
11	6, 7, 9	$\bar{X}_{11} = 7\ 1/3$
12	6, 7, 10	$\bar{X}_{12} = 7\ 2/3$
13	6, 9, 10	$\bar{X}_{13} = 8\ 1/3$
14	7, 9, 10	$\bar{X}_{14} = 8\ 2/3$
15	1, 7, 9	$\bar{X}_{15} = 5\ 2/3$
16	1, 7, 10	$\bar{X}_{16} = 6$
17	1, 9, 10	$\bar{X}_{17} = 6\ 2/3$
18	3, 7, 9	$\bar{X}_{18} = 6\ 1/3$
19	3, 7, 10	$\bar{X}_{19} = 6\ 2/3$
20	3, 9, 10	$\bar{X}_{20} = 7\ 1/3$

$$\mu_{\bar{X}} = \frac{120}{20} = 6 \qquad\qquad \text{This is equal to } \mu, \text{ the population mean.}$$

(c)   The distribution for $n = 3$ has less variability. The larger sample size has resulted in sample means being closer to μ.

(d)   (a)   Sampling Distribution of the Mean for $n = 2$ (with replacement)

7.18
cont.

Sample Number	Outcomes	Sample Means $\bar{X}_i$
1	1, 1	$\bar{X}_1 = 1$
2	1, 3	$\bar{X}_2 = 2$
3	1, 6	$\bar{X}_3 = 3.5$
4	1, 7	$\bar{X}_4 = 4$
5	1, 9	$\bar{X}_5 = 5$
6	1, 10	$\bar{X}_6 = 5.5$
7	3, 1	$\bar{X}_7 = 2$
8	3, 3	$\bar{X}_8 = 3$
9	3, 6	$\bar{X}_9 = 4.5$
10	3, 7	$\bar{X}_{10} = 5$
11	3, 9	$\bar{X}_{11} = 6$
12	3, 10	$\bar{X}_{12} = 6.5$
13	6, 1	$\bar{X}_{13} = 3.5$
14	6, 3	$\bar{X}_{14} = 4.5$
15	6, 6	$\bar{X}_{15} = 6$
16	6, 7	$\bar{X}_{16} = 6.5$
17	6, 9	$\bar{X}_{17} = 7.5$
18	6, 10	$\bar{X}_{18} = 8$
19	7, 1	$\bar{X}_{19} = 4$
20	7, 3	$\bar{X}_{20} = 5$
21	7, 6	$\bar{X}_{21} = 6.5$
22	7, 7	$\bar{X}_{22} = 7$
23	7, 9	$\bar{X}_{23} = 8$
24	7, 10	$\bar{X}_{24} = 8.5$
25	9, 1	$\bar{X}_{25} = 5$
26	9, 3	$\bar{X}_{26} = 6$
27	9, 6	$\bar{X}_{27} = 7.5$
28	9, 7	$\bar{X}_{28} = 8$
29	9, 9	$\bar{X}_{29} = 9$
30	9, 10	$\bar{X}_{30} = 9.5$
31	10, 1	$\bar{X}_{31} = 5.5$
32	10, 3	$\bar{X}_{32} = 6.5$
33	10, 6	$\bar{X}_{33} = 8$
34	10, 7	$\bar{X}_{34} = 8.5$
35	10, 9	$\bar{X}_{35} = 9.5$
36	10, 10	$\bar{X}_{36} = 10$

7.18   (d)   (a)   Mean of All Possible   Mean of All
cont.   Sample Means: Population Elements:

$$\mu_{\bar{X}} = \frac{216}{36} = 6 \qquad\qquad \mu = \frac{1+3+6+7+7+12}{6} = 6$$

Both means are equal to 6. This property is called unbiasedness.

(b)   Repeat the same process for the sampling distribution of the mean for $n = 3$ (with replacement). There will be $6^3 = 216$ different samples.

$\mu_{\bar{X}} = 6$ This is equal to μ, the population mean.

(c)   The distribution for $n = 3$ has less variability. The larger sample size has resulted in more sample means being close to μ.

7.20   (a)   When $n = 2$, the shape of the sampling distribution of $\bar{X}$ should closely resemble the shape of the distribution of the population from which the sample is selected. Because the mean is larger than the median, the distribution of the sales price of new houses is skewed to the right, and so is the sampling distribution of $\bar{X}$ although it will be less skewed than the population.

(b)   If you select samples of $n = 100$, the shape of the sampling distribution of the sample mean will be very close to a normal distribution with a mean of \$270,100 and a standard deviation of $\sigma_{\bar{X}} = \dfrac{\sigma}{\sqrt{n}} = \$9,000$.

(c) $\sigma_{\bar{X}} = \dfrac{\sigma}{\sqrt{n}} = \dfrac{90000}{\sqrt{100}} = 9000$

PHStat output:

Probability for X <=	
X Value	300000
Z Value	3.0666667
P(X<=300000)	0.9989177

$P(\bar{X} < 300,000) = P(Z < 3.0667) = 0.9989$

(d)   PHStat output:

Probability for a Range	
From X Value	275000
To X Value	290000
Z Value for 275000	0.288889
Z Value for 290000	1.955556
P(X<=275000)	0.6137
P(X<=290000)	0.9747
P(275000<=X<=290000)	0.3611

$P(275,000 < \bar{X} < 290,000) = P(0.6137 < Z < 0.9747) = 0.3611$

7.22   PHStat output:

Probability for X >		Find X and Z Given Cum. Pctage.	
X Value	3	Cumulative Percentage	85.00%
Z Value	-1	Z Value	1.036433
P(X>3)	0.8413	X Value	3.203643

(a) $P(\bar{X} > 3) = P(Z > -1.00) = 1 - 0.1587 = 0.8413$

(b) $P(\bar{X} < A) = P(Z < 1.04) = 0.85$ $\bar{X} = 3.10 + 1.04(0.1) = 3.204$

(c) To be able to use the standard normal distribution as an approximation for the area under the curve, we must assume that the population is symmetrically distributed such that the central limit theorem will likely hold for samples of $n = 16$.

(d) PHStat output:

Probability for X >		Find X and Z Given Cum. Pctage.	
X Value	3	Cumulative Percentage	85.00%
Z Value	-2	Z Value	1.036433
P(X>3)	0.9772	X Value	3.151822

$P(\bar{X} < A) = P(Z < 1.04) = 0.85$ $\bar{X} = 3.10 + 1.04(0.05) = 3.152$

7.24 (a) $p = 20/50 = 0.40$ (b) $\sigma_p = \sqrt{\dfrac{(0.45)(0.55)}{50}} = 0.0704$

7.26 (a) $\mu_p = \pi = 0.501$, $\sigma_p = \sqrt{\dfrac{\pi(1-\pi)}{n}} = \sqrt{\dfrac{0.501(1-0.501)}{100}} = 0.05$

Partial PHstat output:

Probability for X >	
X Value	0.55
Z Value	0.98
P(X>0.55)	0.1635

$P(p > 0.55) = P(Z > 0.98) = 1 - 0.8365 = 0.1635$

(b) $\mu_p = \pi = 0.60$, $\sigma_p = \sqrt{\dfrac{\pi(1-\pi)}{n}} = \sqrt{\dfrac{0.6(1-0.6)}{100}} = 0.04899$

Partial PHstat output:

Probability for X >	
X Value	0.55
Z Value	-1.020621
P(X>0.55)	0.8463

$P(p > 0.55) = P(Z > -1.021) = 1 - 0.1539 = 0.8461$

(c) $\mu_p = \pi = 0.49$, $\sigma_p = \sqrt{\dfrac{\pi(1-\pi)}{n}} = \sqrt{\dfrac{0.49(1-0.49)}{100}} = 0.05$

Partial PHstat output:

Probability for X >	
X Value	0.55
Z Value	1.2002401
P(X>0.55)	0.1150

$P(p > 0.55) = P(Z > 1.20) = 1 - 0.8849 = 0.1151$

(d) Increasing the sample size by a factor of 4 decreases the standard error by a factor of 2.

7.26   (d)   (a)   Partial PHstat output:
cont.

Probability for X >	
X Value	0.55
Z Value	1.9600039
P(X>0.55)	0.0250

$P(p > 0.55) = P(Z > 1.96) = 1 - 0.9750 = 0.0250$

(b)   Partial PHstat output:

Probability for X >	
X Value	0.55
Z Value	-2.041241
P(X>0.55)	0.9794

$P(p > 0.55) = P(Z > -2.04) = 1 - 0.0207 = 0.9793$

(c)   Partial PHstat output:

Probability for X >	
X Value	0.55
Z Value	2.4004801
P(X>0.55)	0.0082

$P(p > 0.55) = P(Z > 2.40) = 1 - 0.9918 = 0.0082$

If the sample size is increased to 400, the probably in (a), (b) and (c) is smaller, larger, and smaller, respectively because the standard error of the sampling distribution of the sample proportion becomes smaller and, hence, the sampling distribution is more concentrated around the true population proportion.

7.28   (a) $\mu_p = \pi = 0.46,\ \sigma_p = \sqrt{\dfrac{\pi(1-\pi)}{n}} = \sqrt{\dfrac{0.46(1-0.46)}{100}} = 0.0498$

Partial PHStat output:

Common Data	
Mean	0.46
Standard Deviation	0.0498397
Probability for X <=	
X Value	0.5
Z Value	0.8025724
P(X<=0.5)	0.788889

$P(p < 0.5) = P(Z < 0.8026) = 0.7889$

7.28   (b)   Partial PHStat output:

cont.

Probability for a Range	
From X Value	0.4
To X Value	0.5
Z Value for 0.4	-1.203859
Z Value for 0.5	0.802572
P(X<=0.4)	0.1143
P(X<=0.5)	0.7889
P(0.4<=X<=0.5)	0.6746

$P(0.4 < p < 0.5) = P(-1.2039 < Z < 0.8026) = 0.6746$

(c)   Partial PHStat output:

Probability for X >	
X Value	0.4
Z Value	-1.203859
P(X>0.4)	0.8857

$P(p > 0.4) = P(Z > -1.2039) = 0.8857$

(d) $\mu_p = \pi = 0.46$, $\sigma_p = \sqrt{\dfrac{\pi(1-\pi)}{n}} = \sqrt{\dfrac{0.46(1-0.46)}{400}} = 0.0249$

(a)   Partial PHStat output:

Probability for X <=	
X Value	0.5
Z Value	1.6051447
P(X<=0.5)	0.945769

$P(p < 0.5) = P(Z < 1.6051) = 0.9458$

(b)   Partial PHStat output:

Probability for a Range	
From X Value	0.4
To X Value	0.5
Z Value for 0.4	-2.407717
Z Value for 0.5	1.605145
P(X<=0.4)	0.0080
P(X<=0.5)	0.9458
P(0.4<=X<=0.5)	0.9377

$P(0.4 < p < 0.5) = P(-2.4077 < Z < 1.6051) = 0.9377$

(c)   Partial PHStat output:

Probability for X >	
X Value	0.4
Z Value	-2.407717
P(X>0.4)	0.9920

$P(p > 0.4) = P(Z > -2.4077) = 0.9920$

7.30   (a)   PHStat output:

Probability for a Range	
From X Value	0.3
To X Value	0.4
Z Value for 0.3	-1.767767
Z Value for 0.4	1.178511
P(X<=0.3)	0.0385
P(X<=0.4)	0.8807
P(0.3<=X<=0.4)	0.8422

Since $n = 200$, which is quite large, we use the sample proportion to approximate the population proportion and, hence, $\pi = 0.36$. Also the sampling distribution of the sample proportion will be close to a normal distribution according to the central limit theorem.

$$\mu_p = \pi = 0.36, \ \sigma_p = \sqrt{\frac{\pi(1-\pi)}{n}} = \sqrt{\frac{0.36(1-0.36)}{200}} = 0.0339$$

$P(0.3 < p < 0.4) = P(-1.7678 < Z < 1.1785) = 0.8422$

(b)

Find X and Z Given Cum. Pctage.	
Cumulative Percentage	5.00%
Z Value	-1.644854
X Value	0.304172

Find X and Z Given Cum. Pctage.	
Cumulative Percentage	95.00%
Z Value	1.644854
X Value	0.415828

$P(A < p < B) = P(-1.6449 < Z < 1.6449) = 0.90$

$A = 0.3041$

$B = 0.4158$

The probability is 90% that the sample percentage will be contained within 5.5828% symmetrically around the population percentage.

(c)   PHStat output:

Find X and Z Given Cum. Pctage.	
Cumulative Percentage	2.50%
Z Value	-1.959964
X Value	0.293477

Find X and Z Given Cum. Pctage.	
Cumulative Percentage	97.50%
Z Value	1.959964
X Value	0.426523

$P(A < p < B) = P(-1.96 < Z < 1.96) = 0.95$

$A = 0.2935$

$B = 0.4265$

The probability is 95% that the sample percentage will be contained within 6.6523% symmetrically around the population percentage.

7.32   (a) $\mu_p = \pi = 0.59$, $\sigma_p = \sqrt{\dfrac{\pi(1-\pi)}{n}} = \sqrt{\dfrac{0.59(1-0.59)}{100}} = 0.0492$

Partial PHStat output:

Probability for X <=	
X Value	0.5
Z Value	-1.829888
P(X<=0.5)	0.0336333

$P(p < 0.5) = P(Z < -1.8299) = 0.0336$

(b) $\mu_p = \pi = 0.59$, $\sigma_p = \sqrt{\dfrac{\pi(1-\pi)}{n}} = \sqrt{\dfrac{0.59(1-0.59)}{500}} = 0.0220$

Probability for X <=	
X Value	0.5
Z Value	-4.091755
P(X<=0.5)	2.141E-05

$P(p < 0.5) = P(Z < -4.0918) =$ essentially 0

(c)   Increasing the sample size by a factor of 5 decreases the standard error by a factor of $\sqrt{5}$. The sampling distribution of the proportion becomes more concentrated around the true proportion of 0.59 and, hence, the probability in (b) becomes smaller than that in (a).

7.34   The variation of the sample means becomes smaller as larger sample sizes are taken. This is due to the fact that an extreme observation will have a smaller effect on the mean in a larger sample than in a small sample. Thus, the sample means will tend to be closer to the population mean as the sample size increases.

7.36   The population distribution is the distribution of a particular variable of interest, while the sampling distribution represents the distribution of a statistic.

7.38   A probability sample is one in which the individuals or items are selected based on known probabilities. A nonprobability sample is one in which the individuals or items are selected without regard to their probability of occurrence.

7.40   Sampling with replacement means that once a person or item is selected, it is returned to the frame where it has the same probability of being selected again. Sampling without replacement means that a person or item once selected is not returned to the frame and therefore cannot be selected again.

7.42   In a stratified sample, the N individuals or items in the population are first subdivided into separate subpopulations, or strata, according to some common characteristic. In a simple random sample, each individual item is selected randomly.

7.44 $\mu_{\bar{X}} = 0.753$ $\sigma_{\bar{X}} = \dfrac{\sigma}{\sqrt{n}} = \dfrac{0.004}{5} = 0.0008$

PHStat output:

Common Data	
Mean	0.753
Standard Deviation	0.0008

Probability for X <=	
X Value	0.74
Z Value	-16.25
P(X<=0.74)	1.117E-59

Probability for X >	
X Value	0.76
Z Value	8.75
P(X>0.76)	0.0000

Probability for X<0.74 or X >0.76	
P(X<0.74 or X >0.76)	0.0000

Probability for a Range	
From X Value	0.75
To X Value	0.753
Z Value for 0.75	-3.75
Z Value for 0.753	0
P(X<=0.75)	0.0001
P(X<=0.753)	0.5000
P(0.75<=X<=0.753)	0.4999

Find X and Z Given Cum. Pctage.	
Cumulative Percentage	7.00%
Z Value	-1.475791
X Value	0.751819

Probability for a Range	
From X Value	0.74
To X Value	0.75
Z Value for 0.74	-16.25
Z Value for 0.75	-3.75
P(X<=0.74)	0.0000
P(X<=0.75)	0.0001
P(0.74<=X<=0.75)	0.00009

(a) $P(0.75 < \bar{X} < 0.753) = P(-3.75 < Z < 0) = 0.5 - 0.00009 = 0.4999$

(b) $P(0.74 < \bar{X} < 0.75) = P(-16.25 < Z < -3.75) = 0.00009$

(c) $P(\bar{X} > 0.76) = P(Z > 8.75) = $ virtually zero

(d) $P(\bar{X} < 0.74) = P(Z < -16.25) = $ virtually zero

(e) $P(\bar{X} < A) = P(Z < -1.48) = 0.07$ $X = 0.753 - 1.48(0.0008) = 0.7518$

7.46 $\mu_{\bar{X}} = 4.7$ $\sigma_{\bar{X}} = \dfrac{\sigma_X}{\sqrt{n}} = \dfrac{0.40}{5} = 0.08$

PHstat output:

Common Data	
Mean	4.7
Standard Deviation	0.08

Probability for X >	
X Value	4.6
Z Value	-1.25
P(X>4.6)	0.8944

Find X and Z Given Cum. Pctage.	
Cumulative Percentage	23.00%
Z Value	-0.738847
X Value	4.640892

Find X and Z Given Cum. Pctage.	
Cumulative Percentage	15.00%
Z Value	-1.036433
X Value	4.6170853

Find X and Z Given Cum. Pctage.	
Cumulative Percentage	85.00%
Z Value	1.036433
X Value	4.782915

(a) $P(4.60 < \bar{X}) = P(-1.25 < Z) = 1 - 0.1056 = 0.8944$

(b) $P(A < \bar{X} < B) = P(-1.04 < Z < 1.04) = 0.70$

$A = 4.70 - 1.04(0.08) = 4.6168$ ounces $X = 4.70 + 1.04(0.08) = 4.7832$ ounces

(c) $P(\bar{X} > A) = P(Z > -0.74) = 0.77$ $A = 4.70 - 0.74(0.08) = 4.6408$

7.48 $\mu_{\bar{X}} = \mu = 49.6$, $\sigma_{\bar{X}} = \dfrac{\sigma}{\sqrt{n}} = \dfrac{20}{\sqrt{16}} = 5$

(a)   PHStat output:

Probability for X <=	
X Value	50
Z Value	0.08
P(X<=50)	0.5318814

$P(\bar{X} < 50) = P(Z < 0.08) = 0.5319$

(b)   PHStat output:

Probability for a Range	
From X Value	40
To X Value	60
Z Value for 40	-1.92
Z Value for 60	2.08
P(X<=40)	0.0274
P(X<=60)	0.9812
P(40<=X<=60)	0.9538

$P(40 < \bar{X} < 60) = P(-1.92 < Z < 2.08) = 0.9538$

7.48   (c)   PHStat output:
cont.

Probability for X >	
X Value	40
Z Value	-1.92
P(X>40)	0.9726

$P(\overline{X} > 40) = P(Z > -1.92) = 0.9726$

CHAPTER 8

OBJECTIVES

In this chapter, you learn:
- To construct and interpret confidence interval estimates for the mean and the proportion
- How to determine the sample size necessary to develop a confidence interval for the mean or proportion

OVERVIEW AND KEY CONCEPTS

Why We Need Confidence Interval Estimates in Addition to Point Estimates
- Confidence interval estimates take into consideration variation in sample statistics from sample to sample.
- They provide information about closeness to unknown population parameters.
- The interval estimates are always stated in level of confidence, which is lower than 100%.

Confidence Interval Estimate for the Mean when the Population Variance is Known
- **Assumptions:**
    - Population variance σ^2 is known.
    - Population is normally distributed or the sample size is large.
- **Point estimate for the population mean, μ: $\bar{X}$**
- **Confidence interval estimate:**
    - $\bar{X} \pm Z_{\alpha/2} \dfrac{\sigma}{\sqrt{n}}$ where $Z_{\alpha/2}$ is the value corresponding to a cumulative area of

    $\left(1 - \dfrac{\alpha}{2}\right)$ from a standardized normal distribution, i.e., the right-tail probability of

    $\alpha/2$.
- **Elements of confidence interval estimate**
    - **Level of confidence:** Measures the level of confidence in which the interval will contain the unknown population parameter.
    - **Precision (range):** Represents the closeness to the unknown parameter.
    - **Cost:** The cost required to obtain a sample of size n.
- **Factors affecting interval width (precision)**
    - **Data variation measured by σ^2:** The larger is the σ^2, the wider is the interval estimate.
    - **Sample size n:** The larger is the sample size, the narrower is the interval estimate.
    - **The level of confidence $100(1-\alpha)\%$:** The higher is the level of confidence, the wider is the interval estimate.

- **Interpretation of a $100(1-\alpha)\%$ confidence interval estimate:** If all possible samples of size n are taken and their sample means are computed, $100(1-\alpha)\%$ of the intervals contain the true population mean somewhere within the interval around their sample means and only $100(\alpha)\%$ of them do not.

Confidence Interval Estimate for the Mean when the Population Variance is Unknown

- **Assumptions:**
  - Population variance σ^2 is unknown.
  - Population is normally distributed or the sample size is large.
- **Confidence interval estimate:**
  - $\bar{X} \pm t_{\alpha/2,n-1} \dfrac{S}{\sqrt{n}}$ where $t_{\alpha/2,n-1}$ is the value corresponding to a cumulative area of $\left(1-\dfrac{\alpha}{2}\right)$ from a Student's distribution with n-1 degrees of freedom, i.e., the right-tail probability of $\alpha/2$.

Confidence Interval Estimate for the Proportion

- **Assumptions:**
  - Two categorical outcomes
  - Population follows Binomial distribution
  - Normal approximation can be used if $np \geq 5$ and $n(1-p) \geq 5$.
- **Point estimate for the population proportion of success, π:** $p = \dfrac{X}{n}$
- **Confidence interval estimate:**
  - $p \pm Z_{\alpha/2} \sqrt{\dfrac{p(1-p)}{n}}$

Determining Sample Size

- **The sample size needed when estimating the population mean:**
  - $n = \dfrac{Z^2 \sigma^2}{e^2}$ where e is the acceptable sampling error and σ^2 is estimated from past data, by an educated guess or by the data obtained from a pilot study.
- **The sample size needed when estimating the population proportion:**
  - $n = \dfrac{Z^2 \pi (1-\pi)}{e^2}$ where e is the acceptable sampling error and π is estimated from past information, by an educated guess or use 0.5.

SOLUTIONS TO END OF SECTION
AND CHAPTER REVIEW EVEN PROBLEMS

8.2 $\bar{X} \pm Z \cdot \dfrac{\sigma}{\sqrt{n}} = 125 \pm 2.58 \cdot \dfrac{24}{\sqrt{36}}$ $114.68 \le \mu \le 135.32$

8.4   Yes, it is true since 5% of intervals will not include the population mean.

8.6   (a)   You would compute the mean first because you need the mean to compute the standard deviation. If you had a sample, you would compute the sample mean. If you had the population mean, you would compute the population standard deviation.

            (b)   If you have a sample, you are computing the sample standard deviation not the population standard deviation needed in Equation 8.1. If you have a population, and have computed the population mean and population standard deviation, you don't need a confidence interval estimate of the population mean since you already have computed it.

8.8   Equation (8.1) assumes that you know the population standard deviation. Because you are selecting a sample of 100 from the population, you are computing a sample standard deviation, not the population standard deviation.

8.10   (a)

	A	B
1	Light Bulbs	
2		
3	Population Standard Deviation	100
4	Sample Mean	350
5	Sample Size	64
6	Confidence Level	95%
7	Standard Error of the Mean	12.5
8	Z Value	-1.95996108
9	Interval Half Width	24.49951353
10	Interval Lower Limit	325.5004865
11	Interval Upper Limit	374.4995135

$$\bar{X} \pm Z \cdot \frac{\sigma}{\sqrt{n}} = 350 \pm 1.96 \cdot \frac{100}{\sqrt{64}}$$ $325.5 \le \mu \le 374.50$

            (b)   No. The manufacturer cannot support a claim that the bulbs last an average 400 hours. Based on the data from the sample, a mean of 400 hours would represent a distance of 4 standard deviations above the sample mean of 350 hours.

            (c)   No. Since σ is known and $n = 64$, from the Central Limit Theorem, we may assume that the sampling distribution of $\bar{X}$ is approximately normal.

8.10   (d)   The confidence interval is narrower based on a process standard deviation of 80
cont.   hours rather than the original assumption of 100 hours.

        (a) $\bar{X} \pm Z \cdot \dfrac{\sigma}{\sqrt{n}} = 350 \pm 1.96 \cdot \dfrac{80}{\sqrt{64}}$ $330.4 \le \mu \le 369.6$

        (b)   Based on the smaller standard deviation, a mean of 400 hours would
represent a distance of 5 standard deviations above the sample mean of 350
hours. No, the manufacturer cannot support a claim that the bulbs have a
mean life of 400 hours.

8.12   (a) $df = 9$, $\alpha = 0.05$, $t_{\alpha/2} = 2.2622$

        (b) $df = 9$, $\alpha = 0.01$, $t_{\alpha/2} = 3.2498$

        (c) $df = 31$, $\alpha = 0.05$, $t_{\alpha/2} = 2.0395$

        (d) $df = 64$, $\alpha = 0.05$, $t_{\alpha/2} = 1.9977$

        (e) $df = 15$, $\alpha = 0.1$, $t_{\alpha/2} = 1.7531$

8.14   Original data: $5.8571 \pm 2.4469 \cdot \dfrac{6.4660}{\sqrt{7}}$ $-0.1229 \le \mu \le 11.8371$

      Altered data: $4.00 \pm 2.4469 \cdot \dfrac{2.1602}{\sqrt{7}}$ $2.0022 \le \mu \le 5.9978$

The presence of an outlier in the original data increases the value of the sample mean and
greatly inflates the sample standard deviation.

8.16   (a) $\bar{X} \pm t \cdot \dfrac{S}{\sqrt{n}} = 32 \pm 2.0096 \cdot \dfrac{9}{\sqrt{50}}$ $29.44 \le \mu \le 34.56$

        (b)   The quality improvement team can be 95% confident that the population mean
turnaround time is now somewhere between 29.44 hours and 34.56 hours.

        (c)   The project was a success because the initial turnaround time of 68 hours does not
fall inside the 95% confidence interval.

8.18   PHStat output:

Confidence Interval Estimate for the Mean	
Data	
Sample Standard Deviation	1.812487548
Sample Mean	7.03
Sample Size	9
Confidence Level	95%
Intermediate Calculations	
Standard Error of the Mean	0.604162516
Degrees of Freedom	8
t Value	2.306004133
Interval Half Width	1.393201259
Confidence Interval	
Interval Lower Limit	5.64
Interval Upper Limit	8.42

(a) $\bar{X} \pm t\dfrac{S}{\sqrt{n}} = 7.03 \pm 2.3060\dfrac{1.8125}{\sqrt{9}}$ $5.64 \le \mu \le 8.42$

(b)   You can be 95% confident that the population mean amount spent for lunch ($) at a fast-food restaurant is somewhere between $5.64 and $8.42.

8.20   PHStat output:

Confidence Interval Estimate for the Mean	
Data	
Sample Standard Deviation	2.297099621
Sample Mean	21.12
Sample Size	25
Confidence Level	95%
Intermediate Calculations	
Standard Error of the Mean	0.459419924
Degrees of Freedom	24
t Value	2.063898547
Interval Half Width	0.948196114
Confidence Interval	
Interval Lower Limit	20.17
Interval Upper Limit	22.07

(a) $\bar{X} \pm t\dfrac{S}{\sqrt{n}} = 21.12 \pm 2.0639\left(\dfrac{2.2971}{\sqrt{25}}\right)$ $20.17 \le \mu \le 22.07$

(b)   You can be 95% confident that the population mean MPG of 2011 small SUVs is somewhere between 20.17 and 22.07.

(c)   Because the 95% confidence interval for population mean miles per gallon of 2011 small SUVs overlaps with that for the population mean miles per gallon of 2011 family sedans, you are unable to conclude that the population mean miles per gallon of 2011 small SUVs is different from that of 2011 family sedans.

8.22   (a) $\bar{X} \pm t \cdot \dfrac{S}{\sqrt{n}} = 43.04 \pm 2.0096 \cdot \dfrac{41.9261}{\sqrt{50}}$ $31.12 \le \mu \le 54.96$

(b)   The population distribution needs to be normally distribution.

(c)

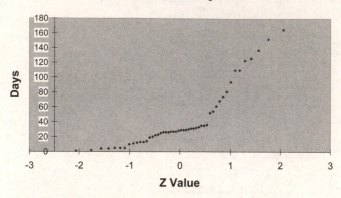

(c)

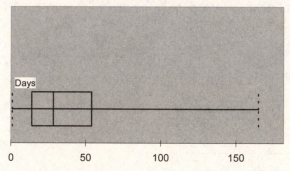

Both the normal probability plot and the boxplot suggest that the distribution is skewed to the right.

(d)   Even though the population distribution is not normally distributed, with a sample of 50, the t distribution can still be used due to the Central Limit Theorem.

8.24   (a)   PHStat output:

Confidence Interval Estimate for the Mean	
Data	
Sample Standard Deviation	0.327289904
Sample Mean	0.93
Sample Size	14
Confidence Level	95%
Intermediate Calculations	
Standard Error of the Mean	0.087471906
Degrees of Freedom	13
t Value	2.160368652
Interval Half Width	0.188971564
Confidence Interval	
Interval Lower Limit	**0.7367**
Interval Upper Limit	**1.1147**

$$\bar{X} \pm t\frac{S}{\sqrt{n}} = 0.93 \pm 2.1604\left(\frac{0.3273}{\sqrt{14}}\right) \qquad 0.7367 \le \mu \le 1.1147$$

(b)   The population distribution needs to be normally distributed.

(c)

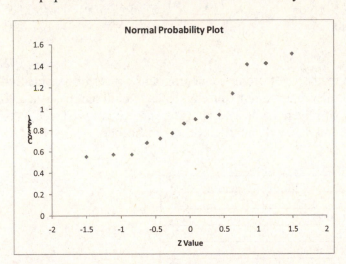

(c)

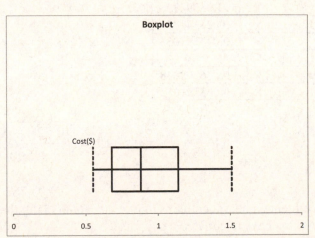

Both the normal probability plot and the boxplot show that the distribution for the cost per ounce is right-skewed.

8.26 $p = \dfrac{X}{n} = \dfrac{50}{200} = 0.25$ $p \pm Z \cdot \sqrt{\dfrac{p(1-p)}{n}} = 0.25 \pm 1.96 \sqrt{\dfrac{0.25(0.75)}{200}}$

$$0.19 \leq \pi \leq 0.31$$

8.28   (a)

	A	B
1	Purchase Additional Telephone Line	
2		
3	Sample Size	500
4	Number of Successes	135
5	Confidence Level	99%
6	Sample Proportion	0.27
7	Z Value	-2.57583451
8	Standard Error of the Proportion	0.019854471
9	Interval Half Width	0.05114183
10	Interval Lower Limit	0.21885817
11	Interval Upper Limit	0.32114183

$$p = \dfrac{X}{n} = \dfrac{135}{500} = 0.27 \qquad p \pm Z \cdot \sqrt{\dfrac{p(1-p)}{n}} = 0.27 \pm 2.5758 \sqrt{\dfrac{0.27(1-0.27)}{500}}$$

$$0.22 \leq \pi \leq 0.32$$

(b)   The manager in charge of promotional programs concerning residential customers can infer that the proportion of households that would purchase an additional telephone line if it were made available at a substantially reduced installation cost is between 0.22 and 0.32 with a 99% level of confidence.

8.30   (a)   PHStat output:

Data	
Sample Size	500
Number of Successes	260
Confidence Level	95%
Intermediate Calculations	
Sample Proportion	0.52
Z Value	-1.95996398
Standard Error of the Proportion	0.022342784
Interval Half Width	0.043791052
Confidence Interval	
Interval Lower Limit	0.476208948
Interval Upper Limit	0.563791052

$$p = \dfrac{X}{n} = \dfrac{260}{500} = 0.52 \qquad p \pm Z \cdot \sqrt{\dfrac{p(1-p)}{n}} = 0.52 \pm 1.96 \sqrt{\dfrac{0.52(1-0.52)}{500}}$$

$$0.4762 \leq \pi \leq 0.5638$$

(b)   Since the 95% confidence interval contains 0.50, you cannot claim that more than half of all U.S. workers have negotiated a pay raise.

8.30   (c)   (a) $p = \dfrac{X}{n} = \dfrac{2600}{5000} = 0.52$ $p \pm Z \cdot \sqrt{\dfrac{p(1-p)}{n}} = 0.52 \pm 1.96\sqrt{\dfrac{0.52(1-0.52)}{5000}}$

cont.

$$0.5062 \leq \pi \leq 0.5338$$

(b)   Since the lower limit of the 95% confidence interval is greater than 0.50, you can claim that more than half of all U.S. workers have negotiated a pay raise.

(d)   The larger the sample size, the narrow is the confidence interval holding everything else constant.

8.32   (a)   PHStat output:

Data	
Sample Size	2395
Number of Successes	1916
Confidence Level	95%
Intermediate Calculations	
Sample Proportion	0.8
Z Value	-1.95996398
Standard Error of the Proportion	0.008173484
Interval Half Width	0.016019735
Confidence Interval	
Interval Lower Limit	0.783980265
Interval Upper Limit	0.816019735

$p = \dfrac{X}{n} = \dfrac{1916}{2395} = 0.8$ $p \pm Z \cdot \sqrt{\dfrac{p(1-p)}{n}} = 0.8 \pm 1.96\sqrt{\dfrac{0.8(1-0.8)}{2395}}$

$$0.7840 \leq \pi \leq 0.8160$$

(b)   PHStat output:

Data	
Sample Size	2395
Number of Successes	1269
Confidence Level	95%
Intermediate Calculations	
Sample Proportion	0.529853862
Z Value	-1.95996398
Standard Error of the Proportion	0.010198628
Interval Half Width	0.019988943
Confidence Interval	
Interval Lower Limit	0.50986492
Interval Upper Limit	0.549842805

8.32   (b) $p = \dfrac{X}{n} = \dfrac{1269}{2395} = 0.5299$

cont. $p \pm Z \cdot \sqrt{\dfrac{p(1-p)}{n}} = 0.5299 \pm 1.96 \sqrt{\dfrac{0.5299(1-0.5299)}{2395}}$

$0.5099 \leq \pi \leq 0.5498$

(c)   Since the two confidence intervals do not overlap, you can conclude that with 95% confidence that the population proportion of adults who report that emails are easy to misinterpret is higher than the population proportion of adults who report that telephone conversations are easy to misinterpret.

8.34 $n = \dfrac{Z^2 \sigma^2}{e^2} = \dfrac{1.96^2 \cdot 15^2}{5^2} = 34.57$ Use $n = 35$

8.36 $n = \dfrac{Z^2 \pi(1-\pi)}{e^2} = \dfrac{2.58^2 (0.5)(0.5)}{(0.04)^2} = 1{,}040.06$ Use $n = 1{,}041$

8.38   (a) $n = \dfrac{Z^2 \sigma^2}{e^2} = \dfrac{1.96^2 \cdot 400^2}{50^2} = 245.86$ Use $n = 246$

(b) $n = \dfrac{Z^2 \sigma^2}{e^2} = \dfrac{1.96^2 \cdot 400^2}{25^2} = 983.41$ Use $n = 984$

8.40 $n = \dfrac{Z^2 \sigma^2}{e^2} = \dfrac{1.96^2 \cdot (100)^2}{(20)^2} = 96.04$ Use $n = 97$

8.42   (a) $n = \dfrac{Z^2 \sigma^2}{e^2} = \dfrac{2.58^2 \cdot 25^2}{5^2} = 166.41$ Use $n = 167$

(b) $n = \dfrac{Z^2 \sigma^2}{e^2} = \dfrac{1.96^2 \cdot 25^2}{5^2} = 96.04$ Use $n = 97$

8.44   (a) $n = \dfrac{Z^2 \sigma^2}{e^2} = \dfrac{1.96^2 \cdot 2^2}{0.25^2} = 245.85$ Use $n = 246$

(b) $n = \dfrac{Z^2 \sigma^2}{e^2} = \dfrac{1.96^2 \cdot 2.5^2}{0.25^2} = 384.15$ Use $n = 385$

(c) $n = \dfrac{Z^2 \sigma^2}{e^2} = \dfrac{1.96^2 \cdot 3.0^2}{0.25^2} = 553.17$ Use $n = 554$

(d)   When there is more variability in the population, a larger sample is needed to accurately estimate the mean.

8.46 (a) $p = 0.28$ $p \pm Z\sqrt{\dfrac{p(1-p)}{n}} = 0.28 \pm 1.96\sqrt{\dfrac{0.28(1-0.28)}{1000}}$

$0.2522 \le \pi \le 0.3078$

(b) $p = 0.19$ $p \pm Z\sqrt{\dfrac{p(1-p)}{n}} = 0.19 \pm 1.96\sqrt{\dfrac{0.19(1-0.19)}{1000}}$

$0.1657 \le \pi \le 0.2143$

(c) $p = 0.07$ $p \pm Z\sqrt{\dfrac{p(1-p)}{n}} = 0.07 \pm 1.96\sqrt{\dfrac{0.07(1-0.07)}{1000}}$

$0.0542 \le \pi \le 0.0858$

(d) (a) $n = \dfrac{Z^2 \pi(1-\pi)}{e^2} = \dfrac{1.96^2(0.28)(1-0.28)}{0.02^2} = 1{,}936.0952$ Use $n = 1{,}937$

(b) $n = \dfrac{Z^2 \pi(1-\pi)}{e^2} = \dfrac{1.96^2(0.19)(1-0.19)}{0.02^2} = 1{,}478.0013$ Use $n = 1{,}479$

(c) $n = \dfrac{Z^2 \pi(1-\pi)}{e^2} = \dfrac{1.96^2(0.07)(1-0.07)}{0.02^2} = 625.1974$ Use $n = 626$

8.48 (a) If you conduct a follow-up study to estimate the population proportion of individuals who said that the most important way to judge a company was how a company responded to a crisis, you would use a π of 0.84 in the sample size formula since it provides the most conservative value based on past information on the proportion. If you are really paranoid, you could use 0.5 to ensure that you would never underestimate the sample size needed.

(b) $n = \dfrac{Z^2 \pi(1-\pi)}{e^2} = \dfrac{1.96^2(0.84)(1-0.84)}{0.03^2} = 573.67$ Use $n = 574$

8.50 The only way to have 100% confidence is to obtain the parameter of interest, rather than a sample statistic. From another perspective, the range of the normal and t distribution is infinite, so a Z or t value that contains 100% of the area cannot be obtained.

8.52 If the confidence level is increased, a greater area under the normal or t distribution needs to be included. This leads to an increased value of Z or t, and thus a wider interval.

8.54 $\bar{X} \pm t\dfrac{S}{\sqrt{n}} = 974 \pm 2.0345\left(\dfrac{96}{\sqrt{34}}\right)$ $940.50 \le \mu \le 1007.50$

Based on the evidence gathered from the sample of 34 stores, the 95% confidence interval for the mean per-store count in all of the franchise's stores is from 940.50 to 1007.50. With a 95% level of confidence, the franchise can conclude that the mean per-store count in all of its stores is somewhere between 940.50 and 1007.50, which is larger than the original average of 900 mean per-store count before the price reduction. Hence, reducing coffee prices is a good strategy to increase the mean customer count.

8.56   (a) $\bar{X} \pm t \cdot \dfrac{S}{\sqrt{n}} = 15.3 \pm 2.0227 \cdot \dfrac{3.8}{\sqrt{40}}$ $\qquad\qquad$ $14.085 \le \mu \le 16.515$

(b) $p \pm Z \cdot \sqrt{\dfrac{p(1-p)}{n}} = 0.675 \pm 1.96 \cdot \sqrt{\dfrac{0.675(0.325)}{40}}$ $\qquad$ $0.530 \le \pi \le 0.820$

(c) $n = \dfrac{Z^2 \cdot \sigma^2}{e^2} = \dfrac{1.96^2 \cdot 5^2}{2^2} = 24.01$ $\qquad\qquad\qquad$ Use $n = 25$

(d) $n = \dfrac{Z^2 \cdot \pi \cdot (1-\pi)}{e^2} = \dfrac{1.96^2 \cdot (0.5) \cdot (0.5)}{(0.035)^2} = 784$ $\qquad$ Use $n = 784$

(e)   If a single sample were to be selected for both purposes, the larger of the two sample sizes ($n = 784$) should be used.

8.58   (a) $\bar{X} \pm t \cdot \dfrac{S}{\sqrt{n}} = 9.7 \pm 2.0639 \cdot \dfrac{4}{\sqrt{25}}$ $\qquad\qquad$ $8.049 \le \mu \le 11.351$

(b) $p \pm Z \cdot \sqrt{\dfrac{p(1-p)}{n}} = 0.48 \pm 1.96 \cdot \sqrt{\dfrac{0.48(0.52)}{25}}$ $\qquad$ $0.284 \le \pi \le 0.676$

(c) $n = \dfrac{Z^2 \cdot \sigma^2}{e^2} = \dfrac{1.96^2 \cdot 4.5^2}{1.5^2} = 34.57$ $\qquad\qquad\qquad$ Use $n = 35$

(d) $n = \dfrac{Z^2 \cdot \pi \cdot (1-\pi)}{e^2} = \dfrac{1.645^2 \cdot (0.5) \cdot (0.5)}{(0.075)^2} = 120.268$ $\qquad$ Use $n = 121$

(e)   If a single sample were to be selected for both purposes, the larger of the two sample sizes ($n = 121$) should be used.

8.60   (a) $\bar{X} \pm t \cdot \dfrac{S}{\sqrt{n}} = \$28.52 \pm 1.9949 \cdot \dfrac{\$11.39}{\sqrt{70}}$ $\qquad\qquad$ $\$25.80 \le \mu \le \$31.24$

(b) $p \pm Z \cdot \sqrt{\dfrac{p(1-p)}{n}} = 0.40 \pm 1.645 \cdot \sqrt{\dfrac{0.40(0.60)}{70}}$ $\qquad$ $0.3037 \le \pi \le 0.4963$

(c) $n = \dfrac{Z^2 \cdot \sigma^2}{e^2} = \dfrac{1.96^2 \cdot 10^2}{2^2} = 96.04$ $\qquad\qquad\qquad$ Use $n = 97$

(d) $n = \dfrac{Z^2 \cdot \pi \cdot (1-\pi)}{e^2} = \dfrac{1.645^2 \cdot (0.5) \cdot (0.5)}{(0.04)^2} = 422.82$ $\qquad$ Use $n = 423$

(e)   If a single sample were to be selected for both purposes, the larger of the two sample sizes ($n = 423$) should be used.

8.62   (a) $\bar{X} \pm t \cdot \dfrac{S}{\sqrt{n}} = \$38.54 \pm 2.0010 \cdot \dfrac{\$7.26}{\sqrt{60}}$ $\$36.66 \le \mu \le \$40.42$

(b) $p \pm Z \cdot \sqrt{\dfrac{p(1-p)}{n}} = 0.30 \pm 1.645 \cdot \sqrt{\dfrac{0.30(0.70)}{60}}$ $0.2027 \le \pi \le 0.3973$

(c) $n = \dfrac{Z^2 \cdot \sigma^2}{e^2} = \dfrac{1.96^2 \cdot 8^2}{1.5^2} = 109.27$ Use $n = 110$

(d) $n = \dfrac{Z^2 \cdot \pi \cdot (1-\pi)}{e^2} = \dfrac{1.645^2 \cdot (0.5) \cdot (0.5)}{(0.04)^2} = 422.82$ Use $n = 423$

(e)   If a single sample were to be selected for both purposes, the larger of the two sample sizes ($n = 423$) should be used.

8.64   (a) $n = \dfrac{Z^2 \cdot \sigma^2}{e^2} = \dfrac{2.5758^2 \cdot 200^2}{100^2} = 26.5396$ Use $n = 27$

(b)

Confidence Interval Estimate for the Mean	
Data	
Sample Standard Deviation	184.62
Sample Mean	1654.27
Sample Size	27
Confidence Level	99%
Intermediate Calculations	
Standard Error of the Mean	35.53013557
Degrees of Freedom	26
t Value	2.778714523
Interval Half Width	98.72810372
Confidence Interval	
Interval Lower Limit	1555.54
Interval Upper Limit	1753.00

$\bar{X} \pm t \cdot \dfrac{S}{\sqrt{n}} = \$1654.27 \pm 2.7787 \cdot \dfrac{\$184.62}{\sqrt{27}}$ $\$1555.54 \le \mu \le \$1753.00$

8.66   (a) $\bar{X} \pm t \cdot \dfrac{S}{\sqrt{n}} = 8.4209 \pm 2.0106 \cdot \dfrac{0.0461}{\sqrt{49}}$ $8.41 \le \mu \le 8.43$

(b)   With 95% confidence, the population mean width of troughs is somewhere between 8.41 and 8.43 inches. Hence, the company's requirement of troughs being between 8.31 and 8.61 is being met with a 95% level of confidence.

(c)   The assumption is valid as the width of the troughs is approximately normally distributed.

8.68   (a) $\bar{X} \pm t \cdot \dfrac{S}{\sqrt{n}} = 0.2641 \pm 1.9741 \cdot \dfrac{0.1424}{\sqrt{170}}$ $0.2425 \le \mu \le 0.2856$

        (b) $\bar{X} \pm t \cdot \dfrac{S}{\sqrt{n}} = 0.218 \pm 1.9772 \cdot \dfrac{0.1227}{\sqrt{140}}$ $0.1975 \le \mu \le 0.2385$

        (c)

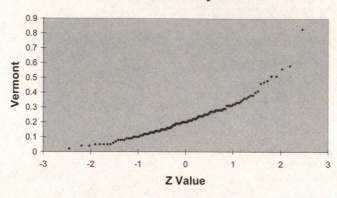

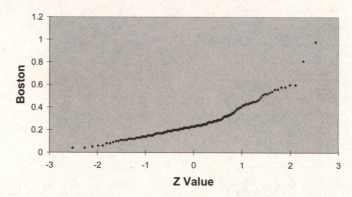

The amount of granule loss for both brands are skewed to the right but the sample sizes are large enough so the violation of the normality assumption is not critical.

        (d)   Because the two confidence intervals do not overlap, you can conclude that the mean granule loss of Boston shingles is higher than that of Vermont shingles

8.70   The 95% confidence interval for the various parameters:

Type:
    Average risk:
        Intermediate Government: $0.35 \le \pi \le 0.58$
        Short Term Corporate: $0.42 \le \pi \le 0.65$
    Above average risk:
        Intermediate Government: $0.36 \le \pi \le 0.62$
        Short Term Corporate: $0.38 \le \pi \le 0.64$
    Below average risk:
        Intermediate Government: $0.33 \le \pi \le 0.59$
        Short Term Corporate: $0.41 \le \pi \le 0.67$

Asset:
    Average risk: $381.36 \le \mu \le 1550.20$
    Above average risk: $302.76 \le \mu \le 1636.06$
    Below average risk: $344.85 \le \mu \le 1216.79$

Fee:
    Average risk:
        Yes: $0.18 \le \pi \le 0.40$
        No: $0.60 \le \pi \le 0.82$
    Above average risk:
        Yes: $0.25 \le \pi \le 0.50$
        No: $0.50 \le \pi \le 0.75$
    Below average risk:
        Yes: $0.11 \le \pi \le 0.32$
        No: $0.68 \le \pi \le 0.89$

Expense ratio:
    Average risk: $0.66 \le \mu \le 0.78$
    Above average risk: $0.63 \le \mu \le 0.79$
    Below average risk: $0.65 \le \mu \le 0.76$

Return 2009:
    Average risk: $5.82 \le \mu \le 7.93$
    Above average risk: $5.91 \le \mu \le 10.72$
    Below average risk: $5.59 \le \mu \le 7.04$

3-year return:
    Average risk: $4.64 \le \mu \le 5.38$
    Above average risk: $3.17 \le \mu \le 5.16$
    Below average risk: $4.33 \le \mu \le 5.17$

8.70   **5-year return:**
cont.

Average risk:	$3.97 \leq \mu \leq 4.43$
Above average risk:	$3.05 \leq \mu \leq 4.19$
Below average risk:	$3.85 \leq \mu \leq 4.36$

CHAPTER 9

OBJECTIVES
In this chapter, you learn:
- The basic principles of hypothesis testing
- How to use hypothesis testing to test a mean or proportion
- The assumptions of each hypothesis-testing procedure, how to evaluate them, and the consequences if they are seriously violated
- How to avoid the pitfalls involved in hypothesis testing
- Ethical issues involved in hypothesis testing

OVERVIEW AND KEY CONCEPTS
Some Basic Concepts in Hypothesis Testing
- **Null hypothesis** (H_0): The hypothesis that is always tested.
    - The null hypothesis always refers to a specified value of the population parameter, not a sample statistic.
    - The statement of the null hypothesis always contains an equal sign regarding the specified value of the population parameter.
- **Alternative hypothesis:** The opposite of the null hypothesis and represents the conclusion supported if the null hypothesis is rejected.
    - The statement of the alternative hypothesis never contains an equal sign regarding the specified value of the population parameter.
- **Critical value:** A value or values that separate the rejection region or regions from the remaining values.
- **Type I error:** A Type I error occurs if the null hypothesis is rejected when in fact it is true and should not be rejected.
- **Type II error:** A Type II error occurs if the null hypothesis is not rejected when in fact it is false and should be rejected.
- **Level of significance** (α): The probability of committing a Type I error.
- **The β risk (the consumer's risk level):** The probability of committing a Type II error.
- **Factors that affect the β risk:** Holding everything else constant,
    - β increases when the difference between the hypothesized parameter and its true value decreases.
    - β increases when α decreases.
    - β increases when σ increases.
    - β increases when the sample size n decreases.
- **The confidence coefficient** $(1-\alpha)$: The probability that the null hypothesis is not rejected when in fact it is true and should not be rejected.
- **The confidence level:** $100(1-\alpha)\%$
- **The power of a test** $(1-\beta)$: The probability of rejecting the null hypothesis when in fact it is false and should be rejected.

- **Risk in decision making:** There is a delicate balance between the probability of committing a Type I error and the probability of a Type II error.

E.g. Jury Trial — The Truth			Hypothesis Test — The Truth		
Verdict	Innocent	Guilty	Decision	H_0 True	H_0 False
Innocent	Correct	Error	Do Not Reject H_0	$1 - \alpha$	Type II Error (β)
Guilty	Error	Correct	Reject H_0	Type I Error (α)	Power ($1 - \beta$)

- Reducing the probability of Type I error will inevitably increase the probability of committing a Type II error holding everything else constant.
- One should choose a smaller Type I error when the cost of rejecting the maintained hypothesis is high.
- One should choose a larger Type I error when there is an interest in changing the status quo.

- ***p*-value (the observed level of significance):** The probability of obtaining a test statistic equal to or more extreme than the result obtained from the sample data, given the null hypothesis is true.
  - It is also the smallest level of significance at which the null hypothesis can be rejected.
  - Roughly speaking, it measures the amount of evidence against the null hypothesis. The smaller the *p*-value, the stronger is the evidence against the null hypothesis.
  - The statistical decision rule is to reject the null hypothesis if the *p*-value is less than the level of significance (α), and do not reject otherwise.

The Six-Step Method in the Traditional Critical Value Approach to Hypothesis Testing

1. State the null hypothesis, H_0 and the alternative hypothesis, H_1.
2. Choose the level of significance, α and the sample size, n. The level of significance is specified according to the relative importance of the risks of committing Type I and Type II errors in the problem.
3. Determine the appropriate test statistic and sampling distribution.
4. Determine the critical values that divide the rejection and nonrejection regions.
5. Collect the data and compute the value of the test statistic.
6. Make the statistical decision and state the managerial conclusion. Compare the computed test statistic to the critical values. Reject H_0 when the computed test statistic falls in a rejection region; do not reject H_0 otherwise. The managerial conclusion is written in the context of the real-world problem.

The Five-Step Method in the *p*-Value Approach to Hypothesis Testing
1. State the null hypothesis, H_0 and the alternative hypothesis, H_1.
2. Choose the level of significance, α and the sample size, n. The level of significance is specified according to the relative importance of the risks of committing Type I and Type II errors in the problem.
3. Determine the appropriate test statistic and sampling distribution.
4. Collect the data, compute the value of the test statistic and obtain the *p*-value based on the computed test statistic.
5. Make the statistical decision and state the managerial conclusion. If the *p*-value is greater than or equal to α, you do not reject the null hypothesis H_0. If the *p*-value is less than α, you reject the null hypothesis. Remember the phrase "if the *p*-value is low, the H_0 must go." The managerial conclusion is written in the context of the real-world problem.

Z Test for the Population Mean (μ) when σ is Known
- **Assumptions:**
  - Population is normally distributed or large sample size.
  - σ is known.
- **Test statistic:**
  - $$Z = \frac{\bar{X} - \mu_{\bar{X}}}{\sigma_{\bar{X}}} = \frac{\bar{X} - \mu}{\sigma / \sqrt{n}}$$
  - The alternative hypothesis can be one-tail with a right-tail rejection region, one-tail with a left-tail rejection region or two-tail with both right-tail and left-tail rejection regions.

t Test for the Population Mean (μ) when σ Is Unknown
- **Assumptions:**
  - Population is normally distributed or large sample size.
  - σ is unknown.
- **Test statistic:**
  - $$t = \frac{\bar{X} - \mu}{S / \sqrt{n}}$$ with $(n-1)$ degrees of freedom.
  - The alternative hypothesis can be one-tail with a right-tail rejection region, one-tail with a left-tail rejection region or two-tail with both right-tail and left-tail rejection regions.

Z Test for the Population Proportion (π)
- **Assumptions:**
  - Population involves 2 categorical values.
  - Both np and $n(1-p)$ are at least 5.
- **Test statistic:**
  - $$Z = \frac{p - \mu_p}{\sigma_p} = \frac{p - \pi}{\sqrt{\dfrac{\pi(1-\pi)}{n}}}$$

  ▪ The alternative hypothesis can be one-tail with a right-tail rejection region, one-tail with a left-tail rejection region or two-tail with both right-tail and left-tail rejection regions.

Potential Hypothesis-Testing Pitfalls

- To avoid potential hypothesis-testing pitfalls, you should:
  1. Consult with a person with substantial statistical training early in the process.
  2. Build in adequate controls from the beginning to avoid biases.
  3. Plan ahead by asking the following questions:
     i.   What is the goal of the survey, study, or experiment? How can you translate into a null hypothesis and an alternative hypothesis?
     ii.   Is the hypothesis test a two-tail test or one-tail test?
     iii. Can you select a random sample from the underlying population of interest?
     iv.   What kinds of measurements will you collect from the sample? Are the sampled outcomes numerical or categorical?
     v.   At what significance level, or risk of committing a Type I error, should you conduct the hypothesis test?
     vi.   Is the intended sample size large enough to achieve the desired power of the test for the level of significance chosen?
     vii. What statistical test procedure should you use and why?
     viii. What conclusions and interpretations can you make from the results of the hypothesis test?

Ethical Issues

- Ethical considerations arise when the hypothesis-testing process is manipulated.
  - **Data collection method should be randomized:** The data must be the outcome of a random sample from a population or from an experiment in which a randomization process was used. Potential respondents should not be permitted to self-select for a study nor should they be purposely selected.
  - **Informed Consent from Human Respondents Being "Treated":** Any individual who is to be subjected to some "treatment" in an experiment should be made aware of the research endeavor and any potential behavioral or physical side effects. The subject should also provide informed consent with respect to participation.
  - **Type of Test—Two-Tail or One-Tail:** If prior information is available that leads you to test the null hypothesis against a specifically directed alternative, then a one-tail test is more powerful than a two-tail test. On the other hand, if you are interested only in differences from the null hypothesis, not in the direction of the difference, the two-tail test is the appropriate procedure to use.
  - **Choice of Level of Significance:** The level of significance should be selected before data collection occurs. It is also good practice to always report the p-value, not just the conclusions of the hypothesis test.
  - **Data Snooping:** It is unethical to perform a hypothesis test on a set of data, look at the results, and then decide on the level of significance or decide between a one-tail or two-tail test.
  - **Cleansing and Discarding of Data:** If a measurement is incomplete or grossly in error because of some equipment problem or unusual behavioral occurrence unrelated to the study, you can discard the value. In a well-designed experiment or study, you should decide, in advance, on all rules regarding the possible discarding of data.

- **Reporting of Findings:** In conducting research, you should document both good and bad results. It is inappropriate to report the results of hypothesis tests that show statistical significance but not those for which there is insufficient evidence in the findings.
- **Statistical Significance versus Practical Significance:** You need to make the distinction between the existence of a statistically significant result and its practical significance in the context within a field of application. Sometimes, due to a very large sample size, you will get a result that is statistically significant, but has little practical significance.

SOLUTIONS TO END OF SECTION
AND CHAPTER REVIEW EVEN PROBLEMS

9.2   Decision rule: Reject H_0 if $Z_{STAT} < -1.96$ or $Z_{STAT} > +1.96$.
        Decision: Since $Z_{STAT} = +2.21$ is greater than the upper critical value of $+1.96$, reject H_0.

9.4   Decision rule: Reject H_0 if $Z_{STAT} < -2.58$ or $Z_{STAT} > +2.58$.

9.6 p-value $= 2(1 - .9772) = 0.0456$

9.8 p-value $= 0.1676$

9.10   Under the French judicial system, unlike ours in the United States, the null hypothesis
        assumes the defendant is guilty, the alternative hypothesis assumes the defendant is innocent.
        A Type I error would be not convicting a guilty person and a Type II error would be
        convicting an innocent person.

9.12 H_0: $\mu = 20$ minutes. 20 minutes is adequate travel time between classes.
        H_1: $\mu \neq 20$ minutes. 20 minutes is not adequate travel time between classes.

9.14   (a)   PHStat output:

Data		
Null Hypothesis $\mu=$		375
Level of Significance		0.05
Population Standard Deviation		100
Sample Size		64
Sample Mean		350
Intermediate Calculations		
Standard Error of the Mean		12.5
Z Test Statistic		-2
Two-Tail Test		
Lower Critical Value		-1.959963985
Upper Critical Value		1.959963985
p-Value		0.045500264
Reject the null hypothesis		

H_0: $\mu = 375$. The mean life of a large shipment of light bulbs is equal to 375 hours.

H_1: $\mu \neq 375$. The mean life of a large shipment of light bulbs differs from 375 hours.

Decision rule: Reject H_0 if $|Z_{STAT}| > 1.96$

Test statistic: $Z_{STAT} = \dfrac{\bar{X} - \mu}{\sigma / \sqrt{n}} = \dfrac{350 - 375}{100/\sqrt{64}} = -2$

Decision: Since $|Z_{STAT}| > 1.96$, reject H_0. There is enough evidence to conclude that
the mean life of a large shipment of light bulbs differs from 375 hours.

9.14   (b)   *p*-value = 0.0455. If the population mean life of a large shipment of light bulbs is
cont.   indeed equal to 375 hours, the probability of obtaining a test statistic that is more
               than 2 standard error units away from 0 is 0.0455.

(c)   PHStat output:

Data	
Population Standard Deviation	100
Sample Mean	350
Sample Size	64
Confidence Level	95%
Intermediate Calculations	
Standard Error of the Mean	12.5
Z Value	-1.95996398
Interval Half Width	24.49954981
Confidence Interval	
Interval Lower Limit	325.5004502
Interval Upper Limit	374.4995498

(c) $\bar{X} \pm Z_{a/2}\dfrac{\sigma}{\sqrt{n}} = 350 \pm 1.96\dfrac{100}{\sqrt{64}}$ $325.5005 \le \mu \le 374.4995$

(d)   You are 95% confident that the population mean life of a large shipment of light bulbs
       is somewhere between 325.5005 and 374.4995 hours.
       Since the 95% confidence interval does not contain the hypothesized value of 375, you
       will reject H_0. The conclusions are the same.

9.16   (a)   PHStat output:

Data	
Null Hypothesis $\mu =$	1
Level of Significance	0.01
Population Standard Deviation	0.02
Sample Size	50
Sample Mean	0.995
Intermediate Calculations	
Standard Error of the Mean	0.002828427
Z Test Statistic	-1.767766953
Two-Tail Test	
Lower Critical Value	-2.575829304
Upper Critical Value	2.575829304
***p*-Value**	0.077099872
Do not reject the null hypothesis	

H_0: $\mu = 1$. The mean amount of paint is 1 gallon.

H_1: $\mu \neq 1$. The mean amount of paint differs from 1 gallon.

Decision rule: Reject H_0 if $|Z_{STAT}| > 2.5758$

9.16   (a)   Test statistic: $Z_{STAT} = \dfrac{\overline{X} - \mu}{\sigma / \sqrt{n}} = \dfrac{.995 - 1}{.02 / \sqrt{50}} = -1.7678$

cont.

         Decision: Since $|Z_{STAT}| < 2.5758$, do not reject H_0. There is not enough evidence to conclude that the mean amount of paint contained in 1-gallon cans purchased from a nationally known manufacturer is different from 1 gallon.

   (b) p-value = 0.0771. If the population mean amount of paint contained in 1-gallon cans purchased from a nationally known manufacturer is actually 1 gallon, the probability of obtaining a test statistic that is more than 1.7678 standard error units away from 0 is 0.0771.

   (c)   PHStat output:

Data	
Population Standard Deviation	0.02
Sample Mean	0.995
Sample Size	50
Confidence Level	99%
Intermediate Calculations	
Standard Error of the Mean	0.002828427
Z Value	-2.5758293
Interval Half Width	0.007285545
Confidence Interval	
Interval Lower Limit	0.987714455
Interval Upper Limit	1.002285545

$$\overline{X} \pm Z_{a/2} \dfrac{\sigma}{\sqrt{n}} = .995 \pm 2.5758 \dfrac{.02}{\sqrt{50}} \qquad\qquad 0.9877 \le \mu \le 1.0023$$

         You are 99% confident that population mean amount of paint contained in 1-gallon cans purchased from a nationally known manufacturer is somewhere between 0.9877 and 1.0023 gallons.

   (d)   Since the 99% confidence interval does not contain the hypothesized value of 1, you will reject H_0. The conclusions are the same.

9.18 $t_{STAT} = \dfrac{\overline{X} - \mu}{S / \sqrt{n}} = \dfrac{56 - 50}{12 / \sqrt{16}} = 2.00$

9.20   For a two-tailed test with a 0.05 level of confidence, the critical values are ± 2.1315.

9.22   No, you should not use the t test to test the null hypothesis that $\mu = 60$ on a population that is left-skewed because the sample size ($n = 16$) is less than 30. The t test assumes that, if the underlying population is not normally distributed, the sample size is sufficiently large to enable the test to be valid. If sample sizes are small ($n < 30$), the t test should not be used because the sampling distribution does not meet the requirements of the Central Limit Theorem.

9.24   PHStat output:

t Test for Hypothesis of the Mean	
Data	
Null Hypothesis $\mu =$	3.7
Level of Significance	0.05
Sample Size	64
Sample Mean	3.57
Sample Standard Deviation	0.8
Intermediate Calculations	
Standard Error of the Mean	0.1
Degrees of Freedom	63
t Test Statistic	-1.3
Two-Tail Test	
Lower Critical Value	-1.9983405
Upper Critical Value	1.9983405
p-Value	0.1983372
Do not reject the null hypothesis	

(a) $H_0 : \mu = 3.7 \quad H_1 : \mu \neq 3.7$

Decision rule: Reject H_0 if $|t_{STAT}| > 1.9983 \quad d.f. = 63$

Test statistic: $t_{STAT} = \dfrac{\overline{X} - \mu}{S / \sqrt{n}} = \dfrac{3.57 - 3.7}{0.8/\sqrt{64}} = -1.3$

Decision: Since $|t_{STAT}| < 1.9983$, do not reject H_0. There is not enough evidence to conclude that the population mean waiting time is different from 3.7 minutes at the 0.05 level of significance.

(b)   The sample size of 64 is large enough to apply the Central Limit Theorem and, hence, you do not need to be concerned about the shape of the population distribution when conducting the *t*-test in (a). In general, the *t* test is appropriate for this sample size except for the case where the population is extremely skewed or bimodal.

9.26   PHStat output:

t Test for Hypothesis of the Mean	
Data	
Null Hypothesis $\mu=$	2.5
Level of Significance	0.05
Sample Size	100
Sample Mean	2.55
Sample Standard Deviation	0.44
Intermediate Calculations	
Standard Error of the Mean	0.044
Degrees of Freedom	99
t Test Statistic	1.136363636
Two-Tail Test	
Lower Critical Value	-1.9842169
Upper Critical Value	1.9842169
p-Value	0.258547677
Do not reject the null hypothesis	

9.26   (a) $H_0 : \mu = \$2.5$ $H_1 : \mu \neq \$2.5$

cont.   Decision rule: Reject H_0 if $|t_{STAT}| > 1.9842$ or p-value < 0.05

                   Test statistic: $t_{STAT} = \dfrac{\overline{X} - \mu}{S / \sqrt{n}} = \dfrac{2.55 - 2.5}{.44 / \sqrt{100}} = 1.1364$

                   p-value $= 0.2585$

                   Decision: Since $|t_{STAT}| < 1.9842$ and the p-value of $0.2585 > 0.05$, do not reject H_0.

                   There is not enough evidence to conclude that the population mean retail value of the greeting cards is different from $2.50.

        (b)   The p-value is 0.2585. If the population mean is indeed $2.5, the probability of obtaining a test statistic that is more than 1.1364 standard error units away from 0 in either direction is 0.2585.

9.28   PHStat output:

t Test for Hypothesis of the Mean	
Data	
Null Hypothesis μ=	6.5
Level of Significance	0.05
Sample Size	9
Sample Mean	7.03
Sample Standard Deviation	1.812487548
Intermediate Calculations	
Standard Error of the Mean	0.604162516
Degrees of Freedom	8
t Test Statistic	0.875408313
Two-Tail Test	
Lower Critical Value	-2.306004133
Upper Critical Value	2.306004133
p-Value	0.406866177
Do not reject the null hypothesis	

        (a) $H_0 : \mu = \$6.50$ $H_1 : \mu \neq \$6.50$

                   Decision rule: Reject H_0 if $|t_{STAT}| > 2.3060$ or p-value < 0.05

                   Test statistic: $t_{STAT} = \dfrac{\overline{X} - \mu}{S / \sqrt{n}} = \dfrac{7.03 - 6.5}{1.8125 / \sqrt{9}} = 0.8754$

                   Decision: Since $|t_{STAT}| < 2.3060$, do not reject H_0. There is not enough evidence to conclude that the mean amount spent for lunch is different from $6.50.

        (b)   The p-value is 0.4069. If the population mean is indeed $6.50, the probability of obtaining a test statistic that is more than 0.8754 standard error units away from 0 in either direction is 0.4069.

        (c)   That the distribution of the amount spent on lunch is normally distributed.

        (d)   With a small sample size, it is difficult to evaluate the assumption of normality. However, the distribution may be symmetric since the mean and the median are close in value.

9.30   (a) $H_0 : \mu = 2$ $H_1 : \mu \neq 2$ $d.f. = 49$

Decision rule: Reject H_0 if $|t_{STAT}| > 2.0096$

Test statistic: $t_{STAT} = \dfrac{\overline{X} - \mu}{S / \sqrt{n}} = \dfrac{2.0007 - 2}{0.0446 / \sqrt{50}} = 0.1143$

Decision: Since $|t_{STAT}| < 2.0096$, do not reject H_0. There is not enough evidence to conclude that the mean amount of soft drink filled is different from 2.0 liters.

(b) p-value = 0.9095. If the population mean amount of soft drink filled is indeed 2.0 liters, the probability of observing a sample of 50 soft drinks that will result in a sample mean amount of fill more different from 2.0 liters is 0.9095.

(c)

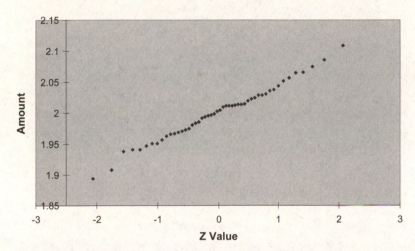

(d)   The normal probability plot suggests that the data are rather normally distributed. Hence, the results in (a) are valid in terms of the normality assumption.

(e)

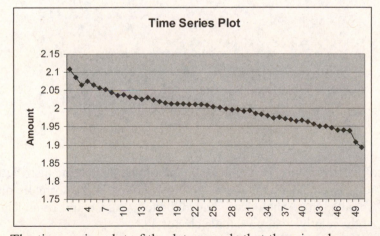

The time series plot of the data reveals that there is a downward trend in the amount of soft drink filled. This violates the assumption that data are drawn independently from a normal population distribution because the amount of fill in consecutive bottles appears to be closely related. As a result, the t test in (a) becomes invalid.

9.32   (a) $H_0 : \mu = 8.46$ $H_1 : \mu \neq 8.46$

Decision rule: Reject H_0 if $|t_{STAT}| > 2.0106$ $d.f. = 48$

Test statistic: $t_{STAT} = \dfrac{\bar{X} - \mu}{S / \sqrt{n}} = \dfrac{8.4209 - 8.46}{0.0461 / \sqrt{49}} = -5.9355$

Decision: Since $|t_{STAT}| > 2.0106$, reject H_0. There is enough evidence to conclude that mean widths of the troughs is different from 8.46 inches.

(b)   The population distribution needs to be normal.

(c)

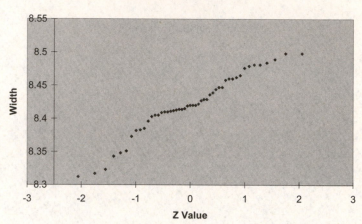

(c)

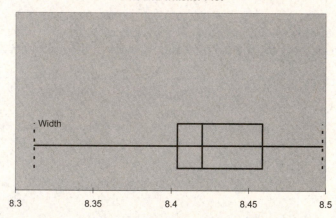

(d)   The normal probability plot and the boxplot indicate that the distribution is skewed to the left. Even though the population distribution is not normally distributed, the result obtained in (a) should still be valid due to the Central Limit Theorem as a result of the relatively large sample size of 49.

9.34   (a) $H_0 : \mu = 5.5$ $H_1 : \mu \neq 5.5$

Decision rule: Reject H_0 if $|t_{STAT}| > 2.680$ $d.f. = 49$

Test statistic: $t_{STAT} = \dfrac{\overline{X} - \mu}{S / \sqrt{n}} = \dfrac{5.5014 - 5.5}{0.1058 / \sqrt{50}} = 0.0935$

Decision: Since $|t_{STAT}| < 2.680$, do not reject H_0. There is not enough evidence to conclude that the mean amount of tea per bag is different from 5.5 grams.

(b) $\overline{X} \pm t \cdot \dfrac{s}{\sqrt{n}} = 5.5014 \pm 2.6800 \cdot \dfrac{0.1058}{\sqrt{50}}$ $5.46 < \mu < 5.54$

With 99% confidence, you can conclude that the population mean amount of tea per bag is somewhere between 5.46 and 5.54 grams.

(c)   The conclusions are the same.

9.36 p-value $= 1 - 0.9772 = 0.0228$

9.38 p-value $= 0.0838$

9.40 p-value $= P(Z < 1.38) = 0.9162$

9.42 $t = 2.7638$

9.44 $t = -2.5280$

9.46   (a) $H_0 : \mu \geq 36.5$ $H_1 : \mu < 36.5$

Decision rule: Reject H_0 if $t_{STAT} < -1.6604$ or p-value < 0.05 $d.f. = 99$

Test statistic: $t_{STAT} = \dfrac{\overline{X} - \mu}{S / \sqrt{n}} = \dfrac{34.5 - 36.5}{11.7 / \sqrt{100}} = -1.7094$

p-value $= 0.0453$

Decision: Since $t_{STAT} < -1.6604$ and the p-value of $0.0453 < 0.05$, reject H_0. There is enough evidence to conclude that the population mean amount is different from 36.5 hours.

(b)   The p-value is 0.0453. If the population mean is indeed at least 36.5 hours, the probability of obtaining a test statistic that is less than -1.7094 is 0.0453.

9.48   PHStat output:

t Test for Hypothesis of the Mean	
Data	
Null Hypothesis μ=	68
Level of Significance	0.01
Sample Size	50
Sample Mean	32
Sample Standard Deviation	9
Intermediate Calculations	
Standard Error of the Mean	1.272792206
Degrees of Freedom	49
t Test Statistic	-28.28427125
Lower-Tail Test	
Lower Critical Value	-2.40489175
***p*-Value**	2.61548E-32
Reject the null hypothesis	

(a) $H_0: \mu \geq 68$ $H_1: \mu < 68$

Decision rule: If $t_{STAT} < -2.4049$ or p-value < 0.01, reject H_0.

Test statistic: $t_{STAT} = \dfrac{\bar{X} - \mu}{S/\sqrt{n}} = \dfrac{32 - 68}{9/\sqrt{50}} = -28.2843$

Decision: Since $t_{STAT} = -28.2843$ is less than -2.4049, reject H_0. There is enough evidence to conclude the new process has reduced turnaround time.

(b)   The probability of obtaining a sample whose mean is 32 hours or less when the null hypothesis is true is essentially zero.

9.50   PHStat output:

t Test for Hypothesis of the Mean	
Data	
Null Hypothesis μ=	900
Level of Significance	0.01
Sample Size	34
Sample Mean	974
Sample Standard Deviation	96
Intermediate Calculations	
Standard Error of the Mean	16.46386417
Degrees of Freedom	33
t Test Statistic	4.494692086
Upper-Tail Test	
Upper Critical Value	2.444794184
***p*-Value**	4.05368E-05
Reject the null hypothesis	

9.50   (a) H_0: $\mu \leq 900$
cont.   The mean customer count is not more than 900.
               H_1: $\mu > 900$
               The mean customer count is more than 900.

        (b)   A Type I error occurs when you conclude the mean customer count is more than 900
               when in fact the mean number is not more than 900.
               A Type II error occurs when you conclude the mean customer count is not more than
               900 when in fact the mean number is more than 900.

        (c)   Decision rule: If $t_{STAT} > 2.4448$ or when the p-value < 0.01, reject H_0.

               Test statistic: $t_{STAT} = \dfrac{\bar{X} - \mu}{S/\sqrt{n}} = \dfrac{974 - 900}{96/\sqrt{34}} = 4.4947$

               p-value is virtually 0.
               Decision: Since $t_{STAT} = 4.4947$ is greater than 2.4448 or the p-value is less than 0.01,
               reject H_0. There is enough evidence to conclude that reducing coffee prices is a good
               strategy for increasing the mean customer count.

        (d)   When the null hypothesis is true, the probability of obtaining a sample whose mean
               is 974 or more is virtually 0.

9.52 $p = \dfrac{X}{n} = \dfrac{88}{400} = 0.22$

9.54 H_0: $\pi = 0.20$
        H_1: $\pi \neq 0.20$
        Decision rule: If $Z < -1.96$ or $Z > 1.96$, reject H_0.

        Test statistic: $Z_{STAT} = \dfrac{p - \pi}{\sqrt{\dfrac{\pi(1-\pi)}{n}}} = \dfrac{0.22 - 0.20}{\sqrt{\dfrac{0.20(0.8)}{400}}} = 1.00$

        Decision: Since $Z = 1.00$ is between the critical bounds of ± 1.96, do not reject H_0.

9.56   (a)   PHStat output:

Z Test of Hypothesis for the Proportion	
Data	
Null Hypothesis $\pi =$	0.192
Level of Significance	0.05
Number of Items of Interest	25
Sample Size	100
Intermediate Calculations	
Sample Proportion	0.25
Standard Error	0.039387308
Z Test Statistic	1.47255559
Upper-Tail Test	
Upper Critical Value	1.644853627
p-Value	0.070435453
Do not reject the null hypothesis	

9.56
cont.

H_0: $\pi \le 0.192$ H_1: $\pi > 0.192$

Decision rule: If p-value < 0.05, reject H_0.

Test statistic: $Z_{STAT} = \dfrac{p - \pi}{\sqrt{\dfrac{\pi(1-\pi)}{n}}} = \dfrac{0.25 - 0.192}{\sqrt{\dfrac{0.192(0.192)}{100}}} = 1.4726$,

p-value = 0.0704.

Decision: Since p-value > 0.05, do not reject H_0. There is not enough evidence that the market share for the Mozilla Firefox web browser at your university is greater than the worldwide market share of 19.2%..

(b)   PHStat output:

Z Test of Hypothesis for the Proportion	
Data	
Null Hypothesis $\pi =$	**0.192**
Level of Significance	**0.05**
Number of Items of Interest	**100**
Sample Size	**400**
Intermediate Calculations	
Sample Proportion	0.25
Standard Error	0.019693654
Z Test Statistic	**2.945111181**
Upper-Tail Test	
Upper Critical Value	**1.644853627**
_p_-Value	**0.001614193**
Reject the null hypothesis	

H_0: $\pi \le 0.192$ H_1: $\pi > 0.192$

Decision rule: If p-value < 0.05, reject H_0.

Test statistic: $Z_{STAT} = \dfrac{p - \pi}{\sqrt{\dfrac{\pi(1-\pi)}{n}}} = \dfrac{0.25 - 0.192}{\sqrt{\dfrac{0.192(0.192)}{400}}} = 2.9451$,

p-value = 0.0016.

Decision: Since p-value < 0.05, reject H_0. There is enough evidence that the market share for the Mozilla Firefox web browser at your university is greater than the worldwide market share of 19.2%..

(c)   A larger sample size reduces the standard error (variation) of the sample proportion and, hence, reduces the p-value and makes it easier to reject H_0 holding everything else constant.

(d)   You would be very unlikely to reject the null hypothesis with a sample of 20.

9.58   PHStat output:

Z Test of Hypothesis for the Proportion	
Data	
Null Hypothesis $\pi =$	**0.6**
Level of Significance	**0.05**
Number of Successes	**650**
Sample Size	**1000**
Intermediate Calculations	
Sample Proportion	0.65
Standard Error	0.015491933
Z Test Statistic	**3.227486122**
Two-Tail Test	
Lower Critical Value	**-1.959963985**
Upper Critical Value	**1.959963985**
_p_-Value	**0.001248831**
Reject the null hypothesis	

H_0: $\pi = 0.60$

H_1: $\pi \neq 0.60$

Decision rule: If $Z_{STAT} < -1.96$ or $Z_{STAT} > 1.96$, reject H_0.

Test statistic: $Z_{STAT} = \dfrac{p - \pi}{\sqrt{\dfrac{\pi(1-\pi)}{n}}} = \dfrac{0.65 - 0.60}{\sqrt{\dfrac{0.60(1-0.60)}{1000}}} = 3.2275$

Decision: Since $Z_{STAT} = 3.2275$ is greater than the upper critical bound of 1.96, reject H_0. You conclude that there is enough evidence that the proportion of all young jobseekers aged 24 to 35 who preferred to "look for a job in a place where I would like to live" rather than "look for the best job I can find, the place where I live is secondary" is different from 60%.

9.60   (a) H_0: $\pi \leq 0.08$ No more than 8% of students at your school are Omnivores

H_1: $\pi > 0.08$ More than 8% of students at your school are Omnivores

(b)   Decision rule: If p-value < 0.05, reject H_0.

Test statistic: $Z_{STAT} = \dfrac{p - \pi}{\sqrt{\dfrac{\pi(1-\pi)}{n}}} = \dfrac{0.15 - 0.08}{\sqrt{\dfrac{0.08(1-0.08)}{200}}} = 3.6490$, p-value $= 0.0001316$

Decision: Since p-value $= 0.0001316 < 0.05$, reject H_0. There is enough evidence to show that the percentage of Omnivores at your school is greater than 8%.

9.62   A Type I error represents rejecting a true null hypothesis, while a Type II error represents not rejecting a false null hypothesis.

9.64   In a one-tailed test for a mean or proportion, the entire rejection region is contained in one tail of the distribution. In a two-tailed test, the rejection region is split into two equal parts, one in the lower tail of the distribution, and the other in the upper tail.

9.66   Assuming a two-tailed test is used, if the hypothesized value for the parameter does not fall into the confidence interval, then the null hypothesis can be rejected.

9.68   The following are the 5-step p-value approach to hypothesis testing: (1) State the null hypothesis, H_0, and the alternative hypothesis, H_1. (2) Choose the level of significance, α, and the sample size, n. (3) Determine the appropriate test statistic and the sampling distribution. (4) Collect the sample data, compute the value of the test statistic, and compute the p-value. (5) Make the statistical decision and state the managerial conclusion. If the p-value is greater than or equal to α, you do not reject the null hypothesis, H_0. If the p-value is less than α, you reject the null hypothesis.

9.70   (a)   La Quinta Motor Inns commits a Type I error when it purchases a site that is not profitable.

(b)   Type II error occurs when La Quinta Motor Inns fails to purchase a profitable site. The cost to the Inns when a Type II error is committed is the loss on the amount of profit the site could have generated had the Inns decided to purchase the site.

(c)   The executives at La Quinta Motor Inns are trying to avoid a Type I error by adopting a very stringent decision criterion. Only sites that are classified as capable of generating high profit will be purchased.

(d)   If the executives adopt a less stringent rejection criterion by buying sites for which the computer model predicts moderate or large profit, the probability of committing a Type I error will increase. Many more of the sites the computer model predicts that will generate moderate profit may end up not being profitable at all. On the other hand, the less stringent rejection criterion will lower the probability of committing a Type II error since more potentially profitable sites will be purchased.

9.72   (a) H_0: $\mu = 10.0$ gallons. The mean gasoline purchase is equal to 10 gallons.
H_1: $\mu \neq 10.0$ gallons. The mean gasoline purchase differs from 10 gallons.
Decision rule: $d.f. = 59$. If $t_{STAT} < -2.0010$ or $t_{STAT} > 2.0010$, reject H_0.

Test statistic: $t_{STAT} = \dfrac{\overline{X} - \mu}{S/\sqrt{n}} = \dfrac{11.3 - 10.0}{3.1/\sqrt{60}} = 3.2483$

Decision: Since $t_{STAT} = 3.2483$ is greater than the upper critical value of 2.0010, reject H_0. There is enough evidence to conclude that the mean gasoline purchase differs from 10 gallons.

(b) p-value $= 0.0019$.
Note: The p value was found using Excel.

(c) H_0: $\pi \geq 0.20$. At least 20% of the motorists purchase premium-grade gasoline.
H_1: $\pi < 0.20$. Less than 20% of the motorists purchase premium-grade gasoline.
Decision rule: If $Z_{STAT} < -1.645$, reject H_0.

Test statistic: $Z_{STAT} = \dfrac{p - \pi}{\sqrt{\dfrac{\pi(1 - \pi)}{n}}} = \dfrac{0.1833 - 0.20}{\sqrt{\dfrac{0.20(1 - 0.20)}{60}}} = -0.32$

Decision: Since $Z_{STAT} = -0.32$ is greater than the critical bound of -1.645, do not reject H_0. There is not sufficient evidence to conclude that less than 20% of the motorists purchase premium-grade gasoline.

9.72   (d) H_0: $\mu = 10.0$ gallons. The mean gasoline purchase is equal to 10 gallons.
cont. H_1: $\mu \neq 10.0$ gallons. The mean gasoline purchase differs from 10 gallons.
                Decision rule: $d.f. = 59$. If $t_{STAT} < -2.0010$ or $t_{STAT} > 2.0010$, reject H_0.

$$\text{Test statistic: } t = \frac{\overline{X} - \mu}{S/\sqrt{n}} = \frac{10.3 - 10.0}{3.1/\sqrt{60}} = 0.7496$$

Decision: Since the test statistic of $t_{STAT} = 0.7496$ is between the critical bounds of ± 2.0010, do not reject H_0. There is not enough evidence to conclude that the mean gasoline purchase differs from 10 gallons.

(e) H_0: $\pi \geq 0.20$. At least 20% of the motorists purchase premium-grade gasoline.
        H_1: $\pi < 0.20$. Less than 20% of the motorists purchase premium-grade gasoline.
        Decision rule: If $Z_{STAT} < -1.645$, reject H_0.

$$\text{Test statistic: } Z_{STAT} = \frac{p - \pi}{\sqrt{\dfrac{\pi(1 - \pi)}{n}}} = \frac{0.1167 - 0.20}{\sqrt{\dfrac{0.20(1 - 0.20)}{60}}} = -1.61$$

Decision: Since $Z_{STAT} = -1.61$ is greater than the critical bound of -1.645, do not reject H_0. There is not sufficient evidence to conclude that less than 20% of the motorists purchase premium-grade gasoline.

9.74   (a) H_0: $\mu \geq 5$ minutes. The mean waiting time at a bank branch in a commercial district of the city is at least 5 minutes during the 12:00 p.m. to 1 p.m. peak lunch period.
                H_1: $\mu < 5$ minutes. The mean waiting time at a bank branch in a commercial district of the city is less than 5 minutes during the 12:00 p.m. to 1 p.m. peak lunch period.
                Decision rule: $d.f. = 14$. If $t_{STAT} < -1.7613$, reject H_0.

$$\text{Test statistic: } t_{STAT} = \frac{\overline{X} - \mu}{S/\sqrt{n}} = \frac{4.28\overline{6} - 5.0}{1.637985/\sqrt{15}} = -1.6867$$

Decision: Since $t_{STAT} = -1.6867$ is greater than the critical bound of -1.7613, do not reject H_0. There is not enough evidence to conclude that the mean waiting time at a bank branch in a commercial district of the city is less than 5 minutes during the 12:00 p.m. to 1 p.m. peak lunch period.

(b)   To perform the t-test on the population mean, you must assume that the observed sequence in which the data were collected is random and that the data are approximately normally distributed.

(c)   Normal probability plot:

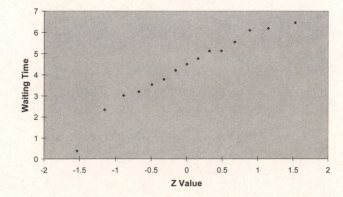

9.74   (d)   With the exception of one extreme point, the data are approximately normally
cont.   distributed.
        (e)   Based on the results of (a), the manager does not have enough evidence to make that
                statement.

9.76   (a) $H_0 : \mu \geq 0.35$ $H_1 : \mu < 0.35$

                Decision rule: Reject H_0 if $t_{STAT} < -1.690$ $d.f. = 35$

                Test statistic: $t_{STAT} = \dfrac{\overline{X} - \mu}{S/\sqrt{n}} = \dfrac{0.3167 - 0.35}{0.1357/\sqrt{36}} = -1.4735$

                Decision: Since $t_{STAT} > -1.690$, do not reject H_0. There is not enough evidence to
                conclude that the mean moisture content for Boston shingles is less than 0.35 pounds
                per 100 square feet.

        (b) p-value = 0.0748. If the population mean moisture content is in fact no less than
                0.35 pounds per 100 square feet, the probability of observing a sample of 36 shingles
                that will result in a sample mean moisture content of 0.3167 pounds per 100 square
                feet or less is .0748.

        (c) $H_0 : \mu \geq 0.35$ $H_1 : \mu < 0.35$

                Decision rule: Reject H_0 if $t_{STAT} < -1.6973$ $d.f. = 30$

                Test statistic: $t_{STAT} = \dfrac{\overline{X} - \mu}{S/\sqrt{n}} = \dfrac{0.2735 - 0.35}{0.1373/\sqrt{31}} = -3.1003$

                Decision: Since $t_{STAT} < -1.6973$, reject H_0. There is enough evidence to conclude
                that the mean moisture content for Vermont shingles is less than 0.35 pounds per 100
                square feet.

        (d) p-value = 0.0021. If the population mean moisture content is in fact no less than
                0.35 pounds per 100 square feet, the probability of observing a sample of 31 shingles
                that will result in a sample mean moisture content of 0.2735 pounds per 100 square
                feet or less is .0021.

        (e)   In order for the t test to be valid, the data are assumed to be independently drawn
                from a population that is normally distributed. Since the sample sizes are 36 and 31,
                respectively, which are considered quite large, the t distribution will provide a good
                approximation to the sampling distribution of the mean as long as the population
                distribution is not very skewed.

9.76   (f)
cont.

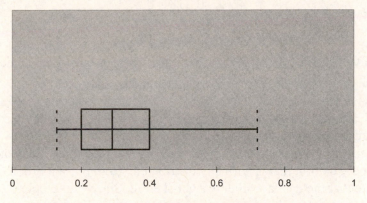

Box-and-whisker Plot (Vermont)

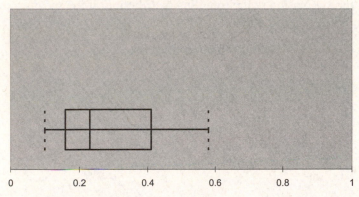

Both boxplots suggest that the data are skewed slightly to the right, more so for the Boston shingles. However, the very large sample sizes mean that the results of the *t* test are relatively insensitive to the departure from normality.

9.78   (a) $H_0 : \mu = 0.5$ $H_1 : \mu \neq 0.5$

Decision rule: Reject H_0 if $|t_{STAT}| > 1.9741$ *d.f.* = 169

Test statistic: $t_{STAT} = \dfrac{\overline{X} - \mu}{S / \sqrt{n}} = \dfrac{0.2641 - 0.5}{0.1424 / \sqrt{170}} = -21.6059$

Decision: Since $t_{STAT} < -1.9741$, reject H_0. There is enough evidence to conclude that the mean granule loss for Boston shingles is different from 0.5 grams.

(b)   *p*-value is virtually zero. If the population mean granule loss is in fact 0.5 grams, the probability of observing a sample of 170 shingles that will yield a test statistic more extreme than −21.6059 is virtually zero.

9.78   (c) $H_0 : \mu = 0.5$ $H_1 : \mu \neq 0.5$

cont.   Decision rule: Reject H_0 if $|t_{STAT}| > 1.977$ $d.f. = 139$

Test statistic: $t_{STAT} = \dfrac{\overline{X} - \mu}{S/\sqrt{n}} = \dfrac{0.218 - 0.5}{0.1227/\sqrt{140}} = -27.1940$

Decision: Since $t_{STAT} < -1.977$, reject H_0. There is enough evidence to conclude that the mean granule loss for Vermont shingles is different from 0.5 grams.

(d) p-value is virtually zero. The probability of observing a sample of 140 shingles that will yield a test statistic more extreme than -27.1940 is virtually zero if the population mean granule loss is in fact 0.5 grams.

(e)   In order for the t test to be valid, the data are assumed to be independently drawn from a population that is normally distributed. Both normal probability plots indicate that the data are slightly right-skewed. Since the sample sizes are 170 and 140, respectively, which are considered large enough, the t distribution will provide a good approximation to the sampling distribution of the mean even if the population is not normally distributed.

Normal Probability Plot

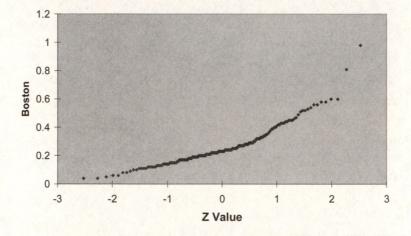

Normal Probability Plot

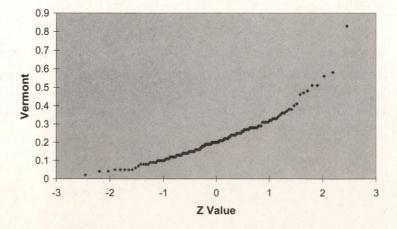

CHAPTER 10

OBJECTIVES
In this chapter, you learn how to use hypothesis testing for comparing the difference between:
- The means of two independent populations
- The means of two related populations
- The proportions of two independent populations
- The variances of two independent populations
- The means of more than two populations

OVERVIEW AND KEY CONCEPTS

Pooled-Variance t Test for Difference in Two Means $(\mu_1 - \mu_2)$

- **Assumptions:**
  - The two samples are randomly and independently drawn.
  - Both populations are normally distributed.
  - Population variances are unknown but assumed equal.
  - If the two populations are not normally distributed, large sample sizes are needed ($n_1 \geq 30$ and $n_2 \geq 30$).

- **Test statistic:**
  - $$t = \frac{\left(\bar{X}_1 - \bar{X}_2\right) - \left(\mu_1 - \mu_2\right)}{\sqrt{S_p^2\left(\dfrac{1}{n_1} + \dfrac{1}{n_2}\right)}}$$ with $n_1 + n_2 - 2$ degrees of freedom

    where $S_p^2 = \dfrac{\left(n_1 - 1\right)S_1^2 + \left(n_2 - 1\right)S_2^2}{\left(n_1 - 1\right) + \left(n_2 - 1\right)}$

  - The alternative hypothesis can be one-tail with a right-tail rejection region, one-tail with a left-tail rejection region or two-tail with both right-tail and left-tail rejection regions.

- **Confidence interval estimate:** Use the $100\left(1 - \alpha\right)\%$ confidence interval for the difference in two means.

  - $$\left(\bar{X}_1 - \bar{X}_2\right) \pm t_{\alpha/2, n_1 + n_2 - 2}\sqrt{S_p^2\left(\frac{1}{n_1} + \frac{1}{n_2}\right)}$$

Paired t Test for the Mean Difference (μ_D) with Unknown Variance

- **Assumptions:**
  - Both populations are normally distributed.
  - Observations are matched or paired.
  - Variance is unknown.
  - The test is robust to the normal distribution assumption as long as the sample size is not too small and the population is not highly skewed.

- **Test statistic:**

  - $t = \dfrac{\bar{D} - \mu_D}{\dfrac{S_D}{\sqrt{n}}}$ with $n-1$ degrees of freedom

    where $\bar{D} = \dfrac{\displaystyle\sum_{i=1}^{n} D_i}{n}$ and $S_D = \sqrt{\dfrac{\displaystyle\sum_{i=1}^{n}(D_i - \bar{D})^2}{n-1}}$

  - The alternative hypothesis can be one-tail with a right-tail rejection region, one-tail with a left-tail rejection region or two-tail with both right-tail and left-tail rejection regions.

- **Confidence interval estimate:** Use the $100(1-\alpha)\%$ confidence interval for the mean difference.

  - $\bar{D} \pm t_{\alpha/2,n-1} \dfrac{S_D}{\sqrt{n}}$

Z Test for Differences in Two Proportions $(\pi_1 - \pi_2)$

- **Assumptions:**
  - Samples are independently drawn.
  - Populations follow the binomial distribution.
  - Both sample sizes are large enough: $n_1 p_1 \geq 5$, $n_1(1-p_1) \geq 5$, $n_2 p_2 \geq 5$, $n_2(1-p_2) \geq 5$

- **Test statistic:**

  - $Z = \dfrac{(p_1 - p_2) - (\pi_1 - \pi_2)}{\sqrt{\bar{p}(1-\bar{p})\left(\dfrac{1}{n_1} + \dfrac{1}{n_2}\right)}}$ where $\bar{p} = \dfrac{X_1 + X_2}{n_1 + n_2}$ is the pooled estimate of the

    population proportion.

  - The alternative hypothesis can be one-tail with a right-tail rejection region, one-tail with a left-tail rejection region or two-tail with both right-tail and left-tail rejection regions.

- **Confidence interval estimate:** Use the $100(1-\alpha)\%$ confidence interval for the difference in two proportions.

  - $(p_1 - p_2) \pm Z_{\alpha/2} \sqrt{\dfrac{p_1(1-p_1)}{n_1} + \dfrac{p_2(1-p_2)}{n_2}}$

F Test for Difference in Two Variances $(\sigma_1^2 - \sigma_2^2)$

- **Assumptions:**
  - The two samples are randomly and independently drawn.
  - Both populations are normally distributed.
  - The test is not robust to violation of the normality assumption.

- **Test statistic:**

  - $F_{STAT} = \dfrac{S_1^2}{S_2^2}$ with $n_1 - 1$ numerator degrees of freedom and $n_2 - 1$ denominator degrees of freedom.

  - S_1^2 variance of sample 1 (the larger sample variance)

  - S_2^2 variance of sample 2 (the smaller sample variance)

  - The upper-tail critical value has $n_1 - 1$ numerator degrees of freedom and $n_2 - 1$ denominator degrees of freedom.

  - The alternative hypothesis can be one-tail with a right-tail rejection region, one-tail with a left-tail rejection region or two-tail with both right-tail and left-tail rejection regions.

General Experimental Setting

- Investigators have control over one or more independent variables called treatment variables or factors.
- Each treatment factor has two or more levels.
- Investigators observe the effects on the dependent variable, i.e., the response to the levels of the independent variable(s).
- **Experimental Design:** The plan used to test a hypothesis.

The Completely Randomized Design

- The experimental units (subjects) are assigned randomly to treatments.
- The subjects are assumed to be homogenous.
- There is only one factor or independent variable with two or more treatment levels.
- The completely randomized design will be analyzed by one-way ANOVA.

Some Important Identities in the Completely Randomized Design

- $SST = SSA + SSW$

- $SST = \displaystyle\sum_{j=1}^{c} \sum_{i=1}^{n_j} (X_{ij} - \bar{\bar{X}})^2$

- $SSA = \displaystyle\sum_{j=1}^{c} n_j (\bar{X}_j - \bar{\bar{X}})^2$

- $SSW = \displaystyle\sum_{j=1}^{c} \sum_{i=1}^{n_j} (X_{ij} - \bar{X}_j)^2$

- $MSA = \dfrac{SSA}{c-1}$

- $MSW = \dfrac{SSW}{n-c}$

    where n: the total number of observations in the sample

    c: the number of groups

    n_j: the number of observations in group j

    X_{ij}: the ith observation in group j

$$\overline{\overline{X}} = \frac{\sum_{j=1}^{c}\sum_{i=1}^{n_j} X_{ij}}{c} : \text{the overall or grand mean}$$

$\overline{X}_j$: the sample mean of group j

F Test for Differences in More than Two Means

- **Assumptions:**
  - Samples are randomly and independently drawn.
  - Populations are normally distributed. The *F* test is robust to violation of this assumption.
  - Populations have equal variances. The *F* test is less sensitive to violation of this assumption when samples are of equal size from each population.
- **The null and alternative hypotheses:**
  - $H_0 : \mu_1 = \mu_2 = \cdots = \mu_c$ There is no treatment effect
  - $H_1 :$ Not all μ_j are the same. There is some treatment effect.
- **Test statistic:**
  - $F = \dfrac{MSA}{MSW}$ with $(c-1)$ numerator degrees of freedom and $(n-c)$ denominator degrees of freedom
  - The *F* test always has the rejection region in the right tail.

One-way ANOVA Summary Table

Source of Variation	Degrees of Freedom	Sum of Squares	Mean Squares (Variance)	F Statistic
Among (Factor)	$c-1$	SSA	MSA = SSA/(c − 1)	MSA/MSW
Within (Error)	$n-c$	SSW	MSW = SSW/(n − c)	
Total	$n-1$	SST = SSA + SSW		

The Tukey-Kramer Procedure for the Completely Randomized Design

- A post hoc (a posteriori) procedure performed after rejection of the null hypothesis of equal means.
- Enables pair-wise comparison to see which pair of means is significantly different.
- **The Tukey-Kramer procedure:**

1. Compute the absolute difference between any pair of sample means $\left| \overline{X}_j - \overline{X}_{j'} \right|$

2. Compute the critical range for that pair of sample means using

$$\text{Critical Range} = Q_{U(c,n-c)}\sqrt{\frac{MSW}{2}\left(\frac{1}{n_j}+\frac{1}{n_{j'}}\right)}$$ where $Q_{U(c,n-c)}$ is the upper-tail critical

value from the Studentized range distribution with c numerator degrees of freedom and

$(n-c)$ denominator degrees of freedom, and n_j and $n_{j'}$ are the two sample sizes for the pair of samples.

3. The population means of a specific pair are declared significantly different if $\left| \overline{X}_j - \overline{X}_{j'} \right|$ is greater than the critical range.

Levene's Test for Homogeneity of Variance

- Used to test the assumption of equal group variances required in the F test for difference in more than two means.
- **The null and alternative hypotheses:**
  - $H_0 : \sigma_1^2 = \sigma_2^2 = \cdots = \sigma_c^2$ All group variances are the same.
  - H_1 : Not all σ_j^2 are the same. Not all group variances are the same.
- **The Levene's test procedure:**
  - For each observation in each group, obtain the absolute value of the difference between each observation and the median of the group.
  - Carry out a one-way analysis of variance on these absolute differences.

SOLUTIONS TO END OF SECTION
AND CHAPTER REVIEW EVEN PROBLEMS

10.2   (a) $S_p^2 = \dfrac{(n_1 - 1) \cdot S_1^2 + (n_2 - 1) \cdot S_2^2}{(n_1 - 1) + (n_2 - 1)} = \dfrac{(7) \cdot 4^2 + (14) \cdot 5^2}{7 + 14} = 22$

$t_{STAT} = \dfrac{(\bar{X}_1 - \bar{X}_2) - (\mu_1 - \mu_2)}{\sqrt{S_p^2 \left(\dfrac{1}{n_1} + \dfrac{1}{n_2} \right)}} = \dfrac{(42 - 34) - 0}{\sqrt{22 \left(\dfrac{1}{8} + \dfrac{1}{15} \right)}} = 3.8959$

(b) $d.f. = (n_1 - 1) + (n_2 - 1) = 7 + 14 = 21$

(c)   Decision rule: $d.f. = 21$. If $t_{STAT} > 2.5177$, reject H_0.

(d)   Decision: Since $t = 3.8959$ is greater than the critical bound of 2.5177, reject H_0.
There is enough evidence to conclude that the first population mean is larger than the second population mean.

10.4

$$(\bar{X}_1 - \bar{X}_2) \pm t \sqrt{S_p^2 \left(\dfrac{1}{n_1} + \dfrac{1}{n_2} \right)} = (42 - 34) \pm 2.0796 \sqrt{22 \left(\dfrac{1}{8} + \dfrac{1}{15} \right)}$$

$$3.7296 \leq \mu_1 - \mu_2 \leq 12.2704$$

10.6   PHStat output:

Data	
Hypothesized Difference	0
Level of Significance	0.01
Population 1 Sample	
Sample Size	5
Sample Mean	42
Sample Standard Deviation	4
Population 2 Sample	
Sample Size	4
Sample Mean	34
Sample Standard Deviation	5
Intermediate Calculations	
Population 1 Sample Degrees of Freedom	4
Population 2 Sample Degrees of Freedom	3
Total Degrees of Freedom	7
Pooled Variance	19.85714
Difference in Sample Means	8
t **Test Statistic**	2.676242
Upper-Tail Test	
Upper Critical Value	2.997949
p-**Value**	0.015856
Do not reject the null hypothesis	

10.6 H_0: $\mu_1 \leq \mu_2$ H_1: $\mu_1 > \mu_2$

cont.   Test statistic: $t_{STAT} = \dfrac{(\overline{X}_1 - \overline{X}_2) - (\mu_1 - \mu_2)}{\sqrt{S_p^2\left(\dfrac{1}{n_1} + \dfrac{1}{n_2}\right)}} = 2.6762$

Decision: Since $t_{STAT} = 2.6762$ is smaller than the upper critical bounds of 2.9979, do not reject H_0. There is not enough evidence of a difference in the means of the two populations.

10.8   (a)   PHStat output:

Pooled-Variance t Test for the Difference Between Two Means				Confidence Interval Estimate	
(assumes equal population variances)				for the Difference Between Two Means	
Data				**Confidence Interval Estimate**	
Hypothesized Difference	**0**			**for the Difference Between Two Means**	
Level of Significance	**0.05**			**Data**	
Population 1 Sample				Data	
Sample Size	59			**Confidence Level**	**95%**
Sample Mean	28.5				
Sample Standard Deviation	8.6			Intermediate Calculations	
Population 2 Sample				Degrees of Freedom	116
Sample Size	59			t Value	1.980625937
Sample Mean	19.7			Interval Half Width	3.01117417
Sample Standard Deviation	7.9				
				Confidence Interval	
Intermediate Calculations				**Interval Lower Limit**	**5.78882583**
Population 1 Sample Degrees of Freedom	58			**Interval Upper Limit**	**11.81117417**
Population 2 Sample Degrees of Freedom	58				
Total Degrees of Freedom	116				
Pooled Variance	68.185				
Difference in Sample Means	8.8				
t Test Statistic	5.788276				
Upper-Tail Test					
Upper Critical Value	1.658096				
p-Value	3.09E-08				
Reject the null hypothesis					

H_0: $\mu_1 \leq \mu_2$ H_1: $\mu_1 > \mu_2$

where population 1 = children who watched food ads
        population 2 = children who do not watch food ads

Decision rule: If p-value < 0.05, reject H_0.

Test statistic: $t_{STAT} = \dfrac{(\overline{X}_1 - \overline{X}_2) - (\mu_1 - \mu_2)}{\sqrt{S_p^2\left(\dfrac{1}{n_1} + \dfrac{1}{n_2}\right)}} = 5.7883$, $df = 116$

p-value is virtually 0.

Decision: Since the p-value is smaller than 0.05, reject H_0. There is enough evidence that the mean amount of Goldfish crackers eaten was significantly higher for the children who watched food ads.

10.8   (b) $\left(\bar{X}_1 - \bar{X}_2\right) \pm t_{\alpha/2}\sqrt{S_p^2\left(\dfrac{1}{n_1} + \dfrac{1}{n_2}\right)} = (28.5 - 19.7) \pm 1.9806\sqrt{68.185\left(\dfrac{1}{59} + \dfrac{1}{59}\right)}$

cont.

$$5.7888 \le \mu_1 - \mu_2 \le 11.8112$$

(c)   The results cannot be compared because (a) is a one-tail test and (b) is a confidence interval that is comparable only to the results of a two-tail test.

10.10   (a) H_0: $\mu_1 = \mu_2$ where Populations: 1 = Males, 2 = Females

Mean computer anxiety experienced by males and females is the same.

H_1: $\mu_1 \ne \mu_2$

Mean computer anxiety experienced by males and females is different.

Decision rule: $d.f. = 170$. If $t_{STAT} < -1.974$ or $t_{STAT} > 1.974$, reject H_0.
Test statistic:

$$S_p^2 = \frac{(n_1 - 1)\cdot S_1^2 + (n_2 - 1)\cdot S_2^2}{(n_1 - 1) + (n_2 - 1)} = \frac{(99)\cdot 13.35^2 + (71)\cdot 9.42^2}{99 + 71} = 140.8489$$

$$t_{STAT} = \frac{\left(\bar{X}_1 - \bar{X}_2\right) - \left(\mu_1 - \mu_2\right)}{\sqrt{S_p^2\left(\dfrac{1}{n_1} + \dfrac{1}{n_2}\right)}} = 1.859$$

Decision: Since $t_{STAT} = 1.859$ is between the lower and upper critical bound of -1.974 and 1.974, do not reject H_0. There is not enough evidence to conclude that the mean computer anxiety experienced by males and females is different.

(b)   Using PHStat, the p-value = 0.0648. The probability of obtaining a sample that yields a t test statistic farther away from 0 in either direction is 0.0648 if there is no difference in the mean computer anxiety experienced by males and females.

(c)   In order to use the pooled-variance t test, you need to assume that the populations are normally distributed with equal variances.

10.12 (a) $H_0 : \mu_1 = \mu_2$ Mean waiting times of Bank 1 and Bank 2 are the same.

$H_1 : \mu_1 \neq \mu_2$ Mean waiting times of Bank 1 and Bank 2 are different.

PHStat output:

t Test for Differences in Two Means	
Data	
Hypothesized Difference	0
Level of Significance	0.05
Population 1 Sample	
Sample Size	15
Sample Mean	4.286667
Sample Standard Deviation	1.637985
Population 2 Sample	
Sample Size	15
Sample Mean	7.114667
Sample Standard Deviation	2.082189
Intermediate Calculations	
Population 1 Sample Degrees of Freedom	14
Population 2 Sample Degrees of Freedom	14
Total Degrees of Freedom	28
Pooled Variance	3.509254
Difference in Sample Means	-2.828
t-Test Statistic	-4.13431
Two-Tailed Test	
Lower Critical Value	-2.04841
Upper Critical Value	2.048409
p-Value	0.000293
Reject the null hypothesis	

Since the *p*-value of 0.000293 is less than the 5% level of significance, reject the null hypothesis. There is enough evidence to conclude that the mean waiting time is different in the two banks.

(b)   *p*-value = 0.000293. The probability of obtaining a sample that will yield a *t* test statistic more extreme than –4.13431 is 0.000293 if, in fact, the mean waiting times of Bank 1 and Bank 2 are the same.

(c)   We need to assume that the two populations are normally distributed.

(d)
$$\left(\bar{X}_1 - \bar{X}_2 \right) + t \sqrt{ S_p^2 \left(\frac{1}{n_1} + \frac{1}{n_2} \right) } = \left(4.2867 - 7.1147 \right) + 2.0484 \sqrt{ 3.5093 \left(\frac{1}{15} + \frac{1}{15} \right) }$$

$$-4.2292 \leq \mu_1 - \mu_2 \leq -1.4268$$

You are 95% confident that the difference in mean waiting time between Bank 1 and Bank 2 is between –4.2292 and –1.4268 minutes.

10.14 (a) $H_0: \mu_1 = \mu_2$ $H_1: \mu_1 \neq \mu_2$
Excel output:

t-Test: Two-Sample Assuming Equal Variances	Untreated	Treated
Mean	165.0948	155.7314
Variance	41.6934168	62.4141
Observations	20	20
Pooled Variance	52.05375826	
Hypothesized Mean Difference	0	
df	38	
t Stat	4.104023608	
P(T<=t) one-tail	0.000103572	
t Critical one-tail	1.685953066	
P(T<=t) two-tail	0.000207144	
t Critical two-tail	2.024394234	

Decision: Since $t_{STAT} = 4.104$ is greater than the upper critical bound of 2.024, reject H_0. There is evidence that the mean surface hardness of untreated steel plates is different from the mean surface hardness of treated steel plates.

(b)   p-value = 0.0002. The probability of obtaining two samples with a mean difference of 9.3634 or more is 0.0002 if the mean surface hardness of untreated steel plates is not different from the mean surface hardness of treated steel plates

(c)   Since both sample sizes are smaller than 30, you need to assume that the population of hardness of both untreated and treated steel plates is normally distributed.

(d)

$$\left(\bar{X}_1 - \bar{X}_2\right) + t\sqrt{S_p^2\left(\frac{1}{n_1} + \frac{1}{n_2}\right)}$$

$$= \left(165.0948 - 155.7314\right) + 2.0244\sqrt{52.0538\left(\frac{1}{20} + \frac{1}{20}\right)}$$

$$4.7447 \leq \mu_1 - \mu_2 \leq 13.9821$$

You are 95% confident that the difference in the mean surface hardness between untreated and treated steel plates is between 4.7447 and 13.9821.

10.16 (a)   PHStat output:

Pooled-Variance *t* Test for the Difference Between Two Means				Confidence Interval Estimate	
(assumes equal population variances)				for the Difference Between Two Means	
Data					
Hypothesized Difference	0				
Level of Significance	0.05			**Data**	
Population 1 Sample				Confidence Level	95%
Sample Size	50				
Sample Mean	137			Intermediate Calculations	
Sample Standard Deviation	51.7			Degrees of Freedom	98
Population 2 Sample				*t* Value	1.984467404
Sample Size	50			Interval Half Width	23.88403599
Sample Mean	231				
Sample Standard Deviation	67.6			Confidence Interval	
				Interval Lower Limit	-117.884036
Intermediate Calculations				Interval Upper Limit	-70.11596401
Population 1 Sample Degrees of Freedom	49				
Population 2 Sample Degrees of Freedom	49				
Total Degrees of Freedom	98				
Pooled Variance	3621.325				
Difference in Sample Means	-94				
t Test Statistic	-7.81024				
Two-Tail Test					
Lower Critical Value	-1.98447				
Upper Critical Value	1.984467				
p-Value	6.43E-12				
Reject the null hypothesis					

H_0: $\mu_1 = \mu_2$ H_1: $\mu_1 \neq \mu_2$
where Populations: 1 = users under 12 years of age; 2 = users 13 to 17 years of age
Decision rule: $d.f. = 98$. If $t_{STAT} < -1.9845$ or $t_{STAT} > 1.9845$, reject H_0.
Test statistic:

$$t_{STAT} = \frac{(\bar{X}_1 - \bar{X}_2) - (\mu_1 - \mu_2)}{\sqrt{S_p^2\left(\frac{1}{n_1} + \frac{1}{n_2}\right)}} = \frac{(137 - 231) - 0}{\sqrt{3621.325\left(\frac{1}{50} + \frac{1}{50}\right)}} = -7.8102$$

Decision: Since $t_{STAT} = -7.8102$ is below the lower critical bound of -1.9845, reject H_0. There is enough evidence of a difference in the mean cellphone usage between cellphone users under 12 years of age and cellphone users 13 to 17 years of age.

(b)   You must assume that each of the two independent populations is normally distributed.

10.18 $d.f. = n - 1 = 20 - 1 = 19$, where n = number of pairs of data

10.20   Excel output:
t-Test: Paired Two Sample for Means

	A	B
Mean	24	25.55555556
Variance	7	3.527777778
Observations	9	9
Pearson Correlation	0.85524255	
Hypothesized Mean Difference	0	
Df	8	
t Stat	-3.277152121	
P(T<=t) one-tail	0.00561775	
t Critical one-tail	1.859548033	
P(T<=t) two-tail	0.011235501	
t Critical two-tail	2.306004133	

(a)   Define the difference in summated rating as the rating on brand A minus the rating on brand B.

$$H_0 : \mu_D = 0 \quad \text{vs.} \quad H_1 : \mu_D \neq 0$$

Test statistic: $t_{STAT} = \dfrac{\bar{D} - \mu_D}{\dfrac{S_D}{\sqrt{n}}} = -3.2772$, p-value $= 0.0112$

Decision: Since the p-value $= 0.0112 < 0.05$, reject H_0. There is enough evidence of a difference in the mean summated ratings between the two brands.

(b)   You must assume that the distribution of the differences between the two ratings is approximately normal.

(c) p-value is 0.0112. The probability of obtaining a mean difference in ratings that gives rise to a test statistic that deviates from 0 by 3.2772 or more in either direction is 0.0112 if there is no difference in the mean summated ratings between the two brands.

(d) $\bar{D} \pm t \dfrac{S_D}{\sqrt{n}} = -1.5556 \pm 2.3060 \dfrac{1.4240}{\sqrt{9}}$ $-2.6501 \leq \mu_D \leq -0.4610$

You are 95% confident that the mean difference in summated ratings between brand A and brand B is somewhere between -2.6501 and -0.4610.

10.22 (a) Define the difference in price as the price of Costco minus the price of store-brands.
PHStat output:
t-Test: Paired Two Sample for Means

	Costco	Store Brand
Mean	6.049	6.025
Variance	34.17881	28.75756111
Observations	10	10
Pearson Correlation	0.920273316	
Hypothesized Mean Difference	0	
df	9	
t Stat	0.033176962	
P(T<=t) one-tail	0.487128804	
t Critical one-tail	1.833112923	
P(T<=t) two-tail	0.974257608	
t Critical two-tail	2.262157158	

$H_0: \mu_{\bar{D}} = 0$ There is no difference between the mean price of Costco purchases and store brand purchases.

$H_1: \mu_{\bar{D}} \neq 0$ There is a difference between the mean price of Costco purchases and store brand purchases.

Decision rule: If $t_{STAT} < -2.2622$ or $t_{STAT} > 2.2622$, reject H_0.

Test statistic: $t_{STAT} = \dfrac{\bar{D} - \mu_D}{\dfrac{S_D}{\sqrt{n}}} = 0.0332$

Decision: Since $t_{STAT} = 0.0332$ falls between the lower and upper critical bound, do not reject H_0. There is not enough evidence to conclude that there is a difference between the mean price of Costco purchases and store brand purchases.

(b) You must assume that the distribution of the differences between the price of Costco and price of store band is approximately normal.

(c) $\bar{D} \pm t_{a/2}\dfrac{S_D}{\sqrt{n}} = 0.02 \pm 2.2622\left(\dfrac{2.2876}{\sqrt{10}}\right)$ $\$-1.61 \leq \mu_D \leq \$1.66$

You are 95% confident that the mean difference between the prices is between $-1.61 and $1.66.

(d) The results in (a) and (c) are the same. The hypothesized value of 0 for the difference between the mean price of Costco purchases and store brand purchases is not inside the 95% confidence interval and, hence, the null hypothesis that there is no difference between the mean price of Costco purchases and store brand purchases should not be rejected.

10.24   (a)   Define the difference in bone marrow microvessel density as the density before the transplant minus the density after the transplant and assume that the difference in density is normally distributed.

$$H_0 : \mu_D \leq 0 \quad \text{vs.} \quad H_1 : \mu_D > 0$$

Excel output:

t-Test: Paired Two Sample for Means

	Before	After
Mean	312.1429	226
Variance	15513.14	4971
Observations	7	7
Pearson Correlation	0.295069	
Hypothesized Mean Difference	0	
df	6	
t Stat	1.842455	
P(T<=t) one-tail	0.057493	
t Critical one-tail	1.943181	
P(T<=t) two-tail	0.114986	
t Critical two-tail	2.446914	

Test statistic: $t_{STAT} = \dfrac{\overline{D} - \mu_D}{\dfrac{S_D}{\sqrt{n}}} = 1.8425$

Decision: Since $t_{STAT} = 1.8425$ is less than the critical value of 1.943, do not reject H_0. There is not enough evidence to conclude that the mean bone marrow microvessel density is higher before the stem cell transplant than after the stem cell transplant.

(b) p-value = 0.0575. The probability of obtaining a mean difference in density that gives rise to a t test statistic that deviates from 0 by 1.8425 or more is .0575 if the mean density is not higher before the stem cell transplant than after the stem cell transplant.

(c) $\overline{D} \pm t \dfrac{S_D}{\sqrt{n}} = 86.1429 \pm 2.4469 \dfrac{123.7005}{\sqrt{7}}$ $-28.26 \leq \mu_D \leq 200.55$

You are 95% confident that the mean difference in bone marrow microvessel density before and after the stem cell transplant is somewhere between -28.26 and 200.55.

(d)   You must assume that the distribution of differences between the mean density of before and after stem cell transplant is approximately normal.

10.26 (a) H_0: $\mu_{\bar{D}} \geq 0$

H_1: $\mu_{\bar{D}} < 0$

Decision rule: $d.f. = 39$. If $t_{STAT} < -2.4258$, reject H_0.

Test statistic: $t_{STAT} = \dfrac{\overline{D} - \mu_D}{\dfrac{S_D}{\sqrt{n}}} = -9.372$

Decision: Since $t_{STAT} = -9.372$ is less than the critical bound of -2.4258, reject H_0. There is enough evidence to conclude that the mean strength is lower at two days than at seven days.

(b) You must assume that the distribution of the differences between the mean strength of the concrete is approximately normal.

(c) p-value is virtually 0. The probability of obtaining a mean difference that gives rise to a test statistic that is -9.372 or less when the null hypothesis is true is virtually 0.

10.28 (a) $p_1 = \dfrac{X_1}{n_1} = \dfrac{45}{100} = 0.45$, $p_2 = \dfrac{X_2}{n_2} = \dfrac{25}{50} = 0.50$,

and $\overline{p} = \dfrac{X_1 + X_2}{n_1 + n_2} = \dfrac{45 + 25}{100 + 50} = 0.467$

H_0: $\pi_1 = \pi_2$ H_1: $\pi_1 \neq \pi_2$

Decision rule: If $Z < -2.58$ or $Z > 2.58$, reject H_0.

$$Z_{STAT} = \dfrac{(p_1 - p_2) - (\pi_1 - \pi_2)}{\sqrt{\overline{p}(1-\overline{p})\left(\dfrac{1}{n_1} + \dfrac{1}{n_2}\right)}} = \dfrac{(0.45 - 0.50) - 0}{\sqrt{0.467(1 - 0.467)\left(\dfrac{1}{100} + \dfrac{1}{50}\right)}} = -0.58$$

Decision: Since $Z_{STAT} = -0.58$ is between the critical bound of ± 2.58, do not reject H_0. There is insufficient evidence to conclude that the population proportion differs for group 1 and group 2

(b) $(p_1 - p_2) \pm Z \sqrt{\left(\dfrac{p_1(1-p_1)}{n_1} + \dfrac{p_2(1-p_2)}{n_2}\right)} = -0.05 \pm 2.5758 \sqrt{\left(\dfrac{.45(.55)}{100} + \dfrac{.5(.5)}{50}\right)}$

$$-0.2727 \leq \pi_1 - \pi_2 \leq 0.1727$$

10.30   (a) H_0: $\pi_1 \leq \pi_2$ H_1: $\pi_1 > \pi_2$ Population 1 = 2009, 2 = 2008

   (b)   PHStat output:

Z Test for Differences in Two Proportions	
Data	
Hypothesized Difference	**0**
Level of Significance	**0.05**
Group 1	
Number of Items of Interest	39
Sample Size	100
Group 2	
Number of Items of Interest	7
Sample Size	100
Intermediate Calculations	
Group 1 Proportion	0.39
Group 2 Proportion	0.07
Difference in Two Proportions	0.32
Average Proportion	0.23
Z Test Statistic	**5.376822502**
Upper-Tail Test	
Upper Critical Value	**1.644853627**
p-Value	**3.79059E-08**
Reject the null hypothesis	

   (b)   Decision rule: If $Z_{STAT} > 1.6449$, reject H_0.
             Test statistic:

$$\bar{p} = \frac{X_1 + X_2}{n_1 + n_2} = \frac{39 + 7}{100 + 100} = 0.23$$

$$Z_{STAT} = \frac{(p_1 - p_2) - (\pi_1 - \pi_2)}{\bar{p}(1 - \bar{p})\left(\frac{1}{n_1} + \frac{1}{n_2}\right)} = \frac{(0.39 - 0.07) - 0}{\sqrt{0.23(1 - 0.23)\left(\frac{1}{100} + \frac{1}{100}\right)}} = 5.3768$$

             Decision: Since $Z_{STAT} = 5.3768$ is greater than the critical bound of 1.6449, reject H_0.
             There is sufficient evidence to conclude that it takes more time to be removed from
             an e-mail list than it used to.

   (c)   Yes, the result in (b) makes it appropriate to claim that it takes more time to be
             removed from an email list than it used to.

10.32 (a)   PHStat output:

Z Test for Differences in Two Proportions	
Data	
Hypothesized Difference	0
Level of Significance	0.01
Group 1	
Number of Items of Interest	707
Sample Size	1000
Group 2	
Number of Items of Interest	536
Sample Size	1000
Intermediate Calculations	
Group 1 Proportion	0.707
Group 2 Proportion	0.536
Difference in Two Proportions	0.171
Average Proportion	0.6215
Z Test Statistic	7.883654882
Two-Tail Test	
Lower Critical Value	-2.575829304
Upper Critical Value	2.575829304
p-Value	3.10862E-15
Reject the null hypothesis	

H_0: $\pi_1 = \pi_2$ H_1: $\pi_1 \neq \pi_2$

Population: 1 = users over 70 years of age; 2 = users 12 to 50 years of age.

Decision rule: If $|Z_{STAT}| > 2.5758$, reject H_0.

Test statistic:

$$Z_{STAT} = \frac{(p_1 - p_2) - (\pi_1 - \pi_2)}{\sqrt{\bar{p}(1-\bar{p})\left(\frac{1}{n_1} + \frac{1}{n_2}\right)}} = \frac{(0.707 - 0.536) - 0}{\sqrt{0.6215(1 - 0.6215)\left(\frac{1}{1000} + \frac{1}{1000}\right)}} = 7.8837$$

Decision: Since $Z_{STAT} = 7.8837$ is greater than the upper critical bound of 2.5758, reject H_0. There is sufficient evidence of a significant difference between the two age groups who believe that e-mail messages should be answered quickly.

(b)   p-value is virtually 0. The probability of obtaining a difference in proportions that gives rise to a test statistic that deviates from 0 by 7.8847 or more in either direction is virtually 0 if there is no difference between the two age groups who believe that e-mail messages should be answered quickly.

10.34   (a) $H_0: \pi_1 = \pi_2$ $H_1: \pi_1 \neq \pi_2$

Z Test for Differences in Two Proportions	
Data	
Hypothesized Difference	**0**
Level of Significance	**0.05**
Group 1	
Number of Items of Interest	**670**
Sample Size	**1000**
Group 2	
Number of Items of Interest	**510**
Sample Size	**1000**
Intermediate Calculations	
Group 1 Proportion	0.67
Group 2 Proportion	0.51
Difference in Two Proportions	0.16
Average Proportion	0.59
Z Test Statistic	**7.274230368**
Two-Tail Test	
Lower Critical Value	**-1.959963985**
Upper Critical Value	**1.959963985**
p-Value	**3.48388E-13**
Reject the null hypothesis	

Decision rule: If $\left| Z_{STAT} \right| > 1.96$, reject H_0.

Test statistic:

$$Z_{STAT} = \frac{(p_1 - p_2) - (\pi_1 - \pi_2)}{\bar{p}(1 - \bar{p})\left(\dfrac{1}{n_1} + \dfrac{1}{n_2} \right)} = 7.2742$$

Decision: Since $|Z_{STAT}| = 7.2742$ is greater than 1.96, reject H_0. There is sufficient evidence of a difference between adult Internet users and Internet users age 12 – 17 in the proportion who oppose ads.

  (b)   p-value is virtually 0. The probability of obtaining a difference in proportions that gives rise to a test statistic that deviates from 0 by 7.2742 or more in either direction is virtually 0 if there is not a difference between adult Internet users and Internet users age 12 – 17 in the proportion who oppose ads.

10.36   (a) $\alpha = 0.10$, $n_1 = 16$, $n_2 = 21$, $F_{0.10/2} = 2.20$

     (b) $\alpha = 0.05$, $n_1 = 16$, $n_2 = 21$, $F_{0.05/2} = 2.57$

     (c) $\alpha = 0.01$, $n_1 = 16$, $n_2 = 21$, $F_{0.01/2} = 3.50$

10.38 (a)   You place the larger sample variance $S^2 = 25$ in the numerator of F_{STAT}.

     (b) $F_{STAT} = \dfrac{S_1^{\,2}}{S_2^{\,2}} = \dfrac{25}{16} = 1.5625$

10.40 The degrees of freedom for the numerator is 24 and for the denominator is 24.

10.42 Since $F_{STAT} = 1.2109$ is lower than $F_{0.05/2} = 2.27$, do not reject H_0. There is not enough evidence to conclude that the two population variances are different.

10.44 (a) H_0: $\sigma_1^{\,2} = \sigma_2^{\,2}$ The population variances are the same.
           H_1: $\sigma_1^{\,2} \neq \sigma_2^{\,2}$ The population variances are different.
           Decision rule: If $F_{STAT} > 3.18$ reject H_0.

           Test statistic: $F_{STAT} = \dfrac{S_1^{\,2}}{S_2^{\,2}} = \dfrac{47.3}{36.4} = 1.2995$

           Decision: Since $F_{STAT} = 1.2995$ is less than $F_{\alpha/2} = 3.18$, do not reject H_0. There is not enough evidence to conclude that the two population variances are different.

     (b) H_0: $\sigma_1^{\,2} \leq \sigma_2^{\,2}$ The variance for population 1 is less than or equal to the variance for population 2.
           H_1: $\sigma_1^{\,2} > \sigma_2^{\,2}$ The variance for population 1 is greater than the variance for population 2.
           Decision rule: If $F_{STAT} > 2.62$, reject H_0.

           Test statistic: $F_{STAT} = \dfrac{S_1^{\,2}}{S_2^{\,2}} = \dfrac{47.3}{36.4} = 1.2995$

           Decision: Since $F_{STAT} = 1.2995$ is less than the critical bound of $F_\alpha = 2.62$, do not reject H_0. There is not enough evidence to conclude that the variance for population 1 is greater than the variance for population 2.

10.46 (a) H_0: $\sigma_1^{\,2} = \sigma_2^{\,2}$ The population variances are the same.
           H_1: $\sigma_1^{\,2} \neq \sigma_2^{\,2}$ The population variances are different.
           Decision rule: If $F_{STAT} > 1.556$, reject H_0.

           Test statistic: $F_{STAT} = \dfrac{S_1^{\,2}}{S_2^{\,2}} = \dfrac{13.35^2}{9.42^2} = 2.008$

           Decision: Since $F_{STAT} = 2.008$ is greater than $F_{\alpha/2} = 1.556$, reject H_0. There is enough evidence to conclude that the two population variances are different.

     (b) p-value $= 0.0022$. The probability of obtaining a sample that yields a test statistic more extreme than 2.008 is 0.0022 if the null hypothesis that there is no difference in the two population variances is true.

     (c)   The test assumes that the two populations are both normally distributed.

     (d)   Based on (a) and (b), a separate variance t test should be used.

10.48   (a)   PHStat output:

F Test for Differences in Two Variances	
Data	
Level of Significance	0.05
Larger-Variance Sample	
Sample Size	16
Sample Standard Deviation	111.9952
Smaller-Variance Sample	
Sample Size	29
Sample Standard Deviation	49.20676
Intermediate Calculations	
F Test Statistic	5.180229
Population 1 Sample Degrees of Freedom	15
Population 2 Sample Degrees of Freedom	28
Two-Tail Test	
Upper Critical Value	2.343847
p-Value	0.000181
Reject the null hypothesis	

H_0: $\sigma_1^{\,2} = \sigma_2^{\,2}$ The population variances are the same.

H_1: $\sigma_1^{\,2} \neq \sigma_2^{\,2}$ The population variances are different.

Decision rule: If $F_{STAT} > 2.3438$, reject H_0.

Test statistic: $F_{STAT} = \dfrac{S_1^{\,2}}{S_2^{\,2}} = 5.1803$

Decision: Since $F_{STAT} = 5.1803$ is greater than the upper critical value of 2.3438, reject H_0. There is enough evidence of a difference in the variability of the battery life between the two types of digital cameras.

(b)   *p*-value = 0.0002. The probability of obtaining a sample that yields a test statistic greater than 5.1803 is 0.0002 if the null hypothesis that there is no difference in the two population variances is true.

(c)   The test assumes that the two populations are both normally distributed.

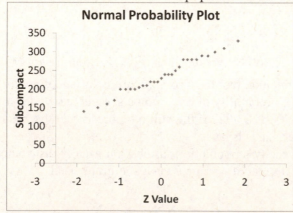

10.48   (c)
cont.

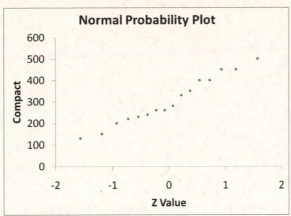

The probability plots do not indicate any departure from the normality assumption.

(d)   Based on (a), a separate-variance t test should be used.

10.50   PHStat output:

F Test for Differences in Two Variances	
Data	
Level of Significance	0.05
Larger-Variance Sample	
Sample Size	9
Sample Standard Deviation	0.681909
Smaller-Variance Sample	
Sample Size	9
Sample Standard Deviation	0.496516
Intermediate Calculations	
F Test Statistic	1.886197
Population 1 Sample Degrees of Freedom	8
Population 2 Sample Degrees of Freedom	8
Two-Tail Test	
Upper Critical Value	4.43326
p-Value	0.388157
Do not reject the null hypothesis	

H_0: $\sigma_1^2 = \sigma_2^2$ The population variances are the same.

H_1: $\sigma_1^2 \neq \sigma_2^2$ The population variances are different.

Decision rule: If $F_{STAT} > 4.4333$, reject H_0.

Test statistic: $F_{STAT} = \dfrac{S_1^2}{S_2^2} = 1.8862$

Decision: Since $F_{STAT} = 1.8862$ is smaller than the upper critical value of 4.4333, do not reject H_0. There is not enough evidence of a difference in the variance of the yield of five-year CDs in the two cities.

10.52 (a) $SSW = SST - SSA = 210 - 60 = 150$

(b) $MSA = \dfrac{SSA}{c-1} = \dfrac{60}{5-1} = 15$

(c) $MSW = \dfrac{SSW}{n-c} = \dfrac{150}{35-5} = 5$

(d) $F_{STAT} = \dfrac{MSA}{MSW} = \dfrac{15}{5} = 3$

10.54 (a) $df\ A = c - 1 = 3 - 1 = 2$
(b) $df\ W = n - c = 21 - 3 = 18$
(c) $df\ T = n - 1 = 21 - 1 = 20$

10.56 (a)   Decision rule: If $F_{STAT} > 2.95$, reject H_0.
(b)   Since $F_{STAT} = 4$ is greater than the critical bound of 2.95, reject H_0.
(c)   There are $c = 4$ degrees of freedom in the numerator and $n - c = 32 - 4 = 28$ degrees of freedom in the denominator. The table does not have 28 degrees of freedom in the denominator so use the next larger critical value, $Q_\alpha = 3.90$.

(d)   To perform the Tukey-Kramer procedure, the critical range is

$$Q_\alpha \sqrt{\frac{MSW}{2}\left(\frac{1}{n_j} + \frac{1}{n_j}\right)} = 3.90\sqrt{\frac{20}{2}\left(\frac{1}{8} + \frac{1}{8}\right)} = 6.166.$$

10.58 (a) $H_0: \mu_A = \mu_B = \mu_C = \mu_D$ H_1: At least one mean is different.

$$MSA = \frac{SSA}{c-1} = \frac{1986.475}{3} = 662.1583$$

$$MSW = \frac{SSW}{n-c} = \frac{495.5}{36} = 13.7639$$

$$F_{STAT} = \frac{MSA}{MSW} = \frac{662.1583}{13.7639} = 48.1084$$

$$F_{\alpha,c-1,n-c} = F_{0.05,3,36} = 2.8663$$

Minitab output:

One-way ANOVA: KROGER, GLAD, HEFTY, TUFFSTUFF

```
Source   DF      SS      MS      F       P
Factor    3   1986.5   662.2   48.11   0.000
Error    36    495.5    13.8
Total    39   2482.0

S = 3.710    R-Sq = 80.04%    R-Sq(adj) = 78.37%

                                    Individual 95% CIs For Mean Based on
                                    Pooled StDev
Level        N    Mean   StDev   --+---------+---------+---------+------
KROGER      10   35.400  4.326                              (---*---)
GLAD        10   36.300  4.423                               (---*--)
HEFTY       10   34.900  2.923                             (---*---)
TUFFSTUFF   10   19.300  2.869    (---*---)
                                 --+---------+---------+---------+------
                                 18.0      24.0      30.0      36.0
```

10.58 (a)   Excel output:
cont.

ANOVA

Source of Variation	SS	df	MS	F	P-value	F crit
Between Groups	1986.475	3	662.1583	48.10838	1.12E-12	2.866265
Within Groups	495.5	36	13.76389			
Total	2481.975	39				

Since the p-value is essentially zero and $F = 48.1084 > 2.8663$, you can reject H_0. There is sufficient evidence to conclude there is a difference in the mean strength of the four brands of trash bags.

(b)

Minitab output:

```
Pooled StDev = 3.710
Tukey 95% Simultaneous Confidence Intervals
All Pairwise Comparisons
Individual confidence level = 98.93%

KROGER subtracted from:

                Lower    Center    Upper    ---------+---------+---------+---------+-
GLAD           -3.570     0.900    5.370                      (---*--)
HEFTY          -4.970    -0.500    3.970                      (---*--)
TUFFSTUFF     -20.570   -16.100  -11.630     (---*--)
                                            ---------+---------+---------+---------+-
                                                -12        0        12       24


GLAD subtracted from:

                Lower    Center    Upper    ---------+---------+---------+---------+-
HEFTY          -5.870    -1.400    3.070                      (---*---)
TUFFSTUFF     -21.470   -17.000  -12.530     (---*---)
                                            ---------+---------+---------+---------+-
                                                -12        0        12       24


HEFTY subtracted from:

                Lower    Center    Upper    ---------+---------+---------+---------+-
TUFFSTUFF     -20.070   -15.600  -11.130     (---*---)
                                            ---------+---------+---------+---------+-
                                                -12        0        12       24
```

10.58   (b)   PHStat output:
cont.

Tukey Kramer Multiple Comparisons

Group	Sample Mean	Sample Size	Comparison	Absolute Difference	Std. Error of Difference	Critical Range	Results
1	35.4	10	Group 1 to Group 2	0.9	1.17319601	4.446	Means are not different
2	36.3	10	Group 1 to Group 3	0.5	1.17319601	4.446	Means are not different
3	34.9	10	Group 1 to Group 4	16.1	1.17319601	4.446	Means are different
4	19.3	10	Group 2 to Group 3	1.4	1.17319601	4.446	Means are not different
			Group 2 to Group 4	17	1.17319601	4.446	Means are different
Other Data			Group 3 to Group 4	15.6	1.17319601	4.446	Means are different
Level of significance	0.05						
Numerator d.f.	4						
Denominator d.f.	36						
MSW	13.76389						
Q Statistic	3.79						

$Q_\alpha = 3.79$

(b)   Critical range $= Q_\alpha \sqrt{\dfrac{MSW}{2}\left(\dfrac{1}{n_j}+\dfrac{1}{n_{j'}}\right)} = 3.79\sqrt{\dfrac{13.7639}{2}\left(\dfrac{1}{10}+\dfrac{1}{10}\right)} = 4.446$

From the Tukey-Kramer procedure, there is a difference in mean strength between Kroger and Tuffstuff, Glad and Tuffstuff, and Hefty and Tuffstuff.

(c) $H_0: \sigma_A^2 = \sigma_B^2 = \sigma_C^2 = \sigma_D^2$ H_1: At least one variance is different.

ANOVA output for Levene's test for homogeneity of variance:

ANOVA

Source of Variation	SS	df	MS	F	P-value	F crit
Between Groups	24.075	3	8.025	1.457619	0.242358	2.866265
Within Groups	198.2	36	5.505556			
Total	222.275	39				

$$MSA = \frac{SSA}{c-1} = \frac{24.075}{3} = 8.025$$

$$MSW = \frac{SSW}{n-c} = \frac{198.2}{36} = 5.5056$$

$$F_{STAT} = \frac{MSA}{MSW} = \frac{8.025}{5.5056} = 1.4576$$

$$F_{\alpha,c-1,n-c} = F_{0.05,3,36} = 2.8663$$

Since the p-value $= 0.2423 > 0.05$ and $F_{STAT} = 1.458 < 2.866$, do not reject H_0. There is not sufficient evidence to conclude that the variances in strength among the four brands of trash bags are different.

10.58   (d)   From the results obtained in (a) and (b), Tuffstuff has the lowest mean strength and
cont.   should be avoided.

10.60   (a) H_0: $\mu_A = \mu_B = \mu_C = \mu_D = \mu_E$ H_1: At least one mean is different.

Minitab output:

One-way ANOVA: Rating versus Ad
```
Source  DF      SS      MS      F       P
Ad       4   377.87   94.47   12.56   0.000
Error   25   188.00    7.52
Total   29   565.87
S = 2.742    R-Sq = 66.78%    R-Sq(adj) = 61.46%
```

PHStat output:

ANOVA

Source of Variation	SS	df	MS	F	P-value	F crit
Between Groups	377.8667	4	94.46667	12.56206	9.74E-06	2.758711
Within Groups	188	25	7.52			
Total	565.8667	29				

Since the p-value is essentially zero, reject H_0. There is evidence of a difference in
the mean rating of the five advertisements.

(b)   Minitab output:
```
Tukey 95% Simultaneous Confidence Intervals
All Pairwise Comparisons among Levels of Ad

Individual confidence level = 99.29%

Ad = 1 subtracted from:

Ad     Lower   Center   Upper   ---------+---------+---------+---------+
2     -4.979  -0.333   4.313                  (------*-----)
3    -11.313  -6.667  -2.021        (-----*------)
4    -13.646  -9.000  -4.354   (------*------)
5     -7.313  -2.667   1.979             (-----*------)
                               ---------+---------+---------+---------+
                                    -7.0      0.0       7.0      14.0


Ad = 2 subtracted from:

Ad     Lower   Center   Upper   ---------+---------+---------+---------+
3    -10.979  -6.333  -1.687       (-------*------)
4    -13.313  -8.667  -4.021   (-------*-----)
5     -6.979  -2.333   2.313          (------*-----)
                               ---------+---------+---------+---------+
                                    -7.0      0.0       7.0      14.0


Ad = 3 subtracted from:

Ad   Lower   Center  Upper   ---------+---------+---------+---------+
4   -6.979  -2.333   2.313        (------*-----)
5   -0.646   4.000   8.646             (------*-----)
                             ---------+---------+---------+---------+
                                  -7.0      0.0       7.0      14.0


Ad = 4 subtracted from:

Ad  Lower   Center   Upper   ---------+---------+---------+---------+
5   1.687   6.333   10.979                 (------*------)
                             ---------+---------+---------+---------+
                                  -7.0      0.0       7.0      14.0
```

10.60   (b)
cont.

Tukey Kramer Multiple Comparisons

Group	Sample Mean	Sample Size	Comparison	Absolute Difference	Std. Error of Difference	Critical Range	Results
1	18	6	Group 1 to Group 2	0.333333	1.11952371	4.668	Means are not different
2	17.66667	6	Group 1 to Group 3	6.666667	1.11952371	4.668	Means are different
3	11.33333	6	Group 1 to Group 4	9	1.11952371	4.668	Means are different
4	9	6	Group 1 to Group 5	2.666667	1.11952371	4.668	Means are not different
5	15.33333	6	Group 2 to Group 3	6.333333	1.11952371	4.668	Means are different
			Group 2 to Group 4	8.666667	1.11952371	4.668	Means are different
Other Data			Group 2 to Group 5	2.333333	1.11952371	4.668	Means are not different
Level of significance	0.05		Group 3 to Group 4	2.333333	1.11952371	4.668	Means are not different
Numerator d.f.	5		Group 3 to Group 5	4	1.11952371	4.668	Means are not different
Denominator d.f.	25		Group 4 to Group 5	6.333333	1.11952371	4.668	Means are different
MSW	7.52						
Q Statistic	4.17						

There is a difference in the mean rating between advertisement A and C, between A and D, between B and C, between B and D and between D and E.

(c) H_0: $\sigma_A^2 = \sigma_B^2 = \sigma_C^2 = \sigma_D^2 = \sigma_E^2$ H_1: At least one variance is different.

ANOVA output for Levene's test for homogeneity of variance:
ANOVA

Source of Variation	SS	df	MS	F	P-value	F crit
Between Groups	14.13333	4	3.533333	1.927273	0.137107	2.758711
Within Groups	45.83333	25	1.833333			
Total	59.96667	29				

Since the p-value $= 0.137 > 0.05$, do not reject H_0. There is not enough evidence to conclude there is a difference in the variation in rating among the five advertisements.

(d)   There is no significant difference between advertisements A and B, and they have the highest mean rating among the five and should be used. There is no significant difference between advertisements C and D, and they are among the lowest in mean rating and should be avoided.

10.62 (a) H_0: $\mu_1 = \mu_2 = \mu_3$ H_1: At least one mean is different.

Population: 1 = new method 1, 2 = new method 2, 3 = standard

Decision rule: df: 2, 15. If p-value < 0.05, reject H_0.

Excel output:

ANOVA

Source of Variation	SS	df	MS	F	P-value	F crit
Between Groups	6.333333	2	3.166667	0.081662	0.92199	3.68232
Within Groups	581.6667	15	38.77778			
Total	588	17				

Test statistic: $F_{STAT} = 0.0817$ p-value $= 0.92199$

Decision: Since p-value > 0.05, do not reject H_0. There is not enough evidence of a difference in the yield among the methods used in the cleansing steps.

(b) Since you do not reject H_0, it is not appropriate to perform a Tukey-Kramer procedure to decide which methods differ in mean yields.

(c) H_0: $\sigma_1^2 = \sigma_2^2 = \sigma_3^2$ H_1: At least one variance is different.

Excel output for Levene's test for homogeneity of variance:

ANOVA

Source of Variation	SS	df	MS	F	P-value	F crit
Between Groups	8.333333	2	4.166667	0.172811	0.842948	3.68232
Within Groups	361.6667	15	24.11111			
Total	370	17				

Since the p-value $= 0.8429 > 0.05$, do not reject H_0. There is not enough evidence to conclude there is a significant difference in the variation in yields among the different methods.

(d) Since there is no evidence of a difference in the variation between the methods, the validity of the conclusion reached in (a) is not affected.

10.64 (a) To test at the 0.05 level of significance whether there is any evidence of a difference in the mean distance traveled by the golf balls differing in design, you conduct an F test:

H_0: $\mu_1 = \mu_2 = \mu_3 = \mu_4$ H_1: At least one mean is different.

Decision rule: df: 3, 36. If $F_{STAT} > 2.866$, reject H_0.

Minitab output:

One-way ANOVA: Distance versus Design

```
Source  DF     SS     MS     F       P
Design   3  2991.0  997.0  53.03  0.000
Error   36   676.8   18.8
Total   39  3667.8

S = 4.336   R-Sq = 81.55%   R-Sq(adj) = 80.01%
```

10.64   (a)   PHStat output:
cont.

ANOVA

Source of Variation	SS	df	MS	F	P-value	F crit
Between Groups	2990.99	3	996.9966	53.02982	2.73E-13	2.866265
Within Groups	676.8244	36	18.80068			
Total	3667.814	39				

Since $F_{STAT} = 53.03$ is greater than the critical bound of 2.866, reject H_0. There is enough evidence to conclude that there is significant difference in the mean distance traveled by the golf balls differing in design.

Note: The critical bound of F is obtained using Excel. The critical bound of F using the Table in the text with 3 numerator and 30 denominator degrees of freedom is 2.92.

(b)   Minitab output:

```
Tukey 95% Simultaneous Confidence Intervals
All Pairwise Comparisons among Levels of Design
Individual confidence level = 98.93%

Design = 1 subtracted from:
Design  Lower  Center  Upper   ---+---------+---------+---------+----
--
2        6.678  11.902  17.126                        (---*---)
3       14.750  19.974  25.198                           (----*---)
4       16.784  22.008  27.232                             (---*----)
                                ---+---------+---------+---------+----
--
                                -12        0        12       24

Design = 2 subtracted from:
Design  Lower  Center  Upper   ---+---------+---------+---------+-----
-
3        2.848   8.072  13.296                    (----*---)
4        4.882  10.106  15.330                      (---*----)
                                ---+---------+---------+---------+-----
-
                                -12        0        12       24

Design = 3 subtracted from:
Design  Lower  Center  Upper   ---+---------+---------+---------+-----
-
4       -3.190   2.034   7.258              (----*---)
                                ---+---------+---------+---------+-----
-
                                -12        0        12       24
```

10.64 (b)
cont.

To determine which of the means are significantly different from one another, you use the Tukey-Kramer procedure to establish the critical range:

$Q_\alpha = 3.79$

critical range $= Q_\alpha \sqrt{\dfrac{MSW}{2}\left(\dfrac{1}{n_j}+\dfrac{1}{n_j}\right)} = 3.79\sqrt{\dfrac{18.8007}{2}\left(\dfrac{1}{10}+\dfrac{1}{10}\right)} = 5.1967$

PHStat output:

Tukey Kramer Multiple Comparisons					
Group	Sample Mean	Sample Size	Comparison	Absolute Difference	Results
1	206.614	10	Group 1 to Group 2	11.902	Means are different
2	218.516	10	Group 1 to Group 3	19.974	Means are different
3	226.588	10	Group 1 to Group 4	22.008	Means are different
4	228.622	10	Group 2 to Group 3	8.072	Means are different
			Group 2 to Group 4	10.106	Means are different
MSW	18.800677		Group 3 to Group 4	2.034	Means are not different

At 5% level of significance, there is enough evidence to conclude that mean traveling distances between all pairs of designs are different with the only exception of the pair between design 3 and design 4.

(c)   The assumptions needed in (a) are (i) the samples are randomly and independently drawn, (ii) populations are normally distributed, and (iii) populations have equal variances.

(d)   To test at the 0.05 level of significance whether the variation within the groups is similar for all groups, you conduct a Levene's test for homogeneity of variance:

H_0: $\sigma_1^2 = \sigma_2^2 = \sigma_3^2 = \sigma_4^2$ H_1: At least one variance is different.

Minitab output:

Test for Equal Variances: Distance versus Design
Levene's Test (Any Continuous Distribution)
Test statistic = 2.09, p-value = 0.118

PHStat output:
ANOVA

Source of Variation	SS	df	MS	F	P-value	F crit
Between Groups	40.63675	3	13.54558	2.093228	0.118276	2.866265
Within Groups	232.9613	36	6.471147			
Total	273.598	39				

Since p-value = 0.1183 > 0.05, do not reject the null hypothesis. There is not enough evidence to conclude that there is any difference in the variation of the distance traveled by the golf balls differing in design.

(e)   In order to produce golf balls with the farthest traveling distance, either design 3 or 4 can be used.

10.66   The pooled variance t-test should be used when the populations are approximately normally distributed and the variances of the two populations are equal.

10.68   With independent populations, the outcomes in one population do not depend on the outcomes in the second population. With two related populations, either repeated measurements are obtained on the same set of items or individuals, or items or individuals are paired or matched according to some characteristic.

10.70   They are two different ways of investigating the concern of whether there is significant difference between the means of two independent populations. If the hypothesized value of 0 for the difference in two population means is not in the confidence interval, then, assuming a two-tailed test is used, the null hypothesis of no difference in the two population means can be rejected.

10.72   The among-groups variance MSA represents variation among the means of the different groups. The within groups-variance MSW measures variation within each group.

10.74   If the populations are approximately normally distributed and the variances of the groups are approximately equal, you select the one-way ANOVA F test to examine possible differences among the means of c independent populations.

10.76   (a)   **Stores that priced the small coffee at \$0.59**
              $H_0 : \mu \le 900$ vs. $H_1 : \mu > 900$

t Test for Hypothesis of the Mean	
Data	
Null Hypothesis $\mu=$	900
Level of Significance	0.05
Sample Size	15
Sample Mean	964
Sample Standard Deviation	88
Intermediate Calculations	
Standard Error of the Mean	22.7215023
Degrees of Freedom	14
t **Test Statistic**	2.816715161
Upper-Tail Test	
Upper Critical Value	1.761310115
p-**Value**	0.006860614
Reject the null hypothesis	

Since the p-value = 0.0069 < 0.05, reject H_0. There is evidence that reducing the price of a small coffee to \$0.59 increases per store average daily customer count.

10.76 (a)
cont.

Stores that priced the small coffee at $0.79

$H_0 : \mu \leq 900$ vs. $H_1 : \mu > 900$

t Test for Hypothesis of the Mean	
Data	
Null Hypothesis μ=	900
Level of Significance	0.05
Sample Size	15
Sample Mean	941
Sample Standard Deviation	76
Intermediate Calculations	
Standard Error of the Mean	19.62311562
Degrees of Freedom	14
t Test Statistic	2.089372595
Upper-Tail Test	
Upper Critical Value	1.761310115
p-Value	0.027705582
Reject the null hypothesis	

Since the *p*-value = 0.0277 < 0.05, reject H_0. There is evidence that reducing the price of a small coffee to $0.79 increases per store average daily customer count.

(b) $H_0 : \sigma_1^2 = \sigma_2^2$ vs. $H_1 : \sigma_1^2 \neq \sigma_2^2$

F Test for Differences in Two Variances	
Data	
Level of Significance	0.05
Larger-Variance Sample	
Sample Size	15
Sample Standard Deviation	88
Smaller-Variance Sample	
Sample Size	15
Sample Standard Deviation	76
Intermediate Calculations	
F Test Statistic	1.34072
Population 1 Sample Degrees of Freedom	14
Population 2 Sample Degrees of Freedom	14
Two-Tail Test	
Upper Critical Value	2.978588
p-Value	0.590648
Do not reject the null hypothesis	

Since the *p*-value = 0.5906 > 0.05, do not reject H_0. There is not enough evidence that the two variances are different. Hence, a pooled-variance *t* test is appropriate.

10.76   (a) $H_0 : \mu_1 = \mu_2$ vs. $H_1 : \mu_1 \neq \mu_2$
cont.

Pooled-Variance *t* Test for the Difference Between Two Means	
(assumes equal population variances)	
Data	
Hypothesized Difference	**0**
Level of Significance	**0.05**
Population 1 Sample	
Sample Size	**15**
Sample Mean	**964**
Sample Standard Deviation	**88**
Population 2 Sample	
Sample Size	**15**
Sample Mean	**941**
Sample Standard Deviation	**76**
Intermediate Calculations	
Population 1 Sample Degrees of Freedom	14
Population 2 Sample Degrees of Freedom	14
Total Degrees of Freedom	28
Pooled Variance	6760
Difference in Sample Means	23
t Test Statistic	0.766099
Two-Tail Test	
Lower Critical Value	-2.04841
Upper Critical Value	2.048407
p-Value	0.450028
Do not reject the null hypothesis	

Since the *p*-value = 0.45 > 0.05, do not reject H_0. There is not enough evidence of a difference in the per store daily customer count between stores in which a small coffee was priced at $0.59 and stores in which a small coffee was priced at $0.79 for a 12 ounce cup.

(c)   Since there is not enough evidence of a difference in the per store mean daily customer count between stores in which a small coffee was priced at $0.59 and stores in which a small coffee was priced at $0.79 for a 12 ounce cup, you will recommend that a small coffee should be priced at $0.79 since that will bring in more profit per cup.

10.78   (a) H_0: $\sigma_1^2 = \sigma_2^2$ The population variances are the same.   1 = Green Belt

H_1: $\sigma_1^2 \neq \sigma_2^2$ The population variances are different.   2 = Master Black Belt

PHStat output:

F Test for Differences in Two Variances	
Data	
Level of Significance	0.05
Larger-Variance Sample	
Sample Size	15
Sample Standard Deviation	29000
Smaller-Variance Sample	
Sample Size	86
Sample Standard Deviation	26466
Intermediate Calculations	
F Test Statistic	1.200658
Population 1 Sample Degrees of Freedom	14
Population 2 Sample Degrees of Freedom	85
Two-Tail Test	
Upper Critical Value	2.024394
p-Value	0.580431
Do not reject the null hypothesis	

Decision rule: If $F_{STAT} > 2.0244$, reject H_0.

Test statistic: $F_{STAT} = \dfrac{S_1^2}{S_2^2} = 1.2007$

Decision: Since $F_{STAT} = 1.2007$ is smaller than the upper critical bound of 2.0244, do not reject H_0. There is not enough evidence of any difference in the variability of salaries between Black Belts and Green Belts.

(b)   Since there is not enough evidence of any difference in the variability of salaries between Master Black Belts and Green Belts, a pooled-variance t test should be used.

10.78   (c) H_0: $\mu_1 = \mu_2$ H_1: $\mu_1 \neq \mu_2$ 1 = Green Belt, 2 = Master Black Belt
cont.

Pooled-Variance *t* Test for the Difference Between Two Means	
(assumes equal population variances)	
Data	
Hypothesized Difference	0
Level of Significance	0.05
Population 1 Sample	
Sample Size	15
Sample Mean	75917
Sample Standard Deviation	29000
Population 2 Sample	
Sample Size	86
Sample Mean	113276
Sample Standard Deviation	26466
Intermediate Calculations	
Population 1 Sample Degrees of Freedom	14
Population 2 Sample Degrees of Freedom	85
Total Degrees of Freedom	99
Pooled Variance	7.2E+08
Difference in Sample Means	-37359
t Test Statistic	-4.97468
Lower-Tail Test	
Lower Critical Value	-1.66039
***p*-Value**	1.38E-06
Reject the null hypothesis	

Decision rule: If $t_{STAT} < -1.6604$, reject H_0.

Decision: Since $t_{STAT} = -4.9747$ is less than -1.6604, reject H_0. There is enough evidence that the mean salary of Green Belts is less than the mean salary of Master Black Belts.

10.80   (a) H_0: $\sigma_1^2 = \sigma_2^2$ The population variances are the same.
H_1: $\sigma_1^2 \neq \sigma_2^2$ The population variances are different.
Decision rule: If $F_{STAT} > 1.6275$, reject H_0.

Test statistic: $F_{STAT} = \dfrac{S_1^2}{S_2^2} = \dfrac{(6.29)^2}{(1.32)^2} = 22.7067$

Decision: Since $F_{STAT} = 22.7067$ is greater than the upper critical bound of 1.6275, reject H_0. There is enough evidence to conclude that there is a difference between the variances in age of students at the Western school and at the Eastern school.

(b)   Since there is a difference between the variances in age of students at the Western school and at the Eastern school, schools should take that into account when designing their curriculum to accommodate the larger variance in age of students in the state university in the "Western" U.S.

(c)   It is more appropriate to use a separate-variance t test.

(d) H_0: $\sigma_1^2 = \sigma_2^2$ The population variances are the same.
H_1: $\sigma_1^2 \neq \sigma_2^2$ The population variances are different.
Decision rule: If $F_{STAT} > 1.6275$, reject H_0.

Test statistic: $F_{STAT} = \dfrac{S_1^2}{S_2^2} = \dfrac{(2.4)^2}{(2.1)^2} = 1.3061$

Decision: Since $F_{STAT} = 1.3061$ is lower than the upper critical bound 1.6275, do not reject H_0. There is not enough evidence to conclude that there is a difference between the variances in years of spreadsheet usage of students at the Western school and at the Eastern school.

(e) H_0: $\mu_1 = \mu_2$ H_1: $\mu_1 \neq \mu_2$
Decision rule: $d.f. = 226$. If $t_{STAT} < -2.5978$ or $t_{STAT} > 2.5978$, reject H_0.
Test statistic:

$$S_p^2 = \frac{(n_1 - 1)S_1^2 + (n_2 - 1)S_2^2}{(n_1 - 1) + (n_2 - 1)} = \frac{(93 - 1)(2.4)^2 + (135 - 1)(2.1)^2}{(93 - 1) + (135 - 1)} = 4.9596$$

$$t_{STAT} = \frac{(\bar{X}_1 - \bar{X}_2) - (\mu_1 - \mu_2)}{\sqrt{S_p^2 \left(\dfrac{1}{n_1} + \dfrac{1}{n_2}\right)}} = \frac{(2.6 - 4) - 0}{\sqrt{4.9596 \left(\dfrac{1}{93} + \dfrac{1}{135}\right)}} = -4.6650$$

Decision: Since $t_{STAT} = -4.6650$ is smaller than the lower critical bound of -2.5978, reject H_0. There is enough evidence of a difference in the mean years of spreadsheet usage of students at the Western school and at the Eastern school.

10.82   (a) H_0: $\mu \le 10$ minutes. Introductory computer students required no more than a mean of 10 minutes to write and run a program in Visual Basic.

H_1: $\mu > 10$ minutes. Introductory computer students required more than a mean of 10 minutes to write and run a program in Visual Basic.

Decision rule: $d.f. = 8$. If $t_{STAT} > 1.8595$, reject H_0.

Test statistic: $t_{STAT} = \dfrac{\overline{X} - \mu}{S/\sqrt{n}} = \dfrac{12 - 10}{1.8028/\sqrt{9}} = 3.3282$

Decision: Since $t_{STAT} = 3.3282$ is greater than the critical bound of 1.8595, reject H_0. There is enough evidence to conclude that the introductory computer students required more than a mean of 10 minutes to write and run a program in Visual Basic.

(b) H_0: $\mu \le 10$ minutes. Introductory computer students required no more than a mean of 10 minutes to write and run a program in Visual Basic.

H_1: $\mu > 10$ minutes. Introductory computer students required more than a mean of 10 minutes to write and run a program in Visual Basic.

Decision rule: $d.f. = 8$. If $t_{STAT} > 1.8595$, reject H_0.

Test statistic: $t_{STAT} = \dfrac{\overline{X} - \mu}{S/\sqrt{n}} = \dfrac{16 - 10}{13.2004/\sqrt{9}} = 1.3636$

Decision: Since $t_{STAT} = 1.3636$ is less than the critical bound of 1.8595, do not reject H_0. There is not enough evidence to conclude that the introductory computer students required more than a mean of 10 minutes to write and run a program in Visual Basic.

(c)   Although the mean time necessary to complete the assignment increased from 12 to 16 minutes as a result of the increase in one data value, the standard deviation went from 1.8 to 13.2, which in turn brought the t-value down because of the increased denominator.

(d) H_0: $\sigma_{IC}^2 = \sigma_{CS}^2$ H_1: $\sigma_{IC}^2 \ne \sigma_{CS}^2$

Decision rule: If $F_{STAT} > 3.8549$, reject H_0.

Test statistic: $F_{STAT} = \dfrac{S_{IC}^2}{S_{CS}^2} = \dfrac{2.0^2}{1.8028^2} = 1.2307$

Decision: Since $F_{STAT} = 1.2307$ is lower than the critical bound 3.8549, do not reject H_0. There is not enough evidence to conclude that the population variances are different for the Introduction to Computers students and computer majors. Hence, the pooled variance t test is a valid test to see whether computer majors can write a Visual Basic program (on average) in less time than introductory students, assuming that the distributions of the time needed to write a Visual Basic program for both the Introduction to Computers students and the computer majors are approximately normal.

10. 82   (d) H_0: $\mu_{IC} \leq \mu_{CS}$ The mean amount of time needed by Introduction to Computers
cont.   students is not greater than the mean amount of time needed by computer majors.
         H_1: $\mu_{IC} > \mu_{CS}$ The mean amount of time needed by Introduction to Computers
                  students is greater than the mean amount of time needed by computer majors.

PHStat output:

Pooled-Variance *t* Test for the Difference Between Two Means	
(assumes equal population variances)	
Data	
Hypothesized Difference	0
Level of Significance	0.05
Population 1 Sample	
Sample Size	9
Sample Mean	12
Sample Standard Deviation	1.802776
Population 2 Sample	
Sample Size	11
Sample Mean	8.5
Sample Standard Deviation	2
Intermediate Calculations	
Population 1 Sample Degrees of Freedom	8
Population 2 Sample Degrees of Freedom	10
Total Degrees of Freedom	18
Pooled Variance	3.666667
Difference in Sample Means	3.5
t Test Statistic	4.066633
Upper-Tail Test	
Upper Critical Value	1.734064
***p*-Value**	0.000362
Reject the null hypothesis	

Decision rule: *d.f.* = 18. If $t_{STAT} > 1.7341$, reject H_0.

Test statistic:

$$S_p^{\,2} = \frac{(n_{IC}-1)\cdot S_{IC}^{\,2} + (n_{CS}-1)\cdot S_{CS}^{\,2}}{(n_{IC}-1)+(n_{CS}-1)} = \frac{9\cdot 1.8028^2 + 11\cdot 2.0^2}{8+10} = 3.6667$$

$$t_{STAT} = \frac{(\overline{X}_{IC} - \overline{X}_{CS}) - (\mu_{IC} - \mu_{CS})}{\sqrt{S_p^{\,2}\left(\dfrac{1}{n_{IC}} + \dfrac{1}{n_{CS}}\right)}} = \frac{12.0 - 8.5}{\sqrt{3.6667\left(\dfrac{1}{9} + \dfrac{1}{11}\right)}} = 4.0666$$

Decision: Since $t_{STAT} = 4.0666$ is greater than 1.7341, reject H_0. There is enough evidence to support a conclusion that the mean time is higher for Introduction to Computers students than for computer majors.

10. 82 (e)   *p*-value = 0.0052. If the true population mean amount of time needed for
cont.   Introduction to Computer students to write a Visual Basic program is indeed no more
               than 10 minutes, the probability for observing a sample mean greater than the 12
               minutes in the current sample is 0.0052, which means it will be a quite unlikely
               event. Hence, at a 95% level of confidence, you can conclude that the population
               mean amount of time needed for Introduction to Computer students to write a Visual
               Basic program is more than 10 minutes.
               As illustrated in part (d) in which there is not enough evidence to conclude that the
               population variances are different for the Introduction to Computers students and
               computer majors, the pooled variance *t* test performed is a valid test to determine
               whether computer majors can write a Visual Basic program in less time than in
               introductory students, assuming that the distributions of the time needed to write a
               Visual Basic program for both the Introduction to Computers students and the
               computer majors are approximately normal.

10.84

	Manufacturer A	Manufacturer B
Minimum	684	819
First Quartile	852	943
Median	916.5	1015.5
Third Quartile	972	1096
Interquartile Range	120	153
Maximum	1093	1230
Range	409	411
Mean	909.65	1018.35
Median	916.5	1015.5
Mode	926	1077
Standard Deviation	94.3052	96.9014
Sample Variance	8893.4641	9389.8744
Count	40	40

Box-and-whisker Plot

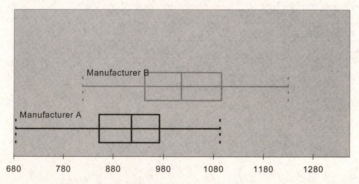

From the box plot and the summary statistics, both data seem to have come
from rather symmetrical distributions that are quite normally distributed.

The following *F* test for any evidence of difference between two population variances
suggests that there is insufficient evidence to conclude that the two population variances are
significantly different at 5% level of significance.

10. 84
cont.   PHStat output:

F Test for Differences in Two Variances	
Data	
Level of Significance	0.05
Larger-Variance Sample	
Sample Size	40
Sample Standard Deviation	96.90136
Smaller-Variance Sample	
Sample Size	40
Sample Standard Deviation	94.30516
Intermediate Calculations	
F Test Statistic	1.055817
Population 1 Sample Degrees of Freedom	39
Population 2 Sample Degrees of Freedom	39
Two-Tail Test	
Upper Critical Value	1.890719
p-Value	0.866186
Do not reject the null hypothesis	

Since both data are drawn from independent populations, the most appropriate test for any difference in the life of the bulbs between the two manufacturers is the pooled-variance *t* test.
PHStat output:

Pooled Variance t Test for Differences in Two Means	
Data	
Hypothesized Difference	0
Level of Significance	0.05
Population 1 Sample	
Sample Size	40
Sample Mean	909.65
Sample Standard Deviation	94.3052
Population 2 Sample	
Sample Size	40
Sample Mean	1018.35
Sample Standard Deviation	96.9014
Intermediate Calculations	
Population 1 Sample Degrees of Freedom	39
Population 2 Sample Degrees of Freedom	39
Total Degrees of Freedom	78
Pooled Variance	9141.676
Difference in Sample Means	-108.7
t-Test Statistic	-5.08431
Two-Tailed Test	
Lower Critical Value	-1.99085
Upper Critical Value	1.990848
p-Value	2.47E-06
Reject the null hypothesis	

Since the p-value is virtually zero, at the 5% level of significance, there is sufficient evidence to reject the null hypothesis of no difference in the mean life of the bulbs between the two manufacturers. You can conclude that there is significant difference in the mean life of the bulbs between the two manufacturers.

Based on the above analyses, you can conclude that there is significant difference in the life of the bulbs between the two manufacturers.

10.86 $H_0: \pi_1 = \pi_2$ $H_1: \pi_1 \neq \pi_2$ where Populations: 1 = Boys, 2 = Girls

Decision rule: If p-value < 0.05, reject H_0.

Played a game on a video game system:

PHStat output:

Z Test for Differences in Two Proportions	
Data	
Hypothesized Difference	0
Level of Significance	0.05
Group 1	
Number of Items of Interest	498
Sample Size	600
Group 2	
Number of Items of Interest	243
Sample Size	623
Intermediate Calculations	
Group 1 Proportion	0.83
Group 2 Proportion	0.390048154
Difference in Two Proportions	0.439951846
Average Proportion	0.605887163
Z Test Statistic	15.74002429
Two-Tail Test	
Lower Critical Value	-1.959963985
Upper Critical Value	1.959963985
p-Value	0
Reject the null hypothesis	

Test statistic: $Z_{STAT} = \dfrac{(p_1 - p_2) - (\pi_1 - \pi_2)}{\sqrt{\bar{p}(1 - \bar{p})\left(\dfrac{1}{n_1} + \dfrac{1}{n_2}\right)}} = 15.74$, p-value is virtually 0.

Decision: Since the p-value is smaller than 0.05, reject H_0. There is enough evidence that there is a difference between boys and girls in the proportion who played a game on a video game system.

10.86   **Read a book for fun:**
cont.   PHStat output:
f

Z Test for Differences in Two Proportions	
Data	
Hypothesized Difference	**0**
Level of Significance	**0.05**
Group 1	
Number of Items of Interest	**276**
Sample Size	**600**
Group 2	
Number of Items of Interest	**324**
Sample Size	**623**
Intermediate Calculations	
Group 1 Proportion	0.46
Group 2 Proportion	0.520064205
Difference in Two Proportions	-0.060064205
Average Proportion	0.490596893
Z Test Statistic	**-2.10053037**
Two-Tail Test	
Lower Critical Value	**-1.959963985**
Upper Critical Value	**1.959963985**
p-Value	**0.035682212**
Reject the null hypothesis	

Test statistic: $Z_{STAT} = \dfrac{(p_1 - p_2) - (\pi_1 - \pi_2)}{\sqrt{\bar{p}(1-\bar{p})\left(\dfrac{1}{n_1} + \dfrac{1}{n_2}\right)}} = -2.1005$, p-value $= 0.0357$

Decision: Since the p-value $= 0.0357$ is smaller than 0.05, reject H_0. There is enough evidence that there is a difference between boys and girls in the proportion who read a book for fun.

10.86   **Gave product advice to parents:**
cont.   PHstat output:

Z Test for Differences in Two Proportions	
Data	
Hypothesized Difference	0
Level of Significance	0.05
Group 1	
Number of Items of Interest	186
Sample Size	600
Group 2	
Number of Items of Interest	181
Sample Size	623
Intermediate Calculations	
Group 1 Proportion	0.31
Group 2 Proportion	0.290529695
Difference in Two Proportions	0.019470305
Average Proportion	0.300081766
Z Test Statistic	**0.742738125**
Two-Tail Test	
Lower Critical Value	-1.959963985
Upper Critical Value	1.959963985
p-Value	0.457640243
Do not reject the null hypothesis	

Test statistic: $Z_{STAT} = \dfrac{(p_1 - p_2) - (\pi_1 - \pi_2)}{\sqrt{\bar{p}(1-\bar{p})\left(\dfrac{1}{n_1} + \dfrac{1}{n_2}\right)}} = 0.7427$, *p*-value = 0.4576

Decision: Since the *p*-value = 0.4576 is larger than 0.05, do not reject H_0. There is not enough evidence that there is a difference between boys and girls in the proportion who gave product advice to parents.

10.86 **Shopped at a mall:**
cont. PHStat output:

Z Test for Differences in Two Proportions	
Data	
Hypothesized Difference	0
Level of Significance	0.05
Group 1	
Number of Items of Interest	144
Sample Size	600
Group 2	
Number of Items of Interest	262
Sample Size	623
Intermediate Calculations	
Group 1 Proportion	0.24
Group 2 Proportion	0.420545746
Difference in Two Proportions	-0.180545746
Average Proportion	0.331970564
Z Test Statistic	**-6.702643071**
Two-Tail Test	
Lower Critical Value	-1.959963985
Upper Critical Value	1.959963985
p-Value	2.04683E-11
Reject the null hypothesis	

Test statistic: $Z_{STAT} = \dfrac{(p_1 - p_2) - (\pi_1 - \pi_2)}{\sqrt{\bar{p}(1-\bar{p})\left(\dfrac{1}{n_1} + \dfrac{1}{n_2}\right)}}$ = -6.7026, *p*-value is virtually 0.

Decision: Since the *p*-value is smaller than 0.05, reject H_0. There is enough evidence that there is a difference between boys and girls in the proportion who shopped at a mall.

10.88

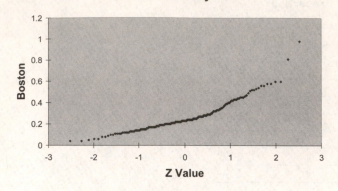

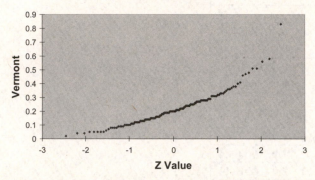

The normal probability plots suggest that the two populations are not normally distributed so an F test is inappropriate for testing the difference in two variances. The sample variances for Boston and Vermont shingles are 0.0203 and 0.015, respectively, which are not very different. It appears that a pooled-variance t test is appropriate for testing the difference in means.

$H_0 : \mu_B = \mu_V$ Mean granule loss of Boston and Vermont shingles are the same.

$H_1 : \mu_B \neq \mu_V$ Mean granule loss of Boston and Vermont shingles are different.

Excel output:
t-Test: Two-Sample Assuming Equal Variances

	Boston	Vermont
Mean	0.264059	0.218
Variance	0.020273	0.015055
Observations	170	140
Pooled Variance	0.017918	
Hypothesized Mean Difference	0	
Df	308	
t Stat	3.014921	
P(T<=t) one-tail	0.001392	
t Critical one-tail	1.649817	
P(T<=t) two-tail	0.002784	
t Critical two-tail	1.967696	

Since the p-value = 0.0028 is less than the 5% level of significance, reject H_0. There is sufficient evidence to conclude that there is a difference in the mean granule loss of Boston and Vermont shingles.

10.90 **3-year return:**

Populations: 1 = Foreign Large-Cap Blend, 2 = Small-Cap Blend, 3 = Mid-Cap Blend, 4 = Large-Cap Blend, 5 = Diversified Emerging Markets

H_0: $\sigma_1^2 = \sigma_2^2 = \cdots = \sigma_5^2$ The population variances are the same.

H_1: Not all σ_i^2 are the same.

ANOVA output for Levene's test for homogeneity of variance:

ANOVA

Source of Variation	SS	df	MS	F	P-value	F crit
Between Groups	3.9852	4	0.9963	0.414783	0.797068	2.578739
Within Groups	108.089	45	2.401978			
Total	112.0742	49				

Since the p-value is greater than 0.05, do not reject H_0. There is not enough evidence that the variances are different. Hence, the appropriate test for the difference in the means is the one-way ANOVA.

H_0: $\mu_1^2 = \mu_2^2 = \cdots = \mu_5^2$ The population means are the same.

H_1: Not all μ_i are the same.

ANOVA output:

ANOVA

Source of Variation	SS	df	MS	F	P-value	F crit
Between Groups	280.9188	4	70.2297	14.31273	1.3E-07	2.578739
Within Groups	220.806	45	4.9068			
Total	501.7248	49				

Since p-value < 0.05, reject H_0. There is enough evidence that the means are not all the same.

Tukey-Kramer Multiple Comparison output:

10.90   PHStat output of the Tukey-Kramer multiple comparisons:
cont.

Tukey Kramer Multiple Comparisons								
Group	Sample Mean	Sample Size		Comparison	Absolute Difference	Std. Error of Difference	Critical Range	Results
1	-1.64	10		Group 1 to Group 2	2.01	0.700485546	2.83	Means are not different
2	0.37	10		Group 1 to Group 3	2.42	0.700485546	2.83	Means are not different
3	0.78	10		Group 1 to Group 4	2.34	0.700485546	2.83	Means are not different
4	0.7	10		Group 1 to Group 5	7.19	0.700485546	2.83	Means are different
5	5.55	10		Group 2 to Group 3	0.41	0.700485546	2.83	Means are not different
				Group 2 to Group 4	0.33	0.700485546	2.83	Means are not different
Other Data				Group 2 to Group 5	5.18	0.700485546	2.83	Means are different
Level of significance	0.05			Group 3 to Group 4	0.08	0.700485546	2.83	Means are not different
Numerator d.f.	5			Group 3 to Group 5	4.77	0.700485546	2.83	Means are different
Denominator d.f.	45			Group 4 to Group 5	4.85	0.700485546	2.83	Means are different
MSW	4.9068							
Q Statistic	4.04							

At the 5% level of significance, there is sufficient evidence that the mean three-year returns of group 5 (diversified emerging markets) is lower than the other categories. All other comparisons are not significant.

5-year return:

Populations: 1 = Foreign Large-Cap Blend, 2 = Small-Cap Blend, 3 = Mid-Cap Blend, 4 = Large-Cap Blend, 5 = Diversified Emerging Markets

H_0: $\sigma_1^2 = \sigma_2^2 = \cdots = \sigma_5^2$ The population variances are the same.

H_1: Not all σ_i^2 are the same.

ANOVA output for Levene's test for homogeneity of variance:
ANOVA

Source of Variation	SS	df	MS	F	P-value	F crit
Between Groups	4.5112	4	1.1278	0.967073	0.434889	2.578739
Within Groups	52.479	45	1.1662			
Total	56.9902	49				

Since the p-value is greater than 0.05, do not reject H_0. There is not enough evidence that the variances are different. Hence, the appropriate test for the difference in the means is the one-way ANOVA.

10.90 H_0: $\mu_1^2 = \mu_2^2 = \cdots = \mu_5^2$ The population means are the same.

cont. H_1: Not all μ_i are the same.

ANOVA output:

ANOVA

Source of Variation	SS	df	MS	F	P-value	F crit
Between Groups	821.6968	4	205.4242	62.4512	8.61E-18	2.578739
Within Groups	148.021	45	3.289356			
Total	969.7178	49				

Since p-value < 0.05, reject H_0. There is enough evidence that the means are not all the same.

PHStat output of the Tukey-Kramer multiple comparisons:

Tukey Kramer Multiple Comparisons

Group	Sample Mean	Sample Size		Comparison	Absolute Difference	Std. Error of Difference	Critical Range	Results
1	7.5	10		Group 1 to Group 2	1.19	0.573529036	2.3171	Means are not different
2	6.31	10		Group 1 to Group 3	1.8	0.573529036	2.3171	Means are not different
3	5.7	10		Group 1 to Group 4	2.68	0.573529036	2.3171	Means are different
4	4.82	10		Group 1 to Group 5	8.48	0.573529036	2.3171	Means are different
5	15.98	10		Group 2 to Group 3	0.61	0.573529036	2.3171	Means are not different
				Group 2 to Group 4	1.49	0.573529036	2.3171	Means are not different
Other Data				Group 2 to Group 5	9.67	0.573529036	2.3171	Means are different
Level of significance	0.05			Group 3 to Group 4	0.88	0.573529036	2.3171	Means are not different
Numerator d.f.	5			Group 3 to Group 5	10.28	0.573529036	2.3171	Means are different
Denominator d.f.	45			Group 4 to Group 5	11.16	0.573529036	2.3171	Means are different
MSW	3.289356							
Q Statistic	4.04							

At the 5% level of significance, there is sufficient evidence that the mean five-year returns of the diversified emerging market funds (group 5) is significantly higher than the others. Also, the mean five-year returns of the large-cap blend funds (group 4) is significantly lower than that of the foreign large-cap funds (group 1).

10.90   **10-year return:**
cont.   Populations: 1 = Foreign Large-Cap Blend, 2 = Small-Cap Blend, 3 = Mid-Cap Blend, 4 = Large-Cap Blend, 5 = Diversified Emerging Markets

H_0: $\sigma_1^2 = \sigma_2^2 = \cdots = \sigma_5^2$ The population variances are the same.

H_1: Not all σ_i^2 are the same.

ANOVA output for Levene's test for homogeneity of variance:
ANOVA

Source of Variation	SS	df	MS	F	P-value	F crit
Between Groups	8.6632	4	2.1658	0.78538	0.540725	2.578739
Within Groups	124.094	45	2.757644			
Total	132.7572	49				

Since the *p*-value is greater than 0.05, do not reject H_0. There is not enough evidence that the variances are different. Hence, the appropriate test for the difference in the means is the one-way ANOVA.

H_0: $\mu_1^2 = \mu_2^2 = \cdots = \mu_5^2$ The population means are the same.

H_1: Not all μ_i are the same.

ANOVA output:
ANOVA

Source of Variation	SS	df	MS	F	P-value	F crit
Between Groups	327.3848	4	81.8462	11.99512	1.02E-06	2.578739
Within Groups	307.048	45	6.823289			
Total	634.4328	49				

Since *p*-value < 0.05, reject H_0. There is enough evidence that the means are not all the same.

PHStat output of the Tukey-Kramer multiple comparisons:

Tukey Kramer Multiple Comparisons

Group	Sample Mean	Sample Size		Comparison	Absolute Difference	Std. Error of Difference	Critical Range	Results
1	4.67	10		Group 1 to Group 2	4.02	0.826032014	3.3372	Means are different
2	8.69	10		Group 1 to Group 3	3.17	0.826032014	3.3372	Means are not different
3	7.84	10		Group 1 to Group 4	0.72	0.826032014	3.3372	Means are not different
4	5.39	10		Group 1 to Group 5	7.18	0.826032014	3.3372	Means are different
5	11.85	10		Group 2 to Group 3	0.85	0.826032014	3.3372	Means are not different
				Group 2 to Group 4	3.3	0.826032014	3.3372	Means are not different
Other Data				Group 2 to Group 5	3.16	0.826032014	3.3372	Means are not different
Level of significance	0.05			Group 3 to Group 4	2.45	0.826032014	3.3372	Means are not different
Numerator d.f.	5			Group 3 to Group 5	4.01	0.826032014	3.3372	Means are different
Denominator d.f.	45			Group 4 to Group 5	6.46	0.826032014	3.3372	Means are different
MSW	6.823289							
Q Statistic	4.04							

10.90
cont.

At the 5% level of significance, there is sufficient evidence that the mean 10-year returns of the diversified emerging market funds (group 5) is significantly higher than the others except the small-cap blend (group 2). Also the mean 10-year returns of the foreign large-cap blend (group 1) is significantly lower than that of the small-cap blend (group 2).

Expense ratio:

Populations: 1 = Foreign Large-Cap Blend, 2 = Small-Cap Blend, 3 = Mid-Cap Blend, 4 = Large-Cap Blend, 5 = Diversified Emerging Markets

H_0: $\sigma_1^2 = \sigma_2^2 = \cdots = \sigma_5^2$ The population variances are the same.

H_1: Not all σ_i^2 are the same.

ANOVA output for Levene's test for homogeneity of variance:
ANOVA

Source of Variation	SS	df	MS	F	P-value	F crit
Between Groups	0.171428	4	0.042857	0.590022	0.671568	2.578739
Within Groups	3.26863	45	0.072636			
Total	3.440058	49				

Since the p-value is greater than 0.05, do not reject H_0. There is not enough evidence that the variances are different. Hence, the appropriate test for the difference in the means is the one-way ANOVA.

H_0: $\mu_1^2 = \mu_2^2 = \cdots = \mu_5^2$ The population means are the same.

H_1: Not all μ_i are the same.

ANOVA output:
ANOVA

Source of Variation	SS	df	MS	F	P-value	F crit
Between Groups	2.309468	4	0.577367	4.106873	0.006387	2.578739
Within Groups	6.32635	45	0.140586			
Total	8.635818	49				

Since p-value < 0.05, reject H_0. There is enough evidence that the means are not all the same.

10.90   PHStat output of the Tukey-Kramer multiple comparisons: cont.

Tukey Kramer Multiple Comparisons					Absolute	Std. Error	Critical	
Group	Sample Mean	Sample Size	Comparison		Difference	of Difference	Range	Results
1	0.923	10	Group 1 to Group 2		0.321	0.11856878	0.479017871	Means are not different
2	1.244	10	Group 1 to Group 3		0.162	0.11856878	0.479017871	Means are not different
3	1.085	10	Group 1 to Group 4		0.19	0.11856878	0.479017871	Means are not different
4	1.113	10	Group 1 to Group 5		0.641	0.11856878	0.479017871	Means are different
5	1.564	10	Group 2 to Group 3		0.159	0.11856878	0.479017871	Means are not different
			Group 2 to Group 4		0.131	0.11856878	0.479017871	Means are not different
Other Data			Group 2 to Group 5		0.32	0.11856878	0.479017871	Means are not different
Level of significance	0.05		Group 3 to Group 4		0.028	0.11856878	0.479017871	Means are not different
Numerator d.f.	5		Group 3 to Group 5		0.479	0.11856878	0.479017871	Means are not different
Denominator d.f.	45		Group 4 to Group 5		0.451	0.11856878	0.479017871	Means are not different
MSW	0.140585556							
Q Statistic	4.04							

At the 5% level of significance, there is sufficient evidence that the mean expense ratio of the diversified emerging market funds (group 5) is significantly higher than the foreign large-cap funds (group 1).

10.94   **2009 return:**

Populations: 1 = short term corporate, 2 = intermediate government

H_0: $\sigma_1^2 = \sigma_2^2$ The population variances are the same.

H_1: $\sigma_1^2 \neq \sigma_2^2$ The population variances are different.

PHstat output:

F Test for Differences in Two Variances	
Data	
Level of Significance	0.05
Larger-Variance Sample	
Sample Size	97
Sample Standard Deviation	5.686734
Smaller-Variance Sample	
Sample Size	87
Sample Standard Deviation	5.360641
Intermediate Calculations	
F Test Statistic	1.125362
Population 1 Sample Degrees of Freedom	96
Population 2 Sample Degrees of Freedom	86
Two-Tail Test	
Upper Critical Value	1.516688
p-Value	0.577999
Do not reject the null hypothesis	

Decision: Since p-value > 0.05, reject H_0. There is not enough evidence to conclude that the two population variances are different. Hence, the appropriate test for the difference in two means is the pooled-variance t test.

10.94 cont.

Populations: 1 = short term corporate, 2 = intermediate government

H_0: $\mu_1 = \mu_2$ H_1: $\mu_1 \neq \mu_2$

PHStat output:

Pooled-Variance *t* Test for the Difference Between Two Means	
(assumes equal population variances)	
Data	
Hypothesized Difference	0
Level of Significance	0.05
Population 1 Sample	
Sample Size	97
Sample Mean	9.595876
Sample Standard Deviation	5.686734
Population 2 Sample	
Sample Size	87
Sample Mean	4.452874
Sample Standard Deviation	5.360641
Intermediate Calculations	
Population 1 Sample Degrees of Freedom	96
Population 2 Sample Degrees of Freedom	86
Total Degrees of Freedom	182
Pooled Variance	30.63668
Difference in Sample Means	5.143003
t Test Statistic	6.292635
Two-Tail Test	
Lower Critical Value	-1.97308
Upper Critical Value	1.973084
p-Value	2.27E-09
Reject the null hypothesis	

Decision: Since the *p*-value is virtually zero, reject H_0. There is sufficient evidence to conclude that the mean 2009 return is different between the short term corporate bond funds and the intermediate government bond funds.

10.94   **3-year return:**

cont.

Populations: 1 = short term corporate, 2 = intermediate government

H_0: $\sigma_1^2 = \sigma_2^2$ The population variances are the same.

H_1: $\sigma_1^2 \neq \sigma_2^2$ The population variances are different.

PHstat output:

F Test for Differences in Two Variances	
Data	
Level of Significance	0.05
Larger-Variance Sample	
Sample Size	97
Sample Standard Deviation	2.888542
Smaller-Variance Sample	
Sample Size	87
Sample Standard Deviation	1.570289
Intermediate Calculations	
F Test Statistic	3.383748
Population 1 Sample Degrees of Freedom	96
Population 2 Sample Degrees of Freedom	86
Two-Tail Test	
Upper Critical Value	1.516688
p-Value	2.64E-08
Reject the null hypothesis	

Decision: Since *p*-value < 0.05, reject H_0. There is enough evidence to conclude that the two population variances are different. Hence, the appropriate test for the difference in two means is the separate-variance *t* test.

10.94
cont.

Populations: 1 = short term corporate, 2 = intermediate government

H_0: $\mu_1 = \mu_2$ H_1: $\mu_1 \neq \mu_2$

PHStat output:

Separate-Variances t Test for the Difference Between Two Means	
(assumes unequal population variances)	
Data	
Hypothesized Difference	0
Level of Significance	0.05
Population 1 Sample	
Sample Size	97
Sample Mean	3.819587629
Sample Standard Deviation	2.88854199
Population 2 Sample	
Sample Size	87
Sample Mean	5.602298851
Sample Standard Deviation	1.570289339
Intermediate Calculations	
Numerator of Degrees of Freedom	0.0131
Denominator of Degrees of Freedom	0.0001
Total Degrees of Freedom	151.3445
Degrees of Freedom	151
Separate Variance Denominator	0.3382
Difference in Sample Means	-1.782711222
Separate-Variance t Test Statistic	-5.2716
Two-Tail Test	
Lower Critical Value	-1.9758
Upper Critical Value	1.9758
p-Value	0.0000
Reject the null hypothesis	

Decision: Since the p-value is virtually zero, reject H_0. There is sufficient evidence to conclude that the mean 3-year return is different between the short term corporate bond funds and the intermediate government bond funds.

10.94   **5-year return:**
cont.

Populations: 1 = short term corporate, 2 = intermediate government

H_0: $\sigma_1^2 = \sigma_2^2$ The population variances are the same.

H_1: $\sigma_1^2 \neq \sigma_2^2$ The population variances are different.

PHstat output:

F Test for Differences in Two Variances	
Data	
Level of Significance	0.05
Larger-Variance Sample	
Sample Size	97
Sample Standard Deviation	1.668427
Smaller-Variance Sample	
Sample Size	87
Sample Standard Deviation	0.979634
Intermediate Calculations	
F Test Statistic	2.900596
Population 1 Sample Degrees of Freedom	96
Population 2 Sample Degrees of Freedom	86
Two-Tail Test	
Upper Critical Value	1.516688
p-Value	9.72E-07
Reject the null hypothesis	

Decision: Since p-value < 0.05, reject H_0. There is enough evidence to conclude that the two population variances are different. Hence, the appropriate test for the difference in two means is the separate-variance t test.

10.94
cont.

Populations: 1 = short term corporate, 2 = intermediate government

H_0: $\mu_1 = \mu_2$ H_1: $\mu_1 \neq \mu_2$

Separate-Variances *t* Test for the Difference Between Two Means	
(assumes unequal population variances)	
Data	
Hypothesized Difference	0
Level of Significance	0.05
Population 1 Sample	
Sample Size	97
Sample Mean	3.473195876
Sample Standard Deviation	1.66842712
Population 2 Sample	
Sample Size	87
Sample Mean	4.557471264
Sample Standard Deviation	0.979633556
Intermediate Calculations	
Numerator of Degrees of Freedom	0.0016
Denominator of Degrees of Freedom	0.0000
Total Degrees of Freedom	157.9370
Degrees of Freedom	157
Separate Variance Denominator	0.1993
Difference in Sample Means	-1.084275388
Separate-Variance *t* Test Statistic	-5.4399
Two-Tail Test	
Lower Critical Value	-1.9752
Upper Critical Value	1.9752
p-Value	0.0000
Reject the null hypothesis	

Decision: Since the *p*-value is virtually zero, reject H_0. There is sufficient evidence
to conclude that the mean 5-year return is different between the short term corporate
bond funds and the intermediate government bond funds.

10.94   **Expense Ratio:**

cont.   Populations: 1 = intermediate government, 2 = short term corporate

H_0: $\sigma_1^2 = \sigma_2^2$ The population variances are the same.

H_1: $\sigma_1^2 \neq \sigma_2^2$ The population variances are different.

PHStat output:

F Test for Differences in Two Variances	
Data	
Level of Significance	0.05
Larger-Variance Sample	
Sample Size	87
Sample Standard Deviation	0.300741
Smaller-Variance Sample	
Sample Size	97
Sample Standard Deviation	0.201476
Intermediate Calculations	
F Test Statistic	2.228129
Population 1 Sample Degrees of Freedom	86
Population 2 Sample Degrees of Freedom	96
Two-Tail Test	
Upper Critical Value	1.509473
p-Value	0.000153
Reject the null hypothesis	

Decision: Since p-value < 0.05, reject H_0. There is enough evidence to conclude that the two population variances are different. Hence, the appropriate test for the difference in two means is the separate-variance t test.

10.94
cont.
Populations: 1 = short term corporate, 2 = intermediate government

H_0: $\mu_1 = \mu_2$ H_1: $\mu_1 \neq \mu_2$

PHStat output:

Separate-Variances *t* Test for the Difference Between Two Means	
(assumes unequal population variances)	
Data	
Hypothesized Difference	0
Level of Significance	0.05
Population 1 Sample	
Sample Size	97
Sample Mean	0.670515464
Sample Standard Deviation	0.201475656
Population 2 Sample	
Sample Size	87
Sample Mean	0.757816092
Sample Standard Deviation	0.300741043
Intermediate Calculations	
Numerator of Degrees of Freedom	0.0000
Denominator of Degrees of Freedom	0.0000
Total Degrees of Freedom	147.7279
Degrees of Freedom	147
Separate Variance Denominator	0.0382
Difference in Sample Means	-0.087300628
Separate-Variance *t* Test Statistic	-2.2863
Two-Tail Test	
Lower Critical Value	-1.9762
Upper Critical Value	1.9762
p-Value	0.0237
Reject the null hypothesis	

Decision: Since p-value < 0.05, reject H_0. There is sufficient evidence to conclude that the mean expense ratio is different between the short term corporate bond funds and the intermediate government bond funds.

10.96 (a)   **GPA:**

Population 1 = males, 2 = females

H_0: $\sigma_1^2 = \sigma_2^2$ The population variances are the same.

H_1: $\sigma_1^2 \neq \sigma_2^2$ The population variances are different.

PHstat output:

F Test for Differences in Two Variances	
Data	
Level of Significance	0.05
Larger-Variance Sample	
Sample Size	29
Sample Standard Deviation	1.536902
Smaller-Variance Sample	
Sample Size	33
Sample Standard Deviation	1.354706
Intermediate Calculations	
F Test Statistic	1.287072
Population 1 Sample Degrees of Freedom	28
Population 2 Sample Degrees of Freedom	32
Two-Tail Test	
Upper Critical Value	2.058973
p-Value	0.488273
Do not reject the null hypothesis	

Since the p-value > 0.05, do not reject H_0. There is not enough evidence to conclude that the two population variances are different. Hence, the appropriate test for the difference in two means is the pooled-variance t test.

Population 1 = males, 2 = females

H_0: $\mu_1 = \mu_2$ H_1: $\mu_1 \neq \mu_2$

10.96   (a)   PHStat output:
cont.

Pooled-Variance *t* Test for the Difference Between Two Means	
(assumes equal population variances)	
Data	
Hypothesized Difference	0
Level of Significance	0.05
Population 1 Sample	
Sample Size	29
Sample Mean	21.17241
Sample Standard Deviation	1.536902
Population 2 Sample	
Sample Size	33
Sample Mean	21.09091
Sample Standard Deviation	1.354706
Intermediate Calculations	
Population 1 Sample Degrees of Freedom	28
Population 2 Sample Degrees of Freedom	32
Total Degrees of Freedom	60
Pooled Variance	2.081087
Difference in Sample Means	0.081505
t Test Statistic	0.221972
Two-Tail Test	
Lower Critical Value	-2.0003
Upper Critical Value	2.000298
p-Value	0.82509
Do not reject the null hypothesis	

Decision: Since the p-value > 0.05, do not reject H_0. There is insufficient evidence to conclude that the mean GPA is different between males and females.

Expected Salary:

Population 1 = females, 2 = males

H_0: $\sigma_1^2 = \sigma_2^2$ The population variances are the same.

H_1: $\sigma_1^2 \neq \sigma_2^2$ The population variances are different.

10.96   (a)   PHstat output:
cont.

F Test for Differences in Two Variances	
Data	
Level of Significance	0.05
Larger-Variance Sample	
Sample Size	33
Sample Standard Deviation	13.2724
Smaller-Variance Sample	
Sample Size	29
Sample Standard Deviation	10.79317
Intermediate Calculations	
F Test Statistic	1.512171
Population 1 Sample Degrees of Freedom	32
Population 2 Sample Degrees of Freedom	28
Two-Tail Test	
Upper Critical Value	2.096283
p-Value	0.269804
Do not reject the null hypothesis	

Since the p-value > 0.05, do not reject H_0. There is not enough evidence to conclude that the two population variances are different. Hence, the appropriate test for the difference in two means is the pooled-variance t test.

Population 1 = males, 2 = females

H_0: $\mu_1 = \mu_2$ H_1: $\mu_1 \neq \mu_2$

10.96   (a)   PHStat output:
cont.

Pooled-Variance *t* Test for the Difference Between Two Means	
(assumes equal population variances)	
Data	
Hypothesized Difference	0
Level of Significance	0.05
Population 1 Sample	
Sample Size	29
Sample Mean	48.27586
Sample Standard Deviation	10.79317
Population 2 Sample	
Sample Size	33
Sample Mean	48.78788
Sample Standard Deviation	13.2724
Intermediate Calculations	
Population 1 Sample Degrees of Freedom	28
Population 2 Sample Degrees of Freedom	32
Total Degrees of Freedom	60
Pooled Variance	148.3135
Difference in Sample Means	-0.51202
t Test Statistic	-0.16518
Two-Tail Test	
Lower Critical Value	-2.0003
Upper Critical Value	2.000298
p-Value	0.869359
Do not reject the null hypothesis	

Since the *p*-value > 0.05, do not reject H_0. There is insufficient evidence to conclude that the mean expected salary is different between males and females.

Social Networking:

Population 1 = males, 2 = females

H_0: $\sigma_1^2 = \sigma_2^2$ The population variances are the same.

H_1: $\sigma_1^2 \neq \sigma_2^2$ The population variances are different.

10.96   (a)   PHstat output:
cont.

F Test for Differences in Two Variances	
Data	
Level of Significance	0.05
Larger-Variance Sample	
Sample Size	29
Sample Standard Deviation	0.941647
Smaller-Variance Sample	
Sample Size	33
Sample Standard Deviation	0.751262
Intermediate Calculations	
F Test Statistic	1.571065
Population 1 Sample Degrees of Freedom	28
Population 2 Sample Degrees of Freedom	32
Two-Tail Test	
Upper Critical Value	2.058973
p-Value	0.217459
Do not reject the null hypothesis	

Since the p-value > 0.05, do not reject H_0. There is not enough evidence to conclude that the two population variances are different. Hence, the appropriate test for the difference in two means is the pooled-variance t test.

Population 1 = males, 2 = females

H_0: $\mu_1 = \mu_2$ H_1: $\mu_1 \neq \mu_2$

10.96   (a)   PHStat output:
cont.

Pooled-Variance t Test for the Difference Between Two Means	
(assumes equal population variances)	
Data	
Hypothesized Difference	0
Level of Significance	0.05
Population 1 Sample	
Sample Size	29
Sample Mean	1.62069
Sample Standard Deviation	0.941647
Population 2 Sample	
Sample Size	33
Sample Mean	1.424242
Sample Standard Deviation	0.751262
Intermediate Calculations	
Population 1 Sample Degrees of Freedom	28
Population 2 Sample Degrees of Freedom	32
Total Degrees of Freedom	60
Pooled Variance	0.714803
Difference in Sample Means	0.196447
t Test Statistic	0.912878
Two-Tail Test	
Lower Critical Value	-2.0003
Upper Critical Value	2.000298
p-Value	0.36496
Do not reject the null hypothesis	

Since the p-value > 0.05, do not reject H_0. There is insufficient evidence to conclude that the mean number of social networking sites registered for is different between males and females.

Age:

Population 1 = males, 2 = females

H_0: $\sigma_1^2 = \sigma_2^2$ The population variances are the same.

H_1: $\sigma_1^2 \neq \sigma_2^2$ The population variances are different.

10.96   (a)   PHstat output:
cont.

F Test for Differences in Two Variances	
Data	
Level of Significance	0.05
Larger-Variance Sample	
Sample Size	29
Sample Standard Deviation	1.536902
Smaller-Variance Sample	
Sample Size	33
Sample Standard Deviation	1.354706
Intermediate Calculations	
F Test Statistic	1.287072
Population 1 Sample Degrees of Freedom	28
Population 2 Sample Degrees of Freedom	32
Two-Tail Test	
Upper Critical Value	2.058973
p-Value	0.488273
Do not reject the null hypothesis	

Since the *p*-value > 0.05, do not reject H_0. There is not enough evidence to conclude that the two population variances are different. Hence, the appropriate test for the difference in two means is the pooled-variance *t* test.

Population 1 = males, 2 = females

H_0: $\mu_1 = \mu_2$ H_1: $\mu_1 \neq \mu_2$

10.96 (a)   PHStat output:
cont.

Pooled-Variance *t* Test for the Difference Between Two Means	
(assumes equal population variances)	
Data	
Hypothesized Difference	0
Level of Significance	0.05
Population 1 Sample	
Sample Size	29
Sample Mean	21.17241
Sample Standard Deviation	1.536902
Population 2 Sample	
Sample Size	33
Sample Mean	21.09091
Sample Standard Deviation	1.354706
Intermediate Calculations	
Population 1 Sample Degrees of Freedom	28
Population 2 Sample Degrees of Freedom	32
Total Degrees of Freedom	60
Pooled Variance	2.081087
Difference in Sample Means	0.081505
t Test Statistic	0.221972
Two-Tail Test	
Lower Critical Value	-2.0003
Upper Critical Value	2.000298
p-Value	0.82509
Do not reject the null hypothesis	

Since the *p*-value > 0.05, do not reject H_0. There is insufficient evidence to conclude that the mean age is different between males and females.

Spending:

Population 1 = males, 2 = females
H_0: $\sigma_1^2 = \sigma_2^2$ The population variances are the same.
H_1: $\sigma_1^2 \neq \sigma_2^2$ The population variances are different.

10.96   (a)   PHstat output:
cont.

F Test for Differences in Two Variances	
Data	
Level of Significance	0.05
Larger-Variance Sample	
Sample Size	29
Sample Standard Deviation	239.245
Smaller-Variance Sample	
Sample Size	33
Sample Standard Deviation	204.5843
Intermediate Calculations	
F Test Statistic	1.367544
Population 1 Sample Degrees of Freedom	28
Population 2 Sample Degrees of Freedom	32
Two-Tail Test	
Upper Critical Value	2.058973
p-Value	0.391107
Do not reject the null hypothesis	

Since the p-value > 0.05, do not reject H_0. There is not enough evidence to conclude that the two population variances are different. Hence, the appropriate test for the difference in two means is the pooled-variance t test.

Population 1 = males, 2 = females

H_0: $\mu_1 = \mu_2$ H_1: $\mu_1 \neq \mu_2$

PHStat output:

Pooled-Variance *t* Test for the Difference Between Two Means	
(assumes equal population variances)	
Data	
Hypothesized Difference	0
Level of Significance	0.05
Population 1 Sample	
Sample Size	29
Sample Mean	516.0345
Sample Standard Deviation	239.245
Population 2 Sample	
Sample Size	33
Sample Mean	452.1212
Sample Standard Deviation	204.5843
Intermediate Calculations	
Population 1 Sample Degrees of Freedom	28
Population 2 Sample Degrees of Freedom	32
Total Degrees of Freedom	60
Pooled Variance	49033.67
Difference in Sample Means	63.91327
t Test Statistic	1.133976
Two-Tail Test	
Lower Critical Value	-2.0003
Upper Critical Value	2.000298
p-Value	0.261315
Do not reject the null hypothesis	

Since the p-value > 0.05, do not reject H_0. There is insufficient evidence to conclude that the mean spending is different between males and females.

10.96   (a)
cont.

Text Messages:
Population 1 = males, 2 = females
H_0: $\sigma_1^2 = \sigma_2^2$ The population variances are the same.
H_1: $\sigma_1^2 \neq \sigma_2^2$ The population variances are different.
PHstat output:

F Test for Differences in Two Variances	
Data	
Level of Significance	0.05
Larger-Variance Sample	
Sample Size	29
Sample Standard Deviation	219.0672
Smaller-Variance Sample	
Sample Size	33
Sample Standard Deviation	213.348
Intermediate Calculations	
F Test Statistic	1.054333
Population 1 Sample Degrees of Freedom	28
Population 2 Sample Degrees of Freedom	32
Two-Tail Test	
Upper Critical Value	2.058973
p-Value	0.879489
Do not reject the null hypothesis	

Since the p-value > 0.05, do not reject H_0. There is not enough evidence to conclude that the two population variances are different. Hence, the appropriate test for the difference in two means is the pooled-variance t test.

Population 1 = males, 2 = females
H_0: $\mu_1 = \mu_2$ H_1: $\mu_1 \neq \mu_2$

10.96   (a)   PHStat output:
cont.

Pooled-Variance *t* Test for the Difference Between Two Means	
(assumes equal population variances)	
Data	
Hypothesized Difference	0
Level of Significance	0.05
Population 1 Sample	
Sample Size	29
Sample Mean	256.2069
Sample Standard Deviation	219.0672
Population 2 Sample	
Sample Size	33
Sample Mean	237.4242
Sample Standard Deviation	213.348
Intermediate Calculations	
Population 1 Sample Degrees of Freedom	28
Population 2 Sample Degrees of Freedom	32
Total Degrees of Freedom	60
Pooled Variance	46671.48
Difference in Sample Means	18.78265
t Test Statistic	0.341579
Two-Tail Test	
Lower Critical Value	-2.0003
Upper Critical Value	2.000298
p-Value	0.733861
Do not reject the null hypothesis	

Since the p-value > 0.05, do not reject H_0. There is insufficient evidence to conclude that the mean text messages sent in a week is different between males and females.

Wealth:

Population 1 = males, 2 = females
H_0: $\sigma_1^2 = \sigma_2^2$ The population variances are the same.
H_1: $\sigma_1^2 \neq \sigma_2^2$ The population variances are different.

10.96   (a)   PHstat output:
cont.

F Test for Differences in Two Variances	
Data	
Level of Significance	0.05
Larger-Variance Sample	
Sample Size	29
Sample Standard Deviation	27.34992
Smaller-Variance Sample	
Sample Size	33
Sample Standard Deviation	5.360431
Intermediate Calculations	
F Test Statistic	26.0323
Population 1 Sample Degrees of Freedom	28
Population 2 Sample Degrees of Freedom	32
Two-Tail Test	
Upper Critical Value	2.058973
p-Value	7.69E-15
Reject the null hypothesis	

Since the p-value < 0.05, reject H_0. There is enough evidence to conclude that the two population variances are different. Hence, the appropriate test for the difference in two means is the separate-variance t test.

Population 1 = males, 2 = females

H_0: $\mu_1 = \mu_2$ H_1: $\mu_1 \neq \mu_2$

10.96   (a)   PHStat output:
cont.

Separate-Variances t Test for the Difference Between Two Means	
(assumes unequal population variances)	
Data	
Hypothesized Difference	0
Level of Significance	0.05
Population 1 Sample	
Sample Size	29
Sample Mean	12.55344828
Sample Standard Deviation	27.34991816
Population 2 Sample	
Sample Size	33
Sample Mean	2.403787879
Sample Standard Deviation	5.360431278
Intermediate Calculations	
Numerator of Degrees of Freedom	710.9934
Denominator of Degrees of Freedom	23.7850
Total Degrees of Freedom	29.8925
Degrees of Freedom	29
Separate Variance Denominator	5.1638
Difference in Sample Means	10.1496604
Separate-Variance t Test Statistic	1.9656
Two-Tail Test	
Lower Critical Value	-2.0452
Upper Critical Value	2.0452
p-Value	0.0590
Do not reject the null hypothesis	

Since the p-value > 0.05, do not reject H_0. There is insufficient evidence to conclude that the mean wealth needed to feel rich is different between males and females.

10.96   (b)
cont.

GPA:

Population 1 = do not plan to go to graduate school, 2 = plan to go to graduate school

H_0: $\sigma_1^2 = \sigma_2^2$ The population variances are the same.

H_1: $\sigma_1^2 \neq \sigma_2^2$ The population variances are different.

PHstat output:

F Test for Differences in Two Variances	
Data	
Level of Significance	0.05
Larger-Variance Sample	
Sample Size	12
Sample Standard Deviation	0.425245
Smaller-Variance Sample	
Sample Size	28
Sample Standard Deviation	0.379252
Intermediate Calculations	
F Test Statistic	1.257251
Population 1 Sample Degrees of Freedom	11
Population 2 Sample Degrees of Freedom	27
Two-Tail Test	
Upper Critical Value	2.514294
p-Value	0.599929
Do not reject the null hypothesis	

Decision rule: If $F_{STAT} > 2.5143$, reject H_0.

Test statistic: $F_{STAT} = \dfrac{S_1^2}{S_2^2} = 1.2573$

Decision: Since $F_{STAT} = 1.2573$ is lower than 2.5143, do not reject H_0. There is not enough evidence to conclude that the two population variances are different. Hence, the appropriate test for the difference in two means is the pooled-variance t test.

Population 1 = do not plan to go to graduate school, 2 = plan to go to graduate school

H_0: $\mu_1 = \mu_2$ $\qquad\qquad\qquad$ H_1: $\mu_1 \neq \mu_2$

10.96   (b)   PHStat output:
cont.

Pooled-Variance *t* Test for the Difference Between Two Means	
(assumes equal population variances)	
Data	
Hypothesized Difference	0
Level of Significance	0.05
Population 1 Sample	
Sample Size	12
Sample Mean	3.141667
Sample Standard Deviation	0.425245
Population 2 Sample	
Sample Size	28
Sample Mean	3.077857
Sample Standard Deviation	0.379252
Intermediate Calculations	
Population 1 Sample Degrees of Freedom	11
Population 2 Sample Degrees of Freedom	27
Total Degrees of Freedom	38
Pooled Variance	0.154543
Difference in Sample Means	0.06381
t Test Statistic	0.470436
Two-Tail Test	
Lower Critical Value	-2.02439
Upper Critical Value	2.024394
p-Value	0.640733
Do not reject the null hypothesis	

Decision: Since $t_{STAT} = 0.4704$ is in between the upper critical bound of 2.0244 and the lower critical bound of -2.0244, do not reject H_0. There is insufficient evidence to conclude that the mean GPA is different between those students who plan to go to graduate school and those students who do not plan to go to graduate school.

Expected Salary:

Population 1 = do not plan to go to graduate school, 2 = plan to go to graduate school

H_0: $\sigma_1^2 = \sigma_2^2$ The population variances are the same.

H_1: $\sigma_1^2 \neq \sigma_2^2$ The population variances are different.

10.96   (b)   PHstat output:
cont.

F Test for Differences in Two Variances	
Data	
Level of Significance	0.05
Larger-Variance Sample	
Sample Size	12
Sample Standard Deviation	12.05386
Smaller-Variance Sample	
Sample Size	28
Sample Standard Deviation	10.13942
Intermediate Calculations	
F Test Statistic	1.413272
Population 1 Sample Degrees of Freedom	11
Population 2 Sample Degrees of Freedom	27
Two-Tail Test	
Upper Critical Value	2.514294
p-Value	0.446767
Do not reject the null hypothesis	

Decision rule: If $F_{STAT} > 2.5143$, reject H_0.

Test statistic: $F_{STAT} = \dfrac{S_1^2}{S_2^2} = 1.4133$

Decision: Since $F_{STAT} = 1.4133$ is lower than 2.5143, do not reject H_0. There is not enough evidence to conclude that the two population variances are different. Hence, the appropriate test for the difference in two means is the pooled-variance t test.

$H_0: \mu_1 = \mu_2$ $\qquad\qquad\qquad$ $H_1: \mu_1 \neq \mu_2$

10.96   (b)   PHStat output:
cont.

Pooled-Variance *t* Test for the Difference Between Two Means	
(assumes equal population variances)	
Data	
Hypothesized Difference	0
Level of Significance	0.05
Population 1 Sample	
Sample Size	12
Sample Mean	42.25
Sample Standard Deviation	12.05386
Population 2 Sample	
Sample Size	28
Sample Mean	48.125
Sample Standard Deviation	10.13942
Intermediate Calculations	
Population 1 Sample Degrees of Freedom	11
Population 2 Sample Degrees of Freedom	27
Total Degrees of Freedom	38
Pooled Variance	115.1069
Difference in Sample Means	-5.875
t Test Statistic	-1.58707
Two-Tail Test	
Lower Critical Value	-2.02439
Upper Critical Value	2.024394
p-Value	0.120784
Do not reject the null hypothesis	

Decision: Since $t_{STAT} = -1.5871$ is between the lower critical bound of -2.0244 and the upper critical bound of 2.0244, do not reject H_0. There is insufficient evidence to conclude that the mean expected salary is different between those students who plan to go to graduate school and those students who do not plan to go to graduate school.

Number of Social Networking:
Population 1 = plan to go to graduate school, 2 = do not plan to go to graduate school
H_0: $\sigma_1^2 = \sigma_2^2$ The population variances are the same.
H_1: $\sigma_1^2 \neq \sigma_2^2$ The population variances are different.

10.96   (b)   PHstat output:
cont.

F Test for Differences in Two Variances	
Data	
Level of Significance	0.05
Larger-Variance Sample	
Sample Size	28
Sample Standard Deviation	0.922958
Smaller-Variance Sample	
Sample Size	12
Sample Standard Deviation	0.514929
Intermediate Calculations	
F Test Statistic	3.212698
Population 1 Sample Degrees of Freedom	27
Population 2 Sample Degrees of Freedom	11
Two-Tail Test	
Upper Critical Value	3.142182
p-Value	0.046019
Reject the null hypothesis	

Decision rule: If $F_{STAT} > 3.1422$, reject H_0.

Test statistic: $F_{STAT} = \dfrac{S_1^2}{S_2^2} = 3.2127$

Decision: Since $F_{STAT} = 3.2127$ is larger than the upper critical bound of 3.1422, reject H_0. There is enough evidence to conclude that the two population variances are different. Hence, the appropriate test for the difference in two means is the separate-variance *t* test.

Population 1 = plan to go to graduate school, 2 = do not plan to go to graduate school

H_0: $\mu_1 = \mu_2$ $\qquad\qquad\qquad$ H_1: $\mu_1 \neq \mu_2$

10.96   (b)   Excel output:
cont.

Separate-Variances *t* Test for the Difference Between Two Means	
(assumes unequal population variances)	
Data	
Hypothesized Difference	0
Level of Significance	0.05
Population 1 Sample	
Sample Size	28
Sample Mean	1.5
Sample Standard Deviation	0.922958207
Population 2 Sample	
Sample Size	12
Sample Mean	1.416666667
Sample Standard Deviation	0.514928651
Intermediate Calculations	
Numerator of Degrees of Freedom	0.0028
Denominator of Degrees of Freedom	0.0001
Total Degrees of Freedom	35.0634
Degrees of Freedom	35
Separate Variance Denominator	0.2292
Difference in Sample Means	0.083333333
Separate-Variance *t* Test Statistic	0.3636
Two-Tail Test	
Lower Critical Value	-2.0301
Upper Critical Value	2.0301
p-Value	0.7183
Do not reject the null hypothesis	

Decision: Since $t_{STAT} = 0.3636$ is between the lower critical bound of -2.0301 and the upper critical bound of 2.0301, do not reject H_0. There is insufficient evidence to conclude that the mean number of social networking sites registered for is different between those students who plan to go to graduate school and those students who do not plan to go to graduate school.

10.96   (b)
cont.   **Age:**

Population 1 = plan to go to graduate school, 2 = do not plan to go to graduate school
H_0: $\sigma_1^2 = \sigma_2^2$ The population variances are the same.
H_1: $\sigma_1^2 \neq \sigma_2^2$ The population variances are different.
PHstat output:

F Test for Differences in Two Variances	
Data	
Level of Significance	0.05
Larger-Variance Sample	
Sample Size	28
Sample Standard Deviation	1.634208
Smaller-Variance Sample	
Sample Size	12
Sample Standard Deviation	0.792961
Intermediate Calculations	
F Test Statistic	4.247275
Population 1 Sample Degrees of Freedom	27
Population 2 Sample Degrees of Freedom	11
Two-Tail Test	
Upper Critical Value	3.142182
p-Value	0.015281
Reject the null hypothesis	

Decision rule: If $F_{STAT} > 3.1422$, reject H_0.

Test statistic: $F_{STAT} = \dfrac{S_1^2}{S_2^2} = 4.2473$

Decision: Since $F_{STAT} = 4.2473$ is greater than 3.1422, reject H_0. There is enough evidence to conclude that the two population variances are different. Hence, the appropriate test for the difference in two means is the separate-variance *t* test.

10.96 (b)   Population 1 = plan to go to graduate school, 2 = do not plan to go to graduate school
cont. $H_0: \mu_1 = \mu_2$ $H_1: \mu_1 \neq \mu_2$

Excel output:

Separate-Variances *t* Test for the Difference Between Two Means	
(assumes unequal population variances)	
Data	
Hypothesized Difference	0
Level of Significance	0.05
Population 1 Sample	
Sample Size	28
Sample Mean	21.32142857
Sample Standard Deviation	1.634207735
Population 2 Sample	
Sample Size	12
Sample Mean	20.91666667
Sample Standard Deviation	0.792961461
Intermediate Calculations	
Numerator of Degrees of Freedom	0.0218
Denominator of Degrees of Freedom	0.0006
Total Degrees of Freedom	37.2327
Degrees of Freedom	37
Separate Variance Denominator	0.3844
Difference in Sample Means	0.404761905
Separate-Variance *t* Test Statistic	1.0529
Two-Tail Test	
Lower Critical Value	-2.0262
Upper Critical Value	2.0262
***p*-Value**	0.2992
Do not reject the null hypothesis	

10.96   (b)
cont.

Decision: Since $t_{STAT} = 1.0529$ is between the lower critical bound of -2.0262 and the upper critical bound of 2.0262, do not reject H_0. There is insufficient evidence to conclude that the mean age is different between those students who plan to go to graduate school and those students who do not plan to go to graduate school.

Spending:

Population 1 = plan to go to graduate school, 2 = do not plan to go to graduate school
H_0: $\sigma_1^2 = \sigma_2^2$ The population variances are the same.
H_1: $\sigma_1^2 \neq \sigma_2^2$ The population variances are different.
PHstat output:

F Test for Differences in Two Variances	
Data	
Level of Significance	0.05
Larger-Variance Sample	
Sample Size	28
Sample Standard Deviation	269.1621
Smaller-Variance Sample	
Sample Size	12
Sample Standard Deviation	228.7565
Intermediate Calculations	
F Test Statistic	1.384462
Population 1 Sample Degrees of Freedom	27
Population 2 Sample Degrees of Freedom	11
Two-Tail Test	
Upper Critical Value	3.142182
p-Value	0.584208
Do not reject the null hypothesis	

Decision rule: If $F_{STAT} > 3.1422$, reject H_0.

Test statistic: $F_{STAT} = \dfrac{S_1^2}{S_2^2} = \dfrac{152.5941^2}{75.7109^2} = 1.3845$

Decision: Since $F_{STAT} = 1.3845$ is smaller than 3.1422, do not reject H_0. There is not enough evidence to conclude that the two population variances are different. Hence, the appropriate test for the difference in two means is the pooled-variance t test.

Population 1 = plan to go to graduate school, 2 = do not plan to go to graduate school
H_0: $\mu_1 = \mu_2$ H_1: $\mu_1 \neq \mu_2$

10.96   (b)   Excel output:
cont.

Pooled-Variance *t* Test for the Difference Between Two Means	
(assumes equal population variances)	
Data	
Hypothesized Difference	0
Level of Significance	0.05
Population 1 Sample	
Sample Size	28
Sample Mean	500.8929
Sample Standard Deviation	269.1621
Population 2 Sample	
Sample Size	12
Sample Mean	487.5
Sample Standard Deviation	228.7565
Intermediate Calculations	
Population 1 Sample Degrees of Freedom	27
Population 2 Sample Degrees of Freedom	11
Total Degrees of Freedom	38
Pooled Variance	66624.41
Difference in Sample Means	13.39286
t Test Statistic	0.150382
Two-Tail Test	
Lower Critical Value	-2.02439
Upper Critical Value	2.024394
***p*-Value**	0.881259
Do not reject the null hypothesis	

Decision: Since $t_{STAT} = 0.1504$ is in between the lower critical bound of -2.0244 and the upper critical bound of 2.0244, do not reject H_0. There is insufficient evidence to conclude that the mean spending is different between those students who plan to go to graduate school and those students who do not plan to go to graduate school.

10.96   (b)
cont.   **Text messages sent:**

Population 1 = do not plan to go to graduate school, 2 = plan to go to graduate school

H_0: $\sigma_1^2 = \sigma_2^2$ The population variances are the same.

H_1: $\sigma_1^2 \neq \sigma_2^2$ The population variances are different.

PHstat output:

F Test for Differences in Two Variances	
Data	
Level of Significance	0.05
Larger-Variance Sample	
Sample Size	12
Sample Standard Deviation	253.776
Smaller-Variance Sample	
Sample Size	28
Sample Standard Deviation	207.5808
Intermediate Calculations	
F Test Statistic	1.494607
Population 1 Sample Degrees of Freedom	11
Population 2 Sample Degrees of Freedom	27
Two-Tail Test	
Upper Critical Value	2.514294
p-Value	0.38163
Do not reject the null hypothesis	

Decision rule: If $F_{STAT} > 2.5143$, reject H_0.

Test statistic: $F_{STAT} = \dfrac{S_1^2}{S_2^2} = 1.4946$

Decision: Since $F_{STAT} = 1.4946$ is lower than 2.5143, do not reject H_0. There is not enough evidence to conclude that the two population variances are different. Hence, the appropriate test for the difference in two means is the pooled-variance *t* test.

Population 1 = do not plan to go to graduate school, 2 = plan to go to graduate school

H_0: $\mu_1 = \mu_2$ H_1: $\mu_1 \neq \mu_2$

10.96   (b)   PHStat output:
cont.

Pooled-Variance *t* Test for the Difference Between Two Means	
(assumes equal population variances)	
Data	
Hypothesized Difference	0
Level of Significance	0.05
Population 1 Sample	
Sample Size	12
Sample Mean	292.5
Sample Standard Deviation	253.776
Population 2 Sample	
Sample Size	28
Sample Mean	252.6786
Sample Standard Deviation	207.5808
Intermediate Calculations	
Population 1 Sample Degrees of Freedom	11
Population 2 Sample Degrees of Freedom	27
Total Degrees of Freedom	38
Pooled Variance	49259.19
Difference in Sample Means	39.82143
t Test Statistic	0.520011
Two-Tail Test	
Lower Critical Value	-2.02439
Upper Critical Value	2.024394
p-Value	0.606072
Do not reject the null hypothesis	

Decision: Since $t_{STAT} = 0.5200$ is in between the upper critical bound of 2.0244 and the lower critical bound of -2.0244, do not reject H_0. There is insufficient evidence to conclude that the mean text messages sent in a week is different between those students who plan to go to graduate school and those students who do not plan to go to graduate school.

Wealth:

Population 1 = plan to go to graduate school, 2 = do not plan to go to graduate school
H_0: $\sigma_1^2 = \sigma_2^2$ The population variances are the same.
H_1: $\sigma_1^2 \neq \sigma_2^2$ The population variances are different.

10.96 (b)   PHstat output:
cont.

F Test for Differences in Two Variances	
Data	
Level of Significance	0.05
Larger-Variance Sample	
Sample Size	28
Sample Standard Deviation	28.27505
Smaller-Variance Sample	
Sample Size	12
Sample Standard Deviation	1.578165
Intermediate Calculations	
F Test Statistic	320.9975
Population 1 Sample Degrees of Freedom	27
Population 2 Sample Degrees of Freedom	11
Two-Tail Test	
Upper Critical Value	3.142182
p-Value	2.99E-12
Reject the null hypothesis	

Decision rule: If $F_{STAT} > 3.1422$, reject H_0.

Test statistic: $F_{STAT} = \dfrac{S_1^2}{S_2^2} = 320.9975$

Decision: Since $F_{STAT} = 320.9975$ is greater than 3.1422, reject H_0. There is enough evidence to conclude that the two population variances are different. Hence, the appropriate test for the difference in two means is the separate-variance t test.

Population 1 = plan to go to graduate school, 2 = do not plan to go to graduate school
H_0: $\mu_1 = \mu_2$ H_1: $\mu_1 \neq \mu_2$

10.96   (b)   Excel output:
cont.

Separate-Variances *t* Test for the Difference Between Two Means	
(assumes unequal population variances)	
Data	
Hypothesized Difference	0
Level of Significance	0.05
Population 1 Sample	
Sample Size	28
Sample Mean	12.70535714
Sample Standard Deviation	28.27504573
Population 2 Sample	
Sample Size	12
Sample Mean	1.716666667
Sample Standard Deviation	1.57816541
Intermediate Calculations	
Numerator of Degrees of Freedom	827.1574
Denominator of Degrees of Freedom	30.1988
Total Degrees of Freedom	27.3904
Degrees of Freedom	27
Separate Variance Denominator	5.3629
Difference in Sample Means	10.98869048
Separate-Variance *t* Test Statistic	2.0490
Two-Tail Test	
Lower Critical Value	-2.0518
Upper Critical Value	2.0518
***p*-Value**	0.0503
Do not reject the null hypothesis	

Decision: Since $t_{STAT} = 2.0490$ is between the lower critical bound of -2.0518 and the upper critical bound of 2.0518, do not reject H_0. There is insufficient evidence to conclude that the mean wealth needed to feel rich is different between those students who plan to go to graduate school and those students who do not plan to go to graduate school.

10.98   **Undergrad GPA:**

Population 1 = Females, 2 = Males

H_0: $\sigma_1^2 = \sigma_2^2$ The population variances are the same.

H_1: $\sigma_1^2 \neq \sigma_2^2$ The population variances are different.

PHstat output:

F Test for Differences in Two Variances	
Data	
Level of Significance	0.05
Larger-Variance Sample	
Sample Size	19
Sample Standard Deviation	0.316597
Smaller-Variance Sample	
Sample Size	25
Sample Standard Deviation	0.308869
Intermediate Calculations	
F Test Statistic	1.05067
Population 1 Sample Degrees of Freedom	18
Population 2 Sample Degrees of Freedom	24
Two-Tail Test	
Upper Critical Value	2.364797
p-Value	0.894969
Do not reject the null hypothesis	

Since p-value > 0.05, do not reject H_0. There is not enough evidence to conclude that the two population variances are different. Hence, the appropriate test for the difference in two means is the pooled-variance t test.

Population 1 = Males, 2 = females

H_0: $\mu_1 = \mu_2$ H_1: $\mu_1 \neq \mu_2$

10.98
cont.

PHStat output:

Pooled-Variance *t* Test for the Difference Between Two Means	
(assumes equal population variances)	
Data	
Hypothesized Difference	0
Level of Significance	0.05
Population 1 Sample	
Sample Size	19
Sample Mean	3.463158
Sample Standard Deviation	0.316597
Population 2 Sample	
Sample Size	25
Sample Mean	3.296
Sample Standard Deviation	0.308869
Intermediate Calculations	
Population 1 Sample Degrees of Freedom	18
Population 2 Sample Degrees of Freedom	24
Total Degrees of Freedom	42
Pooled Variance	0.097472
Difference in Sample Means	0.167158
t Test Statistic	1.759171
Two-Tail Test	
Lower Critical Value	-2.01808
Upper Critical Value	2.018082
p-Value	0.085832
Do not reject the null hypothesis	

Since p-value > 0.05, do not reject H_0. There is insufficient evidence to conclude that the mean undergraduate GPA is different between males and females.

Graduate GPA:

Population 1 = Females, 2 = Males

H_0: $\sigma_1^2 = \sigma_2^2$ The population variances are the same.

H_1: $\sigma_1^2 \neq \sigma_2^2$ The population variances are different.

10.98
cont.

PHstat output:

F Test for Differences in Two Variances	
Data	
Level of Significance	0.05
Larger-Variance Sample	
Sample Size	19
Sample Standard Deviation	0.419412
Smaller-Variance Sample	
Sample Size	25
Sample Standard Deviation	0.399917
Intermediate Calculations	
F Test Statistic	1.099873
Population 1 Sample Degrees of Freedom	18
Population 2 Sample Degrees of Freedom	24
Two-Tail Test	
Upper Critical Value	2.364797
p-Value	0.814295
Do not reject the null hypothesis	

Since p-value > 0.05, do not reject H_0. There is not enough evidence to conclude that the two population variances are different. Hence, the appropriate test for the difference in two means is the pooled-variance t test.

Population 1 = Males, 2 = females

H_0: $\mu_1 = \mu_2$ H_1: $\mu_1 \neq \mu_2$

10.98
cont.

PHStat output:

Pooled-Variance *t* Test for the Difference Between Two Means	
(assumes equal population variances)	
Data	
Hypothesized Difference	0
Level of Significance	0.05
Population 1 Sample	
Sample Size	25
Sample Mean	3.308
Sample Standard Deviation	0.399917
Population 2 Sample	
Sample Size	19
Sample Mean	3.357895
Sample Standard Deviation	0.419412
Intermediate Calculations	
Population 1 Sample Degrees of Freedom	24
Population 2 Sample Degrees of Freedom	18
Total Degrees of Freedom	42
Pooled Variance	0.166779
Difference in Sample Means	-0.04989
t Test Statistic	-0.40143
Two-Tail Test	
Lower Critical Value	-2.01808
Upper Critical Value	2.018082
p-Value	0.690142
Do not reject the null hypothesis	

Since the p-value > 0.05, do not reject H_0. There is insufficient evidence to conclude that the mean graduate GPA is different between males and females.

Age:

Population 1 = Females, 2 = Males

H_0: $\sigma_1^2 = \sigma_2^2$ The population variances are the same.

H_1: $\sigma_1^2 \neq \sigma_2^2$ The population variances are different.

10.98
cont.

PHstat output:

F Test for Differences in Two Variances	
Data	
Level of Significance	0.05
Larger-Variance Sample	
Sample Size	19
Sample Standard Deviation	5.919044
Smaller-Variance Sample	
Sample Size	25
Sample Standard Deviation	4.982302
Intermediate Calculations	
F Test Statistic	1.411377
Population 1 Sample Degrees of Freedom	18
Population 2 Sample Degrees of Freedom	24
Two-Tail Test	
Upper Critical Value	2.364797
p-Value	0.425058
Do not reject the null hypothesis	

Since the p-value > 0.05, do not reject H_0. There is not enough evidence to conclude that the two population variances are different. Hence, the appropriate test for the difference in two means is the pooled-variance t test.

Population 1 = Males, 2 = females

H_0: $\mu_1 = \mu_2$ H_1: $\mu_1 \neq \mu_2$

10.98
cont.

PHStat output:

Pooled-Variance *t* Test for the Difference Between Two Means	
(assumes equal population variances)	
Data	
Hypothesized Difference	0
Level of Significance	0.05
Population 1 Sample	
Sample Size	25
Sample Mean	26.36
Sample Standard Deviation	4.982302
Population 2 Sample	
Sample Size	19
Sample Mean	26.57895
Sample Standard Deviation	5.919044
Intermediate Calculations	
Population 1 Sample Degrees of Freedom	24
Population 2 Sample Degrees of Freedom	18
Total Degrees of Freedom	42
Pooled Variance	29.1998
Difference in Sample Means	-0.21895
t Test Statistic	-0.13313
Two-Tail Test	
Lower Critical Value	-2.01808
Upper Critical Value	2.018082
***p*-Value**	0.894728
Do not reject the null hypothesis	

Since the *p*-value > 0.05, do not reject H_0. There is insufficient evidence to conclude that the mean age is different between males and females.

Expected Salary:

Population 1 = Males, 2 = females

H_0: $\sigma_1^2 = \sigma_2^2$ The population variances are the same.

H_1: $\sigma_1^2 \neq \sigma_2^2$ The population variances are different.

10.98
cont.

PHstat output:

F Test for Differences in Two Variances	
Data	
Level of Significance	0.05
Larger-Variance Sample	
Sample Size	25
Sample Standard Deviation	51.06574
Smaller-Variance Sample	
Sample Size	19
Sample Standard Deviation	34.6125
Intermediate Calculations	
F Test Statistic	2.176674
Population 1 Sample Degrees of Freedom	24
Population 2 Sample Degrees of Freedom	18
Two-Tail Test	
Upper Critical Value	2.502697
p-Value	0.094729
Do not reject the null hypothesis	

Since p-value > 0.05, do not reject H_0. There is not enough evidence to conclude that the two population variances are different. Hence, the appropriate test for the difference in two means is the pooled-variance t test.

Population 1 = Males, 2 = females

H_0: $\mu_1 = \mu_2$ H_1: $\mu_1 \neq \mu_2$

10.98
cont.

PHStat output:

Pooled-Variance *t* Test for the Difference Between Two Means	
(assumes equal population variances)	
Data	
Hypothesized Difference	**0**
Level of Significance	**0.05**
Population 1 Sample	
Sample Size	**25**
Sample Mean	**86.72**
Sample Standard Deviation	**51.06574**
Population 2 Sample	
Sample Size	**19**
Sample Mean	**78.05263**
Sample Standard Deviation	**34.6125**
Intermediate Calculations	
Population 1 Sample Degrees of Freedom	24
Population 2 Sample Degrees of Freedom	18
Total Degrees of Freedom	42
Pooled Variance	2003.559
Difference in Sample Means	8.667368
t Test Statistic	0.636219
Two-Tail Test	
Lower Critical Value	**-2.01808**
Upper Critical Value	**2.018082**
***p*-Value**	**0.528086**
Do not reject the null hypothesis	

Since p-value > 0.05, do not reject H_0. There is insufficient evidence to conclude that the mean expected salary is different between males and females.

10.98 **Spending:**
cont.

Population 1 = Males, 2 = Females

H_0: $\sigma_1^2 = \sigma_2^2$ The population variances are the same.

H_1: $\sigma_1^2 \neq \sigma_2^2$ The population variances are different.

PHstat output:

F Test for Differences in Two Variances	
Data	
Level of Significance	0.05
Larger-Variance Sample	
Sample Size	25
Sample Standard Deviation	407.3448
Smaller-Variance Sample	
Sample Size	19
Sample Standard Deviation	296.0216
Intermediate Calculations	
F Test Statistic	1.893553
Population 1 Sample Degrees of Freedom	24
Population 2 Sample Degrees of Freedom	18
Two-Tail Test	
Upper Critical Value	2.502697
p-Value	0.168423
Do not reject the null hypothesis	

Since p-value > 0.05, do not reject H_0. There is not enough evidence to conclude that the two population variances are different. Hence, the appropriate test for the difference in two means is the pooled-variance t test.

Population 1 = Males, 2 = females

H_0: $\mu_1 = \mu_2$ H_1: $\mu_1 \neq \mu_2$

10.98
cont.

PHStat output:

Pooled-Variance *t* Test for the Difference Between Two Means	
(assumes equal population variances)	
Data	
Hypothesized Difference	0
Level of Significance	0.05
Population 1 Sample	
Sample Size	25
Sample Mean	361.2
Sample Standard Deviation	407.3448
Population 2 Sample	
Sample Size	19
Sample Mean	367.3684
Sample Standard Deviation	296.0216
Intermediate Calculations	
Population 1 Sample Degrees of Freedom	24
Population 2 Sample Degrees of Freedom	18
Total Degrees of Freedom	42
Pooled Variance	132372.2
Difference in Sample Means	-6.16842
t Test Statistic	-0.05571
Two-Tail Test	
Lower Critical Value	-2.01808
Upper Critical Value	2.018082
p-Value	0.955841
Do not reject the null hypothesis	

Since p-value > 0.05, do not reject H_0. There is insufficient evidence to conclude that the mean spending is different between males and females.

10.98 **Text Messages:**
cont.
Population 1 = Females, 2 = Males
H_0: $\sigma_1^2 = \sigma_2^2$ The population variances are the same.
H_1: $\sigma_1^2 \neq \sigma_2^2$ The population variances are different.
PHstat output:

F Test for Differences in Two Variances	
Data	
Level of Significance	0.05
Larger-Variance Sample	
Sample Size	19
Sample Standard Deviation	323.4155
Smaller-Variance Sample	
Sample Size	25
Sample Standard Deviation	278.349
Intermediate Calculations	
F Test Statistic	1.350027
Population 1 Sample Degrees of Freedom	18
Population 2 Sample Degrees of Freedom	24
Two-Tail Test	
Upper Critical Value	2.364797
p-Value	0.485676
Do not reject the null hypothesis	

Since *p*-value > 0.05, do not reject H_0. There is not enough evidence to conclude that the two population variances are different. Hence, the appropriate test for the difference in two means is the pooled-variance *t* test.

Population 1 = Males, 2 = females
H_0: $\mu_1 = \mu_2$ $\qquad\qquad$ H_1: $\mu_1 \neq \mu_2$

10.98
cont.

PHStat output:

Pooled-Variance *t* Test for the Difference Between Two Means	
(assumes equal population variances)	
Data	
Hypothesized Difference	0
Level of Significance	0.05
Population 1 Sample	
Sample Size	25
Sample Mean	203.6
Sample Standard Deviation	278.349
Population 2 Sample	
Sample Size	19
Sample Mean	270.4211
Sample Standard Deviation	323.4155
Intermediate Calculations	
Population 1 Sample Degrees of Freedom	24
Population 2 Sample Degrees of Freedom	18
Total Degrees of Freedom	42
Pooled Variance	89100.78
Difference in Sample Means	-66.8211
t Test Statistic	-0.73552
Two-Tail Test	
Lower Critical Value	-2.01808
Upper Critical Value	2.018082
p-Value	0.466112
Do not reject the null hypothesis	

Since p-value > 0.05, do not reject H_0. There is insufficient evidence to conclude that the mean number of text messages sent in a week is different between males and females.

Wealth:

Population 1 = Females, 2 = Males

H_0: $\sigma_1^2 = \sigma_2^2$ The population variances are the same.

H_1: $\sigma_1^2 \neq \sigma_2^2$ The population variances are different.

10.98
cont.

PHstat output:

F Test for Differences in Two Variances	
Data	
Level of Significance	0.05
Larger-Variance Sample	
Sample Size	19
Sample Standard Deviation	24.26602
Smaller-Variance Sample	
Sample Size	25
Sample Standard Deviation	21.2986
Intermediate Calculations	
F Test Statistic	1.298061
Population 1 Sample Degrees of Freedom	18
Population 2 Sample Degrees of Freedom	24
Two-Tail Test	
Upper Critical Value	2.364797
p-Value	0.542857
Do not reject the null hypothesis	

Since p-value > 0.05, do not reject H_0. There is not enough evidence to conclude that the two population variances are different. Hence, the appropriate test for the difference in two means is the pooled-variance t test.

Population 1 = Males, 2 = females

H_0: $\mu_1 = \mu_2$ H_1: $\mu_1 \neq \mu_2$

10.98   PHStat output:
cont.

Pooled-Variance *t* Test for the Difference Between Two Means	
(assumes equal population variances)	
Data	
Hypothesized Difference	0
Level of Significance	0.05
Population 1 Sample	
Sample Size	25
Sample Mean	10.576
Sample Standard Deviation	21.2986
Population 2 Sample	
Sample Size	19
Sample Mean	10.72632
Sample Standard Deviation	24.26602
Intermediate Calculations	
Population 1 Sample Degrees of Freedom	24
Population 2 Sample Degrees of Freedom	18
Total Degrees of Freedom	42
Pooled Variance	511.5772
Difference in Sample Means	-0.15032
t Test Statistic	-0.02184
Two-Tail Test	
Lower Critical Value	-2.01808
Upper Critical Value	2.018082
p-Value	0.982682
Do not reject the null hypothesis	

Since *p*-value > 0.05, do not reject H_0. There is insufficient evidence to conclude that the mean wealth needed to feel rich is different between males and females.

10.100 (a)   1 = Others, 2 = Management, 3 = CIS, 4 = Economics/Finance, 5 = Undecided, 6 = International Business, 7 = Retailing/Marketing, 8 = Accounting

GPA:

$H_0 : \mu_1 = \mu_2 = \mu_3 = \mu_4 = \mu_5 = \mu_6 = \mu_7 = \mu_8$

H_1 : Not all μ_j are equal for j = 1, 2, 3, 4, 5, 6, 7, 8

Anova: Single Factor						
SUMMARY						
Groups	Count	Sum	Average	Variance		
Other	7	20.58	2.94	0.076533		
Management	10	33.64	3.364	0.070982		
CIS	4	11.58	2.895	0.309433		
Economics/Finance	11	33.29	3.026364	0.097045		
Undecided	3	8.6	2.866667	0.303333		
International Business	6	18.2	3.033333	0.138667		
Retailing/Marketing	14	45.49	3.249286	0.149223		
Accounting	7	22.45	3.207143	0.142024		
ANOVA						
Source of Variation	SS	df	MS	F	P-value	F crit
Between Groups	1.643417	7	0.234774	1.788417	0.108577	2.184632
Within Groups	7.08883	54	0.131275			
Total	8.732247	61				

Since p-value > 0.05, do not reject H_0. There is insufficient evidence of a difference based on academic major in GPA.

10.100 (a)
cont.

Expected Salary:

$H_0 : \mu_1 = \mu_2 = \mu_3 = \mu_4 = \mu_5 = \mu_6 = \mu_7 = \mu_8$

H_1 : Not all μ_j are equal for $j = 1, 2, 3, 4, 5, 6, 7, 8$

Anova: Single Factor						
SUMMARY						
Groups	Count	Sum	Average	Variance		
Other	7	362	51.71429	168.9048		
Management	10	459	45.9	169.2111		
CIS	4	190	47.5	75		
Economics/Finance	11	605	55	137.55		
Undecided	3	162	54	523		
International Business	6	242	40.33333	40.66667		
Retailing/Marketing	14	630	45	88.46154		
Accounting	7	360	51.42857	172.619		
ANOVA						
Source of Variation	SS	df	MS	F	P-value	F crit
Between Groups	1330.979	7	190.1398	1.356011	0.242881	2.184632
Within Groups	7571.876	54	140.2199			
Total	8902.855	61				

Since p-value $= > 0.05$, do not reject H_0. There is insufficient evidence of a difference based on academic major in expected starting salary.

10.100 (a)
cont.

Age:

$H_0 : \mu_1 = \mu_2 = \mu_3 = \mu_4 = \mu_5 = \mu_6 = \mu_7 = \mu_8$

$H_1 :$ Not all μ_j are equal for $j = 1, 2, 3, 4, 5, 6, 7, 8$

Anova: Single Factor						
SUMMARY						
Groups	Count	Sum	Average	Variance		
Other	7	148	21.14286	1.142857		
Management	10	216	21.6	2.266667		
CIS	4	80	20	0.666667		
Economics/Finance	11	235	21.36364	2.254545		
Undecided	3	62	20.66667	2.333333		
International Business	6	127	21.16667	0.566667		
Retailing/Marketing	14	292	20.85714	1.208791		
Accounting	7	150	21.42857	6.619048		
ANOVA						
Source of Variation	SS	df	MS	F	P-value	F crit
Between Groups	10.23657	7	1.462368	0.688286	0.681388	2.184632
Within Groups	114.7312	54	2.124651			
Total	124.9677	61				

Since p-value > 0.05, do not reject H_0. There is insufficient evidence of a difference based on academic major in age.

10.100 (a)
cont.

Social Networking:

$H_0 : \mu_1 = \mu_2 = \mu_3 = \mu_4 = \mu_5 = \mu_6 = \mu_7 = \mu_8$

H_1 : Not all μ_j are equal for $j = 1, 2, 3, 4, 5, 6, 7, 8$

Anova: Single Factor						
SUMMARY						
Groups	*Count*	*Sum*	*Average*	*Variance*		
Other	7	11	1.571429	0.619048		
Management	10	15	1.5	1.611111		
CIS	4	8	2	2		
Economics/Finance	11	18	1.636364	0.454545		
Undecided	3	5	1.666667	0.333333		
International Business	6	10	1.666667	0.666667		
Retailing/Marketing	14	17	1.214286	0.489011		
Accounting	7	10	1.428571	0.285714		
ANOVA						
Source of Variation	*SS*	*df*	*MS*	*F*	*P-value*	*F crit*
Between Groups	2.652702	7	0.378957	0.501178	0.829533	2.184632
Within Groups	40.83117	54	0.756133			
Total	43.48387	61				

Since p-value > 0.05, do not reject H_0. There is insufficient evidence of a difference based on academic major in the number of social networking sites registered for.

10.100 (a)
cont.

Spending:

$H_0 : \mu_1 = \mu_2 = \mu_3 = \mu_4 = \mu_5 = \mu_6 = \mu_7 = \mu_8$

H_1 : Not all μ_j are equal for $j = 1, 2, 3, 4, 5, 6, 7, 8$

Anova: Single Factor						
SUMMARY						
Groups	Count	Sum	Average	Variance		
Other	7	2700	385.7143	22261.9		
Management	10	4810	481	15387.78		
CIS	4	1900	475	10833.33		
Economics/Finance	11	4965	451.3636	30090.45		
Undecided	3	1400	466.6667	3333.333		
International Business	6	3550	591.6667	98416.67		
Retailing/Marketing	14	7140	510	123630.8		
Accounting	7	3420	488.5714	22347.62		
ANOVA						
Source of Variation	SS	df	MS	F	P-value	F crit
Between Groups	159571.3	7	22795.9	0.432605	0.877471	2.184632
Within Groups	2845502	54	52694.48			
Total	3005073	61				

Since p-value > 0.05, do not reject H_0. There is insufficient evidence of a difference based on academic major in spending on textbooks and supplies.

10.100 (a)
cont.

Text Messages:

$H_0 : \mu_1 = \mu_2 = \mu_3 = \mu_4 = \mu_5 = \mu_6 = \mu_7 = \mu_8$

H_1 : Not all μ_j are equal for $j = 1, 2, 3, 4, 5, 6, 7, 8$

Anova: Single Factor

SUMMARY					
Groups	Count	Sum	Average	Variance	
Other	7	1850	264.2857	45595.24	
Managem	10	1965	196.5	19289.17	
CIS	4	1150	287.5	22291.67	
Economic	11	1790	162.7273	14416.82	
Undecide	3	850	283.3333	75833.33	
Internatic	6	905	150.8333	31624.17	
Retailing/	14	4285	306.0714	84646.84	
Accountir	7	2470	352.8571	73057.14	

ANOVA					
ce of Varic	SS	df	MS	F	P-value	F crit
Between	298977.9	7	42711.13	0.920074	0.498422	2.184632
Within Gr	2506756	54	46421.41			
Total	2805734	61				

Since p-value > 0.05, do not reject H_0. There is insufficient evidence of a difference based on academic major in the number of text messages sent in a typical week.

10.100 (a)
cont.

Wealth:

$H_0 : \mu_1 = \mu_2 = \mu_3 = \mu_4 = \mu_5 = \mu_6 = \mu_7 = \mu_8$

H_1 : Not all μ_j are equal for $j = 1, 2, 3, 4, 5, 6, 7, 8$

Anova: Single Factor						
SUMMARY						
Groups	Count	Sum	Average	Variance		
Other	7	78.35	11.19286	672.8687		
Management	10	40.5	4.05	14.08278		
CIS	4	101.6	25.4	2473.54		
Economics/Finance	11	54.8	4.981818	76.74964		
Undecided	3	8.5	2.833333	1.583333		
International Business	6	9	1.5	1.536		
Retailing/Marketing	14	131.725	9.408929	689.3888		
Accounting	7	18.9	2.7	12.85917		
ANOVA						
Source of Variation	SS	df	MS	F	P-value	F crit
Between Groups	2051.966	7	293.138	0.73962	0.639463	2.184632
Within Groups	21402.13	54	396.3357			
Total	23454.1	61				

Since p-value > 0.05, do not reject H_0. There is insufficient evidence of a difference based on academic major in the amount of wealth needed to feel rich.

10.100 (b)   1 = yes, 2 = undecided, 3 = no.
cont.

GPA:

$H_0 : \mu_1 = \mu_2 = \mu_3$

H_1 : Not all μ_j are equal for $j = 1, 2, 3$

Anova: Single Factor						
SUMMARY						
Groups	Count	Sum	Average	Variance		
Yes	28	86.18	3.077857	0.143832		
Undecided	22	69.95	3.179545	0.129938		
No	12	37.7	3.141667	0.180833		
ANOVA						
Source of Variation	SS	df	MS	F	P-value	F crit
Between Groups	0.130913	2	0.065457	0.448993	0.640433	3.153123
Within Groups	8.601334	59	0.145785			
Total	8.732247	61				

Test statistic: $F_{STAT} = 0.4490$

Since p-value $= 0.6404 > 0.05$, do not reject H_0. There is insufficient evidence of a difference based on graduate school intention in grade point average.

Expected Starting Salary:

$H_0 : \mu_1 = \mu_2 = \mu_3$

H_1 : Not all μ_j are equal for $j = 1, 2, 3$

Anova: Single Factor						
SUMMARY						
Groups	Count	Sum	Average	Variance		
Yes	28	1347.5	48.125	102.8079		
Undecided	22	1155.5	52.52273	176.2018		
No	12	507	42.25	145.2955		
ANOVA						
Source of Variation	SS	df	MS	F	P-value	F crit
Between Groups	828.5537	2	414.2769	3.027176	0.056038	3.153123
Within Groups	8074.301	59	136.8526			
Total	8902.855	61				

Test statistic: $F_{STAT} = 3.0272$

Since p-value $= 0.0560 > 0.05$, do not reject H_0. There is insufficient evidence of a difference based on graduate school intention in expected starting salary.

10.100 (b) cont.

Age:

$H_0 : \mu_1 = \mu_2 = \mu_3$

H_1 : Not all μ_j are equal for $j = 1, 2, 3$

Anova: Single Factor						
SUMMARY						
Groups	Count	Sum	Average	Variance		
Yes	28	597	21.32143	2.670635		
Undecided	22	462	21	2.095238		
No	12	251	20.91667	0.628788		
ANOVA						
Source of Variation	SS	df	MS	F	P-value	F crit
Between Groups	1.943932	2	0.971966	0.466137	0.629712	3.153123
Within Groups	123.0238	59	2.085149			
Total	124.9677	61				

Test statistic: $F_{STAT} = 0.4661$

Since p-value = 0.6297 > 0.05, do not reject H_0. There is insufficient evidence of a difference based on graduate school intention in age.

Spending:

$H_0 : \mu_1 = \mu_2 = \mu_3$

H_1 : Not all μ_j are equal for $j = 1, 2, 3$

Anova: Single Factor						
SUMMARY						
Groups	Count	Sum	Average	Variance		
Yes	28	14025	500.8929	72448.25		
Undecided	22	10010	455	21283.33		
No	12	5850	487.5	52329.55		
ANOVA						
Source of Variation	SS	df	MS	F	P-value	F crit
Between Groups	26395.31	2	13197.65	0.261412	0.770851	3.153123
Within Groups	2978678	59	50486.06			
Total	3005073	61				

Test statistic: $F_{STAT} = 0.2614$

Since p-value = 0.7709 > 0.05, do not reject H_0. There is insufficient evidence of a difference based on graduate school intention in spending on textbooks and supplies.

10.100 (b)
cont.

Social Networking:

$H_0 : \mu_1 = \mu_2 = \mu_3$

H_1 : Not all μ_j are equal for $j = 1, 2, 3$

Anova: Single Factor						
SUMMARY						
Groups	Count	Sum	Average	Variance		
Yes	28	42	1.5	0.851852		
Undecided	22	35	1.590909	0.824675		
No	12	17	1.416667	0.265152		
ANOVA						
Source of Variation	SS	df	MS	F	P-value	F crit
Between Groups	0.249022	2	0.124511	0.169913	0.84415	3.153123
Within Groups	43.23485	59	0.732794			
Total	43.48387	61				

Test statistic: $F_{STAT} = 0.1699$

Since p-value $= 0.8441 > 0.05$, do not reject H_0. There is insufficient evidence of a difference based on graduate school intention in the number of social networking sites registered for.

Text messages:

$H_0 : \mu_1 = \mu_2 = \mu_3$

H_1 : Not all μ_j are equal for $j = 1, 2, 3$

Anova: Single Factor						
SUMMARY						
Groups	Count	Sum	Average	Variance		
Yes	28	7075	252.6786	43089.78		
Undecided	22	4680	212.7273	42016.02		
No	12	3510	292.5	64402.27		
ANOVA						
Source of Variation	SS	df	MS	F	P-value	F crit
Between Groups	51548.8	2	25774.4	0.552138	0.578663	3.153123
Within Groups	2754185	59	46681.11			
Total	2805734	61				

Test statistic: $F_{STAT} = 0.5521$

Since p-value $= 0.5787 > 0.05$, do not reject H_0. There is insufficient evidence of a difference based on graduate school intention in number of text messages sent in a typical week.

10.100 (b)
cont.

Wealth:

$H_0 : \mu_1 = \mu_2 = \mu_3$

H_1 : Not all μ_j are equal for $j = 1, 2, 3$

Anova: Single Factor						
SUMMARY						
Groups	Count	Sum	Average	Variance		
Yes	28	355.75	12.70536	799.4782		
Undecided	22	67.025	3.046591	11.99823		
No	12	20.6	1.716667	2.490606		
ANOVA						
Source of Variation	SS	df	MS	F	P-value	F crit
Between Groups	1588.824	2	794.4122	2.143596	0.126275	3.153123
Within Groups	21865.27	59	370.5978			
Total	23454.1	61				

Test statistic: $F_{STAT} = 2.1436$

Since p-value $= 0.1263 > 0.05$, do not reject H_0. There is insufficient evidence of a difference based on graduate school intention in the amount of wealth needed to feel rich.

(c)   1 = full-time, 2 = part-time, 3 = unemployed.

GPA:

$H_0 : \mu_1 = \mu_2 = \mu_3$

H_1 : Not all μ_j are equal for $j = 1, 2, 3$

Anova: Single Factor						
SUMMARY						
Groups	Count	Sum	Average	Variance		
Full-Time	10	29.55	2.955	0.114339		
Part-Time	43	136.42	3.172558	0.131534		
Unemployed	9	27.86	3.095556	0.223103		
ANOVA						
Source of Variation	SS	df	MS	F	P-value	F crit
Between Groups	0.393956	2	0.196978	1.393775	0.256186	3.153123
Within Groups	8.338291	59	0.141327			
Total	8.732247	61				

Since p-value > 0.05, do not reject H_0. There is insufficient evidence of a difference based on employment status in grade point average.

10.100 (c)
cont.

Expected Starting Salary:

$H_0 : \mu_1 = \mu_2 = \mu_3$

H_1 : Not all μ_j are equal for $j = 1, 2, 3$

Anova: Single Factor

SUMMARY

Groups	Count	Sum	Average	Variance
Full-Time	10	527	52.7	182.9
Part-Time	43	2030	47.2093	120.729
Unemployed	9	453	50.33333	238.5

ANOVA

Source of Variation	SS	df	MS	F	P-value	F crit
Between Groups	278.1386	2	139.0693	0.951346	0.392065	3.153123
Within Groups	8624.716	59	146.1816			
Total	8902.855	61				

Since p-value > 0.05, do not reject H_0. There is insufficient evidence of a difference based on employment status in expected starting salary.

Age:

$H_0 : \mu_1 = \mu_2 = \mu_3$

H_1 : Not all μ_j are equal for $j = 1, 2, 3$

Anova: Single Factor

SUMMARY

Groups	Count	Sum	Average	Variance
Full-Time	10	217	21.7	1.566667
Part-Time	43	908	21.11628	2.009967
Unemployed	9	185	20.55556	2.527778

ANOVA

Source of Variation	SS	df	MS	F	P-value	F crit
Between Groups	6.226915	2	3.113458	1.547016	0.221393	3.153123
Within Groups	118.7408	59	2.012556			
Total	124.9677	61				

Since p-value > 0.05, do not reject H_0. There is insufficient evidence of a difference based on employment status in age.

10.100 (c)
cont.

Social Networking:

$H_0 : \mu_1 = \mu_2 = \mu_3$

H_1 : Not all μ_j are equal for $j = 1, 2, 3$

Anova: Single Factor						
SUMMARY						
Groups	Count	Sum	Average	Variance		
Full-Time	10	14	1.4	1.155556		
Part-Time	43	65	1.511628	0.636766		
Unemployed	9	15	1.666667	0.75		
ANOVA						
Source of Variation	SS	df	MS	F	P-value	F crit
Between Groups	0.339685	2	0.169842	0.232261	0.793461	3.153123
Within Groups	43.14419	59	0.731257			
Total	43.48387	61				

Since p-value > 0.05, do not reject H_0. There is insufficient evidence of a difference based on employment status in the number of social networking sites registered for.

Spending:

$H_0 : \mu_1 = \mu_2 = \mu_3$

H_1 : Not all μ_j are equal for $j = 1, 2, 3$

Anova: Single Factor						
SUMMARY						
Groups	Count	Sum	Average	Variance		
Full-Time	10	5205	520.5	115146.9		
Part-Time	43	20530	477.4419	41909.97		
Unemployed	9	4150	461.1111	23611.11		
ANOVA						
Source of Variation	SS	df	MS	F	P-value	F crit
Between Groups	19642.99	2	9821.495	0.194099	0.8241	3.153123
Within Groups	2985430	59	50600.51			
Total	3005073	61				

Since p-value > 0.05, do not reject H_0. There is insufficient evidence of a difference based on employment status in spending on textbooks and supplies.

10.100 (c)
cont.

Text Message:

$H_0 : \mu_1 = \mu_2 = \mu_3$

H_1 : Not all μ_j are equal for $j = 1, 2, 3$

Anova: Single Factor						
SUMMARY						
Groups	Count	Sum	Average	Variance		
Full-Time	10	2990	299	53343.33		
Part-Time	43	10445	242.907	48737.18		
Unemployed	9	1830	203.3333	29225		
ANOVA						
Source of Variation	SS	df	MS	F	P-value	F crit
Between Groups	44882.65	2	22441.32	0.479576	0.621438	3.153123
Within Groups	2760852	59	46794.1			
Total	2805734	61				

Since p-value > 0.05, do not reject H_0. There is insufficient evidence of a difference based on employment status in the number of text messages sent in a typical week.

Wealth:

$H_0 : \mu_1 = \mu_2 = \mu_3$

H_1 : Not all μ_j are equal for $j = 1, 2, 3$

Anova: Single Factor						
SUMMARY						
Groups	Count	Sum	Average	Variance		
Full-Time	10	151.85	15.185	969.1534		
Part-Time	43	266.275	6.192442	328.1682		
Unemployed	9	25.25	2.805556	11.71778		
ANOVA						
Source of Variation	SS	df	MS	F	P-value	F crit
Between Groups	854.9074	2	427.4537	1.115959	0.334416	3.153123
Within Groups	22599.19	59	383.0371			
Total	23454.1	61				

Since p-value = 0.3344 > 0.05, do not reject H_0. There is insufficient evidence of a difference based on employment status in the amount of wealth needed to feel rich.

10.102 (a)   1 = Biological Sciences, 2 = Business, 3 = Engineering, 4 = Other

Age:

$H_0 : \mu_1 = \mu_2 = \mu_3 = \mu_4$

H_1 : Not all μ_j are equal for $j = 1, 2, 3, 4$

Anova: Single Factor						
SUMMARY						
Groups	*Count*	*Sum*	*Average*	*Variance*		
Age_Biological Sciences	3	75	25	1		
Age_Business	25	662	26.48	36.42667		
Age_Engineering	3	82	27.33333	2.333333		
Age_Other	13	345	26.53846	28.10256		
ANOVA						
Source of Variation	*SS*	*df*	*MS*	*F*	*P-value*	*F crit*
Between Groups	8.771655	3	2.923885	0.096012	0.961796	2.838745
Within Groups	1218.137	40	30.45344			
Total	1226.909	43				

Since p-value > 0.05, do not reject H_0. There is insufficient evidence of a difference based on undergraduate major in age.

Graduate GPA:

$H_0 : \mu_1 = \mu_2 = \mu_3 = \mu_4$

H_1 : Not all μ_j are equal for $j = 1, 2, 3, 4$

Anova: Single Factor						
SUMMARY						
Groups	*Count*	*Sum*	*Average*	*Variance*		
G-GPA_Biological Sciences	3	9.8	3.266667	0.093333		
G-GPA_Business	25	81.4	3.256	0.157567		
G-GPA_Engineering	3	10.2	3.4	0.13		
G-GPA_Other	13	45.1	3.469231	0.198974		
ANOVA						
Source of Variation	*SS*	*df*	*MS*	*F*	*P-value*	*F crit*
Between Groups	0.415632	3	0.138544	0.837635	0.481262	2.838745
Within Groups	6.615959	40	0.165399			
Total	7.031591	43				

Since p-value = 0.4813 > 0.05, do not reject H_0. There is insufficient evidence of a difference based on undergraduate major in graduate grade point average.

10.102 (a)   **Undergraduate GPA:**
cont.

$H_0 : \mu_1 = \mu_2 = \mu_3 = \mu_4$

H_1 : Not all μ_j are equal for $j = 1, 2, 3, 4$

Anova: Single Factor						
SUMMARY						
Groups	Count	Sum	Average	Variance		
U-GPA_Biological Sciences	3	9.6	3.2	0.13		
U-GPA_Business	25	86	3.44	0.083333		
U-GPA_Engineering	3	9.6	3.2	0.19		
U-GPA_Other	13	43	3.307692	0.117436		
ANOVA						
Source of Variation	SS	df	MS	F	P-value	F crit
Between Groups	0.346224	3	0.115408	1.140048	0.344581	2.838745
Within Groups	4.049231	40	0.101231			
Total	4.395455	43				

Since p-value = 0.3446 > 0.05, do not reject H_0. There is insufficient evidence of a difference based on undergraduate major in undergraduate grade point average.

Expected Salary Upon Graduation:

$H_0 : \mu_1 = \mu_2 = \mu_3 = \mu_4$

H_1 : Not all μ_j are equal for $j = 1, 2, 3, 4$

Anova: Single Factor						
SUMMARY						
Groups	Count	Sum	Average	Variance		
Expected Salary_Biological Scie	3	252.5	84.16667	2352.083		
Expected Salary_Business	25	1970.5	78.82	2399.393		
Expected Salary_Engineering	3	240	80	325		
Expected Salary_Other	13	1188	91.38462	1719.923		
ANOVA						
Source of Variation	SS	df	MS	F	P-value	F crit
Between Groups	1381.794	3	460.5979	0.220438	0.881635	2.838745
Within Groups	83578.68	40	2089.467			
Total	84960.48	43				

Since p-value = 0.8816 > 0.05, do not reject H_0. There is insufficient evidence of a difference based on undergraduate major in expected salary upon graduation.

10.102 (a)
cont.

Text Message:

$H_0 : \mu_1 = \mu_2 = \mu_3 = \mu_4$

H_1 : Not all μ_j are equal for $j = 1, 2, 3, 4$

Anova: Single Factor

SUMMARY

Groups	Count	Sum	Average	Variance
Text Messages_Biological Scienc	3	760	253.3333	50533.33
Text Messages_Business	25	6006	240.24	87260.19
Text Messages_Engineering	3	680	226.6667	104933.3
Text Messages_Other	13	2782	214	114825.5

ANOVA

Source of Variation	SS	df	MS	F	P-value	F crit
Between Groups	7351.016	3	2450.339	0.025908	0.994274	2.838745
Within Groups	3783084	40	94577.1			
Total	3790435	43				

Since p-value $= 0.9943 > 0.05$, do not reject H_0. There is insufficient evidence of a difference based on undergraduate major in the number of text messages sent in a typical week.

Spending:

$H_0 : \mu_1 = \mu_2 = \mu_3 = \mu_4$

H_1 : Not all μ_j are equal for $j = 1, 2, 3, 4$

Anova: Single Factor

SUMMARY

Groups	Count	Sum	Average	Variance
Spending_Biological Sciences	3	1075	358.3333	77708.33
Spending_Business	25	9100	364	158360.4
Spending_Engineering	3	1060	353.3333	34533.33
Spending_Other	13	4775	367.3077	127860.9

ANOVA

Source of Variation	SS	df	MS	F	P-value	F crit
Between Groups	579.0793	3	193.0264	0.001389	0.999927	2.838745
Within Groups	5559464	40	138986.6			
Total	5560043	43				

Since p-value $= 0.9999 > 0.05$, do not reject H_0. There is insufficient evidence of a difference based on undergraduate major in spending on textbooks and supplies.

10.102 (a)
cont.

Wealth:

$H_0 : \mu_1 = \mu_2 = \mu_3 = \mu_4$

H_1 : Not all μ_j are equal for $j = 1, 2, 3, 4$

Anova: Single Factor						
SUMMARY						
Groups	Count	Sum	Average	Variance		
Biological Sciences	3	61	20.33333	680.3333		
Business	25	250.4	10.016	454.9256		
Engineering	3	12	4	27		
Other	13	144.8	11.13846	727.2076		
ANOVA						
Source of Variation	SS	df	MS	F	P-value	F crit
Between Groups	427.1153	3	142.3718	0.27042	0.84634	2.838745
Within Groups	21059.37	40	526.4843			
Total	21486.49	43				

Since p-value $= 0.8463 > 0.05$, do not reject H_0. There is insufficient evidence of a difference based on undergraduate major in the amount of wealth needed to feel rich.

(b)   1 = Accounting, 2 = Economics/Finance, 3 = Management, 4 = Other, 5 = Retailing/Marketing

Age:

$H_0 : \mu_1 = \mu_2 = \mu_3 = \mu_4 = \mu_5$

H_1 : Not all μ_j are equal for $j = 1, 2, 3, 4, 5$

ANOVA						
Source of Variation	SS	df	MS	F	P-value	F crit
Between Groups	42.24877	4	10.56219	0.347716	0.843997	2.612306
Within Groups	1184.66	39	30.37591			
Total	1226.909	43				

Since p-value $= 0.8440 > 0.05$, do not reject H_0. There is insufficient evidence of a difference based on graduate major in age.

Undergraduate GPA:

$H_0 : \mu_1 = \mu_2 = \mu_3 = \mu_4 = \mu_5$

H_1 : Not all μ_j are equal for $j = 1, 2, 3, 4, 5$

ANOVA						
Source of Variation	SS	df	MS	F	P-value	F crit
Between Groups	0.896709	4	0.224177	2.498869	0.058182	2.612306
Within Groups	3.498746	39	0.089711			
Total	4.395455	43				

Since p-value $= 0.0582 > 0.05$, do not reject H_0. There is insufficient evidence of a difference based on graduate major in undergraduate grade point average.

10.102 (b)
cont.

Graduate GPA:

$H_0 : \mu_1 = \mu_2 = \mu_3 = \mu_4 = \mu_5$

H_1 : Not all μ_j are equal for $j = 1, 2, 3, 4, 5$

ANOVA						
Source of Variation	SS	df	MS	F	P-value	F crit
Between Groups	0.626575	4	0.156644	0.9538	0.44358	2.612306
Within Groups	6.405016	39	0.164231			
Total	7.031591	43				

Since p-value = 0.4438 > 0.05, do not reject H_0. There is insufficient evidence of a difference based on graduate major in graduate grade point average.

Expected Salary Upon Graduation:

$H_0 : \mu_1 = \mu_2 = \mu_3 = \mu_4 = \mu_5$

H_1 : Not all μ_j are equal for $j = 1, 2, 3,$

ANOVA						
Source of Variation	SS	df	MS	F	P-value	F crit
Between Groups	16536.79	4	4134.198	2.356402	0.070409	2.612306
Within Groups	68423.69	39	1754.453			
Total	84960.48	43				

Since p-value = 0.0704 > 0.05, do not reject H_0. There is insufficient evidence of a difference based on graduate major in expected salary upon graduation.

Spending:

$H_0 : \mu_1 = \mu_2 = \mu_3 = \mu_4 = \mu_5$

H_1 : Not all μ_j are equal for $j = 1, 2, 3, 4, 5$

ANOVA						
Source of Variation	SS	df	MS	F	P-value	F crit
Between Groups	725704.3	4	181426.1	1.463616	0.231839	2.612306
Within Groups	4834339	39	123957.4			
Total	5560043	43				

Since p-value = 0.2318 > 0.05, do not reject H_0. There is insufficient evidence of a difference based on graduate major in spending on textbooks and supplies.

10.102 (b)
cont.

Text Messages:

$H_0 : \mu_1 = \mu_2 = \mu_3 = \mu_4 = \mu_5$

H_1 : Not all μ_j are equal for $j = 1, 2, 3, 4, 5$

ANOVA						
Source of Variation	*SS*	*df*	*MS*	*F*	*P-value*	*F crit*
Between Groups	396223.5	4	99055.87	1.138167	0.35287	2.612306
Within Groups	3394211	39	87031.06			
Total	3790435	43				

Since p-value = 0.3529 > 0.05, do not reject H_0. There is insufficient evidence of a difference based on graduate major in the number of text messages sent in a typical week.

Wealth:

$H_0 : \mu_1 = \mu_2 = \mu_3 = \mu_4 = \mu_5$

H_1 : Not all μ_j are equal for $j = 1, 2, 3, 4, 5$

ANOVA						
Source of Variation	*SS*	*df*	*MS*	*F*	*P-value*	*F crit*
Between Groups	1140.936	4	285.2341	0.54676	0.702409	2.612306
Within Groups	20345.55	39	521.6808			
Total	21486.49	43				

Since p-value = 0.7024 > 0.05, do not reject H_0. There is insufficient evidence of a difference based on graduate major in the amount of wealth needed to feel rich.

(c)   1 = full-time, 2 = part-time, 3 = unemployed

Age:

$H_0 : \mu_1 = \mu_2 = \mu_3$

H_1 : Not all μ_j are equal for $j = 1, 2, 3$

Anova: Single Factor					
SUMMARY					
Groups	*Count*	*Sum*	*Average*	*Variance*	
Age_Full-Time	28	754	26.92857	21.55026	
Age_Part-Time	7	163	23.28571	15.2381	
Age_Unemployed	9	247	27.44444	58.52778	
ANOVA					
Source of Variation	*SS*	*df*	*MS*	*F*	*P-value*	*F crit*
Between Groups	85.40115	2	42.70058	1.533694	0.227858	3.225684
Within Groups	1141.508	41	27.84166			
Total	1226.909	43				

Since p-value = 0.2279 > 0.05, do not reject H_0. There is insufficient evidence of a difference based on employment status in age.

10.102 (c)
cont.

Undergraduate GPA:

$H_0 : \mu_1 = \mu_2 = \mu_3$

H_1 : Not all μ_j are equal for $j = 1, 2, 3$

Anova: Single Factor						
SUMMARY						
Groups	Count	Sum	Average	Variance		
U-GPA_Full-Time	28	93.3	3.332143	0.108929		
U-GPA_Part-Time	7	24.2	3.457143	0.082857		
U-GPA_Unemployed	9	30.7	3.411111	0.106111		
ANOVA						
Source of Variation	SS	df	MS	F	P-value	F crit
Between Groups	0.108351	2	0.054176	0.518113	0.599491	3.225684
Within Groups	4.287103	41	0.104563			
Total	4.395455	43				

Since p-value $= 0.5995 > 0.05$, do not reject H_0. There is insufficient evidence of a difference based on employment status in undergraduate grade point average.

Graduate GPA:

$H_0 : \mu_1 = \mu_2 = \mu_3$

H_1 : Not all μ_j are equal for $j = 1, 2, 3$

Anova: Single Factor						
SUMMARY						
Groups	Count	Sum	Average	Variance		
G-GPA_Full-Time	28	94.1	3.360714	0.161733		
G-GPA_Part-Time	7	21.1	3.014286	0.001429		
G-GPA_Unemployed	9	31.3	3.477778	0.216944		
ANOVA						
Source of Variation	SS	df	MS	F	P-value	F crit
Between Groups	0.920678	2	0.460339	3.088557	0.056309	3.225684
Within Groups	6.110913	41	0.149047			
Total	7.031591	43				

Since p-value $= 0.0553 > 0.05$, do not reject H_0. There is insufficient evidence of a difference based on employment status in graduate grade point average.

10.102 (c)   **Expected Salary Upon Graduation:**
cont. $H_0 : \mu_1 = \mu_2 = \mu_3$

H_1 : Not all μ_j are equal for $j = 1, 2, 3$

Anova: Single Factor						
SUMMARY						
Groups	*Count*	*Sum*	*Average*	*Variance*		
Expected Salary_Full-Time	28	2675	95.53571	2583.499		
Expected Salary_Part-Time	7	390	55.71429	120.2381		
Expected Salary_Unemployed	9	586	65.11111	249.1111		
ANOVA						
Source of Variation	*SS*	*df*	*MS*	*F*	*P-value*	*F crit*
Between Groups	12491.7	2	6245.848	3.533656	0.038384	3.225684
Within Groups	72468.78	41	1767.531			
Total	84960.48	43				

Since p-value = 0.0384 < 0.05, reject H_0. There is sufficient evidence of a difference based on employment status in expected salary upon graduation.

Tukey Kramer Multiple Comparisons							
	Sample	Sample		Absolute	Std. Error	Critical	
Group	Mean	Size	**Comparison**	Difference	of Difference	Range	**Results**
1	95.53571	28	Group 1 to Group 2	39.821429	12.56245562	43.215	**Means are not different**
2	55.71429	7	Group 1 to Group 3	30.424603	11.39119131	39.186	**Means are not different**
3	65.11111	9	Group 2 to Group 3	9.3968254	14.98160253	51.537	**Means are not different**

Other Data	
Level of significance	0.05
Numerator d.f.	3
Denominator d.f.	41
MSW	1767.531
Q Statistic	3.44

The Turkey-Kramer procedure does not reveal significant difference between any pair

10.102 (c)
cont.

Spending:

$H_0 : \mu_1 = \mu_2 = \mu_3$

H_1 : Not all μ_j are equal for $j = 1, 2, 3$

Anova: Single Factor

SUMMARY

Groups	Count	Sum	Average	Variance
Spending_Full-Time	28	10965	391.6071	195085.3
Spending_Part-Time	7	2105	300.7143	21936.9
Spending_Unemployed	9	2940	326.6667	12400

ANOVA

Source of Variation	SS	df	MS	F	P-value	F crit
Between Groups	61919.07	2	30959.54	0.230868	0.794869	3.225684
Within Groups	5498124	41	134100.6			
Total	5560043	43				

Since p-value = 0.7949 > 0.05, do not reject H_0. There is insufficient evidence of a difference based on employment status in spending on textbooks and supplies.

Text Message:

$H_0 : \mu_1 = \mu_2 = \mu_3$

H_1 : Not all μ_j are equal for $j = 1, 2, 3$

Anova: Single Factor

SUMMARY

Groups	Count	Sum	Average	Variance
Text Messages_Full-Time	28	7308	261	115840.4
Text Messages_Part-Time	7	830	118.5714	23289.29
Text Messages_Unemployed	9	2090	232.2222	51175.69

ANOVA

Source of Variation	SS	df	MS	F	P-value	F crit
Between Groups	113601.6	2	56800.82	0.63338	0.535908	3.225684
Within Groups	3676833	41	89678.86			
Total	3790435	43				

Since p-value = 0.5359 > 0.05, do not reject H_0. There is insufficient evidence of a difference based on employment status in number of text messages sent in a typical week.

10.102 (c)   **Wealth:**
cont.
$H_0 : \mu_1 = \mu_2 = \mu_3$

H_1 : Not all μ_j are equal for $j = 1, 2, 3$

Anova: Single Factor						
SUMMARY						
Groups	*Count*	*Sum*	*Average*	*Variance*		
Wealth_Full-Time	28	416	14.85714	739.6144		
Wealth_Part-Time	7	28.4	4.057143	10.47286		
Wealth_Unemployed	9	23.8	2.644444	9.675278		
ANOVA						
Source of Variation	*SS*	*df*	*MS*	*F*	*P-value*	*F crit*
Between Groups	1376.658	2	688.3292	1.403368	0.257324	3.225684
Within Groups	20109.83	41	490.4836			
Total	21486.49	43				

Since p-value $= 0.2573 > 0.05$, do not reject H_0. There is insufficient evidence of a difference based on employment status in the amount of wealth needed to feel rich.

CHAPTER 11

OBJECTIVES

In this chapter, you learn:

- How and when to use the chi-square test for contingency tables

OVERVIEW AND KEY CONCEPTS

χ^2 Test for Differences in Two Proportions (Independent Samples)

- **Assumptions:**
  - Independent samples
  - Large sample sizes: All expected frequencies ≥ 5.
- **Test statistic:**
  - $$\chi^2 = \sum_{\text{All Cells}} \frac{(f_0 - f_e)^2}{f_e} \text{ with 1 degree of freedom}$$
    where
    f_o : observed frequency in a cell
    f_e = [(row total)(column total)]/n : expected frequency in a cell
  - The rejection region is always in the right tail.

χ^2 Test for Differences among More Than Two Proportions

- **Assumptions:**
  - Independent samples
  - Large sample sizes: All expected frequencies ≥ 1.
- **Test statistic:**
  - $$\chi^2 = \sum_{\text{All Cells}} \frac{(f_0 - f_e)^2}{f_e} \text{ with } (c-1) \text{ degree of freedom}$$
    where
    f_o : observed frequency in a cell
    f_e = [(row total)(column total)]/n: expected frequency in a cell
  - The rejection region is always in the right tail.

χ^2 Test of Independence

- **Assumptions:**
    - One sample is drawn with two factors; each factor has two or more levels (categories) of responses.
    - Large sample sizes: All expected frequencies ≥ 1.
- **Test statistic:**

    - $$\chi^2 = \sum_{\text{All Cells}} \frac{(f_0 - f_e)^2}{f_e} \text{ with } (r-1)(c-1) \text{ degree of freedom}$$

      where

      f_o : observed frequency in a cell

      f_e = [(row total)(column total)]/n: expected frequency in a cell

      r: the number of rows in the contingency table.

      c: the number of columns in the contingency table.
    - The rejection region is always in the right tail.
    - The χ^2 test does not show the nature of any relationship nor causality.

SOLUTIONS TO END OF SECTION
AND CHAPTER REVIEW EVEN PROBLEMS

11.2   (a)   For $df = 1$ and $\alpha = 0.05$, $\chi^2 = 3.841$.

(b)   For $df = 1$ and $\alpha = 0.025$, $\chi^2 = 5.024$.

(c)   For $df = 1$ and $\alpha = 0.01$, $\chi^2 = 6.635$.

11.4   (a)

Observed Freq	*Expected Freq*	Observed Freq	*Expected Freq*	Total Obs, Row 1
20	25	30	25	50
chi-sq contrib= 1.00		chi-sq contrib= 1.00		
Observed Freq	*Expected Freq*	Observed Freq	*Expected Freq*	Total Obs, Row 2
30	25	20	25	50
chi-sq contrib= 1.00		chi-sq contrib= 1.00		
Total Obs, Col 1		Total Obs, Col 2		GRAND TOTAL
50		50		100

(b)   Decision rule: If $\chi^2 > 3.841$, reject H_0.

Test statistic: $\chi^2_{STAT} = \displaystyle\sum_{All\,Cells} \frac{(f_0 - f_e)^2}{f_e} = 1.00 + 1.00 + 1.00 + 1.00 = 4$

Decision: Since $\chi^2_{STAT} = \displaystyle\sum_{All\,Cells} \frac{(f_0 - f_e)^2}{f_e} = 4$ is greater than the critical value of 3.841,

it is significant at the 5% level of significance.

11.6   PHStat output:

Chi-Square Test			
Observed Frequencies			
	Need >= 3 Clicks		
Year	Yes	No	Total
2009	39	61	100
2008	7	93	100
Total	46	154	200

Expected Frequencies			
	Need >= 3 Clicks		
Year	Yes	No	Total
2009	23	77	100
2008	23	77	100
Total	46	154	200

Data	
Level of Significance	0.05
Number of Rows	2
Number of Columns	2
Degrees of Freedom	1

Results	
Critical Value	3.841459
Chi-Square Test Statistic	28.91022
p-Value	7.58E-08
Reject the null hypothesis	

(a) $H_0: \pi_1 = \pi_2$ $H_1: \pi_1 \neq \pi_2$

(b)   Decision rule: $df = 1$. If $\chi^2_{STAT} > 3.8415$, reject H_0.

Test statistic: $\chi^2_{STAT} = 28.9102$

Decision: Since $\chi^2_{STAT} = 28.9102$ is greater than the upper critical bound of 3.8415, reject H_0. There is enough evidence the time to be removed from an email list has changed at the 0.05 level of significance.

(c)   You should not compare the results in (a) to those of Problem 10.30 part (b) because Problem 10.30 was a one-tail test.

11.8   (a) H_0: $\pi_1 = \pi_2$ H_1: $\pi_1 \neq \pi_2$

PHStat output with computation:

Chi-Square Test			
Observed Frequencies			
	Column variable		
Row variable	**Above age 70**	**12-50 years old**	**Total**
Yes	707	536	1243
No	293	464	757
Total	1000	1000	2000
Expected Frequencies			
	Column variable		
Row variable	Above age 70	12-50 years old	Total
Yes	621.5	621.5	1243
No	378.5	378.5	757
Total	1000	1000	2000
Data			
Level of Significance	0.01		
Number of Rows	2		
Number of Columns	2		
Degrees of Freedom	1		
Results			
Critical Value	6.634896		
Chi-Square Test Statistic	62.15201		
p-Value	3.18E-15		
Reject the null hypothesis			

Decision rule: $df = 1$. If $\chi^2_{STAT} > 6.6349$, reject H_0.

Test statistic: $\chi^2_{STAT} = \sum_{\text{All Cells}} \dfrac{(f_0 - f_e)^2}{f_e} = 62.1520$

Decision: Since $\chi^2_{STAT} = 62.1520$ is greater than the upper critical bound of 6.6349, reject H_0. There is enough evidence to conclude that there is a significant difference in the proportion of people who think emails should be answered quickly between the two age groups.

(b) p-value is virtually 0. The probability of obtaining a test statistic of 62.1520 or larger when the null hypothesis is true is virtually 0.

(c)   The results of (a) and (b) are exactly the same as those of Problem 10.32. The χ^2_{STAT} in (a) and the Z_{STAT} in Problem 10.32 (a) satisfy the relationship that $\chi^2_{STAT} = 62.1520 = (Z_{STAT})^2 = (7.8837)^2$ and the p-value in Problem 10.32 (b) is exactly the same as the p-value obtained in (b).

11.10   (a) H_0: $\pi_1 = \pi_2$ H_1: $\pi_1 \neq \pi_2$

PHStat output with computation:

Chi-Square Test

Observed Frequencies			
	Age		
Opposed	**Adults**	**12-17**	**Total**
Yes	670	510	1180
No	330	490	820
Total	1000	1000	2000

Expected Frequencies			
	Age		
Opposed	**Adults**	**12-17**	**Total**
Yes	590	590	1180
No	410	410	820
Total	1000	1000	2000

Data	
Level of Significance	0.05
Number of Rows	2
Number of Columns	2
Degrees of Freedom	1

Results	
Critical Value	3.841459
Chi-Square Test Statistic	52.91443
p-Value	3.48E-13
Reject the null hypothesis	

Decision rule: $df = 1$. If $\chi^2_{STAT} > 3.841$, reject H_0.

Test statistic: $\chi^2_{STAT} = \sum_{\text{All Cells}} \frac{(f_0 - f_e)^2}{f_e} = 52.9144$

Decision: Since $\chi^2_{STAT} = 52.9144$ is larger than the upper critical bound of 3.841, reject H_0. There is enough evidence of a difference between adult Internet users and Internet users age $12 - 17$ in the proportion who oppose ads.

(b)   *p*-value is virtually 0. The probability of obtaining a test statistic of $= 52.9144$ or larger when the null hypothesis is true is virtually 0.

11.12   (a)   The expected frequencies in the first row are 20, 30, and 40.
The expected frequencies in the second row are 30, 45, and 60.

(b) $\chi^2_{STAT} = 12.500$. The critical value with 2 degrees of freedom and $\alpha = 0.05$ is 5.991.
The result is deemed significant.

11.14   PHStat output:

Chi-Square Test

Observed Frequencies						
	Age Group					
Opposed	18-24	25-34	35-49	50-64	65-89	Total
Yes	110	118	132	154	164	678
No	90	82	68	46	36	322
Total	200	200	200	200	200	1000

Expected Frequencies						
	Age Group					
Opposed	18-24	25-34	35-49	50-64	65-89	Total
Yes	135.6	135.6	135.6	135.6	135.6	678
No	64.4	64.4	64.4	64.4	64.4	322
Total	200	200	200	200	200	1000

Data	
Level of Significance	0.05
Number of Rows	2
Number of Columns	5
Degrees of Freedom	4

Results	
Critical Value	9.487729
Chi-Square Test Statistic	48.62676
p-Value	6.99E-10
Reject the null hypothesis	

(a) $H_0: \pi_1 = \pi_2 = \pi_3 = \pi_4 = \pi_5$ H_1: Not all π_j are equal.

Test statistic: $\chi^2_{STAT} = \sum_{\text{All Cells}} \frac{(f_0 - f_e)^2}{f_e} = 48.6268$

Decision: Since the calculated test statistic 48.6268 is greater than the critical value of 9.4877, you reject H_0 and conclude that there is evidence of a difference among the age groups in the opposition to ads on web pages.

(b)   *p*-value is virtually zero. The probability of obtaining a data set which gives rise to a test statistic of 48.6268 or more is virtually zero if there is no difference among the age groups in the opposition to ads on web pages.

11.16 (a) $H_0 : \pi_1 = \pi_2 = \pi_3$ H_1 : at least one proportion differs
where population 1 = under 35, 2 = 35-54, 3 = over 54
PHStat output:

Observed Frequencies						Calculations		
	Column variable						fo-fe	
Row variable	Under 35	35-54	Over 54	Total				
Saturday	48	56	24	128		5.333	13.333	-18.66
A Day other than Saturday	152	144	176	472		-5.333	-13.333	18.66
Total	200	200	200	600				

Expected Frequencies								
	Column variable						(fo-fe)^2/fe	
Row variable	Under 35	35-54	Over 54	Total				
Saturday	42.667	42.667	42.667	128		0.667	4.167	8.16
A Day other than Saturday	157.333	157.333	157.333	472		0.181	1.130	2.21
Total	200	200	200	600				

Data	
Level of Significance	0.05
Number of Rows	2
Number of Columns	3
Degrees of Freedom	2

Results	
Critical Value	5.9915
Chi-Square Test Statistic	16.5254
p-Value	0.0003
Reject the null hypothesis	

Decision rule: $df = (c - 1) = (3 - 1) = 2$. If $\chi^2_{STAT} > 5.9915$, reject H_0.

Test statistic: $\chi^2_{STAT} = \sum_{\text{All Cells}} \frac{(f_0 - f_e)^2}{f_e} = 16.5254$

Decision: Since $\chi^2_{STAT} = 16.5254$ is greater than the upper critical bound of 5.9915, reject H_0. There is enough evidence to conclude that there is a significant relationship between age and major grocery shopping day.

(b)   *p*-value = 0.0003. The probability of obtaining a sample that gives rise to a test statistic that is equal to or more than 16.5254 is 0.0003 if the null hypothesis is true.

(c)   The stores can use this information to target their marketing on the specific group of shoppers on Saturday and the days other than Saturday.

11.18   PHStat output:

Chi-Square Test

Observed Frequencies				
	Age Group			
Often Listen	16 to 29	30 to 49	50 to 64	Total
Yes	90	84	66	240
No	110	116	134	360
Total	200	200	200	600

Expected Frequencies				
	Age Group			
Often Listen	16 to 29	30 to 49	50 to 64	Total
Yes	80	80	80	240
No	120	120	120	360
Total	200	200	200	600

Data	
Level of Significance	0.05
Number of Rows	2
Number of Columns	3
Degrees of Freedom	2

Results	
Critical Value	5.991465
Chi-Square Test Statistic	6.5
p-Value	0.038774
Reject the null hypothesis	

(a) H_0: $\pi_1 = \pi_2 = \pi_3$ H_1 Not all π_j are equal.

Test statistic: $\chi^2_{STAT} = \sum_{\text{All Cells}} \frac{(f_0 - f_e)^2}{f_e} = 6.5$

Decision: Since the calculated test statistic 6.5 is greater than the critical value of 5.9915, you reject H_0 and conclude that there is evidence of a significant difference among the age groups with respect to the proportion who often listened to rock music.

(b)   p-value = 0.0388. The probability of obtaining a data set which gives rise to a test statistic of 6.5 or more is virtually zero if there is no difference among the age groups with respect to the proportion who often listened to rock music.

11.20 $df = (r-1)(c-1) = (3-1)(4-1) = 6$

11.22 H_0: There is no relationship between type of dessert and type of entrée.
H_1: There is a relationship between type of dessert and type of entrée.

Test statistic: $\chi^2_{STAT} = \sum_{All\,Cells} \frac{(f_0 - f_e)^2}{f_e} = 92.1028$

Decision: Since the calculated test statistic 92.1028 is larger than the critical value of 16.9190, you reject H_0 and conclude that there is enough evidence of a relationship between type of dessert and type of entrée.

11.24   (a) H_0: There is no relationship between the commuting time of company employees and the level of stress-related problems observed on the job.
H_1: There is a relationship between the commuting time of company employees and the level of stress-related problems observed on the job.

PHStat output:

Observed Frequencies						Calculations		
	Stress					fo-fe		
Commuting Time	High	Moderate	Low	Total				
Under 15 min.	9	5	18	32		-3.1379	-0.2414	3.3793
15-45 min.	17	8	28	53		-3.1034	-0.6810	3.7845
Over 45 min.	18	6	7	31		6.2414	0.9224	-7.1638
Total	44	19	53	116				
Expected Frequencies								
	Stress							
Commuting Time	High	Moderate	Low	Total		(fo-fe)^2/fe		
Under 15 min.	12.1379	5.2414	14.6207	32		0.8112	0.0111	0.7811
15-45 min.	20.1034	8.6810	24.2155	53		0.4791	0.0534	0.5915
Over 45 min.	11.7586	5.0776	14.1638	31		3.3129	0.1676	3.6233
Total	44	19	53	116				
Level of Significance	0.01							
Number of Rows	3							
Number of Columns	3							
Degrees of Freedom	4							
Results								
Critical Value	13.2767							
Chi-Square Test Statistic	9.8311							
p-Value	0.04337							
Do not reject the null hypothesis								

(a)   Decision rule: If $\chi^2_{STAT} > 13.277$, reject H_0.

Test statistic: $\chi^2_{STAT} = \sum_{All\,Cells} \frac{(f_0 - f_e)^2}{f_e} = 9.831$

Decision: Since $\chi^2_{STAT} = 9.831$ is less than the critical bound of 13.277, do not reject H_0. There is not enough evidence to conclude there is any relationship between the commuting time of company employees and the level of stress-related problems observed on the job.

(b)   Decision rule: If $\chi^2_{STAT} > 9.488$, reject H_0.

Decision: Since the $\chi^2_{STAT} = 9.831$ is greater than the critical bound of 9.488, reject H_0. There is enough evidence at the 0.05 level to conclude there is a relationship between the commuting time of company employees and the level of stress-related problems observed on the job.

11.30 (a) H_0: There is no relationship between a student's gender and his/her pizzeria selection.
H_1: There is a relationship between a student's gender and his/her pizzeria selection.
Decision rule: $d.f. = 1$.   If $\chi^2_{STAT} > 3.841$, reject H_0.   Test statistic: $\chi^2_{STAT} = 0.412$

Decision: Since the $\chi^2_{STAT} = 0.412$ is smaller than the critical bound of 3.841, do not reject H_0. There is not enough evidence to conclude that there is a relationship between a student's gender and his/her pizzeria selection.

(b)   Test statistic: $\chi^2_{STAT} = 2.624$

Decision: Since the $\chi^2_{STAT} = 2.624$ is less than the critical bound of 3.841, do not reject H_0. There is not enough evidence to conclude that there is a relationship between a student's gender and his/her pizzeria selection.

(c) H_0: There is no relationship between price and pizzeria selection.
H_1: There is a relationship between price and pizzeria selection.
Decision rule: $d.f. = 2$.   If $\chi^2_{STAT} > 5.991$, reject H_0.   Test statistic: $\chi^2_{STAT} = 4.956$

Decision: Since the $\chi^2_{STAT} = 4.956$ is smaller than the critical bound of 5.991, do not reject H_0. There is not enough evidence to conclude that there is a relationship between price and pizzeria selection.

(d) p-value = 0.0839. The probability of obtaining a sample that gives a test statistic equal to or greater than 4.956 is 0.0839 if the null hypothesis of no relationship between price and pizzeria selection is true.

11.32 (a) H_0: There is no relationship between the attitudes of employees toward the use of self-managed work teams and employee job classification.
H_1: There is a relationship between the attitudes of employees toward the use of self-managed work teams and employee job classification.
Decision rule: If $\chi^2_{STAT} > 12.592$, reject H_0.

Test statistic: $\chi^2_{STAT} = 11.895$

Decision: Since $\chi^2_{STAT} = 11.895$ is less than the critical bound 12.592, do not reject H_0. There is not enough evidence to conclude that there is a relationship between the attitudes of employees toward the use of self-managed work teams and employee job classification.

(b) H_0: There is no relationship between the attitudes of employees toward vacation time without pay and employee job classification.
H_1: There is a relationship between the attitudes of employees toward vacation time without pay and employee job classification.
Decision rule: If $\chi^2_{STAT} > 12.592$, reject H_0.

Test statistic: $\chi^2_{STAT} = 3.294$

Decision: Since $\chi^2_{STAT} = 3.294$ is less than the critical bound 12.592, do not reject H_0. There is not enough evidence to conclude that there is a relationship between the attitudes of employees toward vacation time without pay and employee job classification.

11.34   (a)

Count of Type	Type		
Fees	Intermediate Government	Short Term Corporate	Grand Total
No	53	77	130
Yes	34	20	54
Grand Total	87	97	184

(b) H_0: There is no relationship between the category of a bond fund and whether or not there is a sales charge.

H_1: There is a relationship between the category of a bond fund and whether or not there is a sales charge.

Chi-Square Test

Observed Frequencies			
	Type		
Fees	Intermediate Government	Short Term Corporate	Total
No	53	77	130
Yes	34	20	54
Total	87	97	184

Expected Frequencies			
	Type		
Fees	Intermediate Government	Short Term Corporate	Total
No	61.4673913	68.5326087	130
Yes	25.5326087	28.4673913	54
Total	87	97	184

Data	
Level of Significance	0.05
Number of Rows	2
Number of Columns	2
Degrees of Freedom	1

Results	
Critical Value	3.841459149
Chi-Square Test Statistic	7.539188998
p-Value	0.006037122
Reject the null hypothesis	

Decision rule: If $\chi^2_{STAT} > 3.8415$, reject H_0.

Test statistic: $\chi^2_{STAT} = \sum_{All\,Cells} \frac{(f_0 - f_e)^2}{f_e} = 7.5392$

Decision: Since $\chi^2_{STAT} = 7.5392$ is greater than the critical bound of 3.8415, reject H_0.

There is enough evidence to conclude there is a relationship between the type of a bond fund and whether or not there is a sales charge.

11.36   (a)

Count of Risk	Risk			
Type	Above average	Average	Below average	Grand Total
Intermediate Government	29	32	26	87
Short Term Corporate	30	37	30	97
Grand Total	59	69	56	184

(b) H_0: There is no relationship between the perceived risk of a mutual fund and its type.

H_1: There is a relationship between the perceived risk of a mutual fund and its type.

Chi-Square Test

Observed Frequencies				
	Column variable			
Type	Above ave	Average	Below ave	Total
Intermediate Government	29	32	26	87
Short Term Corporate	30	37	30	97
Total	59	69	56	184

Expected Frequencies				
	Column variable			
Type	bove avera	Average	elow avera	Total
Intermediate Government	27.89674	32.625	26.47826	87
Short Term Corporate	31.10326	36.375	29.52174	97
Total	59	69	56	184

Data	
Level of Significance	0.05
Number of Rows	2
Number of Columns	3
Degrees of Freedom	2

Results	
Critical Value	5.991465
Chi-Square Test Statistic	0.121864
p-Value	0.940887
Do not reject the null hypothesis	

Decision rule: If $\chi_{STAT}^2 > 5.9915$, reject H_0.

Test statistic: $\chi_{STAT}^2 = \displaystyle\sum_{\text{All Cells}} \frac{(f_0 - f_e)^2}{f_e} = 0.1219$

Decision: Since $\chi_{STAT}^2 = 0.1219$ is smaller than the critical bound of 5.9915, do not reject H_0. There is not enough evidence to conclude there is a relationship between the perceived risk of a bond fund and its type.

CHAPTER 12

OBJECTIVES

In this chapter, you learn:

- How to use regression analysis to predict the value of a dependent variable based on an independent variable
- The meaning of the regression coefficients b_0 and b_1
- How to evaluate the assumptions of regression analysis and know what to do if the assumptions are violated
- How to make inferences about the slope and correlation coefficient
- How to estimate mean values and predict individual values

OVERVIEW AND KEY CONCEPTS

Purpose of Regression Analysis

- Regression analysis is used for predicting the values of a dependent (response) variable based on the value of at least one independent (explanatory) variable.

The Simple Linear Regression Model

- The relationship between the dependent variable (Y) and the explanatory variable (X) is described by a linear function.
- The change of the explanatory variable causes the explained (dependent) variable to change.
- The value of the explained variable depends on the explanatory variable.
- The population linear regression: $Y_i = \beta_0 + \beta_1 X_i + \varepsilon_i$ where β_0 is the intercept and β_1 is the slope of the population regression line $\mu_{Y|X} = \beta_0 + \beta_1 X_i$ and ε_i is called the error term.

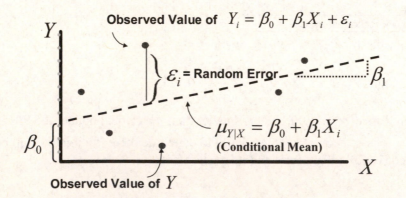

- The parameters β_0 and β_1 are unknown and need to be estimated.
- The least squares estimates for β_0 and β_1 are b_0 and b_1, respectively, obtained by minimizing the sum of squared residuals, $\sum_{i=1}^{n} \left(Y_i - \left(b_0 + b_1 X_i \right) \right)^2 = \sum_{i=1}^{n} e_i^{\,2}$.

- The sample linear regression: $Y_i = b_0 + b_1 X_i + e_i$ where b_0 is the intercept and b_1 is the slope of the simple linear regression equation $\hat{Y} = b_0 + b_1 X_i$ and e_i is called the residual.
- The simple linear regression equation (sample regression line) $\hat{Y} = b_0 + b_1 X_i$ can be used to predict the value of the dependent variable for a given value of the independent variable X.

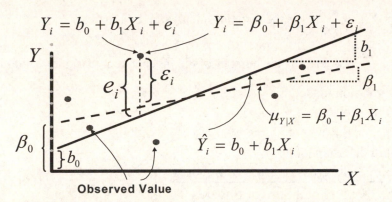

Interpretations of β_0, β_1, b_0 and b_1

- $\beta_0 = E(Y \mid X = 0) = \mu_{Y\mid X=0}$ is the average value of Y when the value of X is zero.
- $b_0 = \hat{E}(Y \mid X = 0) = \hat{Y}(X = 0)$ is the **estimated** average value of Y when the value of X is zero.
- $\beta_1 = \dfrac{\text{change in } E(Y \mid X)}{\text{change in } X} = \dfrac{\text{change in } \mu_{Y\mid X}}{\text{change in } X}$ measures the change in the average value of Y as a result of a one-unit change in X.
- $b_1 = \dfrac{\text{change in } \hat{E}(Y \mid X)}{\text{change in } X} = \dfrac{\text{change in } \hat{Y}}{\text{change in } X}$ measures the **estimated** change in the average value of Y as a result of a one-unit change in X.

Some Important Identities in the Simple Linear Regression Model

- $Y_i = \beta_0 + \beta_1 X_i + \varepsilon_i = \mu_{Y\mid X} + \varepsilon_i$. The value of the dependent variable is decomposed into the value on the population regression line and the error term.
- $Y_i = b_0 + b_1 X_i + e_i = \hat{Y}_i + e_i$. The value of the dependent variable is decomposed into the value on the sample regression line (fitted regression line) and the residual term.
- $\mu_{Y\mid X} = \beta_0 + \beta_1 X_i = E(Y \mid X)$ is the population regression line, which measures the average value of the dependent variable Y for a particular value of the independent variable X. Hence, it is also sometimes called the conditional mean regression line.
- $\hat{Y}_i = b_0 + b_1 X_i$ is the sample regression line (simple linear regression equation), which measures the **estimated** average value of the dependent variable Y for a particular value of the independent variable X. It also provides prediction for the value of Y for a given value of X.
- $\varepsilon_i = Y_i - \mu_{Y\mid X} = Y_i - (\beta_0 + \beta_1 X_i)$ is the error.
- $e_i = Y_i - \hat{Y}_i = Y_i - (b_0 + b_1 X_i)$ is the residual.

- $SST = \sum_{i=1}^{n}(Y_i - \bar{Y})^2$ is the total sum of squares.

- $SSR = \sum_{i=1}^{n}(\hat{Y}_i - \bar{Y})^2$ is the regression (explained) sum of squares.

- $SSE = \sum_{i=1}^{n}(Y_i - \hat{Y}_i)^2 = \sum_{i=1}^{n}e_i^2$ is the error (residual) sum of squares.

- $MSR = \dfrac{SSR}{k} = \dfrac{SSR}{1}$ where k is the number of the independent variable, which is 1 in the simple linear regression model.

- $MSE = \dfrac{SSE}{n-k-1} = \dfrac{SSE}{n-2}$

- The coefficient of determination
  - $r^2 = \dfrac{SSR}{SST} = \dfrac{\text{Regression Sum of Squares}}{\text{Total Sum of Squares}}$
  - The coefficient of determination measures the proportion of variation in Y that is explained by the independent variable X in the regression model.

- Standard error of estimate
  - $S_{YX} = \sqrt{\dfrac{SSE}{n-2}} = \sqrt{\dfrac{\sum_{i=1}^{n}(Y - \hat{Y}_i)^2}{n-2}}$
  - The standard error of estimate is the standard deviation of the variation of observations around the sample regression line $\hat{Y}_i = b_0 + b_1 X_i$.

The ANOVA Table for the Simple Linear Regression Model as Presented in Excel

ANOVA					
	df	SS	MS	F	Significance F
Regression	k	SSR	MSR=SSR/k	MSR/MSE	p-value of the F Test
Residuals	n-k-1	SSE	MSE=SSE/(n-k-1)		
Total	n-1	SST			

Assumptions Needed for the Simple Linear Regression Model

- Normality of error: The errors around the population regression line are normally distributed at each X value. This also implies that the dependent variable is normally distributed at each value of the independent variable.
- Homoscedasticity: The variance (amount of variation) of the errors around the population regression line is the same at each X value.
- Independence of errors: The errors around the population regression line are independent for each value of X.

Residual Analysis

- Residual analysis is used to evaluate whether the regression model that has been fitted to the data is an appropriate model.
- **Residual analysis for linearity:**

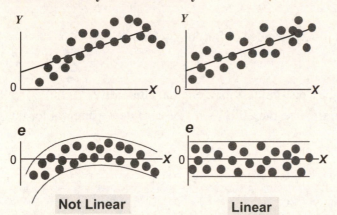

- **Residual analysis for homoscedasticity:**

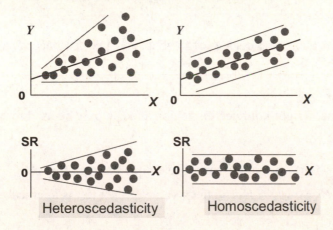

- **Residual analysis for independence:**

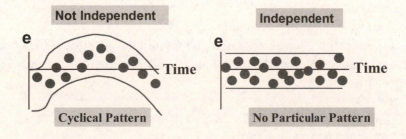

t Test for the Slope Parameter β_1

- $H_0 : \beta_1 = 0$ (*Y* does not depend on *X*)

  $H_1 : \beta_1 \neq 0$ (*Y* depends linearly on *X*)
- **Test statistic:**
  - $t = \dfrac{b_1 - \beta_1}{S_{b_1}}$ with $(n-2)$ degrees of freedom, where $S_{b_1} = \dfrac{S_{YX}}{\sqrt{\sum\limits_{i=1}^{n}(X_i - \bar{X})^2}}$

  - The *t* test can also be a one-tail test for a one-tail alternative.
- **Confidence interval estimate:** Use the $100(1-\alpha)\%$ confidence interval for the slope parameter β_1.
  - $b_1 \pm t_{\alpha/2,n-2} S_{b_1}$

F Test for the Slope Parameter β_1

- $H_0 : \beta_1 = 0$ (*Y* does not depend on *X*)

  $H_1 : \beta_1 \neq 0$ (*Y* depends linearly on *X*)
- **Test statistic:**
  - $F = \dfrac{\dfrac{SSR}{1}}{\dfrac{SSE}{(n-2)}}$ with 1 numerator degrees of freedom and $(n-2)$ denominator degrees of freedom.
  - The *F* test always has a right-tail rejection region and can only be used for the two-tail alternative.

The Relationship between the *t* Test and *F* Test for the Slope Parameter β_1

- For $H_0 : \beta_1 = 0$ vs $H_1 : \beta_1 \neq 0$, $t^2 = F$ and the *p*-value of the *t* test is identical to the *p*-value of the *F* test.

Correlation Analysis

- Correlation analysis is concerned with the strength of any linear relationship between 2 quantitative variables.
- There is no causal effect implied in a correlation analysis.
- The population correlation coefficient ρ is used to measure the strength of the linear relationship between the variables while the sample correlation coefficient r provides an estimate of the strength.
- **Features of ρ and r :**
  - They are unit free.
  - Their values range between −1 and +1.
  - The close is the value to −1, the stronger is the negative linear relationship.
  - The close is the value to +1, the stronger is the positive linear relationship.
  - The close is the value to 0, the weaker is any linear relationship.

t Test for a Linear Relationship

- **Hypotheses:**
  - $H_0 : \rho = 0$ (There is no linear relationship)
  - $H_1 : \rho \neq 0$ (There is some linear relationship)
- **Test statistic:**
  - $t = \dfrac{r - \rho}{\sqrt{\dfrac{1 - r^2}{n - 2}}}$ with $(n - 2)$ degrees of freedom, where

$$r = \sqrt{r^2} = \frac{\displaystyle\sum_{i=1}^{n}(X_i - \bar{X})(Y_i - \bar{Y})}{\sqrt{\displaystyle\sum_{i=1}^{n}(X_i - \bar{X})^2 \sum_{i=1}^{n}(Y_i - \bar{Y})^2}}.$$

  - The *t* test can be a one-tail test for a one-tail alternative.

Confidence Interval Estimate for the Mean of Y $\left(\mu_{Y|X}\right)$

- The point estimate for $\mu_{Y|X=X_i}$ is $\hat{Y}_i$

- The confidence interval estimate for $\mu_{Y|X}$ is $\hat{Y}_i \pm t_{\alpha/2, n-2} S_{YX} \sqrt{\dfrac{1}{n} + \dfrac{(X_i - \bar{X})^2}{\displaystyle\sum_{i=1}^{n}(X_i - \bar{X})^2}}$

Prediction Interval for an Individual Response Y

- The point prediction for an individual response Y_i at a particular X_i, denoted as $Y_{X=X_i}$ is

$$\hat{Y}_i = b_0 + b_1 X_i$$

- The prediction interval for an individual response Y_i is

$$\hat{Y}_i \pm t_{\alpha/2, n-2} S_{YX} \sqrt{1 + \frac{1}{n} + \frac{(X_i - \bar{X})^2}{\displaystyle\sum_{i=1}^{n}(X_i - \bar{X})^2}}$$

Common Pitfalls in Regression Analysis

- Lacking an awareness of the assumptions underlying least-squares regression
- Not knowing how to evaluate the assumptions
- Not knowing what the alternatives to least-squares regression are if a particular assumption is violated
- Using a regression model without knowledge of the subject matter
- Extrapolating outside the relevant range
- Concluding that a significant relationship identified in an observational study is due to a cause-and-effect relationship

Strategy for Avoiding the Pitfalls in Regression

- Always start with a scatter plot to observe the possible relationship between X and Y
- Check the assumptions of the regression after the regression model has been fit, before moving on to using the results of the model
- Plot the residuals versus the independent variable to determine whether the model fit to the data is appropriate and check visually for violations of the homoscedasticity assumption
- Use a histogram, stem-and-leaf display, box plot, or normal probability plot of the residuals to graphically evaluate whether the normality assumption has been seriously violated
- If the evaluations indicate violations in the assumptions, use alternative methods to least-squares regression or alternative least-squares models (quadratic or multiple regression) depending on what the evaluation has indicated
- If the evaluations do not indicate violations in the assumptions, then the inferential aspects of the regression analysis can be undertaken, tests for the significance of the regression coefficients can be done, and confidence and prediction intervals can be developed
- Avoid making predictions and forecasts outside the relevant range of the independent variable
- Always note that the relationships identified in observational studies may or may not be due to a cause-and-effect relationship, and remember that while causation implies correlation, correlation does not imply causation

SOLUTIONS TO END OF SECTION
AND CHAPTER REVIEW EVEN PROBLEMS

12.2   (a)   yes,   (b) no,   (c) no,   (d) yes

12.4   (a)

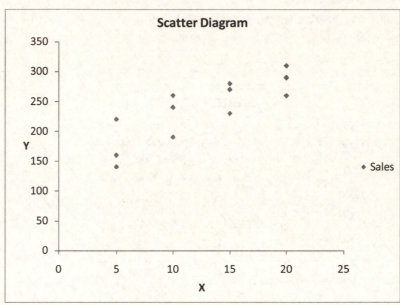

The scatter plot shows a positive linear relationship.

(b)   For each increase in shelf space of an additional foot, there is an expected increase in weekly sales of an estimated $7.40.

(c) $\hat{Y} = 145 + 7.4X = 145 + 7.4(8) = \$204.20$

12.6   (a)

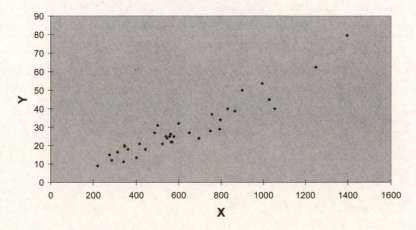

12.6   (b)   Partial Excel output:
cont.

	Coefficients	Standard Error	t Stat	P-value
Intercept	-2.3697	2.0733	-1.1430	0.2610
Feet	0.0501	0.0030	16.5223	0.0000

(c)   The estimated mean amount of labor will increase by 0.05 hour for each additional cubic foot moved.

(d) $\hat{Y} = -2.3697 + 0.0501(500) = 22.6705$

12.8   (a)

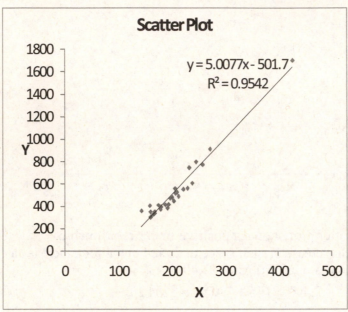

(b)   Partial PHStat output:

	Coefficients	Standard Error	t Stat	P-value
Intercept	-501.7008	43.7544	-11.4663	0.0000
Revenue	5.0077	0.2073	24.1555	0.0000

$b_0 = -501.7008$ $b_1 = 5.0077$

(c)   For each additional million dollars increase in revenue, the mean annual value will increase by an estimated 5.0077 million dollars. Literal interpretation of b_0 is not meaningful because an operating franchise cannot have zero revenue.

(d) $\hat{Y} = -501.7008 + 5.0077(150) = 249.4485$ million dollars

12.10   (a)

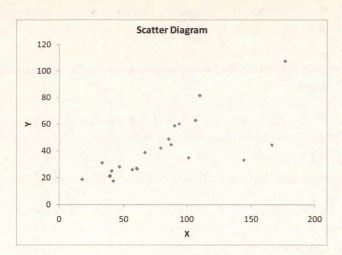

(b)

	Coefficients	Standard Error	t Stat	P-value
Intercept	10.47300676	7.030942955	1.489559342	0.151941591
Gross	0.383904431	0.078405148	4.89641868	8.72425E-05

$$\hat{Y} = b_0 + b_1 X = 10.4730 + 0.3839X$$

(c)   For each increase of one additional million dollars of box office gross, the estimated mean revenue of DVDs sold will increase by 0.3839 million dollars.

(d) $\hat{Y} = b_0 + b_1 X = 10.4730 + 0.3839(75) = 39.2658$ million dollars.

12.12 $SST = 40$ and $r^2 = 0.90$. So, 90% of the variation in the dependent variable can be explained by the variation in the independent variable.

12.14 $r^2 = 0.75$. So, 75% of the variation in the dependent variable can be explained by the variation in the independent variable.

12.16   (a) $r^2 = \dfrac{SSR}{SST} = \dfrac{20,535}{30,025} = 0.684$. So, 68.4% of the variation in weekly sales can be explained by the variation in shelf space.

(b) $S_{YX} = \sqrt{\dfrac{SSE}{n-2}} = \sqrt{\dfrac{\sum_{i=1}^{n}\left(Y_i - \hat{Y}_i\right)^2}{n-2}} = \sqrt{\dfrac{9490}{10}} = 30.8058$

(c)   Based on (a) and (b), the model should be moderately useful for predicting sales.

12.18   (a) $r^2 = 0.8892$. So, 88.92% of the variation in labor hours can be explained by the variation in cubic feet moved.

(b) $S_{YX} = 5.0314$

(c)   Based on (a) and (b), the model should be very useful for predicting labor hours.

12.20   (a) $r^2 = 0.9542$. So, 95.42% of the variation in value of a baseball franchise can be explained by the variation in its annual revenue.

(b) $S_{YX} = 58.9821$

(c)   Based on (a) and (b), the model should be very useful for predicting the value of a baseball franchise.

12.22   (a) $r^2 = 0.5452$. So, 54.52% of the variation in the revenue from DVDs sold can be explained by the variation in box office gross.

(b) $S_{YX} = 15.3782$.

(c)   Based on (a) and (b), the model is moderately useful for predicting the revenue from DVDs sold.

(d)   Other variables that might explain the variation in DVDs revenue could be the amount spent on advertising, the timing of the release of the DVDs and the distribution channels of the DVDs.

12.24   A residual analysis of the data indicates a pattern, with sizable clusters of consecutive residuals that are either all positive or all negative. This pattern indicates a violation of the assumption of linearity. A curvilinear model should be investigated.

12.26

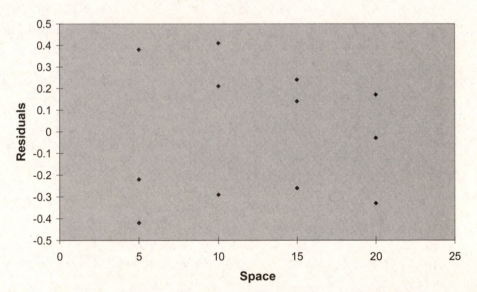

Based on the residual plot, there does not appear to be a pattern in the residual plot.

12.26
cont.

Normal Probability Plot

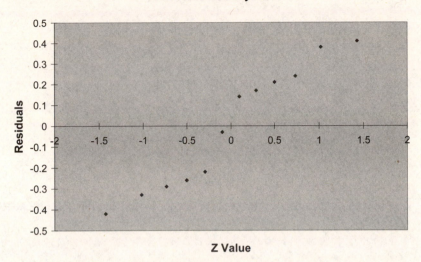

There does not appear to be a pattern in the residual plot. The assumptions of regression do not appear to be seriously violated.

12.28

Feet Residual Plot

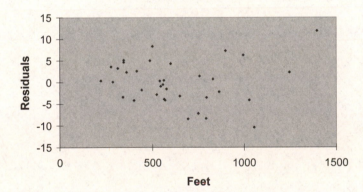

Based on the residual plot, there does not appear to be a curvilinear pattern in the residuals.

12.28
cont.

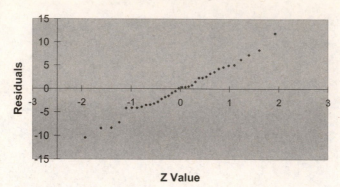

Normal Probability Plot

The assumptions of normality and equal variance do not appear to be seriously violated.

12.30

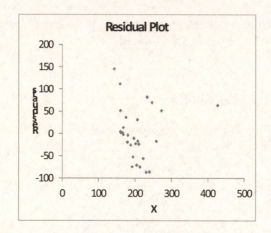

Residual Plot

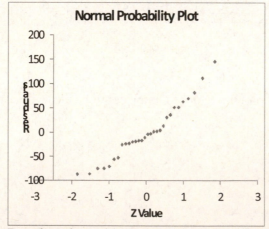

Normal Probability Plot

Based on the residual plot, there appears to be a nonlinear pattern in the residuals. A curvilinear model should be investigated.

The normal probability plot does not reveal serious violation of the normality assumption.

12.32 (a)

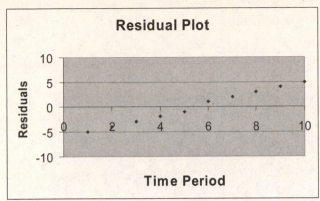

An increasing linear relationship exists.

(b)   There appears to be strong positive autocorrelation among the residuals.

12.34 (a)   No, it is not necessary to compute the Durbin-Watson statistic since the data have been collected for a single period for a set of stores.

(b)   If a single store was studied over a period of time and the amount of shelf space varied over time, computation of the Durbin-Watson statistic would be necessary.

12.36 (a) $b_1 = \dfrac{SSXY}{SSX} = \dfrac{201399.05}{12495626} = 0.0161$

$b_0 = \overline{Y} - b_1\overline{X} = 71.2621 - 0.0161(4393) = 0.458$

(b) $\hat{Y} = 0.458 + 0.0161X = 0.458 + 0.0161(4500) = 72.908$ or $72,908

(c)

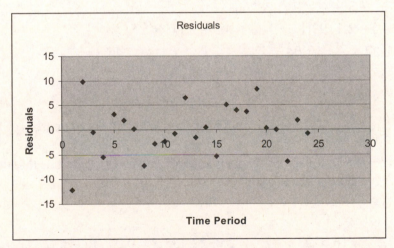

(d) $D = \dfrac{\sum\limits_{i=2}^{n}(e_i - e_{i-1})^2}{\sum\limits_{i=1}^{n}e_i^2} = \dfrac{1243.2244}{599.0683} = 2.08 > 1.45$. There is no evidence of positive autocorrelation among the residuals.

(e)   Based on a residual analysis, the model appears to be adequate.

12.38   (a) $b_0 = -2.535$, $b_1 = 0.060728$

(b) $\hat{Y} = -2.535 + 0.060728X = -2.535 + 0.060728(83) = 2.5054$ or $\$2505.40$

(c)

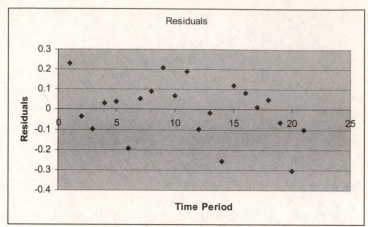

(d) $D = 1.64 > 1.42$. There is no evidence of positive autocorrelation among the residuals.

(e)   The plot of the residuals versus time period shows some clustering of positive and negative residuals for intervals in the domain, suggesting a nonlinear model might be better. Otherwise, the model appears to be adequate.

12.40   (a) $H_0 : \beta_1 = 0$ $H_1 : \beta_1 \neq 0$

Test statistic: $t_{STAT} = (b_1 - 0) / s_{b_1} = 4.5 / 1.5 = 3.00$

(b)   With $n = 18$, df $= 18 - 2 = 16$, $t_{0.05/2} = \pm 2.1199$.

(c)   Reject H_0. There is evidence that the fitted linear regression model is useful.

(d) $b_1 - t_{0.05/2} s_{b_1} \leq \beta_1 \leq b_1 + t_{0.05/2} s_{b_1}$

$4.5 - 2.1199(1.5) \leq \beta_1 \leq 4.5 + 2.1199(1.5)$

$1.32 \leq \beta_1 \leq 7.68$

12.42   (a) $H_0 : \beta_1 = 0$ $H_1 : \beta_1 \neq 0$

$t_{STAT} = \dfrac{b_1 - \beta_1}{S_{b_1}} = \dfrac{7.4}{1.59} = 4.65 > t_{0.05} = 2.2281$ with 10 degrees of freedom for

$\alpha = 0.05$. Reject H_0. There is enough evidence to conclude that the fitted linear regression model is useful.

(b) $b_1 \pm t_{\alpha/2} S_{b_1} = 7.4 \pm 2.2281(1.59)$ $3.86 \leq \beta_1 \leq 10.94$

12.44   (a) $t_{STAT} = 16.5223 > t_{0.05/2} = 2.0322$ for $\alpha = 0.05$. Reject H_0. There is evidence that the fitted linear regression model is useful.

(b) $0.0439 \leq \beta_1 \leq 0.0562$

12.46 (a) $H_0 : \beta_1 = 0$ $H_1 : \beta_1 \neq 0$

	Coefficients	Standard Error	t Stat	P-value	Lower 95%	Upper 95%
Intercept	-501.7008	43.7544	-11.4663	0.0000	-591.3277	-412.0740
Revenue	5.0077	0.2073	24.1555	0.0000	4.5830	5.4323

Since the p-value is essentially zero, reject H_0 at 5% level of significance. There is evidence of a linear relationship between annual revenue sales and franchise value.

(b) $4.5830 \leq \beta_1 \leq 5.4323$

12.48 (a)   Partial Excel output:

	Coefficients	Standard Error	t Stat	P-value	Lower 95%	Upper 95%
Intercept	10.47300676	7.030942955	1.489559342	0.151941591	-4.193283201	25.13929672
Gross	0.383904431	0.078405148	4.89641868	8.72425E-05	0.220354159	0.547454703

p-value is essentially $0 < 0.05$. Reject H_0. There is evidence of a linear relationship between box office gross and DVD revenue.

(b) $0.2204 \leq \beta_1 \leq 0.5475$

12.50 (a)   (% weekly change in BGU) = 0.0 + 3.0 (% weekly change in Russell 1000 Index)
       (b)   If the Russell 1000 Index gains 10% in a year, the BGU is expected to gain an estimated 30% on average.
       (c)   If the Russell 1000 Index loses 20% in a year, the BGU is expected to lose an estimated 60% on average.
       (d)   Risk takers will be attracted to leveraged funds, but risk averse investors will stay away.

12.52 (a)   **First weekend gross and the U. S. gross**
       $r = -0.2526$. There appears to be a weak negative linear relationship.
       First weekend gross and the worldwide gross
       $r = -0.4149$. There appears to be a moderate negative linear relationship.
       U. S. gross, and worldwide gross
       $r = 0.9414$. There appears to be a strong positive linear relationship.
       (b)   **First weekend gross and the U. S. gross**
       $t = -0.5221$, p-value = 0.6292 > 0.05. Do not reject H_0. At the 0.05 level of significance, there is not a significant linear relationship.
       First weekend gross and the worldwide gross
       $t = -0.9120$, p-value = 0.4134 > 0.05. Do not reject H_0. At the 0.05 level of significance, there is not a significant linear relationship.
       U. S. gross, and worldwide gross
       $t = 5.5807$, p-value = 0.0051 < 0.05. Reject H_0. At the 0.05 level of significance, there is a significant linear relationship.

12.54 (a) $r = 0.5497$. There appears to be a moderate positive linear relationship between the average Wonderlic score of football players trying out for the NFL and the graduation rate for football players at selected schools.
       (b) $t = 3.9485$, p-value = 0.0004 < 0.05. Reject H_0. At the 0.05 level of significance, there is a significant linear relationship between the average Wonderlic score of football players trying out for the NFL and the graduation rate for football players at selected schools.
       (c)   There is a significant linear relationship between the average Wonderlic score of football players trying out for the NFL and the graduation rate for football players at selected schools but the positive linear relationship is considered as only moderate.

12.56   (a)   When $X = 4$, $\hat{Y} = 5 + 3X = 5 + 3(4) = 17$

$$h = \frac{1}{n} + \frac{(X_i - \overline{X})^2}{\sum_{i=1}^{n}(X_i - \overline{X})^2} = \frac{1}{20} + \frac{(4-2)^2}{20} = 0.25$$

95% confidence interval: $\hat{Y} \pm t_{0.05/2} s_{YX} \sqrt{h} = 17 \pm 2.1009 \cdot 1 \cdot \sqrt{0.25}$

$$15.95 \leq \mu_{Y|X=4} \leq 18.05$$

(b)   95% prediction interval: $\hat{Y} \pm t_{0.05/2} s_{YX} \sqrt{1 + h} = 17 \pm 2.1009 \cdot 1 \cdot \sqrt{1.25}$

$$14.651 \leq Y_{X=4} \leq 19.349$$

(c)   The intervals in this problem are wider because the value of X is farther from $\overline{X}$.

12.58   (a) $\hat{Y}_i \pm t_{\alpha/2} S_{YX} \sqrt{h_i} = 204.2 \pm 2.2281(30.81)\sqrt{0.1373}$

$$178.76 \leq \mu_{Y|X=8} \leq 229.64$$

(b) $\hat{Y}_i \pm t_{\alpha/2} S_{YX} \sqrt{1 + h_i} = 204.2 \pm 2.2281(30.81)\sqrt{1 + 0.1373}$

$$131.00 \leq Y_{X=8} \leq 277.40$$

(c)   Part (b) provides a prediction interval for the individual response given a specific value of the independent variable, and part (a) provides an interval estimate for the mean value, given a specific value of the independent variable. Because there is much more variation in predicting an individual value than in estimating a mean value, a prediction interval is wider than a confidence interval estimate.

12.60   (a) $0.2543 \leq \mu_{Y|X=0} \leq 1.2457$

(b) $-1.4668 \leq Y_{X=0} \leq 2.9668$

(c)   Part (b) provides an interval prediction for the individual response given a specific value of the independent variable, and part (a) provides an interval estimate for the mean value given a specific value of the independent variable. Since there is much more variation in predicting an individual value than in estimating a mean value, a prediction interval is wider than a confidence interval estimate holding everything else fixed.

12.62   (a) $217.4561 \leq \mu_{Y|X=150} \leq 281.4410$

(b) $124.4653 \leq Y_{X=150} \leq 374.4318$

(c)   Part (b) provides an interval prediction for the individual response given a specific value of the independent variable, and part (a) provides an interval estimate for the mean value given a specific value of the independent variable. Since there is much more variation in predicting an individual value than in estimating a mean value, a prediction interval is wider than a confidence interval estimate holding everything else fixed.

12.64   The slope of the line, b_1, represents the estimated expected change in Y per unit change in X. It represents the estimated mean amount that Y changes (either positively or negatively) for a particular unit change in X. The Y intercept b_0 represents the estimated mean value of Y when X equals 0.

12.66 The unexplained variation or error sum of squares (SSE) will be equal to zero only when the regression line fits the data perfectly and the coefficient of determination equals 1.

12.68 Unless a residual analysis is undertaken, you will not know whether the model fit is appropriate for the data. In addition, residual analysis can be used to check whether the assumptions of regression have been seriously violated.

12.70 The normality of error assumption can be evaluated by obtaining a histogram, boxplot, and/or normal probability plot of the residuals. The homoscedasticity assumption can be evaluated by plotting the residuals on the vertical axis and the X variable on the horizontal axis. The independence of errors assumption can be evaluated by plotting the residuals on the vertical axis and the time order variable on the horizontal axis. This assumption can also be evaluated by computing the Durbin-Watson statistic.

12.72 The confidence interval for the mean response estimates the mean response for a given X value. The prediction interval estimates the value for a single item or individual.

12.74 (a) $b_0 = 24.84$, $b_1 = 0.14$

(b) 24.84 is the portion of estimated mean delivery time that is not affected by the number of cases delivered. For each additional case, the estimated mean delivery time increases by 0.14 minutes.

(c) $\hat{Y} = 24.84 + 0.14X = 24.84 + 0.14(150) = 45.84$

(d) No, 500 cases is outside the relevant range of the data used to fit the regression equation.

(e) $r^2 = 0.972$. So, 97.2% of the variation in delivery time can be explained by the variation in the number of cases.

(f) Based on a visual inspection of the graphs of the distribution of residuals and the residuals versus the number of cases, there is no pattern. The model appears to be adequate.

(g) $t = 24.88 > t_{0.05/2} = 2.1009$ with 18 degrees of freedom for $\alpha = 0.05$. Reject H_0. There is evidence that the fitted linear regression model is useful.

(h) $44.88 \le \mu_{Y|X=150} \le 46.80$

$41.56 \le Y_{X=150} \le 50.12$

12.76   (a)

Scatter Diagram

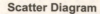
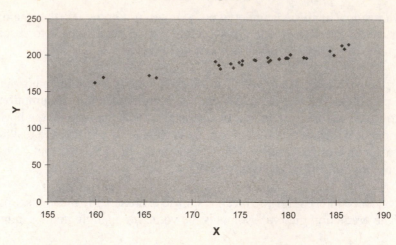

$$b_0 = -122.3439 \qquad b_1 = 1.7817$$

(b)   For each additional thousand dollars in assessed value, the estimated mean selling price of a house increases by 1.7817 thousand dollars. The estimated mean selling price of a house with a 0 assessed value is −122.3439 thousand dollars. However, this interpretation is not meaningful in the current setting since the assessed value is very unlikely to be 0 for a house.

(c) $\hat{Y} = -122.3439 + 1.78171X = -122.3439 + 1.78171(170) = 180.5475$ thousand dollars

(d) $r^2 = 0.9256$. So, 92.56% of the variation in selling price can be explained by the variation in assessed value.

(e)

Assessed Value Residual Plot

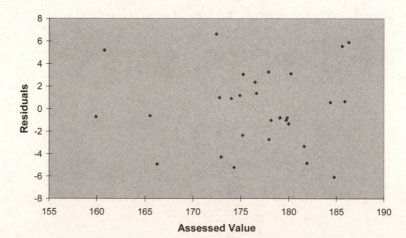

12.76   (e)
cont.

Normal Probability Plot

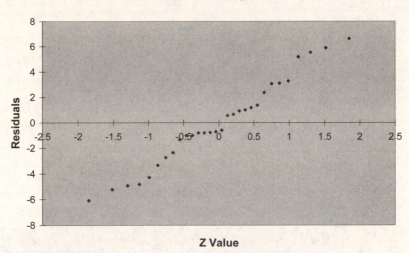

Both the residual plot and the normal probability plot do not reveal any potential violation of the linearity, equal variance and normality assumptions.

(f) $t = 18.6648$ with 28 degrees of freedom, p-value is virtually zero. Since p-value < 0.05, reject H_0. There is evidence of a linear relationship between selling price and assessed value.

(g) $1.5862 \le \beta_1 \le 1.9773$

12.78   (a)

Scatter Diagram

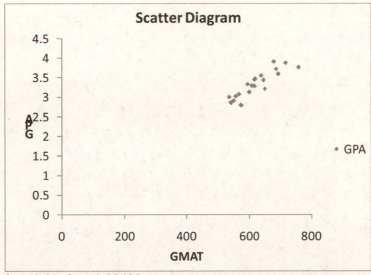

$b_0 = 0.30$, $b_1 = 0.00487$

(b)   0.30 is the portion of estimated mean GPI index (GPA) that is not affected by the GMAT score. The mean GPI index of a student with a zero GMAT score is estimated to be 0.30, which does not have practical meaning. For each additional point on the GMAT score, the estimated GPI increases by an average of 0.00487.

(c) $\hat{Y} = 0.30 + 0.00487 X = 0.30 + 0.00487(600) = 3.222$

12.78   (d) $r^2 = 0.7978$. 79.78% of the variation in the GPI can be explained by the
cont.   variation in the GMAT score.

     (e)   Based on a visual inspection of the graphs of the distribution of residuals and the
                  residuals versus the GMAT score, there is no pattern. The model appears to be
                  adequate.

     (f) $t = 8.428 > t_{0.05/2} = 2.1009$ with 18 degrees of freedom for $\alpha = 0.05$. Reject H_0.
                  There is evidence that the fitted linear regression model is useful.

     (g) $3.144 \le \mu_{Y|X=600} \le 3.301$

                  $2.886 \le Y_{X=600} \le 3.559$

     (h) $0.00366 \le \beta_1 \le 0.00608$

12.80   (a)

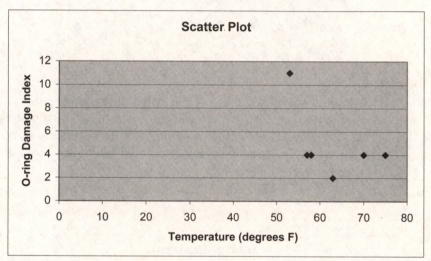

There is not any clear relationship between atmospheric temperature and O-ring
damage from the scatter plot.

    (b),(f)

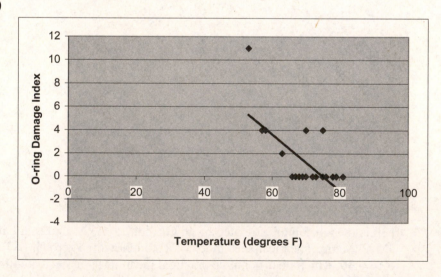

12.80   (c)   In (b), there are 16 observations with an O-ring damage index of 0 for a variety of
cont.   temperatures. If one concentrates on these observations with no O-ring damage,
                there is obviously no relationship between O-ring damage index and temperature. If
                all observations are used, the observations with no O-ring damage will bias the
                estimated relationship. If the intention is to investigate the relationship between the
                degrees of O-ring damage and atmospheric temperature, it makes sense to focus only
                on the flights in which there was O-ring damage.

         (d)   Prediction should not be made for an atmospheric temperature of 31 ^{0}F because it is
                outside the range of the temperature variable in the data. Such prediction will
                involve extrapolation, which assumes that any relationship between two variables
                will continue to hold outside the domain of the temperature variable.

         (e) $\hat{Y} = 18.036 - 0.240X$

         (g)   A nonlinear model is more appropriate for these data.

         (h)

Temperature Residual Plot

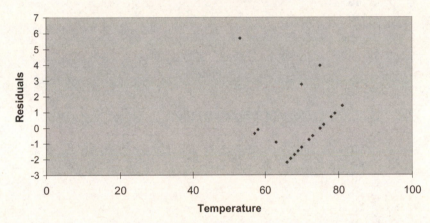

                The string of negative residuals and positive residuals that lie on a straight line with a
                positive slope in the lower-right corner of the plot is a strong indication that a
                nonlinear model should be used if all 23 observations are to be used in the fit.

12.82   (a)

Regression Statistics				
Multiple R	0.990453703			
R Square	0.980998538			
Adjusted R Square	0.980319914			
Standard Error	13.59646521			
Observations	30			
ANOVA				
	df	SS	MS	F
Regression	1	267233.8117	267233.8117	1445.570827
Residual	28	5176.18825	184.8638661	
Total	29	272410		
	Coefficients	Standard Error	t Stat	P-value
Intercept	-6.244798827	10.12588395	-0.616716413	0.542404238
Revenue	2.957565759	0.077788379	38.02066316	1.20611E-25

$b_0 = -6.2448 \quad b_1 = 2.9576$

12.82   (b)   For each additional million-dollars of revenue generated, the mean value of the franchise
cont.   will increase by an estimated \$2.9576 million. Literal interpretation of the intercept is
                 not meaningful because an operating franchise cannot have zero revenue.

(c) $\hat{Y} = -6.2449 + 2.9576X = -6.2449 + 2.9576(150) = \$\,437.3901$ millions

(d) $r^2 = 0.9810$. So, 98.10% of the variation in the value of an NBA franchise can be
        explained by the variation in its annual revenue.

(e)

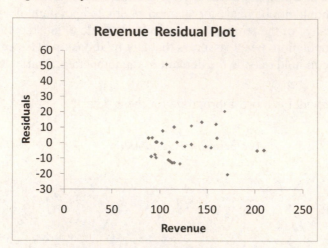

(e)

There does not appear to be a pattern in the residual plot. With the exception of an
outlier on the right-tail, the normal probability plot does not suggest serious departure
from the normality assumption.

(f) $t_{STAT} = 38.0207$ with a p-value that is approximately zero, reject H_0 at the 5% level
        of significance. There is evidence of a linear relationship between annual revenue and
        franchise value.

(g) $431.0467 \leq \mu_{Y|X=150} \leq 443.7334$.

(h) $408.8257 \leq Y_{X=150} \leq 465.9544$.

(i)   The strength of the relationship between revenue and value is stronger for baseball
        and NBA franchises than for European soccer teams.

12.84   (a)

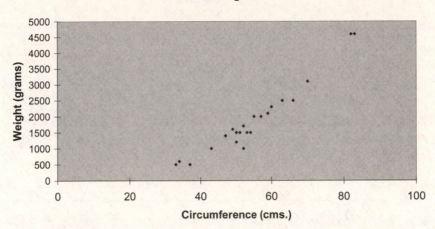

$\hat{Y} = -2629.222 + 82.4717X$

(b)   For each increase of one centimeter in circumference, the estimated mean weight of a pumpkin will increase by 82.4717 grams.

(c) $\hat{Y} = -2629.222 + 82.4717(60) = 2319.080$ grams.

(d)   There appears to be a positive relationship between weight and circumference of a pumpkin. It is a good idea for the farmer to sell pumpkins by circumference instead of weight for circumference is a good predictor of weight, and it is much easier to measure the circumference of a pumpkin than its weight.

(e) $r^2 = 0.9373$.   93.73% of the variation in pumpkin weight can be explained by the variation in circumference.

(f)

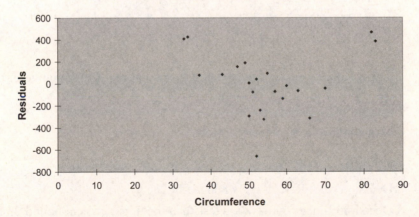

There appears to be a nonlinear relationship between circumference and weight.

(g) p-value is virtually 0. Reject H_0. There is sufficient evidence to conclude that there is a linear relationship between the circumference and the weight of a pumpkin.

(h) $72.7875 < \beta_1 < 92.1559$

12.86   (a)

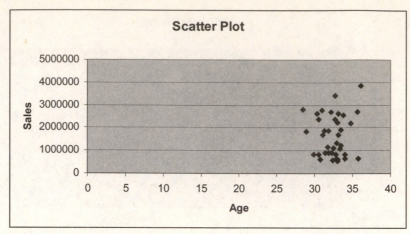

(b) $\hat{Y} = 931626.16 + 21782.76X$

(c)   Since median age of customer base cannot be 0, b_0 just captures the portion of the latest one-month mean sales total that varies with factors other than median age.
$b_1 = 21782.76$ means that as the median age of customer base increases by one year, the estimated mean latest one-month sales total will increase by $21782.76.

(d) $r^2 = 0.0017$. Only 0.17% of the total variation in the franchise's latest one-month sales total can be explained by using the median age of customer base.

(e)

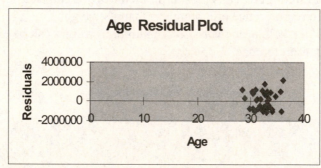

The residuals are very evenly spread out across different range of median age.

(f) $H_0 : \rho = 0$ $H_1 : \rho \neq 0$

Test statistic: $t = \dfrac{r}{\sqrt{\dfrac{1-r^2}{n-2}}} = 0.2482$

Decision rule: Reject H_0 when $|t| > 2.0281$.

Decision: Since $t = 0.2482$ is less than the upper critical bound 2.0281, do not reject H_0. There is not enough evidence to conclude that there is a linear relationship between one-month sales total and median age of customer base.

(g) $b_1 \pm t_{\alpha/2} S_{b_1} = 21782.76354 \pm 2.0281 (87749.63)$

$$-156181.50 \leq \beta_1 \leq 199747.02$$

12.88   (a)

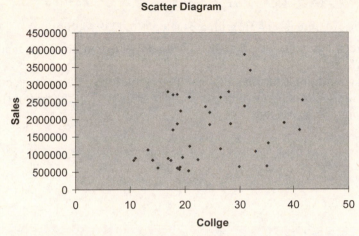

There is a positive linear relationship between total sales and percentage of customer base with a college diploma.

(b) $\hat{Y} = 789847.38 + 35854.15X$

(c) $b_1 = 35854.15$ means that as the percent of customer base with a college diploma increases by one, the estimated mean latest one-month sales total will increase by $35854.15.

(d) $r^2 = 0.1036$. 10.36% of the total variation in the franchise's latest one-month sales total can be explained by the percentage of customer base with a college diploma.

(e)

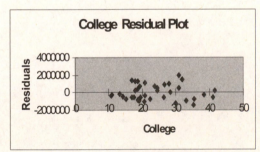

The residuals are evenly spread out around zero.

(f) $H_0 : \rho = 0$ $H_1 : \rho \neq 0$

Test statistic: $t = \dfrac{r}{\sqrt{\dfrac{1-r^2}{n-2}}} = 2.0392$

Decision rule: Reject H_0 when $|t| > 2.0281$.

Decision: Since $t = 2.0392$ is greater than the upper critical bound 2.0281, reject H_0.

There is enough evidence to conclude that there is a linear relationship between one-month sales total and percentage of customer base with a college diploma.

(g) $b_1 \pm t_{\alpha/2} S_{b_1} = 35854.15 \pm 2.0281(17582.269)$

$$195.75 \leq \beta_1 \leq 71512.60$$

12.90   (a)   The correlation between compensation and the investment return in 2009 is - 0.0389.

(b) $H_0 : \rho = 0$ vs. $H_1 : \rho \neq 0$

The t_{STAT} value is -0.4912 with a p-value = 0.6239, do not reject H_0. The correlation between compensation and the investment return in 2010 is not statistically significant.

(c)   You would think that the total compensation for CEOs of large companies is positively correlated with the investment return. But the test in (b) concludes that the two are not correlated.

CHAPTER 13

OBJECTIVES

In this chapter, you learn:
- How to develop a multiple regression model
- How to interpret the regression coefficients
- How to determine which independent variables to include in the regression model
- How to determine which independent variables are most important in predicting a dependent variable
- How to use categorical independent variables in a regression model

OVERVIEW AND KEY CONCEPTS

The Multiple Regression Model

- The multiple regression model describes the relationship between one dependent variable and 2 or more independent variables in a linear function.

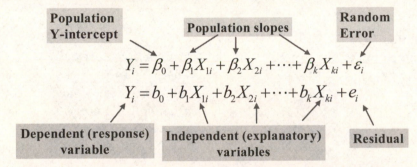

$$Y_i = \beta_0 + \beta_1 X_{1i} + \beta_2 X_{2i} + \cdots + \beta_k X_{ki} + \varepsilon_i$$

$$Y_i = b_0 + b_1 X_{1i} + b_2 X_{2i} + \cdots + b_k X_{ki} + e_i$$

The Simple Linear Regression and Multiple Regression Compared

- Coefficients in a simple regression pick up the impact of that variable plus the impacts of other variables that are correlated with it and the dependent variable.
- Coefficients in a multiple regression net out the impacts of other variables in the equation. Hence, they are called *net regression coefficients*.

Interpretation of the Estimated Coefficients

- **The Y intercept (b_0):** The estimated average value of Y_i when all $X_i = 0$.
- **Slope (b_i):** Estimated that the average value of Y changes by b_i for each one-unit increase in X_i holding constant the effect of all other independent variables.

Predicting the Dependent Variable Y

- Use the estimated sample regression equation (multiple linear regression equation):
$$\hat{Y}_i = b_0 + b_1 X_{1i} + \cdots + b_k X_{ki}$$

The Venn Diagram and Explanatory Power of the Multiple Regression Model

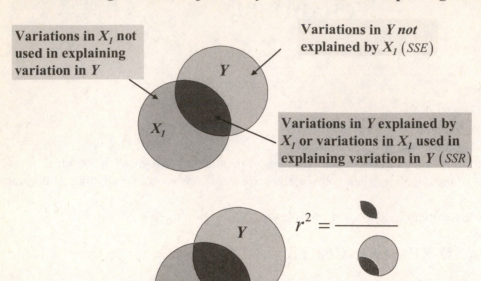

Variations in X_1 not used in explaining variation in Y

Variations in Y *not* explained by X_1 (SSE)

Variations in Y explained by X_1 or variations in X_1 used in explaining variation in Y (SSR)

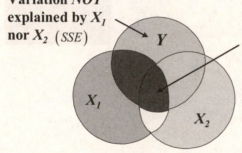

$$r^2 = \frac{}{}$$

$$= \frac{SSR}{SSR + SSE}$$

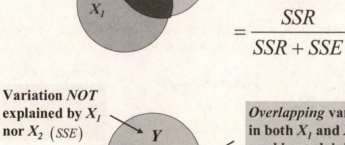

Variation *NOT* explained by X_1 nor X_2 (SSE)

***Overlapping* variation in both X_1 and X_2 are used in explaining the *variation* in Y but *NOT* in the *estimation* of β_1 nor β_2**

Coefficient of Multiple Determination

- Coefficient of multiple determination measures the proportion of total variation in Y explained by all X variables taken together.
- $r^2 = \dfrac{SSR}{SST} = \dfrac{\text{Explained Variation}}{\text{Total Variation}}$
- It never decreases when an additional X variable is added to the model, which is a disadvantage when comparing among models.

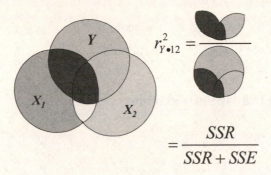

$$r_{Y \bullet 12}^2 = \frac{}{}$$

$$= \frac{SSR}{SSR + SSE}$$

Adjusted Coefficient of Multiple Determination

- It measures the proportion of variation in Y explained by all X variables adjusted for the number of X variables used.
- $r_{adj}^2 = 1 - \left[\left(1 - r^2\right) \dfrac{n-1}{n-k-1} \right]$
- It penalizes excessive use of independent variables.
- It is smaller than r^2.
- It is useful in comparing among models.
- It can have a negative value.
- Its value can decrease when an additional explanatory variable is added to the existing model.

Interpretation of Coefficient of Multiple Determination

- r^2 measures the proportion of total variation in Y that can be explained by all X variables.
- r_{adj}^2 measures the proportion of total variation in Y that can be explained by all X variables after adjusting for the number of independent variables and sample size.

F Test for the Significance of the Entire Multiple Regression Model

- **The hypotheses:**
    - $H_0 : \beta_1 = \beta_2 = \cdots = \beta_k = 0$ (There is no linear relationship)
    - $H_1 :$ At least one $\beta_i \neq 0$ (At least one independent variable affects Y)
- **Test statistic:**
    - $F = \dfrac{MSR}{MSE} = \dfrac{SSR\,(\text{all})/k}{SSE\,(\text{all})/(n-k-1)}$ with k numerator degrees of freedom and $(n-k-1)$ denominator degrees of freedom.
    - The rejection region is always in the right tail.

t Test for the Significance of Individual Variables

- **The hypotheses:**
    - $H_0 : \beta_i = 0$ (X_i does not affect Y)
    - $H_1 : \beta_i \neq 0$ (X_i affects Y)
- **Test statistic:**
    - $t = \dfrac{b_j - \beta_j}{S_{b_j}}$ with $(n-k-1)$ degrees of freedom.
    - The t test can also be a one-tail test for a one-tail alternative.
- Confidence interval estimate for β_j : Use the $100(1-\alpha)\%$ confidence interval for β_j.
    - $b_j \pm t_{\alpha/2, n-k-1} S_{b_j}$

Dummy-Variable Model and Interactions

- Dummy variables are used to represent categorical explanatory variables with two or more levels.
- A dummy variable is always coded as 0 and 1.
- The number of dummy variables needed is equal to the number of levels minus 1.
- **Interpretation of the estimated slope coefficient of a dummy variable:** The slope coefficient of a dummy variable measures the estimated average incremental effect of the presence of the characteristic captured by the dummy variable holding constant the effect of all other independent variables.
- In the dummy-variable model, it is assumed that the slope of the dependent variable Y with an independent variable X is the same for each of the two levels of the dummy variable.

SOLUTIONS TO END OF SECTION
AND CHAPTER REVIEW EVEN PROBLEMS

13.2   (a)   Holding constant the effect of X_2, for each increase of one unit in X_1, the response variable Y is estimated to decrease an average of 2 units. Holding constant the effect of X_1, for each increase of one unit in X_2, the response variable Y is estimated to increase an average of 7 units.

    (b)   The Y-intercept 50 is the estimate of the mean value of Y if X_1 and X_2 are both 0.

13.4   (a) $\hat{Y} = -2.72825 + 0.047114X_1 + 0.011947X_2$

    (b)   For a given number of orders, each increase of $1,000 in sales is estimated to result in a mean increase in distribution cost of $47.114. For a given amount of sales, each increase of one order is estimated to result in a mean increase in distribution cost of $11.95.

    (c)   The interpretation of b_0 has no practical meaning here because it would have been the estimated mean distribution cost when there were no sales and no orders.

    (d) $\hat{Y}_i = -2.72825 + 0.047114(400) + 0.011947(4500) = 69.878$ or $69,878

    (e) $66,419.93 \le \mu_{Y|X} \le $73,337.01

    (f) $59,380.61 \le Y_X \le $80,376.33

    (g)   Since there is much more variation in predicting an individual value than in estimating a mean value, a prediction interval is wider than a confidence interval estimate holding everything else fixed.

13.6   (a) $\hat{Y} = 156.4 + 13.081X_1 + 16.795X_2$

    (b)   For a given amount of newspaper advertising, each increase of $1000 in radio advertising is estimated to result in a mean increase in sales of $13,081. For a given amount of radio advertising, each increase of $1000 in newspaper advertising is estimated to result in the mean increase in sales of $16,795.

    (c)   When there is no money spent on radio advertising and newspaper advertising, the estimated mean amount of sales is $156,430.44.

    (d)   According to the results of (b), newspaper advertising is more effective as each increase of $1000 in newspaper advertising will result in a higher mean increase in sales than the same amount of increase in radio advertising.

13.8   (a) $\hat{Y} = 400.8057 + 456.4485X_1 - 2.4708X_2$ where $X_1 =$ Land, $X_2 =$ Age

    (b)   For a given age, each increase by one acre in land area is estimated to result in a mean increase in appraised value of $456.45 thousands. For a given acreage, each increase of one year in age is estimated to result in the mean decrease in appraised value of $2.47 thousands.

    (c)   The interpretation of b_0 has no practical meaning here because it would have meant the estimated mean appraised value of a new house that has no land area.

    (d) $\hat{Y} = 400.8057 + 456.4485(0.25) - 2.4708(45) = 403.73 thousands.

    (e) $372.7370 \le \mu_{Y|X} \le 434.7243$

13.8   (f) $235.1964 \leq Y_X \leq 572.2649$

13.10   (a) $MSR = SSR / k = 30 / 2 = 15$
$MSE = SSE / (n - k - 1) = 120 / 10 = 12$

(b) $F_{STAT} = MSR / MSE = 15 / 12 = 1.25$

(c) $F_{STAT} = 1.25 < F_{U(2,13-2-1)} = 4.103$. Do not reject H_0. There is not sufficient evidence of a significant linear relationship.

(d) $r^2 = \dfrac{SSR}{SST} = \dfrac{30}{150} = 0.2$

(e) $r_{adj}^2 = 1 - \left[\left(1 - r_{Y.12}^2\right) \dfrac{n-1}{n-k-1} \right] = 0.04$

13.12   (a) $F_{STAT} = 97.69 > F_{U(2,15-2-1)} = 3.89$. Reject H_0. There is evidence of a significant linear relationship with at least one of the independent variables.

(b) p-value = virtually zero. The probability of obtaining an F test statistic of 97.69 or larger is virtually zero if H_0 is true.

(c) $r_{Y.12}^2 = SSR / SST = 12.6102 / 13.38473 = 0.9421$. So, 94.21% of the variation in the long-term ability to absorb shock can be explained by variation in forefoot absorbing capability and variation in midsole impact.

(d) $r_{adj}^2 = 1 - \left[(1 - r_{Y.12}^2) \dfrac{n-1}{n-k-1} \right] = 1 - \left[(1 - 0.9421) \dfrac{15-1}{15-2-1} \right] = 0.93245$

13.14   (a) $MSR = SSR / k = 3368.087 / 2 = 1684.04$
$MSE = SSE / (n - k - 1) = 477.043 / 21 = 22.72$

$F_{STAT} = MSR / MSE = 1684 / 22.7 = 74.13$

$F_{STAT} = 74.13 > F_{U(2,24-2-1)} = 3.467$. Reject H_0. There is evidence of a significant linear relationship.

(b) p-value = virtually zero. The probability of obtaining an F test statistic of 74.13 or larger is virtually zero if H_0 is true.

(c) $r_{Y.12}^2 = SSR / SST = 3368.087 / 3845.13 = 0.8759$. So, 87.59% of the variation in distribution cost can be explained by variation in sales and variation in number of orders.

(d) $r_{adj}^2 = 1 - \left[(1 - r_{Y.12}^2) \dfrac{n-1}{n-k-1} \right] = 1 - \left[(1 - 0.8759) \dfrac{24-1}{24-2-1} \right] = 0.8641$

13.16   (a) $MSR = SSR / k = 2,028,033 / 2 = 1,014,016$
$MSE = SSE / (n - k - 1) = 479,759.9 / 19 = 25,251$

$F_{STAT} = MSR / MSE = 1,014,016 / 25,251 = 40.16$

$F_{STAT} = 40.16 > F_\alpha = 3.522$. Reject H_0. There is evidence of a significant linear relationship.

(b) p-value < 0.001. The probability of obtaining an F test statistic of 40.16 or larger is less than 0.001 if H_0 is true.

13.16   (c) $r_{Y.12}^2 = SSR / SST = 2,028,033 / 2,507,793 = 0.8087$. So, 80.87% of the variation
cont.   in sales can be explained by variation in radio advertising and variation in newspaper
               advertising.

         (d) $r_{adj}^2 = 1 - \left[(1 - r_{Y.12}^2) \dfrac{n-1}{n-k-1} \right] = 1 - \left[(1 - 0.8087) \dfrac{22-1}{22-2-1} \right] = 0.7886$

13.18   (a)   Minitab output:

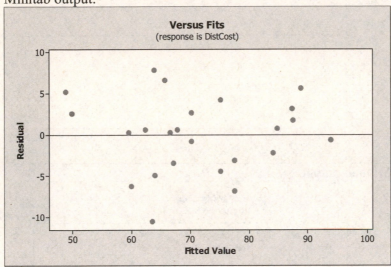

         Based upon a residual analysis the model appears adequate.

         (b)   Minitab output:

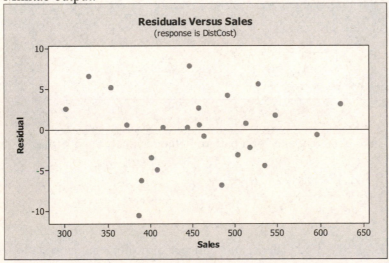

13.18   (c)   Minitab output:
cont.

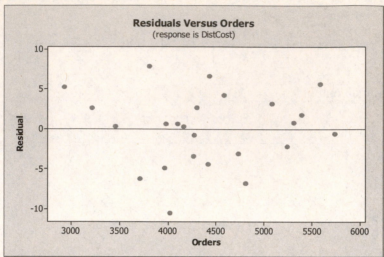

(d)   Minitab output:

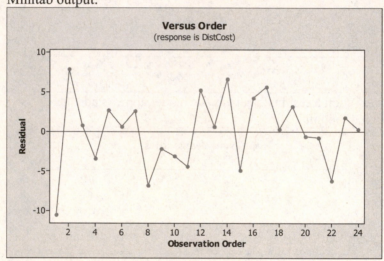

(e)   There is no evidence of a pattern in the residuals versus time.

(f) $D = \dfrac{\sum\limits_{i=2}^{n} (e_i - e_{i-1})^2}{\sum\limits_{i=1}^{n} e_i^2} = \dfrac{1077.0956}{477.0430} = 2.26$

(g) $D = 2.26 > 1.55$. There is no evidence of positive autocorrelation in the residuals.

13.20   (a)   Minitab output:

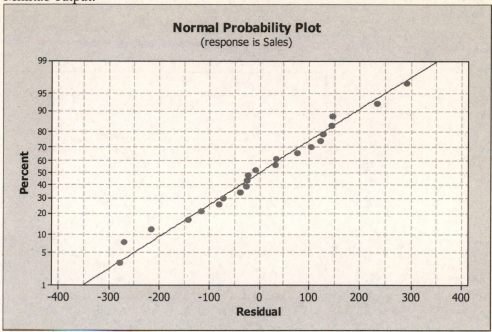

Normal Probability Plot
(response is Sales)

Minitab output:

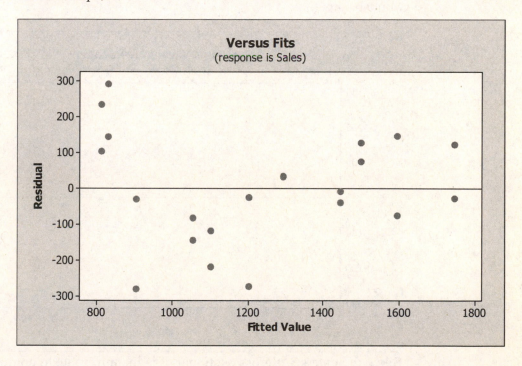

Versus Fits
(response is Sales)

13.20 (a)
cont.

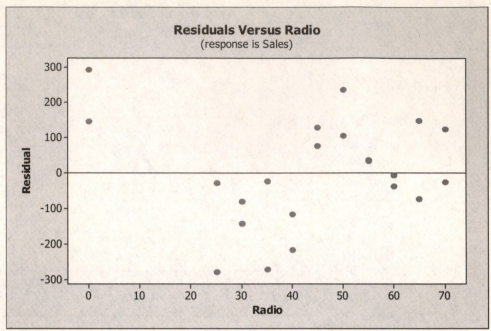

Minitab output:

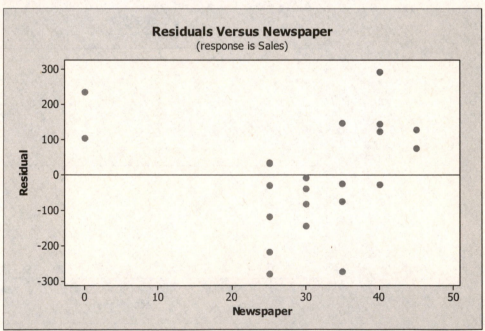

(b)   Since the data set is cross-sectional, it is inappropriate to compute the Durbin-Watson statistic.

(c)   There appears to be a quadratic relationship in the plot of the residuals against the fitted value and both radio and newspaper advertising. Thus, quadratic terms for each of these explanatory models should be considered for inclusion in the model. The normal probability plot suggests that the distribution of the residuals is very close to a normal distribution.

13.22   (a)

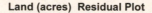

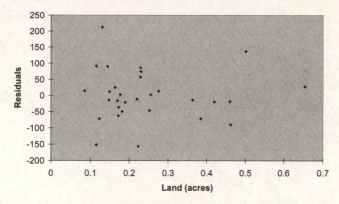

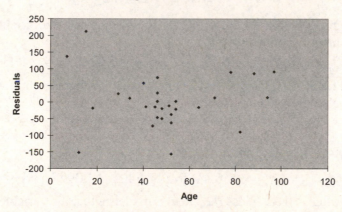

The residual analysis reveals no patterns.

(b)   Since the data is cross-sectional, the Durbin-Watson test is no appropriate.

(c)   There are no apparent violations of the assumptions.

13.24   (a)   The slope of X_2 in terms of the t statistic is 3.75 which is larger than the slope of X_1 in terms of the t statistic which is 3.33.

(b)   95% confidence interval on β_1: $b_1 \pm t_{n-k-1} s_{b_1}$, $4 \pm 2.1098(1.2)$

$$1.46824 \le \beta_1 \le 6.53176$$

(c)   For X_1: $t_{STAT} = b_1 / s_{b_1} = 4/1.2 = 3.33 > t_{17} = 2.1098$ with 17 degrees of freedom for $\alpha = 0.05$. Reject H_0. There is evidence that the variable X_1 contributes to a model already containing X_2.

For X_2: $t_{STAT} = b_2 / s_{b_2} = 3/0.8 = 3.75 > t_{17} = 2.1098$ with 17 degrees of freedom for $\alpha = 0.05$. Reject H_0. There is evidence that the variable X_2 contributes to a model already containing X_1.

Both variables X_1 and X_2 should be included in the model.

13.26 (a)   95% confidence interval on β_1: $b_1 \pm t_{n-k-1} s_{b_1}$, $0.0471 \pm 2.0796(0.0203)$

$$0.00488 \le \beta_1 \le 0.08932$$

(b)   For X_1: $t_{STAT} = b_1/s_{b_1} = 0.0471/0.0203 = 2.32 > t_{21} = 2.0796$ with 21 degrees of freedom for $\alpha = 0.05$. Reject H_0. There is evidence that the variable X_1 contributes to a model already containing X_2.

For X_2: $t_{STAT} = b_2/s_{b_2} = 0.01195/0.00225 = 5.31 > t_{21} = 2.0796$ with 21 degrees of freedom for $\alpha = 0.05$. Reject H_0. There is evidence that the variable X_2 contributes to a model already containing X_1.

Both variables X_1 and X_2 should be included in the model.

13.28 (a)   95% confidence interval on β_1: $b_1 \pm t_{n-k-1} s_{b_1}$, $13.0807 \pm 2.093(1.7594)$

$$9.398 \le \beta_1 \le 16.763$$

(b)   For X_1: $t_{STAT} = b_1/s_{b_1} = 13.0807/1.7594 = 7.43 > t_{19} = 2.093$ with 19 degrees of freedom for $\alpha = 0.05$. Reject H_0. There is evidence that the variable X_1 contributes to a model already containing X_2.

For X_2: $t_{STAT} = b_2/s_{b_2} = 16.7953/2.9634 = 5.67 > t_{19} = 2.093$ with 19 degrees of freedom for $\alpha = 0.05$. Reject H_0. There is evidence that the variable X_2 contributes to a model already containing X_1.

Both variables X_1 and X_2 should be included in the model.

13.30 (a) $227.5865 \le \beta_1 \le 685.3104$

(b)   For X_1: $t_{STAT} = b_1/s_{b_1} = 456.4485/111.5405 = 4.0922$ and p-value $= 0.0003$.

Since p-value < 0.05, reject H_0. There is evidence that the variable X_1 contributes to a model already containing X_2.

For X_2: $t_{STAT} = b_2/s_{b_2} = -2.4708/0.6808 = -3.6295$ and p-value $= 0.0012$. Since p-value < 0.05, reject H_0. There is evidence that the variable X_2 contributes to a model already containing X_1.

Both variables X_1 and X_2 should be included in the model.

13.32 $t = 3.27 > t_{17} = 2.1098$. Reject H_0. The presence of X_2 makes a significant contribution to the model.

13.34 (a) $\hat{Y} = 243.7371 + 9.2189 X_1 + 12.6967 X_2$, where X_1 = number of rooms and X_2 = neighborhood (east = 0).

(b)   Holding constant the effect of neighborhood, for each additional room, the selling price is estimated to increase by a mean of 9.2189 thousands of dollars, or \$9218.9. For a given number of rooms, a west neighborhood is estimated to increase mean selling price over an east neighborhood by 12.6967 thousands of dollars, or \$12,696.7.

(c) $\hat{Y} = 243.7371 + 9.2189(9) + 12.6967(0) = 326.70758$ or \$326,707.58

$\$309,560.04 \le Y_{X=X_i} \le \$343,855.11$ $\$321,471.44 \le \mu_{Y|X=X_i} \le \$331,943.71$

13.34 (d)
cont.

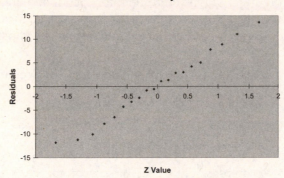

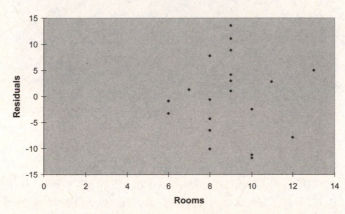

Based on a residual analysis, the model appears adequate.

(e) $F_{STAT} = 55.39$, p-value is virtually 0. Since p-value < 0.05, reject H_0. There is evidence of a significant relationship between selling price and the two independent variables (rooms and neighborhood).

(f)   For X_1: $t_{STAT} = 8.9537$, p-value is virtually 0. Reject H_0. Number of rooms makes a significant contribution and should be included in the model.
       For X_2: $t_{STAT} = 3.5913$, p-value $= 0.0023 < 0.05$. Reject H_0. Neighborhood makes a significant contribution and should be included in the model.
       Based on these results, the regression model with the two independent variables should be used.

(g) $7.0466 \le \beta_1 \le 11.3913$,

(h) $5.2378 \le \beta_2 \le 20.1557$

(i) $r^2_{adj} = 0.851$

(j)   The slope of selling price with number of rooms is the same regardless of whether the house is located in an east or west neighborhood.

(k) $\hat{Y} = 253.95 + 8.032X_1 - 5.90X_2 + 2.089X_1X_2$.
       For $X_1 X_2$: the p-value is 0.330. Do not reject H_0. There is no evidence that the interaction term makes a contribution to the model.

(l)   The two-variable model in (f) should be used.

13.36   (a) $\hat{Y} = 8.0100 + 0.0052X_1 - 2.1052X_2$, where X_1 = depth (in feet) and X_2 = type of
drilling (wet = 0, dry = 1).

(b)   Holding constant the effect of type of drilling, for each foot increase in depth of the
hole, the additional drilling time is estimated to increase by a mean of 0.0052 minute.
For a given depth, a dry drilling is estimated to reduce mean additional drilling time
over wet drilling by 2.1052 minutes.

(c)   Dry drilling: $\hat{Y} = 8.0101 + 0.0052(100) - 2.1052 = 6.4276$ minutes.

$6.2096 \le \mu_{Y|X=X_i} \le 6.6457$, $4.9230 \le Y_{X=X_i} \le 7.9322$

(d)

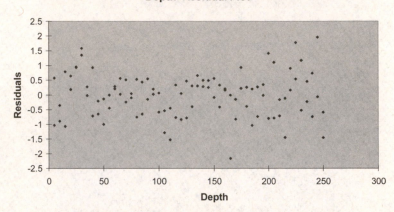

Based on a residual analysis, the model appears adequate.

(e) $F_{STAT} = 111.109$ with 2 and 97 degrees of freedom, $F_{2,97} = 3.09$ using Excel. p-value
is virtually 0. Reject H_0 at 5% level of significance. There is evidence of a
relationship between additional drilling time and the two dependent variables.

(f)   For X_1: $t_{STAT} = 5.0289 > t_{97} = 1.9847$. Reject H_0. Depth of the hole makes
a significant contribution and should be included in the model.
For X_2:: $t_{STAT} = -14.0331 < t_{97} = -1.9847$. Reject H_0. Type of drilling makes a
significant contribution and should be included in the model.
Based on these results, the regression model with the two independent variables
should be used.

(g) $0.0032 \le \beta_1 \le 0.0073$

(h) $-2.4029 \le \beta_2 \le -1.8075$

(i) $r^2_{adj} = 0.6899$

(j)   The slope of additional drilling time with depth of the hole is the same regardless of
whether it is a dry drilling hole or a wet drilling hole.

(k) $\hat{Y} = 7.9120 + 0.0060X_1 - 1.9091X_2 - 0.0015X_1X_2$.
For X_1X_2: the p-value is 0.4624 > 0.05. Do not reject H_0. There is not evidence that
the interaction term makes a contribution to the model.

(l)   The two-variable model in (a) should be used.

13.38 (a) $\hat{Y} = 31.5594 - 0.0296 X_1 + 0.0041 X_2 + 1.7159 \cdot 10^{-5} X_3$.

where X_1 = sales, X_2 = orders, $X_3 = X_1 X_2$
For $X_1 X_2$: the p-value is $0.3249 > 0.05$. Do not reject H_0. There is not enough evidence that the interaction term makes a contribution to the model.

(b)   Since there is not enough evidence of any interaction effect between sales and orders, the model in problem 13.4 should be used.

13.40 (a) $\hat{Y} = -1293.3105 + 43.6600 X_1 + 56.9335 X_2 - 0.8430 X_3$.

where X_1 = radio advertisement, X_2 = newspaper advertisement, $X_3 = X_1 X_2$
For $X_1 X_2$: the p-value is $0.0018 < 0.05$. Reject H_0. There is enough evidence that the interaction term makes a contribution to the model.

(b)   Since there is enough evidence of an interaction effect between radio and newspaper advertisement, the model in this problem should be used.

13.42 (a) $\hat{Y} = 250.4237 + 0.0127 X_1 - 1.4785 X_2 + 0.004 X_3$.

where X_1 = staff present, X_2 = remote hours, $X_3 = X_1 X_2$
For $X_1 X_2$: the p-value is $0.2353 > 0.05$. Do not reject H_0. There is not enough evidence that the interaction term makes a contribution to the model.

(b)   Since there is not enough evidence of an interaction effect between total staff present and remote hours, the model in problem 13.7 should be used.

13.44 In the case of the simple linear regression model, the slope b_1 represents the change in the estimated mean of Y per unit change in X and does not take into account any other variables. In the multiple linear regression model, the slope b_1 represents the change in the estimated mean of Y per unit change in X_1, taking into account the effect of all the other independent variables.

13.46 You test whether the interaction of the dummy variable and each of the independent variables in the model make a significant contribution to the regression model.

13.48 It is assumed that the slope of the dependent variable Y with an independent variable X is the same for each of the two levels of the dummy variable.

13.50 (a) $\hat{Y} = -3.9152 + 0.0319 X_1 + 4.2228 X_2$, where X_1 = amount of cubic feet moved and X_2 = number of pieces of large furniture.

(b)   Holding constant the number of pieces of large furniture, for each additional cubic foot moved, the mean labor hours are estimated to increase by 0.0319. Holding constant the amount of cubic feet moved, for each additional piece of large furniture, the mean labor hours are estimated to increase by 4.2228.

(c) $\hat{Y} = -3.9152 + 0.0319(500) + 4.2228(2) = 20.4926$

13.50   (d)
cont.

Normal Probability Plot

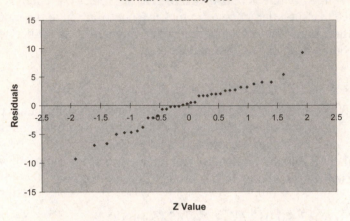

Feet Residual Plot

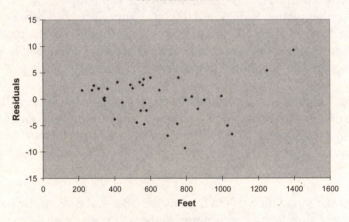

Large Residual Plot

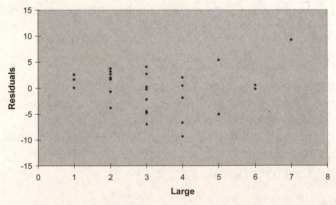

(d)   Based on a residual analysis, the errors appear to be normally distributed. The equal variance assumption might be violated because the variances appear to be larger around the center region of both independent variables. There might also be violation of the linearity assumption. A model with quadratic terms for both independent variables might be fitted.

13.50 (e) $F_{STAT} = 228.80$, p-value is virtually 0. Since p-value < 0.05, reject H_0. There is
cont.   evidence of a significant relationship between labor hours and the two independent
                   variables (the amount of cubic feet moved and the number of pieces of large
                   furniture).

(f)   The p-value is virtually 0. The probability of obtaining a test statistic of 228.80 or
         greater is virtually 0 if there is no significant relationship between labor hours and the
         two independent variables (the amount of cubic feet moved and the number of pieces
         of large furniture).

(g) $r^2 = 0.9327$. 93.27% of the variation in labor hours can be explained by variation in
         the amount of cubic feet moved and the number of pieces of large furniture.

(h) $r^2_{adj} = 0.9287$

(i)   For X_1: $t_{STAT} = 6.9339$, p-value is virtually 0. Reject H_0. The amount of cubic feet
         moved makes a significant contribution and should be included in the model.
         For X_2: $t_{STAT} = 4.6192$, p-value is virtually 0. Reject H_0. The number of pieces of large
         furniture makes a significant contribution and should be included in the model.
         Based on these results, the regression model with the two independent variables
         should be used.

(j)   For X_1: $t_{STAT} = 6.9339$, p-value is virtually 0. The probability of obtaining a sample
         that will yield a test statistic farther away than 6.9339 is virtually 0 if the amount of
         cubic feet moved does not make a significant contribution holding the effect of the
         number of pieces of large furniture constant.
         For X_2: $t_{STAT} = 4.6192$, p-value is virtually 0. The probability of obtaining a sample
         that will yield a test statistic farther away than 4.6192 is virtually 0 if the number of
         pieces of large furniture does not make a significant contribution holding the effect of
         the amount of cubic feet moved constant.

(k) $0.0226 \leq \beta_1 \leq 0.0413$. We are 95% confident that the mean labor hours will
         increase by somewhere between 0.0226 and 0.0413 for each additional cubic foot
         moved holding constant the number of pieces of large furniture. In Problem 12.44,
         we are 95% confident that the mean labor hours will increase by somewhere between
         0.0439 and 0.0562 for each additional cubic foot moved regardless of the number of
         pieces of large furniture.

13.52 (a) $\hat{Y} = -120.0483 + 1.7506 X_1 + 0.3680 X_2$, where $X_1 =$ assessed value and $X_2 =$ time
                 period.

(b)   Holding constant the time period, for each additional thousand dollars of assessed
         value, the mean selling price is estimated to increase by 1.7507 thousand dollars.
         Holding constant the assessed value, for each additional month since assessment, the
         mean selling price is estimated to increase by 0.3680 thousand dollars.

(c) $\hat{Y} = -120.0483 + 1.7506(170) + 0.3680(12) = 181.9692$ thousand dollars

13.52   (d)
cont.

Normal Probability Plot

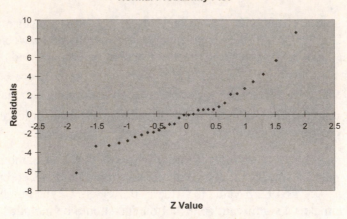

Assessed Value Residual Plot

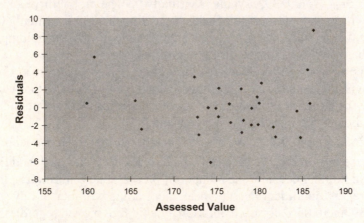

Time Residual Plot

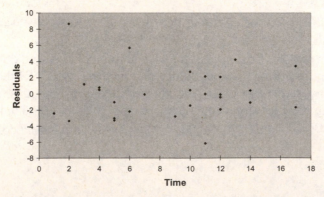

Based on a residual analysis, the model appears adequate.

(e) $F = 223.46$, p-value is virtually 0. Since p-value < 0.05, reject H_0. There is evidence of a significant relationship between selling price and the two independent variables (assessed value and time period).

13.52   (f)   The p-value is virtually 0. The probability of obtaining a test statistic of 223.46 or
cont.   greater is virtually 0 if there is no significant relationship between selling price and
               the two independent variables (assessed value and time period).

        (g) $r^2 = 0.9430$. 94.30% of the variation in selling price can be explained by variation
               in assessed value and time period.

        (h) $r^2_{adj} = 0.9388$

        (i)   For X_1: $t = 20.4137$, p-value is virtually 0. Reject H_0. The assessed value makes a
               significant contribution and should be included in the model.
               For X_2: $t = 2.8734$, p-value $= 0.0078 < 0.05$. Reject H_0. The time period makes a
               significant contribution and should be included in the model.
               Based on these results, the regression model with the two independent variables
               should be used.

        (j)   For X_1: $t = 20.4137$, p-value is virtually 0. The probability of obtaining a sample that
               will yield a test statistic farther away from 0 is virtually 0 if the assessed value does
               not make a significant contribution holding time period constant.
               For X_2: $t = 2.8734$, p-value is virtually 0. The probability of obtaining a sample that
               will yield a test statistic farther away from 0 is virtually 0 if the time period does not
               make a significant contribution holding the effect of the assessed value constant.

        (k) $1.5746 \leq \beta_1 \leq 1.9266$. We are 95% confident that the mean selling price will
               increase by an amount somewhere between 1.5746 thousand dollars and 1.9266
               thousand dollars for each additional thousand dollar increase in assessed value
               holding constant the time period. In Problem 12.76, we are 95% confident that the
               mean selling price will increase by an amount somewhere between 1.5862 thousand
               dollars and 1.9773 thousand dollars for each additional thousand dollar increase in
               assessed value regardless of the time period.

13.54   (a) $\hat{Y} = 163.7751 + 10.7252 X_1 - 0.2843 X_2$, where $X_1 =$ size and $X_2 =$ age.

        (b)   Holding constant the age, for each additional thousand square feet, the assessed value
               is estimated to increase by a mean of 10.7252 thousand dollars. Holding constant the
               size, for each additional year, the assessed value is estimated to decrease by a mean
               of 0.2843 thousand dollars.

        (c) $\hat{Y} = 163.7751 + 10.7252(1.75) - 0.2843(10) = 179.7017$ thousand dollars

13.54   (d)
cont.

Normal Probability Plot

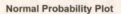

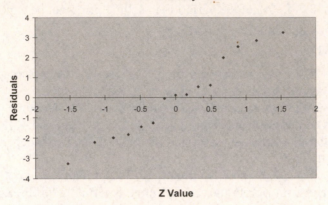

Heating Area Residual Plot

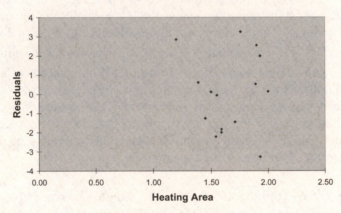

Age Residual Plot

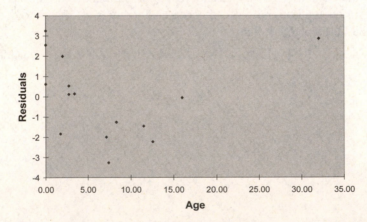

(d)   Based on a residual analysis, the errors appear to be normally distributed. The equal variance assumption appears to be holding up. There might also be violation of the linearity assumption on age. You might want to include a quadratic term for age in the model.

13.54 (e)
cont.
$F_{STAT} = 28.58$, p-value $= 2.72776 \times 10^{-5}$. Since p-value < 0.05, reject H_0. There is evidence of a significant relationship between assessed value and the two independent variables (size and age).

(f) The p-value $= 2.72776 \times 10^{-5}$. The probability of obtaining a test statistic of 28.58 or greater is virtually 0 if there is no significant relationship between assessed value and the two independent variables (size and age).

(g) $r^2 = 0.8265$. 82.65% of the variation in assessed value can be explained by variation in size and age.

(h) $r^2_{adj} = 0.7976$

(i) For X_1: $t_{STAT} = 3.5581$, p-value $= 0.0039 < 0.05$. Reject H_0. The size of a house makes a significant contribution and should be included in the model.
For X_2: $t_{STAT} = -3.4002$, p-value $= 0.0053 < 0.05$. Reject H_0. The age of a house makes a significant contribution and should be included in the model.
Based on these results, the regression model with the two independent variables should be used.

(j) For X_1: p-value $= 0.0039$. The probability of obtaining a sample that will yield a test statistic farther away than 3.5581 is 0.0039 if the size of a house does not make a significant contribution holding age constant.
For X_2: p-value $= 0.0053$. The probability of obtaining a sample that will yield a test statistic farther away than -3.4002 is 0.0053 if the age of a house does not make a significant contribution holding the effect of the size constant.

(k) $4.1575 \le \beta_1 \le 17.2928$. We are 95% confident that the mean assessed value will increase by an amount somewhere between 4.1575 thousand dollars and 17.2928 thousand dollars for each additional thousand square feet increase in size of a house holding constant the age. In Problem 13.77, we are 95% confident that the mean assessed value will increase by an amount somewhere between 9.4695 thousand dollars and 23.7972 thousand dollars for each additional thousand square feet increase in heating area regardless of age.

(l) Based on your answers to (a) through (l), the age of a house does have an effect on its assessed value.

13.56 Excel output:

Regression Statistics						
Multiple R	0.6973					
R Square	0.4862					
Adjusted R Square	0.4482					
Standard Error	8.1748					
Observations	30					
ANOVA						
	df	SS	MS	F	Significance F	
Regression	2	1707.6716	853.8358	12.7768	0.0001	
Residual	27	1804.3284	66.8270			
Total	29	3512.0000				
	Coefficients	Standard Error	t Stat	P-value	Lower 95%	Upper 95%
Intercept	157.8976	15.2939	10.3242	0.0000	126.5172	189.2780
E.R.A.	-18.4490	3.6588	-5.0424	0.0000	-25.9562	-10.9418
League	-3.2787	3.0235	-1.0844	0.2878	-9.4825	2.9250

13.56   (a) $\hat{Y} = 157.8976 - 18.4490X_1 - 3.2787X_2$, where X_1 = ERA and X_2 = League
cont.   (American = 0).

    (b)   Holding constant the effect of the league, for each additional ERA, the number of
wins is estimated to decrease by a mean of 18.4490. For a given ERA, a team in the
National League is estimated to have a mean of 3.2787 fewer wins than a team in the
American League.

    (c) $\hat{Y} = 157.8976 - 18.4490(4.5) - 3.2787(0) = 74.8771$ wins = 75 wins

    (d)   PHStat output:

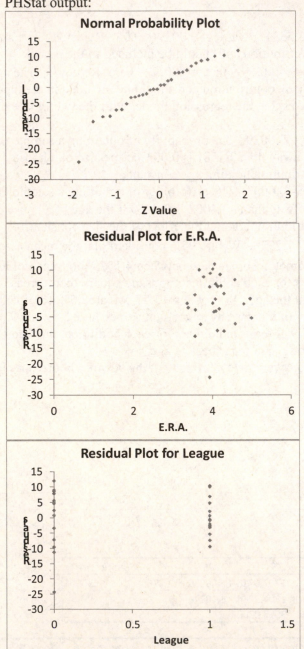

13.56 cont.	(d)	Based on a residual analysis, the errors appear to be left-skewed. There is no apparent violation of other assumptions.

(e) F_{STAT} = 12.7768, p-value = 0.0001. Since p-value < 0.05, reject H_0. There is evidence of a significant relationship between wins and the two independent variables (ERA and league).

(f)   For X_1: t_{STAT} = -5.0424, p-value is virtually 0. Reject H_0. ERA makes a significant contribution and should be included in the model.
For X_2: t_{STAT} = -1.0844, p-value = 0.2878 > 0.05. Do not reject H_0. The league does not make a significant contribution and should not be included in the model.
Based on these results, the regression model with only the ERA as the independent variable should be used.

(g) $-25.9562 \le \beta_1 \le -10.9418$

(h) $-9.4825 \le \beta_2 \le 2.9250$

(i) r^2_{adj} = 0.4477. So 44.77% of the variation in wins can be explained by the variation in ERA and league after adjusting for number of independent variables and sample size.

(j)   The slope of the number of wins with ERA is the same regardless of whether the team belongs to the American or the National League.

(k)   Excel output:

	Coefficients	Standard Error	t Stat	P-value	Lower 95%	Upper 95%
Intercept	151.5015	27.6268	5.4839	0.0000	94.7138	208.2892
E.R.A.	-16.9030	6.6561	-2.5395	0.0174	-30.5848	-3.2212
League	5.9451	33.0622	0.1798	0.8587	-62.0153	73.9055
E.R.A. x League	-2.2499	8.0295	-0.2802	0.7815	-18.7548	14.2551

$$\hat{Y} = 151.5015 - 16.9030X_1 + 5.9451X_2 - 2.2499X_1X_2$$

For $X_1 X_2$: the p-value is 0.7815 > 0.05. Do not reject H_0. There is no evidence that the interaction term makes a contribution to the model.

(l)   The one-variable model in (f) should be used.

13.58   Excel output:

Regression Statistics	
Multiple R	0.2540
R Square	0.0645
Adjusted R Square	0.0247
Standard Error	3.4367
Observations	50

ANOVA

	df	SS	MS	F	Significance F
Regression	2	38.2915	19.1458	1.6211	0.2085
Residual	47	555.0989	11.8106		
Total	49	593.3904			

	Coefficients	Standard Error	t Stat	P-value	Lower 95%	Upper 95%
Intercept	98.7920	15.7539	6.2709	0.0000	67.0992	130.4848
Pressure	-0.0075	0.0350	-0.2150	0.8307	-0.0779	0.0629
Temp	-0.3210	0.1806	-1.7773	0.0820	-0.6843	0.0423

The r^2 of the multiple regression is very low at 0.0645. Only 6.45 of the variation in thickness can be explained by the variation of pressure and temperature.

The F test statistic for the combined significant of pressure and temperature is 1.621 with a p-value of 0.2085. Hence, at a 5% level of significance, there is not enough evidence to conclude that both pressure and temperature affect thickness.

The p-value of the t test for the significance of pressure is 0.8307, which is larger than 5%. Hence, there is not sufficient evidence to conclude that pressure affects thickness holding constant the effect of temperature. The p-value of the t test for the significance of temperature is 0.0820, which is also larger than 5%. There is not enough evidence to conclude that temperature affects thickness at 5% level of significance holding constant the effect of pressure. Hence, neither pressure nor temperature affects thickness individually.

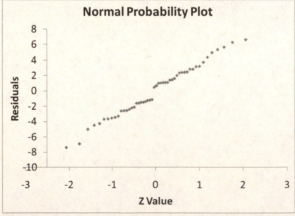

The normal probability plot does not suggest any potential violation of the normality assumption.

13.58
cont.

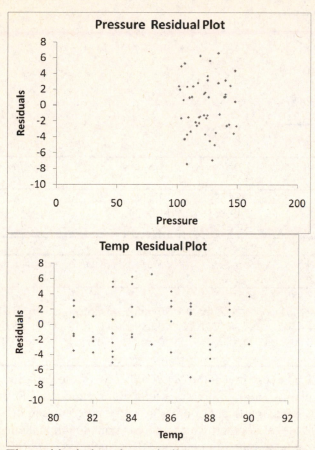

The residual plots do not indicate potential violation of the homoscedasticity assumption. The temperature residual plot, however, suggests that there might be nonlinear relationship between temperature and thickness.

13.58
cont.

Excel output with the interaction term:

Regression Statistics	
Multiple R	0.2709
R Square	0.0734
Adjusted R Square	0.0129
Standard Error	3.4574
Observations	50

ANOVA

	df	SS	MS	F	Significance F
Regression	3	43.5348	14.5116	1.2140	0.3153
Residual	46	549.8556	11.9534		
Total	49	593.3904			

	Coefficients	Standard Error	t Stat	P-value	Lower 95%	Upper 95%
Intercept	197.8857	150.4571	1.3152	0.1950	-104.9687	500.7401
Pressure	-0.8178	1.2240	-0.6682	0.5074	-3.2815	1.6459
Temp	-1.4892	1.7731	-0.8398	0.4053	-5.0583	2.0800
Pressure x Temp	0.0096	0.0144	0.6623	0.5111	-0.0195	0.0386

The r^2 of the multiple regression is very low at 0.0734. Only 7.34 of the variation in thickness can be explained by the variation of pressure, temperature and their interaction. The F test statistic for the combined significant of pressure and temperature is 1.214 with a p-value of 0.3153. Hence, at a 5% level of significance, there is not enough evidence to conclude that pressure, temperature and their interaction affect thickness.
The p-value of the t test for the significance of pressure, temperature and the interaction term are 0.5074, 0.4053 and 0.5111, respectively, which are all larger than 5%. Hence, there is not sufficient evidence to conclude that pressure, temperature or the interaction individually affects thickness holding constant the effect of the other variables.
The pattern in the normal probability plot and residual plots is similar to that in the regression without the interaction term. Hence, the article's suggestion that there is a significant interaction between the pressure and the temperature in the tank cannot be validated.

CHAPTER 14

OBJECTIVES

In this chapter, you learn:
- How to construct various control charts
- Which control chart to use for a particular type of data
- The basic themes of total quality management and Deming's 14 points
- The basic aspects of Six Sigma

OVERVIEW AND KEY CONCEPTS

Themes of Quality Management
1. The primary focus is on process improvement.
2. Most of the variation in a process is due to the system and not the individual.
3. Teamwork is an integral part of a quality management organization.
4. Customer satisfaction is a primary organizational goal.
5. Organizational transformation must occur in order to implement quality management.
6. Fear must be removed from organizations.
7. Higher quality costs less not more but it requires an investment in training.

Deming's 14 Points for Management
1. Create constancy of purpose for improvement of product and service.

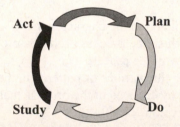

The Shewhart-Deming Cycle Focuses on Constant Improvement

2. Adopt the new philosophy.
3. Cease dependence on inspection to achieve quality.
4. End the practice of awarding business on the basis of price tag alone. Instead, minimize total cost by working with a single supplier.
5. Improve constantly and forever every process for planning, production and service.
6. Institute training on the job.
7. Adopt and institute leadership.
8. Drive out fear.
9. Break down barriers between staff areas.
10. Eliminate slogans, exhortations, and targets for the workforce.
11. Eliminate numerical quotas for the workforce and numerical goals for management.
12. Remove barriers that rob people of pride of workmanship. Eliminate the annual rating or merit system.
13. Institute a vigorous program of education and self-improvement for everyone.
14. Put everyone in the company to work to accomplish the transformation.

Six Sigma Management
- A method for breaking processes into a series of steps in order to eliminate defects and produce near perfect results.
- Has a clear focus on obtaining bottom-line results in a relatively short three to six-month period of time.
- **The Six Sigma DMAIC model:**
    - **Define:** The problem to be solved needs to be defined along with the costs, benefits of the project, and the impact on the customer.
    - **Measure:** Operational definitions for each Critical-To-Quality (CTQ) characteristic must be developed. In addition, the measurement procedure must be verified so that it is consistent over repeated measurements.
    - **Analyze:** The root causes of why defects can occur need to be determined along with the variables in the process that cause these defects to occur. Data are collected to determine the underlying value for each process variable often using control charts.
    - **Improve:** The importance of each process variable on the CTQ characteristic is studied using designed experiments. The objective is to determine the best level for each variable that can be maintained in the long term.
    - **Control:** The objective is to maintain the gains that have been made with a revised process in the long term by avoiding potential problems that can occur when a process is changed.
- Its implementation requires a data-oriented approach using statistical tools such as control charts and designed experiments.
- Involves training everyone in the company in the DMAIC model.

Control Charts
- The **control chart** is a means of monitoring variation in the characteristic of a product or services by focusing on the time dimension in which the process produces products or services and studying the nature of the variability in the process.
- **Special (assignable) causes of variation:** Large fluctuations or patterns in the data that are not inherent to a process. They are often caused by changes in the process that represents either problems to be fixed or opportunities to exploit.
- **Chance (common) causes of variation:** The inherent variability that exists in a process. These consist of the numerous small causes of variability that operate randomly or by chance.
- An **out-of-control process** contains both common causes of variation and assignable causes of variation. Because assignable causes of variation are not part of the process design, an out-of-control process is unpredictable.
- An **in-control process** contains only common causes of variation. Because theses causes of variation are inherent to the process, an in-control process is predictable. An in-control-process is sometimes said to be in a **state of statistical control**.
- **Control limits:**
    - Statistical measure of interest $\pm$ 3 standard deviations

- **Identifying pattern in control charts:**

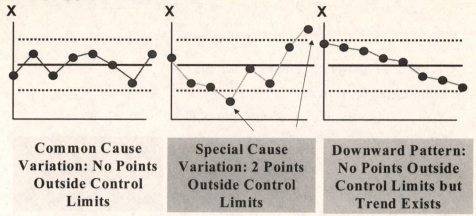

| Common Cause Variation: No Points Outside Control Limits | Special Cause Variation: 2 Points Outside Control Limits | Downward Pattern: No Points Outside Control Limits but Trend Exists |

- ▪ A trend exists if there are 8 consecutive points above (or below) the centerline or 8 consecutive points that are increasing (or decreasing).
- **The first type of control error:** The belief that observed value represents special cause when in fact it is due to common cause.
- **The second type of control error:** Treating special cause variation as if it is common cause variation.
- When a process is out-of-control, the assignable causes of variation must be identified. If the assignable causes of variation are detrimental to the quality of the product or service, a plan to eliminate this source of variation must be implemented. If an assignable cause of variation increases quality, the process should be change so that it is incorporated into the process design and becomes a common cause source of variation and the process is improved.
- When a process is in control, it must be determined whether the amount of common cause variation in the process is small enough to satisfy the customers of the products or services. If it is small enough to consistently satisfy the customers, the control charts can be used to monitor the process on a continuous basis to make sure that it does not go out-of-control. If it is too large, the process should be altered.

Control Chart for the Proportion of Nonconforming Item (the p Chart)
- It is an attribute chart, which is used when sampled items are classified according to whether they conform or do not conform to operationally defined requirement.
- When used with unequal sample sizes over time, the unequal sample sizes should not differ by more than 25% from average sample size.

- $LCL_p = \max\left(0, \bar{p} - 3\sqrt{\dfrac{\bar{p}(1-\bar{p})}{\bar{n}}}\right)$, $UCL_p = \bar{p} + 3\sqrt{\dfrac{\bar{p}(1-\bar{p})}{\bar{n}}}$

  where

  $X_i =$ number of nonforming items in sample i

  $n_i =$ sample size for sample i

  $p_i = X_i / n_i =$ proportion of nonconforming items in sample i

  $$\bar{n} = \frac{\sum_{i=1}^{k} n_i}{k}$$

  $$\bar{p} = \frac{\sum_{i=1}^{k} X_i}{\sum_{i=1}^{k} n_i}$$

  $k =$ number of samples

Morals of the Red Bead Example
- Variation is an inherent part of any process.
- The system is primarily responsible for worker performance.
- Only management can change the system.
- Some workers will always be above average and some will be below.

Control Chart for the Range (R) and Mean $(\bar{X})$
- They are variable control charts.
- They are more sensitive in detecting special-cause variation than the p chart.
- They are typically used in pairs
- The R chart monitors the variation in the process while the $\bar{X}$ chart monitors the process average.
- The R chart should be examined first because if it indicates the process is out-of-control, the interpretation of the $\bar{X}$ chart will be misleading.
- **Control chart for the range (R chart):**
  - $LCL_R = D_3\bar{R}$, $UCL_R = D_4\bar{R}$

    where

    $$\bar{R} = \frac{\sum_{i=1}^{k} R_i}{k}$$

    D_3 and D_4 are to obtained from a table.

- **Control chart for the mean ($\overline{X}$ chart):**
  - $LCL_{\overline{X}} = \overline{\overline{X}} - A_2\overline{R}$, $UCL_{\overline{X}} = \overline{\overline{X}} + A_2\overline{R}$

    where

    $$\overline{\overline{X}} = \frac{\sum\limits_{i=1}^{k} \overline{X}_i}{k}$$

    $$\overline{R} = \frac{\sum\limits_{i=1}^{k} R_i}{k}$$

    $\overline{X}$ = the sample mean of n observations at time i

    R_i = the range of n observations at time i

    k = number of subgroups

    and A_2 is to be obtained from a table.

SOLUTIONS TO END OF SECTION AND CHAPTER REVIEW EVEN PROBLEMS

14.2 (a) Proportion of nonconformances largest on Day 4, smallest on Day 3.

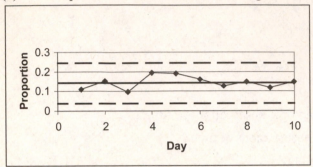

(b) $\bar{n} = 1036/10 = 103.6$, $\bar{p} = 148/1036 = 0.142857$,

$$LCL = \bar{p} - 3\sqrt{\frac{\bar{p}(1-\bar{p})}{\bar{n}}} = 0.142857 - 3\sqrt{\frac{0.142857(1-0.142857)}{103.6}} = 0.039719$$

$$UCL = \bar{p} + 3\sqrt{\frac{\bar{p}(1-\bar{p})}{\bar{n}}} = 0.142857 + 3\sqrt{\frac{0.142857(1-0.142857)}{103.6}} = 0.245995$$

(c) Proportions are within control limits, so there do not appear to be any special causes of variation.

14.4 (a) $n = 500$, $\bar{p} = 761/16000 = 0.0476$

$$LCL = \bar{p} - 3\sqrt{\frac{\bar{p}(1-\bar{p})}{n}} = 0.0476 - 3\sqrt{\frac{0.0476(1-0.0476)}{500}} = 0.0190 > 0$$

$$UCL = \bar{p} + 3\sqrt{\frac{\bar{p}(1-\bar{p})}{n}} = 0.0476 + 3\sqrt{\frac{0.0476(1-0.0476)}{500}} = 0.0761$$

p Chart

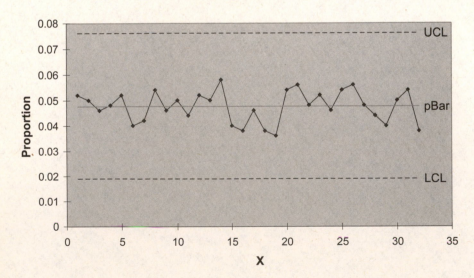

14.4   (b)   Since the individual points are distributed around $\overline{p}$ without any pattern and all the points are within the control limits, the process is in a state of statistical control.

14.6   (a) $\overline{n} = 113345/22 = 5152.0455$, $\overline{p} = 1460/113345 = 0.01288$,

$$LCL = \overline{p} - 3\sqrt{\frac{\overline{p}(1-\overline{p})}{\overline{n}}} = 0.01288 - 3\sqrt{\frac{0.01288(1-0.01288)}{5152.0455}} = 0.00817$$

$$UCL = \overline{p} + 3\sqrt{\frac{\overline{p}(1-\overline{p})}{\overline{n}}} = 0.01288 + 3\sqrt{\frac{0.01288(1-0.01288)}{5152.0455}} = 0.01759$$

PHStat output:

p Chart

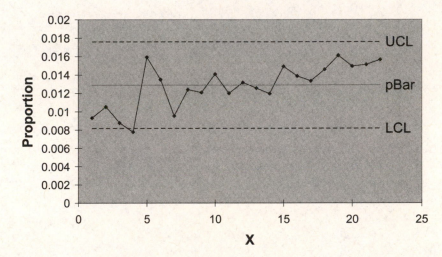

(a)   The proportion of unacceptable cans is below the LCL on Day 4. There is evidence of a pattern over time, since the last eight points are all above the mean and most of the earlier points are below the mean. Thus, the special causes that might be contributing to this pattern should be investigated before any change in the system of operation is contemplated.

(b)   Once special causes have been eliminated and the process is stable, Deming's fourteen points should be implemented to improve the system. They might also look at day 4 to see if they could identify and exploit the special cause that led to such a low proportion of defects on that day.

14.8   (a)

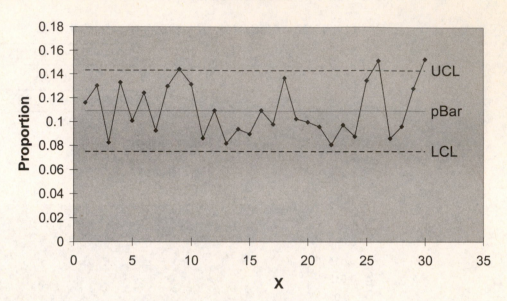

$\overline{p} = 0.1091$, $LCL = 0.0751$, $UCL = 0.1431$. Points 9, 26, and 30 are above the UCL.

(b)   First, the reasons for the special cause variation would need to be determined and local corrective action taken. Once special causes have been eliminated and the process is stable, Deming's fourteen points should be implemented to improve the system.

14.12   (a) $d_2 = 2.059$ (d) $D_4 = 2.282$
        (b) $d_3 = 0.88$ (e) $A_2 = 0.729$
        (c) $D_3 = 0$

14.14   (a) $\bar{R} = \dfrac{\sum\limits_{i=1}^{k} R_i}{k} = 3.275$, $\bar{\bar{X}} = \dfrac{\sum\limits_{i=1}^{k} \bar{X}_i}{k} = 5.9413$.

R chart:

$$UCL = D_4\bar{R} = 2.282(3.275) = 7.4736$$

LCL does not exist.

$\bar{X}$ chart:

$$UCL = \bar{\bar{X}} + A_2\bar{R} = 5.9413 + 0.729(3.275) = 8.3287$$

$$LCL = \bar{\bar{X}} - A_2\bar{R} = 5.9413 - 0.729(3.275) = 3.5538$$

PHStat R Chart output:

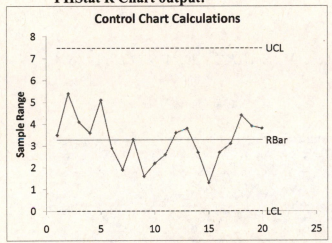

PHStat $\bar{X}$ Chart output:

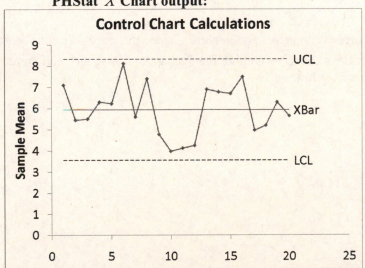

(b)   The process appears to be in control since there are no points outside the control limits and there is no evidence of a pattern in the range chart, and there are no points outside the control limits and there is no evidence of a pattern in the $\bar{X}$ chart.

14.16   (a) $\overline{R}$ = 0.8794, R chart: UCL = 2.0068; LCL does not exist

R Chart

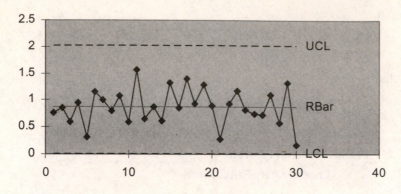

$\overline{\overline{X}}$ = 20.1065, $\overline{X}$ chart: UCL = 20.7476; LCL = 19.4654

XBar Chart

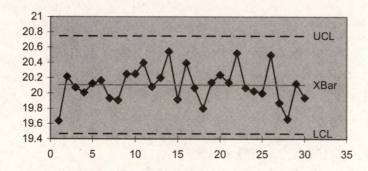

(c)   The process appears to be in control since there are no points outside the lower and upper control limits of either the R-chart and $\overline{X}$-chart, and there is no pattern in the results over time.

14.18   (a)

X Bar Chart

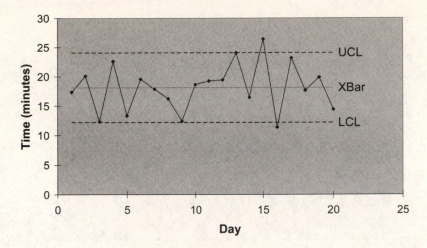

R Chart

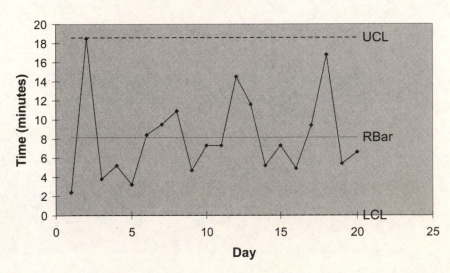

$\overline{R} = 8.145$, $\overline{\overline{X}} = 18.12$.

R chart: $LCL = D_3\,\overline{R} = 0\,(8.145) = 0$. *LCL* does not exist.

$UCL = D_4\,\overline{R} = (2.282)\,(8.145) = 18.58689$.

For $\overline{X}$ chart: $LCL = \overline{\overline{X}} - A_2\,\overline{R} = 18.12 - (0.729)\,(8.145) = 12.1823$

$UCL = \overline{\overline{X}} + A_2\,\overline{R} = 18.12 + (0.729)\,(8.145) = 24.0577$

(b)   There are no sample ranges outside the control limits and there does not appear to be a pattern in the range chart. The sample mean on Day 15 is above the *UCL* and the sample mean on Day 16 is below the *LCL*, which is an indication there is evidence of special cause variation in the sample means.

14.20   (a) $\overline{\overline{R}} = 0.3022$, R chart: $UCL = 0.6389$; LCL does not exist

$\overline{\overline{X}} = 90.1317$, $\overline{X}$ chart: $UCL = 90.3060$; $LCL = 89.9573$

R Chart

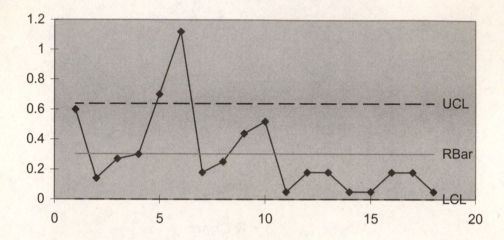

XBar Chart

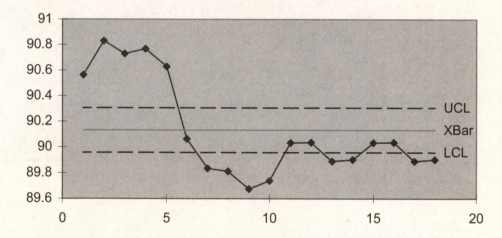

(b)   The R-chart is out-of-control because the 5th and 6th data points fall above the upper control limit. There is also a downward trend in the right tail of the R-chart, which signifies that special causes of variation must be identified and corrected. Even though the $\overline{X}$ chart also appears to be out-of-control because a majority of the data point fall above or below the control limit, any interpretation will be misleading because the R-chart has indicated the presence of out-of-control conditions. There is also a downward trend in both control charts. Special causes of variation should be investigated and eliminated.

14.22   Find the reasons for the special causes and take corrective action to prevent their occurrence in the future or exploit them if they improve the process.

14.24   The p chart is an attribute control chart. It can be used when sampled items are classified according to whether they conform or do not conform to operationally defined requirements. It is based on the proportion of nonconforming items in a sample.

14.26   Since the range is used to obtain the control limits of the chart for the mean, the range needs to be in a state of statistical control. Thus, the range and mean charts are used together.

14.28   (a)   One the main reason that service quality is lower than product quality is because the former involves human interaction which is prone to variation. Also, the most critical aspects of a service are often timeliness and professionalism, and customers can always perceive that the service could be done quicker and with greater professionalism. For products, customers often cannot perceive a better or more ideal product than the one they are getting. For example, a new laptop is better and contains more interesting features than any laptop that he or she has ever imagined.

(b)   Both services and products are the results of processes. However, measuring services is often harder because of the dynamic variation due to the human interaction between the service provider and the customer. Product quality is often a straightforward measurement of a static physical characteristic like the amount of sugar in a can of soda. Categorical data are also more common in service quality.

(c)   Yes.

(d)   Yes.

14.30   (a)

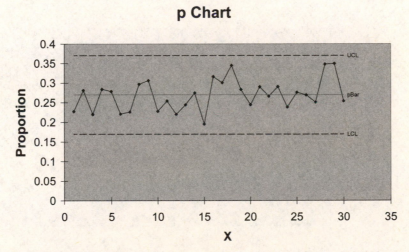

(b)   Yes, RudyBird's market share is in control before the start of the in-store promotion since all sample proportions fall within the control limits.

14.30 (c)
cont.

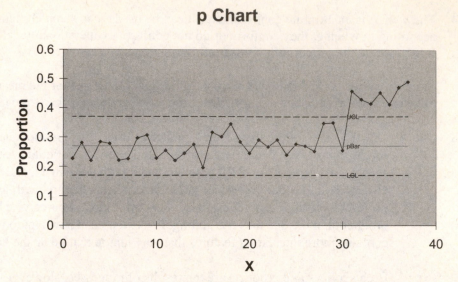

After including the data for days 31-37, there is an apparent upward trend in the p chart during the promotion period and all the market share proportions in that period are above the upper control limit. The process became out-of-control. This assignable-cause variation can be attributed to the in-store promotion. The promotion was successful in increasing the market share of RudyBird.

14.32 (a)

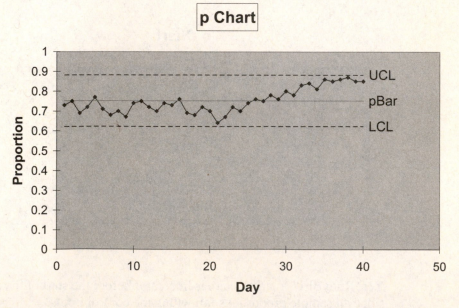

$\bar{p} = 0.75175$, $LCL = 0.62215$, $UCL = 0.88135$. Although none of the points are outside either the LCL or UCL, there is a clear pattern over time with lower values occurring in the first half of the sequence and higher values occurring toward the end of the sequence.

14.32   (b)   This would explain the pattern in the results over time.
cont.   (c)   The control chart would have been developed using the first 20 days and then, using
                 those limits, the additional proportions could have been plotted.

14.34   (a) $\overline{p} = 0.1198$, $LCL = 0.0205$, $UCL = 0.2191$.
        (b)   The process is out of statistical control. The proportion of trades that are undesirable
                 is below the LCL on Day 24 and are above the UCL on Day 4.
        (c)   Special causes of variation should be investigated and eliminated. Next, process
                 knowledge should be improved to decrease the proportion of trades that are
                 undesirable.

14.36   **Kidney- Shift 1**

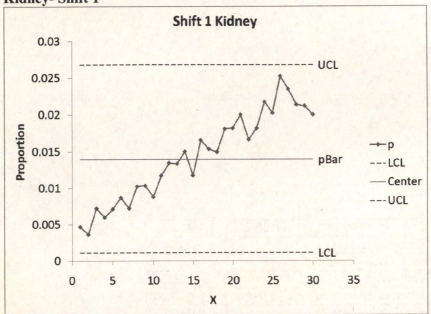

PHStat output:

Shift 1 Kidney	
Intermediate Calculations	
Sum of Subgroup Sizes	22508
Number of Subgroups Taken	30
Average Sample/Subgroup Size	750.266667
Average Proportion of Nonconforming Items	0.0139506
Three Standard Deviations	0.01284574
p Chart Control Limits	
Lower Control Limit	0.00110486
Center	0.0139506
Upper Control Limit	0.02679634

Although there are no points outside the control limits, there is a strong increasing trend in
nonconformances over time.

14.36   **Kidney- Shift 2**
cont.

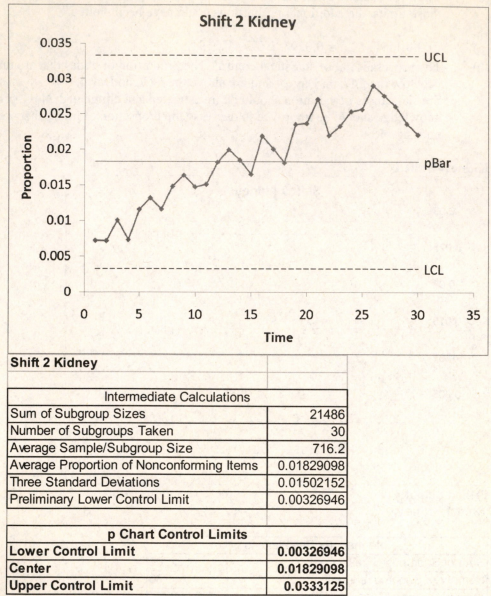

Shift 2 Kidney	

Intermediate Calculations	
Sum of Subgroup Sizes	21486
Number of Subgroups Taken	30
Average Sample/Subgroup Size	716.2
Average Proportion of Nonconforming Items	0.01829098
Three Standard Deviations	0.01502152
Preliminary Lower Control Limit	0.00326946

p Chart Control Limits	
Lower Control Limit	0.00326946
Center	0.01829098
Upper Control Limit	0.0333125

Although there are no points outside the control limits, there is a strong increasing trend in nonconformances over time.

14.36   **Shift 1 Shrimp**
cont.

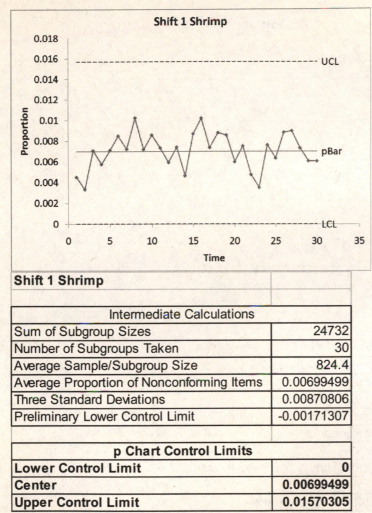

Shift 1 Shrimp	
Intermediate Calculations	
Sum of Subgroup Sizes	24732
Number of Subgroups Taken	30
Average Sample/Subgroup Size	824.4
Average Proportion of Nonconforming Items	0.00699499
Three Standard Deviations	0.00870806
Preliminary Lower Control Limit	-0.00171307

p Chart Control Limits	
Lower Control Limit	**0**
Center	**0.00699499**
Upper Control Limit	**0.01570305**

There are no points outside the control limits and there is no pattern over time.

14.36
cont.

Shift 2 Shrimp

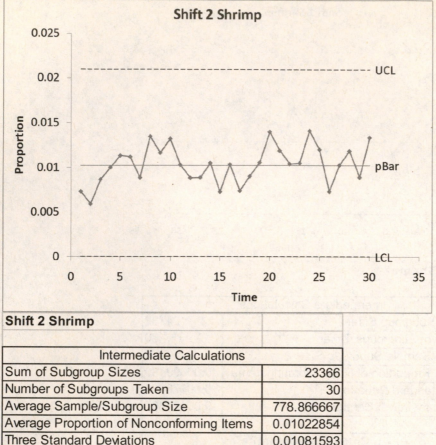

Shift 2 Shrimp	

Intermediate Calculations	
Sum of Subgroup Sizes	23366
Number of Subgroups Taken	30
Average Sample/Subgroup Size	778.866667
Average Proportion of Nonconforming Items	0.01022854
Three Standard Deviations	0.01081593
Preliminary Lower Control Limit	-0.00058739

p Chart Control Limits	
Lower Control Limit	**0**
Center	**0.01022854**
Upper Control Limit	**0.02104447**

There are no points outside the control limits and there is no pattern over time.

The team needs to determine the reasons for the increase in nonconformances for the kidney product. The production volume for kidney is clearly decreasing for both shifts. This can be observed from a plot of the production volume over time. The team needs to investigate the reasons for this.